P9-DDY-110

HILLIER GARDEN PLANNING

HILLIER
GARDEN
PLANNING

The essential guide to garden planning,
planting and maintenance from the
internationally-renowned Hillier Nurseries

KEITH RUSHFORTH • RODERICK GRIFFIN
DENNIS WOODLAND

DAVID & CHARLES

A DAVID & CHARLES BOOK

Copyright © Keith Rushforth, Roderick Griffin, Dennis Woodland and Hillier Nurseries
(Winchester) Ltd. 1988, 1994

Keith Rushforth, Roderick Griffin and Dennis Woodland have asserted their right to be iden-
tified as authors of this work in accordance with the Copyright, Designs and Patents Act 1988.

All rights reserved. No part of this publication may be reproduced, stored in a retrieval
system, or transmitted, in any form or by any means, electronic or mechanical, by photo-
copying, recording or otherwise, without prior permission in writing from the publisher.

A catalogue record for this book is available from the British Library.

ISBN 0 7153 0181 0

Designed and typeset by Les Dominey Design Company, Exeter, Devon
and printed in Germany by Mohndruck GmbH
for David & Charles
Brunel House   Newton Abbot   Devon

NOTE:
Throughout this book an asterisk (*) after a plant name indicates that it
received the Royal Horticultual Society Award of Garden Merit 1993.

Acknowledgements

All photographs by Dennis Woodland except:
pp 30, 38 (centre), 44, 50, 82, 95, 108, 152, 169, 190, 212, 215, 217 Clive Nichols;
pp 69 (bottom right), 71, 106 Photos Horticultural; pp 7 (top), 12, 45 Roderick
Griffin; pp 21, 26, 27, 76, 77 Justyn Willsmore.

All line illustrations by Roderick Griffin except:
pp 68, 75 (left), 109, 111, 113, 115, 116, 144, 145, 146, 147, 148, 149, 150 Ernie
Godden

Pages 2-3: *The corner of a paved walled garden at the Royal Horticultural Society's garden,*
Wisley, Surrey featuring climbing and shrub roses with blending herbaceous plants notably
delphiniums and hardy geraniums. In foreground – modern shrub rose 'Golden Wings'.

CONTENTS

Garden and Home   6

Deciding What You Want   8

Groundwork   20

Designing your Garden   30

Planting Your Garden   72

Maintaining Your Garden   82

Choosing Plants   102

Plants for Personal Collections   151

Further Reading   219

Suppliers and Useful Addresses   220

Index   221

CHAPTER 1

GARDEN AND HOME

A garden gives space, character and beauty to a home's surroundings; it provides scope for outdoor living in summer, and interest and colour all the year round. It adds a dimension that is always changing – with the seasons, with each day's weather and as the plants mature. The aim of this book is to help you plan, plant and look after a garden that is right for you, your lifestyle and your home.

WHY HAVE A GARDEN?

The garden should be an intrinsic part of the home. It can be enjoyed from inside the house, with the view enhanced, perhaps, by well-placed lighting. As your outdoor room, it gives you sheltered spots in which to sit and read, write, sunbathe or do nothing. It gives the children a place for active play or imaginative games. It gives you mental stimulation and a fresh view as it changes from day to day: gradually the new foliage and colour of spring give way to the flowers, warmth and perfume of summer, to the brilliance of autumn leaves and fruits, to the subtle colours and tracery of trees in winter. Your everyday outlook alters hourly with the light – a view is quite different under a cloudless summer sun, in a misty early morning, in low evening sunlight or in a storm. Your view can be framed to give a more dramatic focus; unsightly objects or activities can be masked.

With a garden, you have the chance to develop a hobby or specialist interest, whether growing dahlias for exhibition, or food for the family, conserving rare plants or 'recreating' a patch of the Himalayas or some other plant-rich part of the world. Creating, planting and maintaining the garden also provides useful exercise, while achieving something at the same time.

A garden has educational value for both adults and children. As a microcosm of the world's plant life, it gives an understanding of plant ecology: how plants grow, flower and fruit, how leaves are broken down in autumn, feeding fungi and small invertebrates – in short, how the cycle of life goes on year by year. It will offer a home or feeding-place for wildlife: birds, small mammals and butterflies. If you put up nesting boxes and, in winter, stock your birdtable, you will encourage a healthy bird population, particularly if you provide evergreen trees and shrubs for winter shelter, and berrying plants such as rowans, cotoneasters and berberris. A rich and colourful butterfly population will follow the planting of suitable foodplants for the caterpillar stages, and nectar-producing plants such as buddleia or sedums for the adults. A garden pond becomes a world in itself, holds your fish and attracts magnificent dragonflies.

There is even considerable monetary value in a well-planned and well-kept garden, when you eventually come to sell. A house standing in an open field or an overgrown wilderness deters potential purchasers; a pleasantly laid out garden, whether large, medium or small, makes it far more appealing.

FIRST STEPS

There are always some constraints to be considered before designing or redesigning a garden, such as the time and money available, the size and location of the plot, and perhaps some existing features you do not wish to change, a view that should not be blocked or an eyesore that must be hidden.

Your first consideration is the time you have available. If this is limited, there is no point in planning an intricate rock garden or ornate herbaceous border, however much you like them, as the end result will be only mediocre at best. Instead, design the garden around low-maintenance features, such as trees and shrubs, areas of rough grass and groundcover. However, good design and practice do help you use your time more efficiently: keep the border or rock garden small, and maintenance will take less time.

You may have time at certain seasons but not others: there is little point in designing a good sitting-out area, for example, if no one is free to use it until midwinter! Other hobbies may leave little time in summer for either maintenance or enjoyment, and this must affect how you plan the garden. For instance, you cannot have an ornamental lawn of high standard if you are away for six weeks or more in the summer: 'meadow' lawns rich in bulbs and wild flowers may be an attractive alternative, giving pleasure in spring and autumn when you are there, and needing to be cut only once or twice in late summer and early autumn.

The timescale over which you want the garden to take shape may be critical. If your principal concern is to enhance the value of your house and you are likely to move within five years, the design needs to show strongly within that period; on the other hand, if you expect to stay there for upwards of twenty years, longer-term planning and planting makes sense.

The size and shape of the plot must influence how you plan. A small garden needs a more intricate layout, partly to give an illusion of space, partly to include sufficient plants to give colour and interest at all seasons. A small rock garden that would work well here would look totally lost in a large garden, unless carefully sited in an intimate area.

Look carefully at the existing situation. You may be able to improve it with relatively little effort, perhaps by removing a flowerbed here and

planting a shrub bed there, or adding an area of paving. Usually it is better to develop existing features than to start from scratch and then have to wait several years for the design to come to fruition. Identify the good points that should be retained: mature trees will give an attractive framework to a new design; there may be a pond already rich in wildlife; the soil may be suitable for a specialist plant collection that interests you, such as rhododendrons or rock-roses, and so on.

Next, think about the amount of money you can spend on the garden, both as outlay in plants, paving and other features, and as recurrent expenditure. A patio, or the use of weed-smothering groundcover plants, may be expensive initially but will need little maintenance; conversely, a lawn is cheap to establish from seed, but needs cutting and feeding regularly thereafter. Trees and shrubs work out relatively cheap because they cover large areas and are long lasting; annual summer bedding or perennial plants can be more expensive, as far more plants are needed per unit of area and the annuals need frequent replacement. You can also buy plants

A small paved sitting area well furnished with clematis, roses, honeysuckle and lavender and many scented shrubs and plants.

A sunny house wall (here photographed in late spring) provides an ideal home for Rosa banksiae *'Lutea' and* Clematis *'Nelly Moser' with* Coronilla valentina *ssp* glauca *beneath the window – an excellent evergreen shrub.*

in larger sizes for quicker effect – at a cost. The limits on time, effort and expertise can, of course, be eased if some competent garden help can be employed.

The real costs of a garden are the time required to maintain it, and the effort and the money expended in doing so. Each of these can be tightly controlled by attention to the design, creation and management of your garden. This book will help you to achieve the best result for you.

ADVANTAGES OF A GARDEN

A garden gives you:
• an outdoor room
• a play area for children
• mental stimulation and a fresh view as it changes day to day
• the chance to develop a hobby or specialist interest
• useful exercise
• a home and feeding place for wildlife
• educational value for adults and children
• added value on your home

CHAPTER 2

DECIDING WHAT YOU WANT

Before attempting to design a garden, or redesign part of one, you need to establish its possibilities and decide exactly what you require. The first question to ask is 'Who will be using the garden?' – your design will revolve around the answer. The panel opposite gives three examples of how the owners' requirements can affect garden design.

FEATURES FOR YOUR GARDEN

Next, you will need to make a list of the most important features you want in the new garden, so let's look at the options available.

To help you make your choices, the garden features discussed here have been divided into three categories: Basic, Optional and For Enthusiasts. Treat this as a rough guide only – what is optional for one gardener may well be considered absolutely basic by another!

Basic • PAVED SITTING AREA
Almost certainly you will want this – even the most enthusiastic gardener has to sit down sometimes – and it will probably be the garden's most-used area, acting as the transition between house and garden.

Most people tend to underestimate

the area of paving that they require, whether from financial caution or from being unsure about how it will look. Certainly paving and walling is expensive, but the aftercare costs are minimal. The paved area should be of a reasonable size – it will look better and be far more useful. As a very general guide, a small paved area for entertaining family and a few friends might be 30–40sq m (36–48sq yd), a medium area for entertaining, say, up to 30 people might be 60–80sq m (72–96sq yd).

Even a moderate-sized area of paving should include adequate spaces for planting, to avoid looking

Steps and walling in natural stone become a special feature when aubretia is naturalised in the paving cracks.

WHO WILL USE THE GARDEN?

YOUNG WORKING COUPLE

Due to lack of time, a young working couple will probably want a low-maintenance garden.

• Choose shrubs and groundcover plants to provide seasonal varieties rather than bulbs, annuals and many herbaceous perennials.

• Design a simple layout, omitting work-intensive features such as rockeries or pools.

• Include an area for entertaining, with interesting and more detailed planting, close to the house.

• Garden lighting may be of particular interest.

A FAMILY

There is inevitably a conflict between keeping the garden beautiful and the active habits – or destructive moods – of most children at some stages. By accepting that the whole family should enjoy and use the garden, and planning for children's needs, however, much can be achieved.

• Create a good-sized lawn area for play near, but not too close to, the house and away from vulnerable planting.

• Allocate an area for a climbing frame and sand pit if needed, preferably within sight of the kitchen or workroom.

• In a large garden, provide young children with their own private areas where dens can be constructed and demolished at will. Encouraging this type of activity in any out-of-sight, neglected and over-grown parts of the garden will help keep them out of your own special-interest areas.

• Think ahead as children grow up and the family changes, so must the garden. The sand pit might become an ornamental pool; the neglected area could be tidied and developed as part of the ornamental garden, or extended and managed as a wild garden area, encouraging native flora and fauna.

AN ELDERLY COUPLE

Time available for appreciation of the garden may be greater on retirement, but physical strength and agility will inevitably limit the type of garden that can be maintained.

• Choose a low-maintenance design, where garden work is easy to do though not necessarily quick.

• Keep shrub borders fairly narrow, so that all plants are easy to reach.

• For ease of maintenance, design a very small lawn, or alternatively devote a large part of the garden to grass so that the entire area can be cut by a 'ride-on' mower if necesary.

• Provide a paved sitting area, preferably with some shade for hot days, and incorporate permanent seating and low walls around the garden on which to take a rest.

• Include trees and shrubs that flower throughout the year, and possibly some winter-flowering varieties which will be visible from the house.

too harsh. Plants spilling over walls and spreading over the paved area is a delightful way of displaying different types of foliage, in particular.

There are various materials that can be used for the paved surface:

• Natural stone or secondhand weathered materials such as York stone or traditional brick paviors are ideal and blend well with garden planting, but may be prohibitively expensive, so that artificial equivalents have to be found.

• The effect of artificial stone can be softened by combining it with other materials, such as brick or pebbles – and even artificial stone does weather eventually. You can encourage the growth of algae and lichen by applying liquid manure or, perhaps best and certainly most bizarre, wet the stones with water from boiled rice – worth a try, but perhaps not practical for a large area!

When designing the layout of the paved area remember to include good-sized planting pockets for climbers against the house walls. Even if the roof eaves overhang the pocket, most climbers will find enough soil water, if given a little extra encouragement during their first season.

Adding some low walling around the paved area will provide useful additional seats: 45cm (1ft 6in) is the most comfortable height but to suit the scale of the design any height between 38cm (1ft 3in) and 60cm (2ft) may be considered; 33cm (13in) or 1½ bricks the best width.

Basic • LAWNS

Most gardens in temperate countries, except for the very small, have lawns: the climate is ideal for the cultivation of a fine green lawn, and people are often proud to own one. However, it is easy to become slaves to our lawn, whilst other important areas of the garden are neglected. The space is an important one for recreational use (particularly for a young family) but do we need it to be large?

Consider alternatives, such as bold shrub beds to provide interest, colour and structure. Shrubs and groundcover, although more expensive initially, require very little upkeep once established compared with all the mowing, weedkilling and fertilising that are required for grass cover. Getting the balance right between planting and lawn will save time and money, as well as looking good. The lawn should be considered as a part of the whole garden picture, and not simply as an independent requirement which everything else must fit round: nor should it be simply 'the bit that's left over'.

Basic • SHRUB BORDERS

Shrub borders can form the structure of the garden and give colour and interest throughout the year. This is especially valuable in winter,when other planting, such as an herbaceous border, will have died down. Many shrubs are evergreen, and they can be planned to show variation in height, shape and foliage. The choice is enormous – see Chapters 7 and 8.

For the first three to five years after planting a lot of the soil will be left uncovered; you therefore need to include some short-term items to fill in, as well as the longer-term planting. You can use either annual plants or some of the cheaper, quick-growing groundcover plants. These can be left as a permanent feature and will gradually die out as the larger shrubs grow over them. Groundcover plants have the added advantage of reducing the weeding required in the early establishment period, and provide variety of colour and shape.

Double-sided shrub borders well-furnished with additional blending herbaceous and groundcover plants.
(See also pages 111–115.)
Effective background trees are Pyrus salicifolia 'Pendula' *(left) and purple beech.*

An alternative would be to use a mulch of coarse bark. This both helps to reduce weed growth and gives a neat, attractive finish to the shrub borders. It is especially useful on a very stony soil – the type where however many stones you remove there always seem to be more!

Basic • VEGETABLES
AND SOFT FRUIT
Growing of vegetables can be very rewarding, and some gardeners devote a good proportion of the garden to vegetable cultivation. It is, however, a time-consuming hobby and may take up valuable hours which could otherwise be devoted to the ornamental garden. On the other hand, a well-tended and productive vegetable garden can give great satisfaction.

Even the carefully cultivated vegetable plot is only going to look tidy for a short period during the early summer. As crops mature and are harvested gaps are left, and those plants that remain become unsightly as they die down, so vegetables cannot be relied upon to be ornamental for much of the year.

The size of a vegetable plot is very much a personal choice. A small area for growing a few salad crops and unusual vegetables, not available from the shops, and plants with particularly good flavour when freshly harvested,

is perhaps all that is required. To make access within the vegetable garden easier, small rectangular plots surrounded by paved paths are well worth considering.

As you need to net soft fruit against birds, there may be difficulties in finding a site in the garden where a fruit cage can be screened. However, if a suitable area can be found, soft fruit bushes require very little attention for a considerable crop. It is surprising how few plants are needed and there is always a danger of overplanting; in the summer months, if you are not on holiday anyway, picking and freezing can become a bit of a headache.

Basic • HERBS
There is no real reason to segregate herbs in their own garden, and although formal herb gardens can be extremely pretty, they are not easy to maintain. Many of the more useful culinary herbs are vigorous growers and intricate herb garden paths and patterns can become completely swamped all too quickly. Mint obviously needs to have its roots restricted, but many of the other subjects could be incorporated very successfully into shrub and groundcover plantings elsewhere in the garden. Some of the smaller plants such as the thymes are ideal used between paving; others like rosemary and sage make excellent plants for the front of borders and for

spreading over paved or gravel areas.

Although fresh culinary herbs are now available in shops, there is no better way of keeping herbs fresh than to grow them; it is obviously ideal to position the plot not too far from the kitchen door. Herbs tend to grow best in a sunny position, and shaded sites should be avoided.

Basic • HEDGES AND SCREENS
Under this heading come some important features which provide a link between the areas within your garden, and between your garden and the outside world. At the boundary, overlap fence panels and the Leyland cypress hedge are often our most popular defences. Both are quick to establish and temporarily satisfactory, but the former rots and falls down, and the latter grows to become aesthetically unacceptable, a menace to restrain and often a financial burden. Let's look at some alternatives.
• Brick walls are of course permanent and effective, but due to expense may need to be limited to short runs. Near to the house and sitting area, walls can form an excellent transition from the house to the garden and also provide space for a variety of climbing plants.
• A good, solidly made fence (such as a close-board fence, see Chapter 4) will have similar uses to a brick wall.
• Where height is not of primary concern, there are many types of hedge far more suitable than the Leyland: for example, both beech and yew produce fine hedging which is effective throughout the year and much easier to clip. Given good preparation, including ample farmyard manure dug into the bottom of the planting trench, these will produce an extremely good rate of growth. For instance, a beech hedge four years after planting can be 2m (6ft 6in) tall and will have already been cut back by

90cm (3ft). There are many other shrubs suitable for hedging, all having merits, the main considerations being hardiness, ease of cutting and, most important, their overall height.

• Fast growing evergreen conifers such as the Leyland cypress tend to be the first choice when considering tall screens and may well fulfil many requirements. However, depending on the surrounding countryside, these can look out of place, and a densely branched group of deciduous trees will often successfully achieve the screening required, even in winter. It is not always necessary to have a completely dense, block-type screen, and shade-tolerant evergreen shrubs planted beneath the trees will achieve the screening at low level. The planting of deciduous trees also has the advantage that large specimens up to 4.5m (15ft) or more may be transplanted instantly. Conifers, unless container grown, do not move well as large plants and are generally only planted at less than 1.2m (4ft) in height as anything above this tends to be checked in growth when dug from open ground. (The use of walls, hedges and other screens for sheltering exposed gardens is discussed in detail in Chapter 3.)

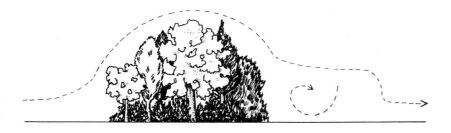

A woodland acts as a solid object and provides less shelter than a narrow belt

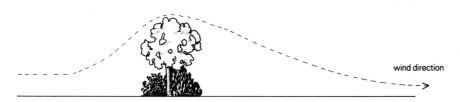

wind direction

A narrow belt increases shelter by filtering wind

FIG 1 *The effects of shape and density on shelter*

Basic • NECESSARY EVILS

There are a few rather less exciting features for which one must remember to allocate some space.

• However small a garden you have there is always garden rubbish to dispose of and, unless you have a convenient space for tipping such material, a bonfire and compost area will need to be provided. There are a variety of ready-made compost bins available which are really quite compact and take up little space. When siting the bonfire area it is vital that this is well away from the garden plants, as they can be very easily damaged by heat.

• Remember to provide a site for the washing line and dustbins; a thoughtful bit of planting or walling will suitably screen the area.

• If you have a good-sized garage the storage of tools and other large equipment such as mowers may not be a problem, but otherwise it will be necessary to provide a garden shed. There are many shapes and sizes, some of which combine storage space and a small area for greenhouse work; likewise, the summerhouse may have space allocated for tools.

• A convenient outside water tap on the house wall is essential. If possible, provide other points as well,

---

BASIC CHECKLIST

Paved sitting area
Lawns
Vegetables and soft fruit
Herbs
Hedges and screens
Bonfire and compost area
Dustbin screen
Washing line
Oil/gas tank screen
Garden shed
Water point

depending on the size of the garden. Suitable frost protection or a draining facility should be included.

Optional • PLAY AREAS

If a growing family is to use the garden, and space permits, a level or near-level area of reasonable lawn will be well used. Obviously there is no point in struggling to establish and maintain a 'perfect' lawn for a games area.

How large this area will be is dictated by the requirements of the family and your site. Put it where the least possible damage will be done from stray footballs and 'other' missiles. (It is also worth considering how easily these can be retrieved from any adjacent impenetrable thicket, river or pond, or even the neighbour's dogs!) Having a definite area for children to play does reduce damage to other parts of the garden.

Optional • CROQUET LAWN

Although in theory a croquet lawn should be 32m x 25.6m (105ft x 84ft), the game can be played on any reasonably level area of lawn. Its advantage is that no permanent features need be left on the lawn when you have finished playing, so a croquet lawn can be considered for most medium-sized gardens.

Optional • SAND PIT

One of the best items to include if you have young children is a sand pit. These are messy, and you do have to cope with the clearing-up involved, but will keep children happily absorbed for long periods. It is essential that the sand pit be adequately covered against animals – especially cats. To avoid the sand becoming waterlogged, it is a good idea to have the pit raised and to provide a free-draining base, as well as covering it. The sand pit need not be large, but if possible have a fair-sized paved surround, so that sand can easily be brushed up and returned to the pit. Portable plastic sandpits are readily available and offer a solution to some of these problems. To avoid bringing more sand than necessary into the house, a nearby cupboard or shed for buckets, spades and related play equipment would be helpful.

Optional • PADDLING POOL
Water is the other big attraction for children, and ways in which to minimise the danger to them from ornamental pools are discussed below. If you would like to give them a paddling pool, buy a temporary one you can set out on the lawn on suitable occasions. This also ensures it is filled with clean water every time. Children grow out of paddling pools very quickly and it is a waste of time and money to construct a permanent feature.

Optional • ORNAMENTAL POOL
Some say that every good garden should have water in it. Certainly water has a fascination; pools, even if quite shallow, seem to have infinite depth and coolness, while sky, sunshine and foliage reflecting from the surface, add another dimension.

Apart from the immediate aesthetic benefit, a pond or stream attracts a wealth of wildlife and provides a completely different planting environment. There are beautiful marginal aquatic plants that can be grown without the slightest difficulty; water lilies and other submersible and floating plants also add a great deal to the garden. Water can be included in almost any part of the garden, in a formal or informal situation.

Water gardening does require regular work. Small pools need periodic draining and clearing out (a messy business); with larger pools the main work is the removal of submerged water weeds and marginal plants which have become over-invasive. Aquatic plants can grow at an alarming rate and often one species will become dominant and need reducing to encourage others.

The safety of young children is an important consideration. We all know

that even the shallowest water may be fatal to a young child, and consequently having a pool is a real responsibility. A smaller pool, particularly a formal one, may be made safer, if not entirely safe, without unduly spoiling its charm by fixing a well-supported heavy-duty mesh just below the water.

A water garden can be enormous fun and waterfalls can be made easily with pumps that circulate the water, but do make sure that it is part of the whole garden landscape. If possible, site the pool near the main paved sitting area, or at least provide an area for sitting near it. From a wildlife point of view, the further away from the house the better, but try to make the pool at least visible from the house: even during winter there is always activity around it.

Optional • CONSERVATORY
OR LEAN-TO GREENHOUSE
These have a number of advantages over the functional greenhouse. They require less heating as they retain and absorb heat from the house itself (the heating system can run from the house central heating). The proximity to the house means that the conservatory is far more likely to be used and hence kept neater and tidier. It is a delight to be able to sit out in it on a day when it is fairly warm but not quite warm enough to be outside. As less heating is required than in an ordinary greenhouse you can more easily afford to maintain a higher temperature; this enables you to grow a large range of unusual plants, climbers and other flowering and fruiting subjects. A conservatory also, of course, makes a very good link between the inside of the house and the garden itself.

There are a wide range of conservatories available now in quite elegant designs. They can also be purpose built to suit the house. In order to make full use of the conservatory or lean-to greenhouse it will be necessary

Small formal pool showing heavy-duty mesh supported below surface – a safety measure for children and proof against cats and herons.

to make an area within it, slightly out of sight of the ornamental planting, for overwintering plants, potting activities and material storage.

Optional • HERBACEOUS BEDS AND BORDERS

A traditional herbaceous border is without question a spectacle. Unfortunately, there is a considerable amount of work involved in creating a successful border. To obtain the traditional effect a good deal of space is required; all other planting types are excluded and the result is a riot of colour during the summer period only. The alternative is to use herbaceous material in groups between widely spaced shrub planting – in effect shrubaceous planting. The great advantage of this type of planting is that a relatively small area is covered with the labour-intensive herbaceous plants, the larger areas being planted with shrubs and ground-smothering perennials, shrub roses, and so on. The effects of mixed planting can in fact be more satisfactory than the traditional herbaceous border, particularly if the effect is extended throughout the winter by the use of evergreen shrubs. Even in a small garden the same principles can be applied. (See p70.)

If, however, you do decide to allocate space to a traditional herbaceous border, remember that in order to achieve diversity of heights it will be necessary to make the border at least 2.5m (8ft) wide, depending on the scale of the garden. A narrow herbaceous border generally does not work satisfactorily, the planting looking thin and weak.

Optional • ROCK GARDEN

The rockery can be the ugliest part of a garden, and yet thousands of gardens have them. One of the problems with a rockery is that unless it is extremely well made it will look out of place. A rock garden should look as if it has always been there: there is nothing worse than the 'pile of stones' or 'bits of concrete' left over from the clearance of building sites, often scattered at random over a mound of soil, giving the effect of a rock bun!

If a rock garden is to be included be sure to use large, well-shaped pieces of natural stone, preferably from a local quarry. Ideally, rocks should be grouped to simulate a natural outcrop of boulders. It may be necessary to employ a contractor with the equipment and skill to manoeuvre and position heavy rocks to achieve the required effect.

Optional • ORCHARD

In a larger garden, there is something rather romantic about having an orchard, and there are few prettier sights than a mature orchard in full flower on a spring day. An orchard is also a very convenient way of using up odd areas of land for which there is otherwise no real use, or which would be difficult to maintain as cultivated garden.

A commercial grower might tell you that there is a lot of pruning to be done and pests to be controlled, and that the trees have to be well spaced. If heavy cropping is important then this would certainly be the case, but on a

OPTIONAL CHECKLIST
Play areas
Croquet lawn
Sand pit
Paddling pool
Ornamental pool
Conservatory or lean-to greenhouse
Herbaceous borders
Rock garden
Orchard

domestic scale an established tree will produce more than one family's requirements with only the minimum of attention. To avoid unnecessary picking problems, trees are available in bush form on dwarfing rootstocks; these also fruit at an earlier age.

For the convenience of mowing and achieving equal spacing between trees, an orchard is often planted on a grid system. This does look rather severe, and there is no reason why orchard trees should not be grouped into informal patches or even interspersed with other tree planting in a more arboretum-like arrangement. Planting in this manner, with longer grass and spring bulbs beneath, can create a most harmonious effect, linking the more formal garden to the wild areas and perhaps the countryside beyond.

An informal white garden featuring shrub roses, foxgloves and Viola cornuta alba *in the foreground. An unusual sculpture in wood forms a focal point.*

Enthusiast • GREENHOUSE

Deciding whether or not to include a greenhouse in your garden is difficult. To think, as a matter of principle, that you must have one is certainly a grave mistake. If a greenhouse is not going to be used enthusiastically and systematically, it will be a waste of money and more than likely unsightly: there are a whole range of shapes and sizes to choose from, but generally the free-standing greenhouse is not an elegant feature. A greenhouse needs to have a reasonably bright position and hence cannot be completely screened. It need not be in the sunniest place, as one of the major problems in summer is trying to keep the greenhouse cool, but as it will probably be used most in winter and early spring it may be necessary to provide an efficient heating system – the main benefit of a greenhouse is often for the overwintering of semi-hardy subjects and particularly for starting flower and vegetable seeds, and cuttings, early in the year. It can be used to extend the gardening year and to grow the increasingly pop-ular tender vegetables such as aubergines and peppers and give enormous pleasure, but the degree of dedication required and the cost of any heating must be considered. In some ways, the conservatory offers greater benefits than the traditional greenhouse and is certainly more ornamental.

Enthusiast • SUMMERHOUSE

A summerhouse can be situated almost anywhere in the garden and may form an interesting focal point. However, it is of most use where the orientation of the house is not ideal, and the space that could be paved for a sitting area is in shade for most of the day. A wide range of prefabricated summerhouses is available, most of them related to garden sheds but generally of more interesting design, although some can be ugly. It is obviously worth getting a number of brochures and having a good look at what is available before buying. Certainly allow sufficient space for keeping all your garden furniture in the summerhouse, as it will probably be sited some distance away from the house.

Enthusiast • ALPINE HOUSE

The alpine house is only mentioned briefly as it will be slightly different in design and function from the greenhouses and conservatories already discussed: for successful cultivation, alpines require greatly increased side and roof ventilation. An alpine house should only be considered for inclusion in the garden design if growing alpines is a specialist hobby.

Enthusiast • SCREE
AND ALPINE GARDEN

These should preferably be associated with rock features and natural slopes. In terms of allocating space, screes and alpine gardens can be as small as you like, even to the point of being an alpine garden in an old stone sink. Those wishing to grow a wide range of the more demanding alpines, or shrubs needing exceptionally well-drained conditions, could have a large

A small scree garden at midsummer but there is always colour and interest.

THE INHERITED GARDEN

Whatever the shape and size of your garden plot there will be features which give the area a certain character. Even an apparently vacant field or the empty plot left by the builder will have features worth retaining. These may not even be tangible structures – simply the aspect, the fact that part of the proposed garden has an area which gets sun late into the evening, or a view to some distant meadowland. The land form itself may have a particularly interesting slope or even a variety of changes in it. More often than not, you inherit an existing garden with numerous features and it is deciding what should remain and what should go that can be difficult.

As far as the plants go, if you intend to replan the entire garden, you must first establish which trees and shrubs are beyond sensibly digging up and moving. Consider also if the plant in question is in good health and, above all, is not nearing the end of its mature life. For example, a mature broom (*Cytisus*) may be an excellent large specimen, but should not be considered as a permanent feature around which to base a planting design: it may only live for another year or two. On the other hand, a mature apple or oak tree, although large, will still have many

years' growth ahead. Gardens are constantly changing as they grow, plants come and go all the time, and this is part of the joy of gardening.

The inherited garden will inevitably include shrubs that have outgrown the space provided, and many of these could be moved to another site. Deciding whether a plant will move satisfactorily is difficult without some previous experience. As a general rule, if you can find out what type of root system is involved this will give some idea. Plants with extensive root growth (such as *Cytisus* and *Cistus*) are unlikely to move, whereas those with dense fibrous roots, like rhododendrons, will probably move well even when quite large. With the exception of conifers, generally if you feel you could physically dig up the plant in question then it is probably worth a try. Do bear in mind that the check in growth may be severe and the planting of a new, vigorously growing specimen might be a better bet in the long run. This is certainly true for conifers and many other evergreen subjects.

Before you resite the plant, ensure that it will be possible to water the specimen frequently in spring and summer for at least two years.

You may have a garden devoid of mature plants, in which case even an old decaying tree may be worth retaining for a period of time until the new planting develops. A very old tree may also provide a sense of maturity to complement the new planting. If you have an old tree that is not too well furnished with leaves, it may be sensible to plant a large rambling rose (such as 'Kiftsgate' or a vigorous vine like *Vitis coignetiae*) to grow up through the tree and extend its decorative value for several years.

It may seem sad to cut down plants that are healthy, but hard decisions have to be made if one is not to fall into the trap of designing around unimportant features, although again it may be possible to resite shrubs or climbers of more recent planting.

When considering hard materials – paving, paths, walls and so on – these too may be movable and reusable. It would be prudent to note down even small quantities of bricks or natural stone which could be included in the planning of a new garden.

ENTHUSIASTS' CHECKLIST

Greenhouse
Summerhouse
Alpine House
Scree and alpine garden
Tennis court
Swimming pool
Lighting
Irrigation

scree feature, but it should preferably be put into the context of the entire garden.

Occasionally, impossible conditions for conventional garden planting occur, for instance where out-cropping rock and very limited soil depth prevent normal planting, and here a scree garden may be the answer.

Enthusiast • TENNIS COURT

If you have the space available, deciding whether to include a tennis court (dimensions 33.5m x 16m/110ft x 53ft) is simply a matter of how committed the family are to playing, and the cost. A large piece of potentially ornamental or productive garden area will be needed, and the boundary netting required is unsightly and will need to be screened from the rest of the garden. Temporary netting may be provided, but the grass itself requires a lot of work.

Enthusiast • SWIMMING POOL

A swimming pool on a hot summer day attracts the envy of everyone who hasn't got one. Unfortunately, some climates do not produce very many hot days and swimming pools are expensive to install. There are other disadvantages too. From an aesthetic point of view swimming pools are difficult to blend into the garden landscape, the pale blue colour which most are painted being a major stumbling block. It would be worth considering using a pale grey or green colour which, though perhaps less inviting, will help blend the pool into a formal garden setting.

Space and money permitting, a separate walled garden for the swimming pool is the ideal, and also provides a good environment for growing climbers and other sun-loving plants. Unfortunately, the design of swimming pools is generally rather traditional, but there is no reason why yours should not be a different shape, although this may be more expensive. When deciding whether you can afford the space, allow – for an average small garden swimming pool – an area of approx 11m x 5.5m (36ft x 18ft), plus adequate paving surround.

Enthusiast • LIGHTING

Outdoor lighting adds another dimension to the garden, and when viewed from the house gives the impression of a rather exotically decorated room. Even the simplest of lighting – one solitary spotlight into the garden – will have this effect; a well-laid-out lighting arrangement can produce something even more inviting and intriguing. The lighting should be used to shine onto foliage plants and up into trees, and not merely as floodlight (light sources at different distances from view will give an exaggerated perspective). In the same way that a photograph tends to highlight the real image, lighting in the garden seems to brighten and strengthen the planting scheme, and even the untidiest garden can look good illuminated at night.

Use only white light as tinted bulbs have a rather disastrous effect on most flower colours. All external lighting should be installed by a qualified electrician, who will provide adequate coverage for the appropriate fuse and cut-out switches. Outside lighting is not particularly expensive, but installation costs may be high since the cables will need to be buried to a good depth to avoid their being disturbed or damaged. Think about lighting at an early stage, and get the necessary cabling done prior to other construction work.

Enthusiast • IRRIGATION

It is now feasible to consider incorporating an automatic irrigation system for the entire garden. With the advent of plastic plumbing materials this is both cheap and virtually maintenance free. There are a number of specialist firms that will suggest suitable systems and provide a quotation for the installation.

Although a useful luxury, an irrigation system is by no means essential unless you live in a very dry climate: most established trees, shrubs and herbaceous plants can withstand or at least recover from drought periods. The real benefit is perhaps to the lawn in dry weather, but even then one has to be very keen on the grass to justify the expense. However, areas that have many mature trees may find a greater need for efficient irrigation as these trees can extract all available moisture during dry summers.

MONEY AND MAINTENANCE

If money and leisure time were no object, it would not be difficult to include a good proportion of the features discussed. In the real world, however, compromises will have to be made. You do not of course have to undertake the development of the garden all in one go. It may be phased over a number of years, but to ensure continuity in the design it is a good idea to have one overall scheme to work to.

In terms of financial outlay, hard landscape materials – paving, walling, pools, greenhouses and so on – are the expensive items. Lawns and plants per square metre are substantially cheaper. However, in terms of maintenance the paving will require no further work, and shrub and ground cover, although initially requiring quite a high work input, soon reduces. The lawn area, on the other hand, requires a very high and constant input. It is necessary therefore to try to achieve a happy balance between:

• Capital outlay
• Further maintenance, your time and possibly someone else's time
• The aesthetic balance between hard paved areas, walls etc, and soft materials

• The importance of the main features as to how much use and pleasure they will give: will you really use the greenhouse, and how often will you use the swimming pool?

Having considered the range of features and options for inclusion in your garden, use the Basic, Optional and For Enthusiasts checklists to make your own features checklist and notes on possible sizes, before proceeding with your garden design.

SURVEYING THE SURROUNDINGS

To plant the garden to its best advantage, first establish the north/south aspect and make a note of where the sun rises and sets. Allow for the difference in the angle of the sun at different times of the year – you may plan a sitting area which is fine in the middle of the summer but towards autumn the neighbour's boundary hedge may well shade the area entirely. Try also to establish the prevailing wind direction and make a note of the more sheltered areas of the garden.

It is a good idea to create a merger between house and garden, and between the garden and its surroundings. Note down the position of adjacent tree groups or abutting woodland, as this will influence the design, and you may wish to link the garden visually to a distant view, such as a glimpse of a river or small picturesque hamlet. Noting the position of views and where best they can be seen from will be helpful when planning the overall scheme.

It is worth having a good look round the adjacent land and taking notes, as a lot of information can be gained about the type of plants which are most likely to thrive in your garden: at the extremes, if there are pines, rhododendrons and bracken, for example, the soil is evidently acid, whereas if there are alders, willows and ash this would suggest a wetter soil which is not necessarily acid, while beech, yew and whitebeam usually indicate an alkaline soil.

FIG 2 *A survey map at a scale of around 1:2500 would be useful to the owners of the rectangular garden plots of The Pines and Wagtails, and particularly to Top Farm with its irregular plot*

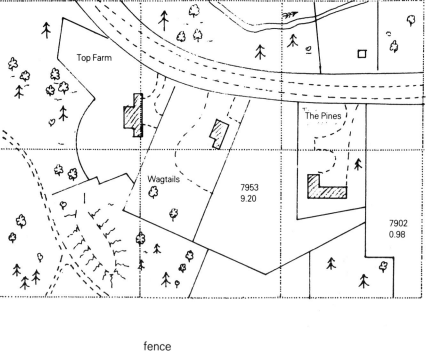

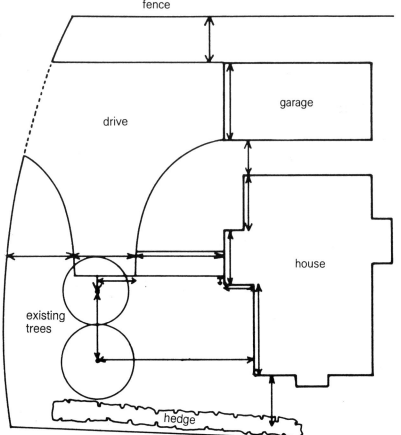

FIG 3 *Arrows indicating the measurements required are marked on the sketch plan before measuring*

PLANNING CHECKLIST

Before you begin to plan your garden on paper, consider:
• the relative scale of the features to be included
• the possibilities for dividing the medium-to-large garden into separate areas of differing character
• the provision of focal points of interest around the garden

SURVEYING THE GARDEN

A certain amount of garden planning can be done on site without the need to prepare a detailed garden plan. However, when you are considering a large area or complete garden, the only way to plan successfully is on paper, in which case it is vital to have accurate information before you start – there is nothing more frustrating than having arrived at an entirely satisfactory detailed garden plan to find on setting it out on the ground that it does not quite fit. The object is therefore to record all the principal features of the garden plot as accurately as possible.

Surveying is a profession in its own right and there are limits to the accuracy required for the average garden. However, if you have a very large garden with a lot of different features to measure, and particularly if there are many changes of level, it may be worth considering employing a qualified surveyor. The electronic equipment now available to the surveyor does mean that a large survey can be done more quickly and hence work out to be less expensive than one might expect.

DOING YOUR OWN SURVEY

For most gardens there are some basic techniques which can be used to establish the main features, such as boundaries and their line: invariably garden walls and fences are not square or parallel, even though they may seem so to the naked eye. Looking through the house deeds will often provide a plan of the plot at 1:2500 or larger, or consult your local library. You can check the accuracy of the plan and its scale by measuring a few dimensions on site; even if you are unable to use the plan due to slightly inaccurate measurements, you may find the various angles of the boundaries very helpful. If you have an architect's drawing of the ground-floor plan of the house, this will also provide detailed information and save time. But beware: check some of the measurements, as the builder may not have followed every detail on the drawings.

Taking Measurements

Before taking any measurements it is a good idea to draw a rough diagram of the main features on paper as you see them, and indicate with arrows the dimensions you need to measure, adding the figures when measured. This will help you to avoid missing any measurements. The simplest procedure is to base all your measure-

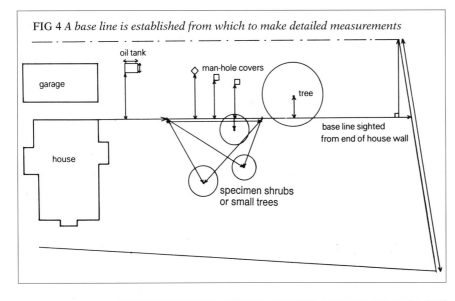

FIG 4 *A base line is established from which to make detailed measurements*

garage

oil tank

man-hole covers

tree

base line sighted from end of house wall

house

specimen shrubs or small trees

TRIANGULATION

Find two fixed points from which to move your measurements; the house wall or treeline sighted from the house are ideal. Measure the distance to each main feature, such as a tree, first from one corner or point and then from the other. Transfer these measurements using compasses set to the correct scale. Make intersecting arcs where the features are sited.

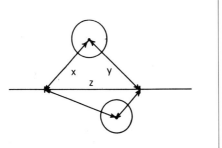

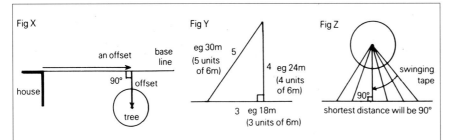

Fig X

an offset

base line

house

90°

offset

tree

Fig Y

eg 30m (5 units of 6m)

5

4 eg 24m (4 units of 6m)

3　eg 18m (3 units of 6m)

Fig Z

swinging tape

90°

shortest distance will be 90°

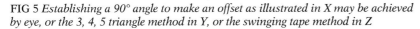

FIG 5 *Establishing a 90° angle to make an offset as illustrated in X may be achieved by eye, or the 3, 4, 5 triangle method in Y, or the swinging tape method in Z*

ments from the house walls. These, apart from being solid and permanent features, are usually square and can be used as a datum point.

In the event that none of the garden boundaries is straight, a line can be extended from a house wall across the area to be surveyed, sighting to the line of the house wall and using garden canes to establish the line. If it is not possible to sight a line from the end of the house, a line at 90° from the house wall can be made using the 3, 4, 5 triangle method. This is now a base line from which measurements can be made from any point along it. These can either be as offsets at 90° (Fig 5x) or by using triangulation (see box); in this way you can plot individual features such as trees. Triangulation may also be done from the house corners as these are fixed points, provided of course that a measurement has been made between them.

Once you have established the perimeter of the site accurately, plotting the internal measurements is relatively simple. Deciding what is, and what is not important to measure is perhaps a more difficult task. Major items such as trees, retaining walls and paths should certainly be included: if in doubt at this stage it is better to mark them in, as they can always be disregarded at a later stage.

Changes of Level
Now is the time to record on the rough diagram important notes on prevailing wind direction, sheltered spots, desirable views and the orientation and level changes. Without special equipment establishing the levels of your site accurately will be difficult. If the level changes are not very great, a little guesswork and at least an appreciation of where the changes in slope occur should suffice. However, you should bear in mind that it can often be very deceptive and you will usually tend to underestimate the extent of the changes in height.

Recording the height of existing retaining walls and steps can often give sufficient information. If you only

USING A LEVEL TRIPOD AND STAFF

1 Accurately locate the position of the points where you wish to record the level heights. You may wish to make a grid in order to get a complete cover of the area, but you will still need to know certain specific positions such as the base of a tree which you intend to retain (you should not change the soil level around trees).

2 Decide on a permanent datum point (or benchmark), such as the top of a manhole or an area of paving that you know you are going to retain.

3 Set up the staff in a position that can be seen from all the points you wish to record, preferably centrally between them, and set the tripod level.

4 With an assistant holding the staff at each point, record all the levels you need to know. If not all the positions you wish to record are visible, you will need to set up a new position. In this case, having moved, refer back to the datum to assess the position of the new location relative to the previous recordings.

5 By adding or subtracting the figure recorded from the original datum, you will have the height difference from the datum to the desired level point.

require a few further levels, it may be possible to do this using a long plank and spirit level and measuring the height difference.

If your garden does slope appreciably, it is advisable to hire a level tripod and staff. You would then need to carry out the procedure shown above.

Drawing up the Completed Survey
If possible, drawing up the plan is best done on a professional drawing board with a parallel motion, enabling you to work on a larger scale. Using unlined paper and tracing paper, copies can easily be printed off your design by most large copying shops. However, it is also quite satisfactory to transfer the information on to graph paper, or alternatively all this could be done on a computer.

It is important that the survey is

drawn to scale. A scale drawing is representative of a unit of measurement on the ground; for example, 1cm on paper might represent 50cm on the ground (1:50) or, in imperial, 1in=4ft on the ground (¼in:1ft). Depending on the area of the garden, a scale should be chosen to make the area fit on to a manageable size of paper, say 1m x 75cm (3ft 3in x 2ft 6in). It may be necessary to divide the garden at a convenient place and make two plans, eg front and back garden, in order to get the survey conveniently on to the paper. A scale of 1:50 (¼in:1ft) is the best scale to work on, as this can be used to include even detailed planting arrangements at a later date without having to enlarge areas from a smaller scale. 1:100 (⅛in:1ft) is quite adequate for designing the layout of the garden, and often the only option for a medium to large garden survey. If you are using graph paper choose squared divisions that suit the scale you have chosen.

The survey should be drawn in pencil, but not too lightly as the information will need to be visible through an overlay of tracing paper. Pencil (H, HB or F) is ideal because it may be desirable at a later stage to remove some information which you decide you do not need.

Having accurately prepared your survey with all the necessary information, you are then in a position to start on the artwork of the garden design as described in Chapter 4.

SURVEY CHECKLIST

Before you begin to survey the garden itself, make notes on the following, to be included later on your diagrams:
• prevailing wind direction
• path of the sun in summer and winter
• sheltered spots
• tree groups or woodland close to your garden
• views
• plants growing in the immediate locality

CHAPTER 3

GROUNDWORK

Diascia spp. from the highlands of South Africa are reasonably hardy, if not long-lived, in well-drained sunny sites like this raised bed.
(See page 127.)

The aim of this chapter is to give you the background knowledge necessary for successful planning and planting. It is thus a reference chapter, rather than one full of inspirational ideas. Here we discuss the soil, how it is formed and how this affects the ease of gardening and which plants can be grown. This is followed by a section on climate, which shows how it affects plants, and how the provision of shelter or other features will modify it and increase the range and quality of plants which can be cultivated. Finally, a brief outline of plant biology is given, as this can help both in successful planting and in the satisfactory control of pests and weeds.

HOW SOIL WORKS

The soil is the medium into which nearly all plants are rooted, the main natural exceptions being epiphytes, which grow on trees or boulders, and algae and other water plants. An understanding of how soil is formed helps to explain how it should be handled to get the best out of it, and also how it affects the plants which can be grown.

The function of the soil is to provide the plants with support, food and water. For support, the plant needs to be in contact with a sufficiently large body of soil to withstand the effects of wind. This is particularly important

for trees and the larger shrubs. Food comes in the form of nutrients, which have to be present in the soil in ways in which the plant can absorb them. Most water, which is essential for all life processes, comes from the soil. The soil also has to be the home for the roots and, apart from a few exceptions like the swamp cypress (*Taxodium distichum*), all plants need oxygen in the soil for these, just as the aerial parts use oxygen for breathing; the soil therefore has to be a fit place in which roots can live. The depth to which plants can root will affect the volume of usable soil on the site, and therefore the size of the reserve of nutrients and water.

COMPOSITION

Soil consists of many different components. It is derived from a mixture of mineral particles and organic matter and is a living world in its own right, including many animals, fungi and bacteria which live out their entire lives there.

The mineral particles in the soil come from the breakdown of rocks. They are graded according to size into stones, sand, silt and clay particles. Stones and larger pieces of rock have a very limited effect upon the soil; they take up space without giving anything in return. Sand is just comfortably visible to the naked eye, whilst silt and clay particles are very much smaller.

Sand particles fit together badly, leaving large empty spaces between the grains. Water can drain through these spaces and air circulates freely through the soil. Even when wet, though, sandy soils hold on to very little water and these soils will dry out quickly. Sand grains have a small surface area in relation to their size and consequently have only a limited capability for holding on to nutrients, which are thus easily washed out of the soil. This makes sandy soils essentially of low fertility.

Clay particles are minute and fit very closely together; in relation to their size, they have a large surface area on to which nutrients and surface water can be held. Because of the tight fitting of the particles, there is little space for the circulation of either water or oxygen through the soil; drainage is therefore very slow and poor, and most plants find rooting in clay soils difficult or impossible. When a clay soil dries out, it can be slow to re-wet. Clay soils generally contain a good supply of nutrients and the problem can be to make these available for plant growth.

Silt particles are smaller than sand and are much more similar in character to clay. Soils derived mainly from silt particles are usually very fertile, as they hold on to large quantities of nutrients and water, while permitting adequate drainage and exchange of gases.

Organic matter is the fourth main component and is essential for a healthy soil, improving the structure and water-holding capacity. Organic matter in the soil acts in part like clay particles, being capable of holding on to both nutrients and water but, unlike clay, the organic matter does not form a dense mass. The effect of organic matter incorporated into clay and other heavy soils is to improve the drainage and structure, making them both more fruitful and much easier to manage in the garden; on light soils, it increases the water- and nutrient-holding capacity.

SOIL ORGANISMS

Organic matter, though, is of no use in the form in which it falls from the tree as a leaf or as a dead root; first it must be broken down into finer particles. This process is carried out by many different organisms in the soil fauna and flora. Bacteria and fungi tend to be used to break down the coarser material such as wood and hard leaves, while animals such as millipedes and earthworms are involved in incorporating the material into the soil.

Earthworms are the most useful animals in the soil. They ingest raw organic matter, especially from the surface layers, where they can prevent the build-up of excess dead material, and mix it with calcium carbonate in the gut. The effect of this action is to produce in the worm-cast soil an improved water- and nutrient-holding capacity. As the worms mainly extract organic matter, this soil also contains more nutrients than the normal soil. The other positive benefit of earthworms is that the burrows they make through the soil act as drainage channels. Most of their activity is concentrated in the top 10–15cm (4–6in), but in dry periods they may burrow much deeper; often it is down such burrows that plant roots can reach greater depths in heavy or compacted soils. The most obvious visible signs of worms are the casts made on the surface, although most species pass the 'processed' soil out underground.

Apart from earthworms, the soil is home to a whole host of organisms, including many species of small invertebrates, like woodlice, and myriads of bacteria and fungi. Some of these organisms, such as cranefly larvae and cutworms, are harmful to garden plants; the overwhelming majority, though, are very positive in their role.

SOIL TYPES

The ideal soil is a loam. Loams are composed of 50 per cent sand, 25 per cent silt, 20 per cent clay particles and

Cytisus do best in neutral or acid soils, or deep soils over chalk, including stiff clay-loam.

5 per cent organic matter or humus. This gives a good combination of water- and nutrient-holding capacity, along with drainage and aeration. These soils are naturally quite fertile and, more importantly in the garden setting, they are able to hold applied nutrients.

Soils with increasing amounts of sand are **sandy loams** or **sandy soils**. As the proportion of sand increases, these become progressively less fertile and more free draining, with a lower capability for holding nutrients and water. One positive aspect of increasing sandiness is that these soils warm up more quickly in the spring, allowing plant growth to start earlier, but they also cool down more quickly. Sandy soils are light and easily worked, whatever the weather.

Soils with higher proportions of clay or silt particles are clay loams or silty loams. Drainage is much poorer, particularly as the amount of clay in the soil increases. They are also cold soils, taking a long time to warm up in the spring, but holding that warmth for longer in the autumn. They are heavy and difficult to cultivate; digging or rotovating should only be carried out when these soils are on the dry side.

Soils with very high proportions of organic matter are **peats**. These are usually low in nutrients and may be poorly drained.

The depth to which plants can root is determined by the nature of the soil and of the drainage. Plants cannot root into compacted or, with few exceptions, airless soil; rooting into pure clays is therefore limited, but roots can be very long though sparse in sands.

Plants must have an adequate supply of oxygen available at the roots. Soils with a greater depth suitable for rooting have a much higher volume of water and nutrients available for plant growth, and are inherently more fertile than those with shallower rooting depths. Drainage can improve rooting and is discussed on p23.

FOOD FOR PLANTS

• The **macro-nutrients** are nitrogen (N), phosphorus (P), potassium (K), calcium (Ca), sulphur (S) and magnesium (Mg), as well as carbon (C), oxygen (O) and hydrogen (H). Shortage of any one of these is very damaging to growth, but equally an excess can kill. The letter in parentheses after the nutrient is the international chemical letter which will be found on fertiliser packets.

• **Nitrogen** is needed by the plant for the formation of proteins, which are essential for growth. Although nitrogen is the main gas in the air, this is inert, and plants have to obtain it from the soil as a nitrate, nitrite or ammonium compound. Nitrogen is usually restricted to the top few inches of soil.

• **Phosphorus** and **potassium** are both needed for cell division and for the ripening of fruits. Potassium is very soluble, and therefore easily lost by leaching from many soils. Phosphorus is much less soluble; in fact, its very insolubility in some soils can create an artificial shortage as far as the plants are concerned.

• **Calcium** is needed by all plants for cell walls.

• **Sulphur** is used in root development and as a component of proteins.

• **Magnesium** is an essential constituent of the chlorophyll molecule (see p27), which is involved in photosynthesis.

• **Carbon**, **hydrogen** and **oxygen** are needed in large quantities to make all organic compounds. Carbon and oxygen come from carbon dioxide in the air and are absorbed by the leaves, while hydrogen comes from water.

• **Trace elements** are required in very small quantities. Molybdenum, for example, is only needed in the plant tissues at a concentration of one part in one hundred million, and may be fatal if more than ten times this amount is present, but is nevertheless important in the plant's use of nitrate and nitrite forms of nitrogen. **Iron** is essential for the manufacture of chlorophyll, **boron** for the uptake from the soil of calcium, and **zinc**, **manganese** and **copper** in the formation of enzymes and proteins.

NUTRIENTS
Plants need to absorb nutrients from the soil to be able to make growth through the action of photosynthesis in the leaves. Half a dozen elements are needed in relatively large amounts and are called major or macro-nutrients, while others are required in much smaller quantities and are termed trace elements (see box).

PH AND NUTRIENT AVAILABILITY
pH is a measure of the alkalinity or acidity of the soil. A neutral soil has a pH of around 6.5 to 7; above pH 7 the soil is alkaline and at pH 6 and below it is acidic. The effect of pH is to alter the way in which nutrients are dissolved in solution, and therefore the way that plants can absorb them.

Some nutrients are only available to plants between certain pH levels. Phosphorus, for instance, may be plentiful in alkaline soils, but most of it is insoluble; bonemeal will not add usable phosphorus to alkaline soils, although it is a satisfactory way of adding phosphorus to acidic ones.

Certain deficiency symptoms are due to the unavailability of nutrients at certain pH levels. Many plants show a yellowing of the foliage, or 'chlorosis', on alkaline sites due to the insolubility of iron on these soils. This form of deficiency cannot be controlled by using rusty nails but is helped by giving iron as iron sequestrene, a compound which makes iron available to plants at higher pH levels. Hydrangeas will tolerate both acidic and alkaline soils, but the aluminium ions which turn the flowers of some hydrangeas blue are not available to the plant on alkaline soils.

Plants differ in their ability to extract nutrients from the soil at different pH levels, and some plants can only grow at certain pH levels. Others may naturally be found in areas where a particular nutrient is scarcely available; if planted in a soil where that nutrient is readily available they may be poisoned by their inability *not* to take it up – rhododendrons and calcium are one such case.

IMPROVING YOUR SOIL

There are several ways to improve soils. These include cultivation techniques, using manures and composts, mulches, drainage and applying fertilisers. In theory, the texture can be altered by incorporating clay into sandy soils and vice versa, but the quantities required are so vast as to make this impractical. The better soils, ie loams, may only need additional nutrients, but other soils will need their structure improved as well.

Soil structure is the way in which the soil holds together: a sandy soil doesn't, while a clay forms a large lump. When rubbed in the hand, the ideal soil breaks into small lumps about a quarter-inch in diameter, and is said to have a 'crumb' structure. Soil improvement must work towards improving the structure, so that on both clay and sandy soils the particles hold together in crumb-sized units. Only as this is achieved does the addition of chemical fertilisers make sense. Otherwise, in sandy soils they will be washed away during the next downpour, whilst on clay ones the added nutrients will either be lost as surface run-off or locked up in the lower part of the soil profile, out of reach of plant roots.

Cultivation can be a good way to improve heavy soils. The act of digging breaks up the soil, incorporating surface organic matter. Even better is the action of frost on the turned clods: alternate freezing and thawing results in the soil forming into crumb-sized particles. Autumn is the best time to cultivate a heavy soil, as it must be carried out when the soil is dryish, otherwise the result will simply be a mud pie. Avoid walking on the soil in winter and wait for it to dry out in the spring before carrying out any further cultivation.

'Ripping', or 'subsoiling', is a method of cultivation which does not turn over the soil. A special plough with deep tines is drawn through the subsoil and shatters it, thereby relieving compaction, although it will also introduce temporary drainage along the line of the tines.

On light soils, cultivation will not improve the structure, although it can be used to relieve compaction.

Drainage is mainly of value on the heavier soils. The object of drainage is to improve the aeration of the soil by removing surplus water which is filling all or many of the spaces that could be occupied by air. Improving the aeration of the soil will increase the potential for plant roots to survive at greater depths, and thus the volume of soil available for plant growth. It will also make it a better environment for soil organisms and will allow them to improve the soil structure at a greater depth. Aeration will also remove toxic compounds caused by the anaerobic (airless) decomposition of organic material.

Drainage will need to be at closer intervals on the heavier soils. On really heavy ones, it may make little impact, as any drainage channels opened may soon close. On light soils, it can be widely spaced, needing only to bypass some impediment.

Cultivation and drainage are the only two methods to increase significantly the depth of soil available for rooting, but the quality of the soil can be improved by **incorporating manures and composts** into the soil. The organic matter added will benefit the soil structure of both clay and sandy soils, as discussed above; also, the nutrients present in the manure will be added to the stock in the soil. The material can either be left on the surface, relying on earthworms and other soil organisms to take the organic matter into the soil (and for the rain to wash in the nutrients), or dug in by some form of cultivation; the latter will be quicker in effect.

Adding organic matter to poorly drained soils can lead to a decrease in fertility. This is because the organic matter can take what little oxygen there is out of the soil as it breaks down, leaving it anaerobic and turning it even more sour. On heavy

CASE STUDY

DRAINAGE

Drainage can be carried out by placing clay pipes or plastic drainage tubes in a trench, which is filled with coarse gravel. A layer of matting over the top will prevent or slow down the rate at which material falls into the trench and clogs up the gravel or pipeworks. Great care must be taken to ensure that the drains are not expected to run uphill, or they will quickly be blocked by silt. On some soils, drainage can be effected by making slits in the soil and filling these with sand.

Provision must always be made for the water drained to be taken off site. Except on a small scale, laying a pattern of drains is best left to a professional drainage contractor. Whatever your drainage, do not expect it to last indefinitely – any scheme will need to be cleaned or relaid at intervals.

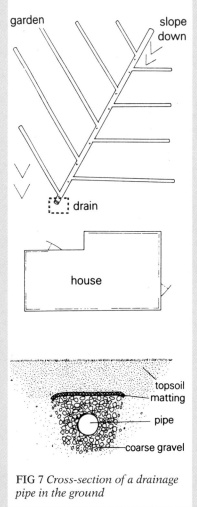

FIG 6 *Herringbone drainage pattern*

FIG 7 *Cross-section of a drainage pipe in the ground*

soils, manures should be used in association with other practices described under Drainage (see Case Study, p23).

Raw material like straw can also be used; it will take longer to break down into useful humus, and while it is doing so it will remove nutrients, primarily nitrogen, from the soil. Where there is time to wait for the material to be broken down, it is a cheaper option than manures for plants which are not sensitive to temporary low levels of nitrogen, or where nitrogen is also added as an inorganic fertiliser.

Organic mulches are similar to manures in their effect upon the soil, but slower. They do not, however, contain any significant quantity of nutrients. Their effect upon soil structure is two-fold: by increasing the level of soil organisms, they lead to an improvement in the organic matter content of the soil, and by covering the surface they prevent compaction and the closing of worm burrows.

Chemicals can be used in three ways to improve soils:

• Artificial or inorganic fertilisers can be used to supplement the nutrient supply. This way, specific deficiencies can be treated very quickly. Special formulations of fertilisers are also available which can give a slow release of the nutrients. However, these are expensive, and the role of fertilisers should be seen as replacing those missing after the soil has been improved, rather than as solving the problem.

• Altering the pH of the soil can be of benefit. It is much easier to increase the pH of an acidic soil, by the addition of limestone or dolomitic limestone, than to reduce the pH. This can be done, however, by adding flowers of sulphur, and will occur if ammonium-sulphate-based fertilisers are added over a period of years. The effect will be to alter the availability of several nutrients, as discussed above.

• On clays, chemicals can also be used to cause the particles to 'flocculate', or stick together in small clusters, so that the soil becomes less sticky and more manageable. Lime is often used for this purpose, and provided the plants you are planning to use are not affected by increasing the pH, it can be an effective way to improve such soils. Alginates, made from seaweed, can have the same effect.

Mulching is very beneficial for young or newly-planted shrubs as it helps conserve water and discourages weed growth

• PROBLEM SOLVER •

MODIFYING YOUR LOCAL ENVIRONMENT

The garden environment can be altered in several ways, although the most effective is to increase the shelter.

• Shelter can be provided either by a living screen, such as a line of carefully chosen trees, or by a structure such as a wall. Shelterbelts can also be made from artificial materials, such as PVC webbing.

Walls are good at creating very local warmer environments. Walled gardens provide some shelter and allow many plants to be grown on the walls: the walls of the house are also extremely effective locations for slightly tender plants. In each case, the wall reduces the wind speed close to it and will retain heat, releasing it slowly overnight.

Shelterbelts can be made either from artificial materials, which usually have a 50 per cent porosity, or by the use of plants. Artificial materials have the advantage of being immediately effective, although of limited lifespan and more expensive. Shelters made out of plants take longer to become effective, but will last much longer. They are also more aesthetically pleasing, fitting into the garden design, and are more economical, although often requiring some regular maintenance.

• Overhead shelter is also very beneficial in many situations. It decreases the wind speed, lowers the temperature during the summer but raises it in winter, and increases the humidity (many rhododendrons, for instance, thrive under the canopy of an oak wood). An overstorey tree must not be too aggressive in its rooting, nor cast too much shade.

• Another way in which the local climate can be modified is by altering the surface of the soil. A grass sward will insulate the soil, keeping it warmer but causing a more severe frost above. If the soil surface is bare, heat will be radiated from it, preventing the temperature just above the soil from dropping so low, and reducing the danger of frost damage.

• Mulches over the root spread will also modify the environment, keeping the soil below damp and thereby reducing moisture stress.

• Banks will have quite a pronounced effect. Water will drain to the bottom, making that moister and generally cooler, except on an east-west bank where one side always faces the sun. The top of the bank will be drier, and more suited to plants which like hot dry sites or dislike damp at the roots.

CASE STUDY

HEDGES VERSUS WALLS AND FENCES
Some gardens are extremely exposed and the use of hedges and screens is particularly important. Walls and fences provide a small amount of local shelter to either side of them, but the ideal way to achieve shelter is to reduce the speed of the wind.

Walls and solid structures do not reduce the speed of wind: they merely deflect it, and can cause it to go faster somewhere else. At a distance of around eight times the height of the structure, the wind will start to eddy back and will often reach half-way back to the structure; in very windy weather, it can reach the whole way back. To slow down the wind, it is necessary to have a barrier that is about half open spaces. This prevents turbulence and gives measurable shelter downwind and also some shelter upwind.

A hedge allows the air to filter through it rather than funnel over and around it, with the extent of the shelter area largely dependent upon the height of the hedge. Effective shelter on the downwind side of a hedge is found up to a distance equivalent to ten times its height, with the measurement being made from the base of the hedge. There is some reduction in wind velocity at distances up to thirty times the height of the hedge.

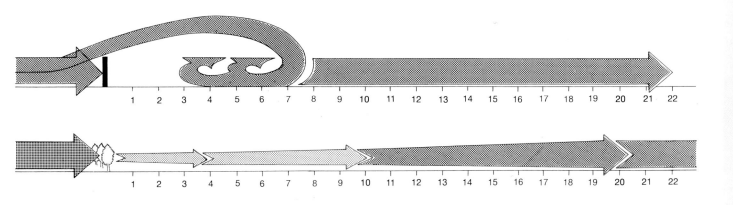

FIG 8 *Modifying the local environment – effects of solid and permeable shelter on wind speed and turbulence (the numerals indicate multiples of the height of the shelter, in the downwind direction)*

A hedge can act as an effective screen, reducing wind speed and producing a microclimate in which less hardy plants or those requiring shelter can survive

CLIMATE

The major elements of climate are common to a large region of a country, but the local climate can be specific to a very limited area. Plants are dependent upon the climate they experience locally, which is set within the general climate of the country, so where your garden is situated will affect the type of climate you experience, how much rain falls, the extremes of frosts recorded and the distribution of sunlight.

LOCAL OR MICROCLIMATE

The local climate is dependent upon the national climate but is influenced by local features, such as the topography, aspect and planting.

Earlier we discussed the differences between light soils, which warm up quickly and cool down as fast, and heavy soils, which do neither quickly.

These differences strongly influence the local environment, although they are insignificant on a national scale.

Local topography has a very pronounced impact on the climate: for example, there will be quite marked differences between the south, east, west and north sides of a hill. In the northern hemisphere, the south side will receive more sunlight and be sheltered from cold north winds. The east side will get the early sunlight in the morning, with the increased chance of damage by unseasonal frosts; it will be exposed to north and east winds and sheltered from the west wind, so having less rainfall. The west side will receive the full force of the west wind, complete with an extra ration of rain, but will be milder overall than the other sides. The north side will be permanently in the shade, and much colder. It will receive the worst of cold northerly winds; growth will start later

in the year but damage from late spring frosts is less likely, although early autumn ones may damage plants if the growth has not ripened in time.

The sides of a hill will tend to be warmer than either the windier top or the bottom. This is because as air cools down, it becomes heavier and will drain down the sides to collect in a frost pocket lower down. Flat land tends to be open and exposed, with no natural air drainage to remove cold air.

The different aspects will receive different amounts of rainfall and sunlight, so that the relative humidity will also be different, and this can affect the growth of some plants.

Again, the wind will vary with the aspect. The most obvious effect of wind is to cause the abrasion and breakage of plant parts; the main effect, however, is a reduction in the rate of growth due to the plant being put under moisture stress.

Local planting will influence the climate. A screen of trees can reduce the wind speed and also shade the garden, giving a less frosty and more humid environment. If on the east side, they will slow down the rate at which the air warms up in the morning, reducing the damage caused by unseasonal frosts. By drying out the soil, they can also cause other plants to slow down their vegetative growth in late summer, leading to better ripening of shoots and possibly a higher set of flowers for next year.

HOW YOUR PLANTS GROW

If you understand a little about the nature of plants, you can enjoy them more, look after their nutrition, and control pests and weeds, with more confidence. But this section can be skipped if you prefer – or left until later!

THE NATURE OF PLANTS

The essential difference between plants and animals is that plants are able to make their own food from raw materials, whilst animals can only eat either plants or other animals.

In making their food, plants use carbon dioxide, water and sunlight to make sugars, by the process called photosynthesis. Sunlight is trapped by the chlorophyll in the leaves – the substance that makes leaves green – and its energy is used in combining water and carbon dioxide; during that process the oxygen which we ourselves need for breathing is released. The carbon dioxide required is extracted by the leaves from the small quantities present in the atmosphere. Water is drawn up from the soil by the roots, although small quantities can also enter through the leaves.

The sugars made in the leaves are converted into other organic products using nutrients extracted from the soil (eg into proteins by incorporating nitrogen). The sugars and other products are moved around through the plant to provide food for growth, for storage or for reproduction. The nutrients and water are carried up to the leaves from the roots in the sap; nearly all of the water extracted from the soil is used not in photosynthesis but to keep the leaves rigid, and is lost in transpiration.

For this essential first stage of sugar manufacture to work, several conditions must be satisfied:
• The leaves must be able to obtain carbon dioxide from the atmosphere, which means that the breathing pores or stomata in them must be open; very windy weather or a shortage of water in the plant will result in them being shut to conserve moisture, thereby preventing photosynthesis.
• The leaves must be exposed to daylight, as photosynthesis cannot take place in the dark.
• Nutrients must be available, both for the manufacture of the next stage (otherwise the concentration of sugars will prove lethal) and the previous one, so that chlorophyll and other enzymes are available.

Details of how each part of a plant performs its functions are given in the box overleaf.

WEEDS
An understanding of weed biology is useful as a prerequisite of control, on the 'know your enemy' principle.

Although 'any plant out of place' is the best definition of a weed, in practice the main ones are those which spring up in no time on bare ground and seem to take ages to remove. These weeds require disturbed ground for germination. In the absence of disturbance the seeds will remain dormant in the soil, in some cases for more than a hundred years. Often they will only germinate if brought sufficiently close to the surface and many need light for germination to take place. One way to reduce the number germinating, therefore, is not to disturb the soil unnecessarily. This can be achieved by avoiding cultivation (only hoe if you find it therapeutic!) and relying upon either herbicides (properly used) or mulches for weed control; as the plants cover the ground, they too will discourage weed-seed germination.

Many weeds produce masses of small seeds. Even in the right conditions, these will not all germinate immediately; some will do so, others will come up after one year and some after several years. If a crop of groundsel (*Senecio vulgaris*), for example, is allowed to seed, sufficient seeds will be produced to make more than enough groundsel plants for the next ten or so years, even if no further plants set seed. This means that you can't blame the neighbours for all the weeds which germinate, as they were already present in your garden soil.

Numerous weeds complete their lifecycle in a very short time. Groundsel takes less than ten weeks, and if cut off from its roots after flowering it can still set viable seed, even if buried in the soil.

Finally, because weeds have very short lifecycles, strains resistant to particular herbicides can be selected within a short number of years.

WHY CONTROL WEEDS?
The two main reasons for controlling weeds are that they can be unsightly

Gravel mulching is an attractive method of controlling the growth of weeds

PLANT PARTS

FLOWERS

The 'perfect' flower consist of sepals, petals, ovaries, stigmas, styles, stamens with anthers and filaments, and nectaries. Its function is to enable the fertilisation of egg cells by pollen, so leading to the production of seeds to make the next generation. Many flowers are not 'perfect' and one or more of the above parts may be missing.

The sepals are often rather green and leafy and are mainly involved in protecting the flower buds. In a few species they become highly coloured and act like petals (eg clematis). The petals are usually the attractive parts of the flowers, giving the floral display. The ovaries are where the seeds are developed, and the stamens where the pollen is manufactured and shed.

Most flowers are designed for pollination by various animals, including birds, but some plants are wind pollinated (eg hazel), and these have no need for showy petals. In wind-pollinated plants, the flowers tend either to be placed where the wind will catch them, or to open before the leaves. To induce insects to visit, many flowers secrete sugar-rich nectar. Fragrance is also used to attract pollinators.

In many plants, the flowers are imperfect: that is, only one sex is present. This is a device to ensure cross-pollination and avoid self-breeding; if these plants are grown for their fruit, both sexes must be present (hollies are an example).

An alternative strategy for ensuring cross-pollination is for the plant's own pollen to be ineffective at fertilising the flowers. Here the flowers must be fertilised by pollen from a different plant of the same species if fruit and seed are to be formed. Many fruit trees, especially apples, have this mechanism and will only crop if two or more compatible trees are growing nearby.

Many garden plants are selected with abnormal flowers, such as extra petals. Some of these abnormalities occur naturally in certain groups of plants: for instance, a number of clematis have extra petal-like structures which are modified stamens and are called staminoides.

In most plants, flowers are only produced by specimens which are growing satisfactorily. The incitement to produce flowers often follows a build-up in the amount of sugars in the top of the plant. In fruit trees, this can be artificially stimulated by partially girdling the stem, thereby restricting the passage of sugars down to the roots. Plants will not flower well if grown in more shade than the species likes, although other plants will not tolerate full sun. A severe pruning will cause the plant to concentrate on vegetative growth at the expense of flower production.

Flowers are produced in several different ways and this has an important impact on pruning. Some species, such as many buddleia or garden roses, produce flowers on the current season's growth. In these, hard pruning in the spring encourages a period of vigorous growth, leading to larger clusters of flowers. Other plants only produce blooms on growth made in the previous year. Many shrub and species roses produce flowers in this way, and if they are cut back severely in the spring there will be no display that year (see Chapter 6).

FRUITS

Fruits are only made if the flowers were successful, and will not be found on male only plants. The purpose of the fruit is to grow and distribute the seeds. Some, like rowan berries, are carried in large showy clusters to attract birds to feed on them and inadvertently carry the seeds away with them. Many plants which have fleshy fruits have seeds which benefit from passing through the gut, as this helps germination and ensures that each seed is planted with its own capsule of nutrients: many bramble plants start life beneath the favoured perches of songbirds. Others, such as sycamore or dandelion, have seeds modified so that the wind carries them to new territory. A few are designed to stick to passing animals and then drop off later.

For good fruit effect, the plants need to flower well (with plants of both sexes present for some species), and have sufficient food and nutrients available to develop the fruits. Potassium fertiliser will assist in their ripening. Early-flowering plants, such as some fruit trees, benefit from shelter so that flowers (and thus fruits) are not lost due to frost or bad weather.

SEEDS

The seed is the blueprint for the next generation. It has to be able to support the new plant until it can carry out its own photosynthesis, and also needs to be able to germinate at the right time. Many plants will germinate immediately the conditions are suitable, but most have some form of dormancy built in to prevent them germinating at the wrong time. This is of special relevance in the context of weed seeds.

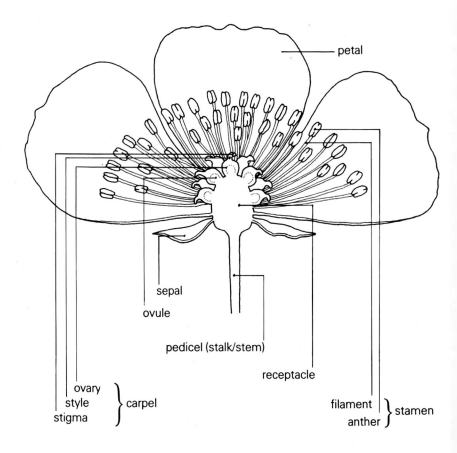

petal
sepal
ovule
pedicel (stalk/stem)
receptacle
ovary
style } carpel
stigma
filament } stamen
anther

STEMS AND BRANCHES

The purpose of the stem is twofold: it acts as the conducting tissue, between the roots and the aerial parts, for the transport of water and nutrients to the foliage, and for the return passage of sugars and proteins to the roots; it also has the function of keeping the aerial parts up in the air. Young trees determine the amount of wood to make for structural needs by the way in which the stem bends in the wind; incorrect and over-staking can stop this feedback and lead to too little stem growth.

ROOTS

The functions of roots are to anchor the plant in the soil and to extract nutrients and water. Roots do the former by being in contact with a large volume of soil.

Roots can only grow in soil conditions which suit them. Few species will root in waterlogged or compacted soil; neither can roots grow through dry soil, although they will not die if part of the soil around them becomes very dry.

In some plants, a bacterium associated with the roots is able to 'fix' nitrogen from the air to convert it into a form usable as a nutrient. Clover and many other legumes (members of the pea family), as well as certain woody plants, such as Alnus and Elaeagnus, are able to do this. The bacterium receives sugars from the plant in return for nitrogen in a form in which the plant can use it.

Another association found on roots is with several species of fungi. The fungus invades the root but does not damage it. Instead, the extensive system of fungal hyphae or strands in the soil extract nutrients and water, which are exchanged for sugars and proteins. These roots are called *mycorrhizae*, literally fungus roots. The association assists plants, like the heathers (*Erica* and *Calluna*) often on very barren sites, but is often destroyed by the generous use of fertiliser. The fungi frequently fruit around the base of the plant and may be mistaken for decay fungi (the strongly coloured fly agaric toadstool (*Amanita muscaria*) is the fruit body of a mycorrhizal fungus beneficial to birch).

FIG 9 Detail of flower parts (buttercup)

and mar the effect of the garden, and they compete for nutrients and water to the detriment of the garden plants.

Controlling weed growth can have a very pronounced impact on the growth of plants, especially newly planted ones. Weeds by their nature grow much faster than newly planted trees and shrubs and most other garden plants – after all, if they didn't they wouldn't be a problem! Their effect on plant growth is threefold:

• Most serious is their use of water, thus drying the soil
• Less significant effects are using the available nutrients, and where growth is rampant
• They swamp valued plants and shade them out.

Experiments with newly planted trees where weeds are not controlled have found that applying extra fertiliser will usually reduce the growth made by the trees. This is because the weeds make a quicker response to the extra fertiliser and therefore compete more effectively against the trees for the available water.

Methods of weed control are fully discussed in Chapter 6.

PATHENOGENIC FUNGI

Most fungi are beneficial in their effect and only exist off dead plant or animal material. A few are pathogens and cause considerable loss.

Fungi are members of the plant kingdom which cannot carry out photosynthesis. They have to rely on finding an existing source of organic matter and reproduce by means of masses of minute spores, the vast majority of which never germinate. However, because there are so many, they are always present in the air, although with most species more are present at certain times of the year. The spores have very precise germination requirements.

Some fungi, such as mildews on roses, can be controlled relatively easily by spraying the susceptible foliage at regular intervals. Others, such as honey fungus (*Armillaria*) cannot be contained by this method,

as most of their growth and spread is carried out underground; for this, the only effective control is to remove infected trees or stumps of felled trees which harbour this disease.

INSECT PESTS

Among a host of insect pests affecting garden plants, Vine Weevil (*Otiorrhynchus sulcatus*), which as a grub chews the roots of plants and as an adult eats portions out of leaves, has become one of the most serious, particularly in nursery plants. Control requires knowledge of the insect to know when and how to disrupt its life-cycle. While several insecticides will deter them, a biological control – a nematode – now available which attacks the larvae stage is likely to be more successful than chemicals currently on the market.

Aphids are equally serious – more than 500 species occur in the British Isles and Northern Europe alone, attacking a very wide range of garden plants. They feed by sucking the sap from plants, but as the sap contains very little protein in comparison to sugars, the excess sugars are excreted as 'honey dew'. Aphids are capable of breeding very quickly and one fertile female and her offspring will produce astronomical quantities of aphids, if allowed to get on with it in peace. Aphids have many natural predators, especially species of ladybirds, and the indiscriminate use of insecticides can kill the predators more completely than the aphids; if this happens, the next generation will be bigger than the first and more difficult to deal with.

Caution should always be exercised before an insecticide is used on aphids. However, careful use in accordance with the manufacturer's instructions of such insecticides as Permethrin and Derris will reduce heavy infestations, while Pirimicarb will kill aphids effectively but will not harm beneficial predators and parasites.

New chemicals appear as each year passes, but biological control of pests should always be used where possible.

CHAPTER 4

DESIGNING YOUR GARDEN

The design and contents of the garden are as unique to its owner as the interior decorations are in the house. The aim of this chapter is to assist the development of your garden in a creative way, rather than enforce rigid designs. We all know what we like and dislike when we see it. However, when faced with an empty plot or vacant corner of the garden, being able to know spontaneously what to do and what will look good can unfortunately be extremely difficult. For most of us, even if we are able to recall some garden theme that we admire, it is unlikely to be adaptable to the particular space in question. If this desired theme could be achieved, reproducing the effects satisfactorily can be a major problem.

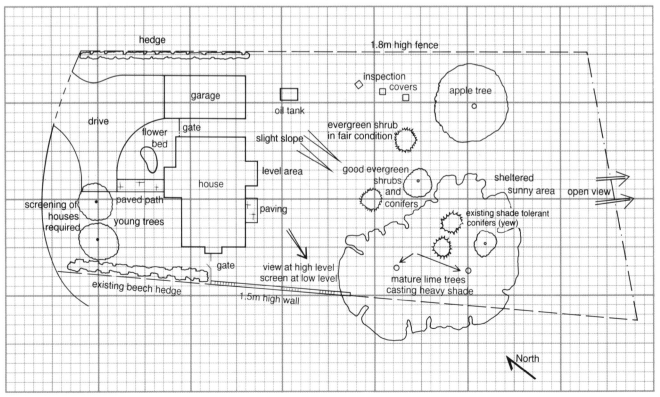

FIG 10 *Completed survey on graph paper*

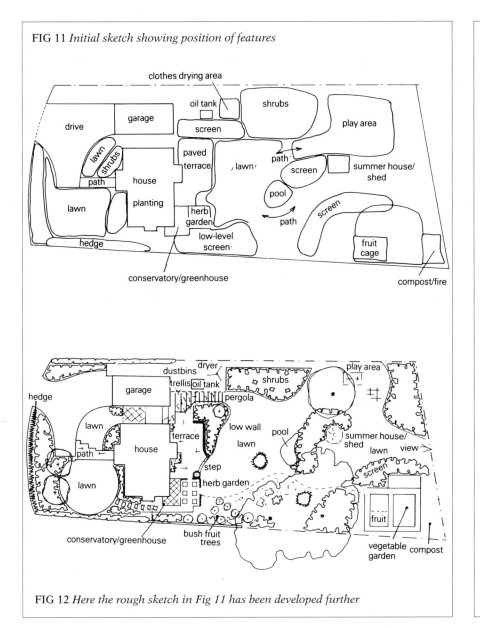

FIG 11 *Initial sketch showing position of features*

FIG 12 *Here the rough sketch in Fig 11 has been developed further*

FIG 13 *Positioning a small tree in a lawn or courtyard*

Central
obvious, static and formal

In one corner
crammed and uncomfortable

Informal and satisfactory

Our first piece of advice, if you are reading this with the idea of finishing the chapter and starting your garden design, is quite simply – don't! Observe other gardens, borrow some glossy gardening books with good illustrations, consider all the options (reading Chapter 2 will help). Do not attempt any designing yet, unless you already have a very clear overall idea as to how the garden should look. Delay doing anything for a few days or a few weeks, and simply observe. Make notes and get a few basic ideas. You may not end up developing any of them, but without them it will be difficult to make a start at all. If some of the ideas you are intending to develop

were directly inspired by books, when you come to start your work it is best to put them away and keep an open mind, allowing your design to develop as the details are added.

DESIGNING STEP-BY-STEP

Before you begin to develop your garden design, there are several important aspects to consider.

ACHIEVING A SENSE OF SCALE

What is scale, and why is it important? The definition of scale is that something is 'in proportion to its surroundings'. Your sense of scale has to do with the spatial relationship between

you and everything that you see around you. In the extreme, if you stood at the top of a mountain looking over a vast valley below, your sense of scale would contrast dramatically with that derived from standing in a narrow alleyway between two buildings.

Getting the relative sizes of the items in your design right and achieving the feeling of good 'scale' in your garden is most important and often extremely difficult. As an example, consider a paving pattern such as paving slabs and brick panels (which can look very effective). By putting brick around one paving slab, or three paving slabs, or nine paving

PLANNING IN THREE DIMENSIONS

Unless you possess artistic ability, it is only possible to draw a garden plan in two dimensions – a sort of bird's-eye view or map. However, although you may not be indicating the third dimension, you must at least be actively considering it. Think not only of the height of a proposed feature, but what it would look like viewed from different places.

An occasional rough three-dimensional sketch may often be useful while designing to check the success or otherwise of the plan that you are drawing in two dimensions. Considering all three dimensions is particularly important when looking at the levels in the garden, getting slopes gentle rather than too steep, retaining walls at convenient heights and, above all, designing steps from one level to another. There is a limit to the height each step riser should be, which in turn will dictate the number of steps required, and hence the area on the plan. It is very easy to underestimate the number of steps necessary: a wonderful design on paper can be spoilt quite significantly by finding out later that having designed for only three steps, you actually need nine, which take you half-way across the lawn. Step building and the correct dimensions are discussed in detail on page 48.

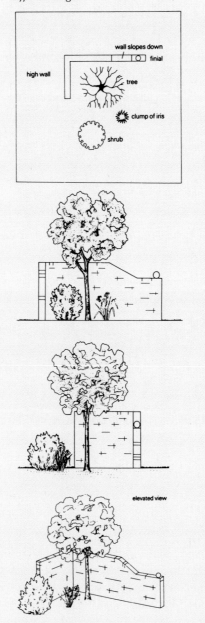

FIGS 14, 15, 16, 17 *Corner of a garden shown as a plan and then from three different angles*

high wall

wall slopes down

finial

tree

clump of iris

shrub

elevated view

uses, divisions encourage the urge to explore and provide an element of surprise: if the whole garden can be seen from one window of the house, do we need to go out? Dividing the garden also enables different design ideas (or even complete 'gardens') to be isolated and successfully included in the garden as a whole. Bold divisions between differently designed areas of the garden will avoid any unfortunate conflicts which might occur if they were simply to merge into one another. Hedges, walls and trellis would provide these divisions in the garden, and by virtue of their height contribute to achieving a good sense of scale.

CREATING POINTS OF INTEREST

When one walks round a garden it is pleasing to come across different focal points, points to walk to and from and to view from different angles. You may already have certain pieces of garden furniture – benches, birdbath, or sundial, perhaps even some sculpture. These need careful siting and will influence the design of the garden considerably. Often there are areas in the garden that apparently have no real purpose and which could be brought to life in this manner.

POSITIONING THE FEATURES

In Chapter 2 the full range of possible garden features was discussed, as well as how to undertake and draw up a detailed survey of your garden. Armed with this information, decisions can now be made on the positions of features on the plot.

In order to cover as many eventualities as possible, let us assume that the garden, after careful consideration of what it is essential to retain, is basically an empty plot apart from a few trees, slightly sloping ground and several isolated large shrubs. Lay a piece of tracing paper over the survey and mark on possible sites for the features you wish to include (see Fig 12), showing the different areas, and how these might relate to the house and paths; the sizes of these items are very important.

slabs, the scale is affected. In a very large area, the size of the paving panels must be large to complement the space. Likewise, a very small area could require brick around only one paving slab.

The really good gardens are those where the designer had an eye to achieving a good sense of scale. Good proportion is a three-dimensional problem and can be a somewhat abstract consideration (see box). To most of us, perhaps, it is sufficient

simply to ask ourselves, 'Is what I have planned on paper going to look and feel right among its surroundings?'

DIVIDING THE GARDEN

Many of the most memorable gardens that one can visit have hedges, walls, trellis or pergolas dividing parts of the garden. These are often good-sized gardens, but the scale of their divisions is very much within the scope of most gardens.

Apart from the obvious screening

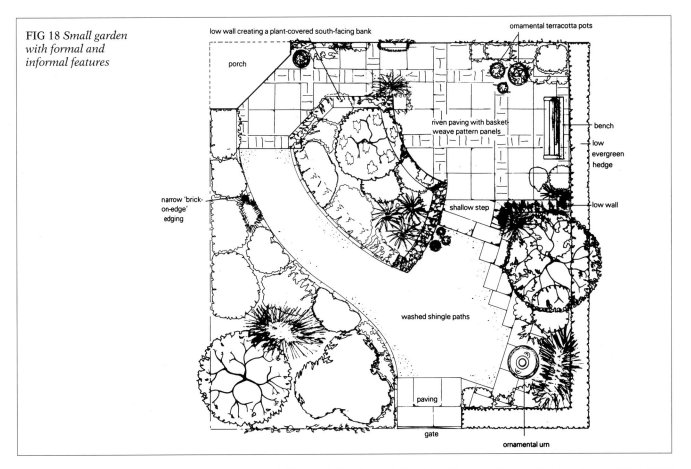

FIG 18 *Small garden with formal and informal features*

low wall creating a plant-covered south-facing bank

ornamental terracotta pots

porch

riven paving with basket-weave pattern panels

bench

low evergreen hedge

narrow 'brick-on-edge' edging

shallow step

low wall

washed shingle paths

paving

gate

ornamental urn

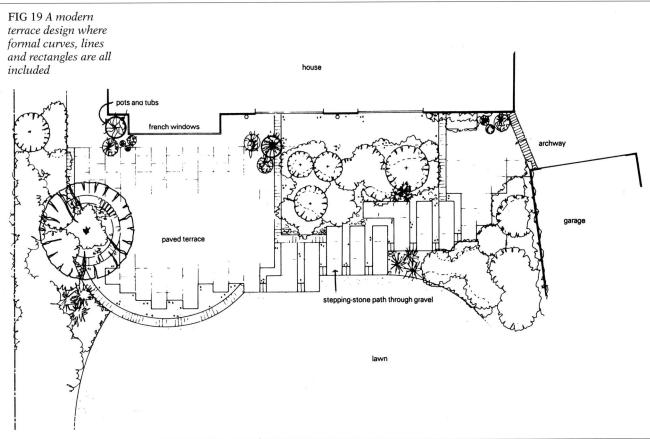

FIG 19 *A modern terrace design where formal curves, lines and rectangles are all included*

house

pots and tubs

french windows

archway

garage

paved terrace

stepping-stone path through gravel

lawn

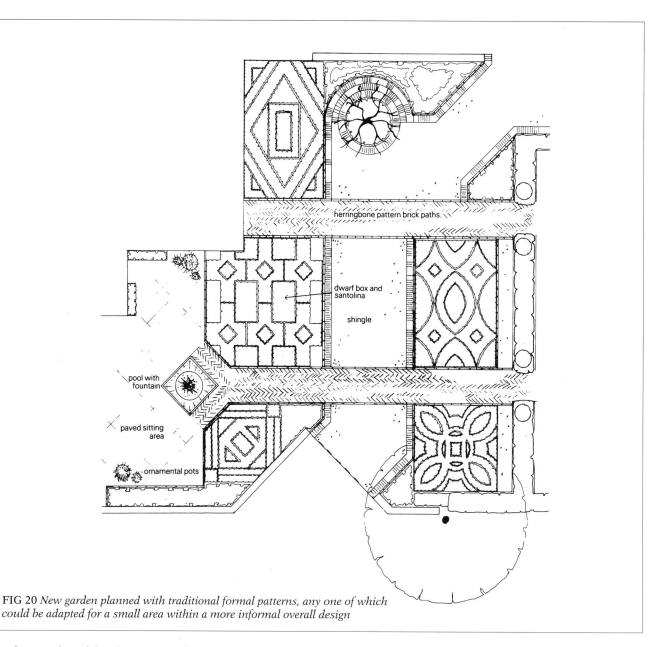

herringbone pattern brick paths

dwarf box and
santolina

shingle

pool with
fountain

paved sitting
area

ornamental pots

FIG 20 *New garden planned with traditional formal patterns, any one of which could be adapted for a small area within a more informal overall design*

If some idea of the shape instantly strikes you, draw in a simple outline developing this idea. At this stage some rethinking will probably be required as to the importance of certain features. For example, can you really afford the space for a tennis court with the attendant loss of orchard area and hence the fruiting potential? It may be that your garden is so small that a lawn, to be effective, would take most of the garden. Would it be better to use planting and paving, or gravel only? By doing this, would there be sufficient room for a greenhouse? At this stage the survey information on orientation, prevailing winds, exposure and other points of interest will be important. Consider alternative sites for the features you are planning at this early stage: good decisions now will save having to discard more detailed work later.

MAKING A GOOD PATTERN

Having decided on the approximate positions of the main items, you will need to consider the shapes in more detail to arrive at a good pattern which will form the basis of the garden design. It is very easy to fall into the trap of going into detail in one part of the garden too soon, and then having to work around this area when designing adjacent features.

The way that one feature is positioned in relation to another can have a profound effect. To take a very simple example, if you decide to plant a small shade tree into a rectangular lawn or courtyard area, the visual effect could be very different depending on the position (see Fig 13, p31). Similarly, how the various other features in the garden are positioned will affect the result.

For a garden design to work well there needs to be a certain unity to the pattern, even to the point of some repetition, and this will add strength to the design.

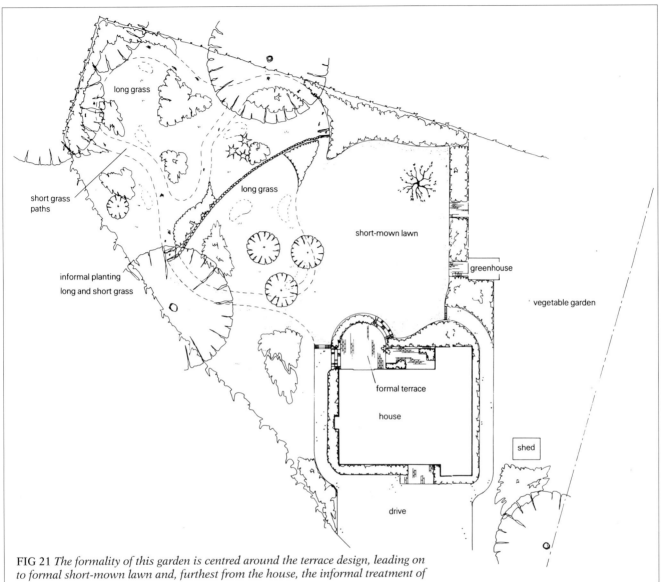

long grass

short grass
paths

long grass

short-mown lawn

greenhouse

vegetable garden

informal planting
long and short grass

formal terrace

house

shed

drive

FIG 21 *The formality of this garden is centred around the terrace design, leading on to formal short-mown lawn and, furthest from the house, the informal treatment of long grass and tree groups*

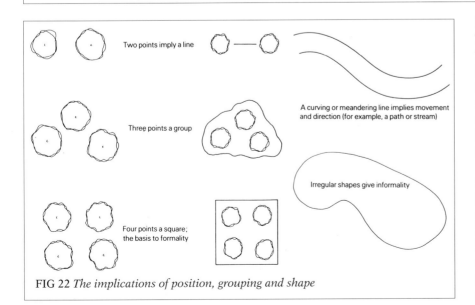

Two points imply a line

A curving or meandering line implies movement and direction (for example, a path or stream)

Three points a group

Irregular shapes give informality

Four points a square;
the basis to formality

FIG 22 *The implications of position, grouping and shape*

FORMAL AND INFORMAL TREATMENTS

Throughout garden history the trend for formal and informal gardens has swung from one to the other. In some cases formal gardens were later ripped out by others, such as Capability Brown, who was more interested in the landscape as a whole.

At the present time we seem to be in a mixed period, with traditional formal layouts becoming increasingly popular, albeit on a smaller scale: Fig 21 illustrates a combination of the formal and informal, whereas Fig 19 concentrates on formality in line and curve. As a formal garden is very expensive to construct and time-

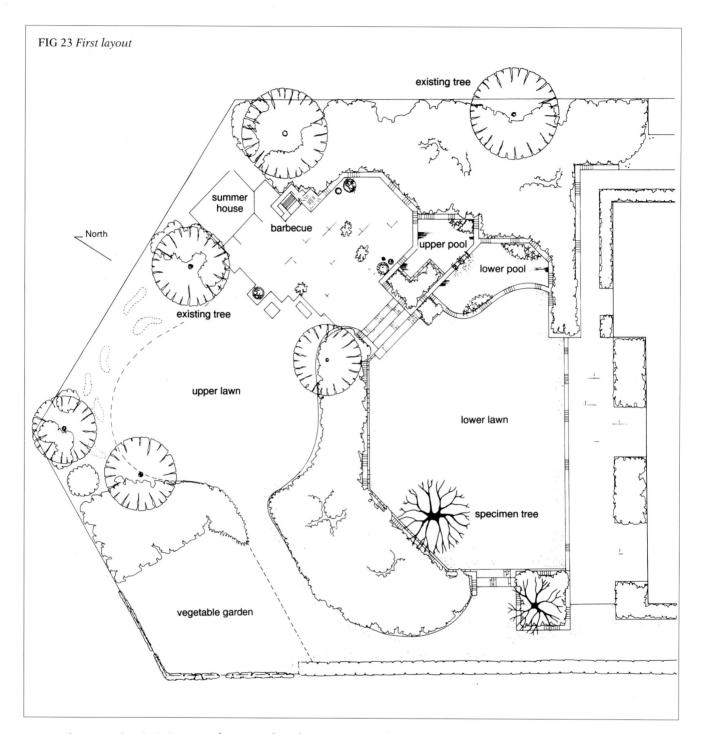

FIG 23 *First layout*

consuming to maintain it is certainly inappropriate to plan a large area on these lines, but this combination can be most suitable for small areas, such as the herb garden (see Fig 20). Formality is not of course only grand pattern-making, and from the design point of view it represents an important part of contemporary thinking. This formality is achieved simply by using straight lines, squares, rectangles and circles, all of which will be combined to a greater or lesser extent with the informal treatment.

As most houses are formal in their planned shape, you can often design the formal garden areas immediately adjacent to the house, gradually becoming more informal towards the perimeter and creating a merger from garden to the surrounding countryside (see Fig 21). Having the formal garden area near the house also has the advantage that it is more likely to get the attention it requires, being seen every day.

Having arrived at a reasonable garden layout plan (Fig 23 shows one example), before going into the final details it is a good idea to use overlays of tracing paper to consider alternative arrangements. In the improved scheme (Fig 24), the pools and vegetable plots have been moved to give a better view from the living room. You will find that although the initial

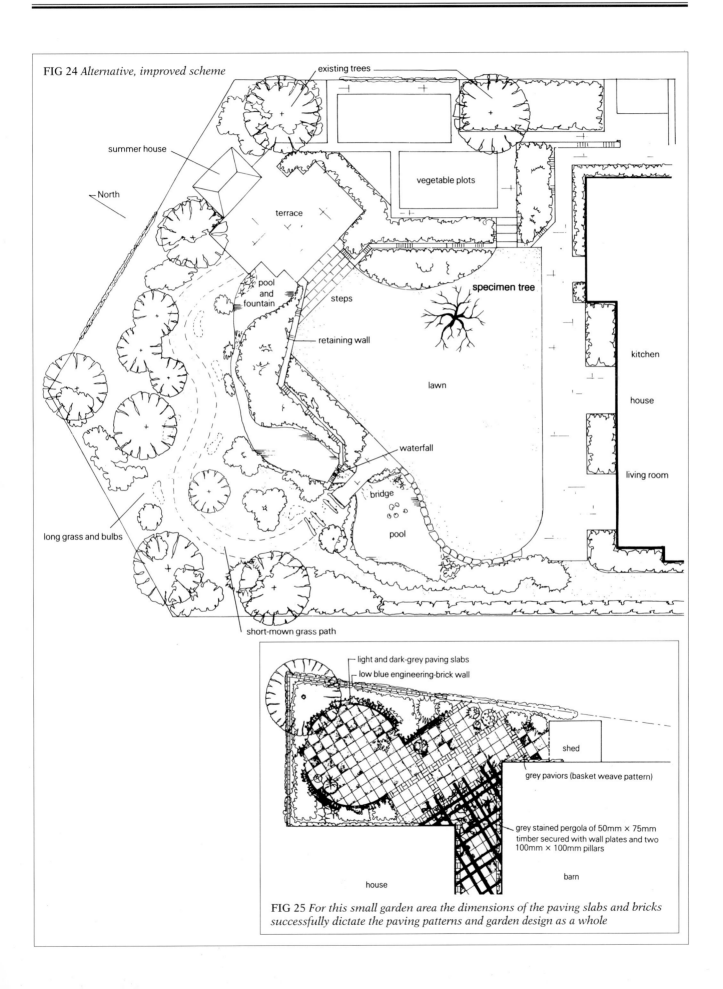

FIG 24 *Alternative, improved scheme*

existing trees

summer house

←North

terrace

vegetable plots

pool
and
fountain

steps

specimen tree

retaining wall

lawn

kitchen

house

living room

waterfall

bridge

pool

long grass and bulbs

short-mown grass path

light and dark-grey paving slabs
low blue engineering-brick wall

shed

grey paviors (basket weave pattern)

grey stained pergola of 50mm × 75mm
timber secured with wall plates and two
100mm × 100mm pillars

barn

house

FIG 25 *For this small garden area the dimensions of the paving slabs and bricks successfully dictate the paving patterns and garden design as a whole*

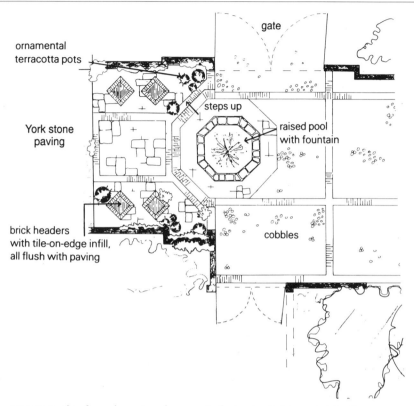

ornamental terracotta pots

York stone paving

brick headers with tile-on-edge infill, all flush with paving

gate

steps up

raised pool with fountain

cobbles

FIG 26 *In this formal courtyard, accurate design is vital to maintain the symmetry and pattern*

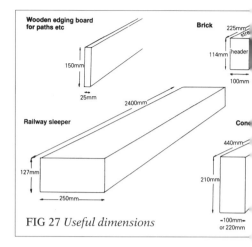

Wooden edging board for paths etc

150mm

25mm

Brick

225mm

114mm header

100mm

2400mm

Railway sleeper

127mm

250mm

Cond

440mm

210mm

100mm or 220mm

FIG 27 *Useful dimensions*

An informal paved path to a modern Agriframe arch with dense herbaceous planting including catmint, Geranium psilostemon* *and Welsh poppy with shrub roses and bold leaves of fig in the background.*

NOTE

You may feel that drawing symbols and making pretty patterns on paper is unnecessary to your garden planning. However, this part of the garden design process is extremely important because it:
• brings your design to life, and gives you a better insight into what your design will look like
• provides an opportunity to make improvements
• clarifies your design
• introduces another creative opportunity, which might result in new ideas that would otherwise have been unexplored.

A formal gravel path to an archway – through hedge – flanked by widely spaced specimens of Chamaecyparis lawsoniana *'Kilmacurragh'* – a columnar form of Lawson cypress. Annual trimming in late summer helps to keep these cypresses narrow, shapely and uniform.*

DESIGN CHECKLIST

For drawing up your design you
will need:
- fine-point ink
or felt-tip pens
- pencils
- eraser
- ruler
- drawing paper
- tracing paper

Optional:
- drawing board
with parallel
motion
- set-square
- scale ruler
- computer

scheme seems satisfactory, a few min-
utes' thought and further drawing
often comes up with alternatives that
are substantial improvements on the
original.

DRAWING AN ACCURATE PLAN

Some basic techniques and symbols
can be used to make your ideas come
to life on paper. By using good graphic
symbols you will get a clearer picture
of the garden you have designed and
hence how successful it looks, or not,
as the case may be. Before starting to
draw up an accurate plan, it is important that you have considered and
decided on the exact materials, both
hard (paving, walling etc) and soft
(trees, shrubs, grass etc).

Different materials and their use
in design work are discussed in detail
on pp 42–7. The dimensions of the
materials, particularly hard materials,
are important from the outset. For
example, you could use paving slabs
that are 45cm (18in) square or 60cm
(2ft) square; likewise, bricks may be
used on edge, 7.5cm (3in) wide, or laid
flat, 10cm (4in) wide. It is vital to
design with the materials in mind.
This will save a lot of time, money and
effort in the construction of the
garden.

Working with the type of information given in Fig 27, you can accurately dimension the features in the
design. This should still be in pencil.
Having completed the design, even if
messy, use a fresh piece of paper to
trace over it to make the final
drawing.

If not using a computer, a professional would choose a selection of

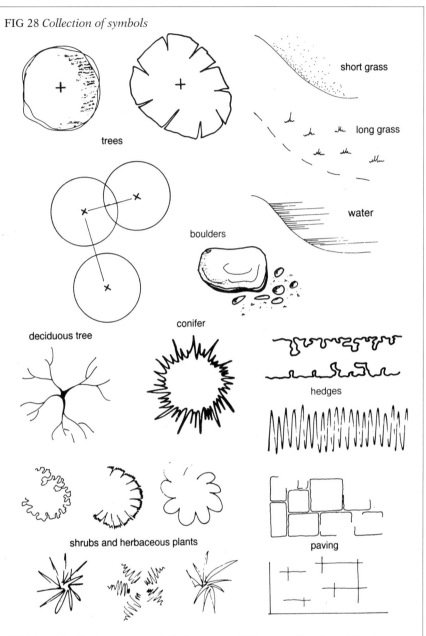

FIG 28 *Collection of symbols*

trees

short grass

long grass

water

boulders

deciduous tree

conifer

hedges

shrubs and herbaceous plants

paving

FIG 29 a & b *The importance of clarity.*
a) *Good, clear and precise combination for trees, shrubs and spiky plants*

b) *Poor, confused combination for the same planting*

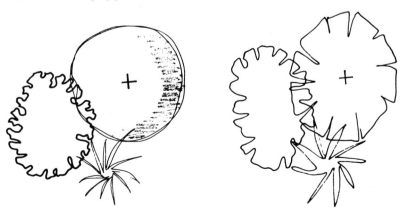

•PROBLEM SOLVER•

DESIGNING A FRONT GARDEN

The design of the front garden needs to be considered in a different way from the rest of the garden. The front garden is your public garden – it is the one that you, your visitors, the postman, milkman and dustman all walk through regularly. From a plantsman's angle, here is the perfect challenge to come up with a planting scheme which provides interest throughout the year, particularly during the winter months, when this garden, unlike the back garden, is used as much as at any other time of the year. At the same time, however, most of us would probably prefer to be doing our gardening out of the public eye. In this respect we need to make this a low-maintenance area, using groundcover planting of a permanent nature, which nevertheless provides an inviting display all year.

Good access needs to be supplied for fuel supplies and, above all, the car. Whatever size your garden may be – so small that only one car space is permissible, or so large with drives and turning circles – you will need to allow adequate space. Remember also to allow for at least one to two visitors' cars to park out of the turning area/driveway. It may be a good idea to include a waterpipe for adequate drainage for car washing. The dustbins will need to be collected and may be permanently located in the front garden, and hence adequate screening and, if possible, a covered walkway to them is going to be much appreciated (log stores and coal bunkers similarly). Likewise, oil and gas tanks need to be within easy reach of the supply lorry and their routes for pipes allocated so that the planting does not get damaged. All these items will need a certain amount of screening by wall, fence, trellis or evergreen shrub planting. Lighting is useful in the front garden, particularly if you have some distance to walk from parking the car to the front door. There are numerous electrical control systems, light sensors and time-delay switches which may be helpful.

If you live near a busy road, apart from the obvious screening requirements, if space permits road noise can be reduced by dense planting; consider also the possibility of soil mounding (see p54). When choosing your plants, a variety of different shrubs with different leaves and branches will tend to absorb more noise than a single hedge or belt of one plant species alone.

FIG 30 *Planting in a dry-stone retaining wall*

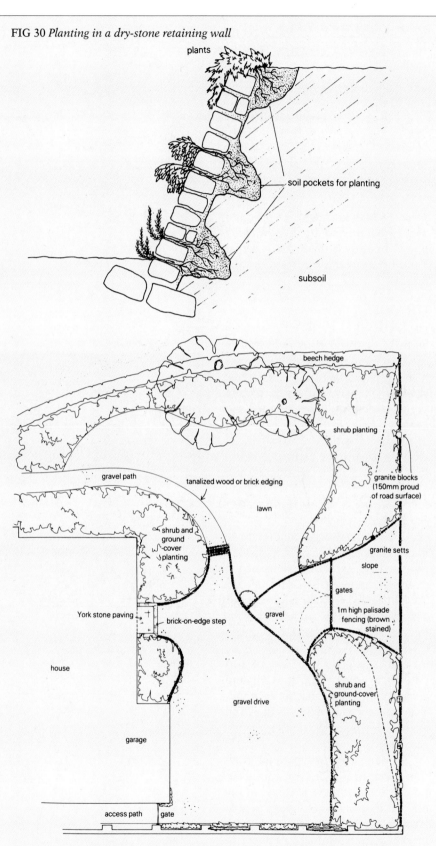

FIG 31 *This simple front-garden design allows adequate space for car turning. The gates are positioned to allow the car to get properly off the main road before they need to be opened*

FIG 32 *Permanent structural interest in a small front garden*

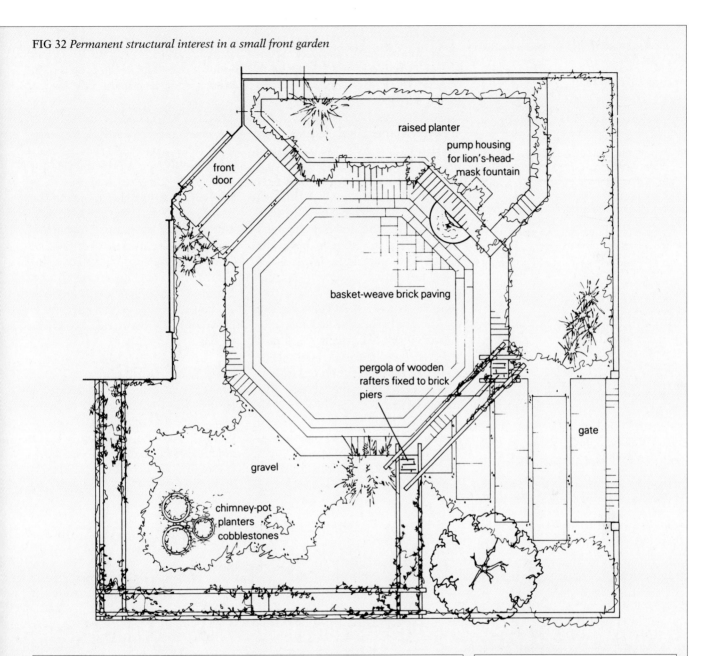

front
door

raised planter

pump housing
for lion's-head-
mask fountain

basket-weave brick paving

pergola of wooden
rafters fixed to brick
piers

gate

gravel

chimney-pot
planters
cobblestones

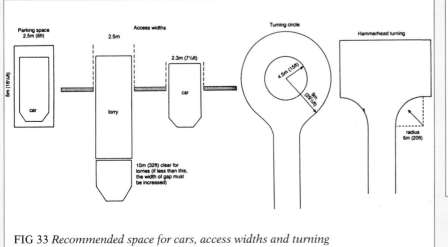

Parking space
2.5m (8ft)

Access widths

2.5m

2.3m (7½ft)

Turning circle

Hammerhead turning

5m (16½ft)

car

lorry

car

4.5m (15ft)

9m
(29ft)

radius
6m (20ft)

10m (32ft) clear for
lorries (if less than this,
the width of gap must
be increased)

FIG 33 *Recommended space for cars, access widths and turning*

FRONT GARDEN CHECKLIST

When designing your front garden,
you will need to include some or
all of the following:

- car space(s)
- turning area
- water supply
- dustbin area
- oil/gas tank area or access
- screening
- lighting

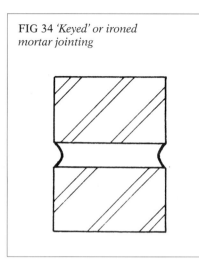

FIG 34 *'Keyed' or ironed mortar jointing*

special ink pens in a variety of sizes. These are, however, relatively expensive and need to be used regularly to prevent them from drying out, so would not be worth purchasing for a one-off design. There are now a variety of fine-point felt-tip pens which are cheap, effective and easy to use. Ink is not essential, though, and pencil is quite adequate, but beware of being too gentle of hand as this will make the pencil line too weak to print successfully. The drawing does not have to be pretty, but to bring the design alive and make it clear and realistic you will need to represent each material you have used with a suitable symbol. Let your natural artistic ability prevail and make up your own symbols, using those provided here as a starting poing. Above all, make up a collection of symbols that work well together but are distinct and clear.

If space permits, you may wish to put all the planting on your design drawing. For clarity, however, it is best to draw in the detailed planting on a separate tracing overlay (or larger scale plan, see pp 36–7) and indicate only trees, hedges and certain other specimen shrubs at this stage.

DESIGN DETAIL

For choosing hard landscape materials (bricks, paving etc) the materials available for use in the garden are endless. Deciding which to use can be very difficult – rather similar to the decisions one makes when decorating a room inside the house. The big difference in the garden is of durability: can your chosen materials stand up to continuous soaking, freezing, and bleaching by the sun, not to mention the battering from garden machinery, heavy boots, bicycles, cricket balls and the like?

WALLS

Walls give a real permanence to a garden. They will make for a pleasant merging of the house with the garden setting, and will store a certain amount of heat, offering a better environment for tender climbers.

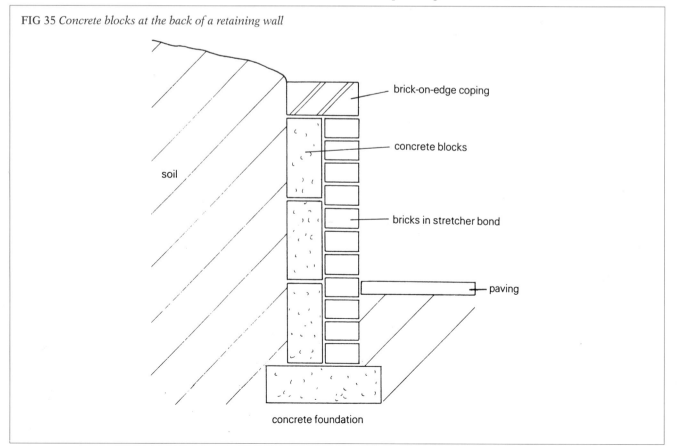

FIG 35 *Concrete blocks at the back of a retaining wall*

brick-on-edge coping

concrete blocks

soil

bricks in stretcher bond

paving

concrete foundation

Generally speaking, the local building material offers the best choice for garden walling: introducing stone walling to a brick area, for instance, needs to be done very carefully if a clash is to be avoided.

Brick

If your house is made of a good-quality brick of mellow colour, consider using either the same brick or, if unsuitable for the garden, another of similar colour. Many house bricks are regretfully not frostproof in the garden, as they are only 'common clay' bricks faced with a sand finish which, although weatherproof when used as a vertical house wall, would absorb water in the open and crack in the frost. Also, once chipped in a garden situation these bricks will expose their true unfaced clay colour and consequently look tatty very quickly. Search out bricks that are not colour faced and are hard (highly baked), resistant types. 'Stock bricks' are ideal; they normally have a good multicolour and some brickworks (and merchants) will sell you seconds or rough stocks which are cheaper and in many ways add interest to the garden wall. A coloured stock brick will blend well in the garden, due to its mellow colour which looks weathered even when only just built.

Avoid building narrow 10cm (4in) brick walls: they may be cheaper to build but also look it, and will not last well. For retaining walls where only one side or part is visible 10cm (4in) wide concrete should be used to save wasting valuable bricks. Brick coping will cover the top concrete block.

When constructing a retaining wall, the wall should taper slightly from bottom to top into the bank.

Brick walls 23cm (9in) wide which are 1.2–2.4m (4–8ft) high will need brick piers at a maximum of 3m (10ft) intervals. Expansion joints will also be necessary and, to avoid the possibility of the wall blowing over, dampproof courses should be avoided. Fig 36 shows a typical brick wall: note the foundations continue 45cm (18in) below the soil to avoid frost damage.

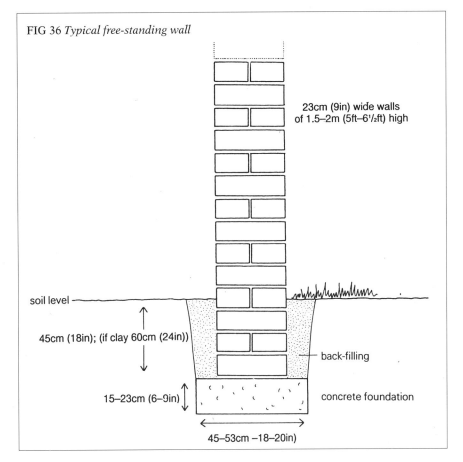

FIG 36 *Typical free-standing wall*

23cm (9in) wide walls of 1.5–2m (5ft–6½ft) high

soil level

45cm (18in); (if clay 60cm (24in))

back-filling

15–23cm (6–9in)

concrete foundation

45–53cm –18–20in)

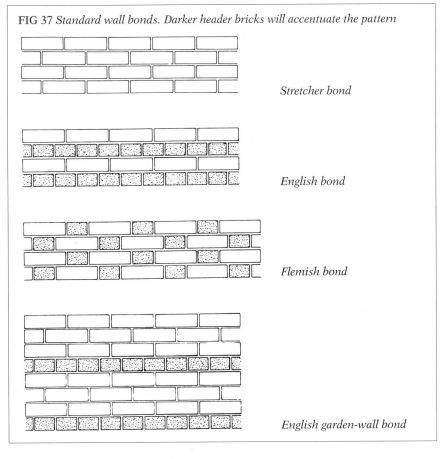

FIG 37 *Standard wall bonds. Darker header bricks will accentuate the pattern*

Stretcher bond

English bond

Flemish bond

English garden-wall bond

In the pebble pool garden, Preen Manor, Shropshire, clipped box grows in wooden tubs and white-flowering hebe in pewter bowls with brick paving in Cordoba pattern.

Most brick manufacturers make special bricks which can add greatly to your walling design, but beware – they are very expensive compared with standard bricks, although for small detailed areas they do add that extra touch.

The way in which bricks are laid in a wall can be varied to give differing patterns and also to strengthen the wall. Standard types are (see Fig 37):
• Stretcher bond – easy to lay but not a strong bonding wall; only suitable for low walls, and metal ties should be included in the brickwork for additional strength
• English bond – a good strong bond
• Flemish bond – not as strong as English bond

• English garden-wall bond (old traditional bond) – this cuts down on the number of header ends of bricks required

The cement mortar jointing between the bricks is also very important visually. The 'keyed' or 'ironed' technique (see Fig 34) is recommended, as this looks softer and is easy to undertake using a stick or the back of a spoon.

If you are going to use a special brick colour, bear in mind that dyes can be added to the mortar mix. With grey engineering bricks, for example, you may wish to add a little black to make the mortar greyer and avoid a big contrast between the light mortar and the dark brick colour.

Stone
The beauty of a stone wall is the fact that plants can survive and be deliberately grown in its crevices. Retaining walls are especially interesting as, being backed by moist soil, these can support a wide range of plants from alpines to ferns. A specially designed alpine garden may not seem appropriate to your plot, or there may simply be inadequate space, but at least a few favourites can be catered for in a length of retaining wall (see Fig 30).

Low retaining walls – that is, those not likely to be taking too much weight – can be constructed quite easily. All you need to worry about is the front face – the back can be packed with any material and a certain amount of soil. Dry stone walls, without mortar pointing, are the best from a planting point of view, but are of course ideal for the uninvited weed!

GARDEN WOODWORK

Regretfully, walls are expensive whether in brick or stone, and the labour costs alone can often mean that you have to use wood rather than brick, especially for long garden boundaries. Wood is a very amenable material and its uses in the garden afford endless possibilities.

Fences

Let's first consider the solid fence as the alternative to wall or hedge. Most garden centres and builders' merchants stock standard 2m (6ft 8in) wide panels at 1.2–2m (4–6ft 8in) high. These are usually made of larch, and either overlap or are interwoven, overlap being stronger and a little more expensive. Both are, however, relatively cheap and certainly instant, but unfortunately look it, and tend not to last more than a few years. They are also often rather unnaturally coloured orange (although they do fade) you will have to accept this or stain them yourself. Do give the fence an extra coat of preservative anyway, particularly at the junction at the level of the soil surface: the fence posts tend to rot at this point considerably in advance of the general decay of the fence itself.

These fences can, and should, be screened by covering with climbers. You will need to provide good training wires (plastic-coated 8-gauge) fixed with galvanised staples, three to four strands for a 1.8m (6ft) high fence. Unfortunately, it is likely that by the time the climbers are fully mature, the fence itself will need replacing. It is for this reason that a stronger fence is preferable.

A much more substantial and longer-lasting fence is the type that is put together on site, called closeboard (or featherboard). To have such a fence erected for you will be more expensive (half as much again), but worth the money. If you can under-

This tiny shady and walled garden contains a satisfying blend of York paving and gravel with a low retaining brick wall and suitable planting.

take the work yourself, the cost is of course much more reasonable. Be sure to have the timber 'tanalised', as this will increase the lifespan to approximately 20 years. The only disadvantage to the closeboard fence is that it is usual to face the fence outward towards your neighbour, ie with the less attractive side facing into your garden. This is obviously a matter of goodwill and frequently the fence will be within your garden, abutting another hedge. You will probably be covering the fence with climbers and, in fact, the posts make the securing of climbing wires much easier. If you are putting climbing wires on the outer face, it may be necessary to have 25mm (1in) square battens at intervals along the fence on to which to fix the wires and staples.

Boundaries and Stockproofing

A complete visual block may not be required. Where the purpose of the fence is merely to keep livestock out and mark the boundary, there is little to compare with the simplicity of the post-and-rail fence, with the exception perhaps of the ha-ha. If you are creating a cottage garden or have that type of property, there is still a place for traditional low-level palisade fencing.

Chestnut paling is used extensively as temporary movable fencing, particularly in the landscape industry, to protect planting in public areas during their establishment period. Chestnut as a wood is a very durable timber and will last 20–30 years. The temporary chestnut paling with its wire fastening is not a particularly tidy fence; how-

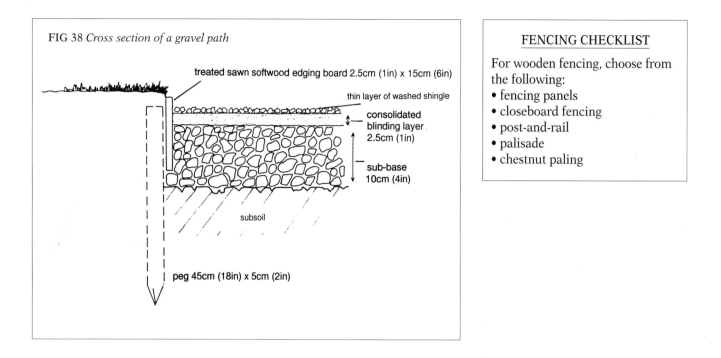

FIG 38 *Cross section of a gravel path*

treated sawn softwood edging board 2.5cm (1in) x 15cm (6in)

thin layer of washed shingle

consolidated blinding layer 2.5cm (1in)

sub-base 10cm (4in)

subsoil

peg 45cm (18in) x 5cm (2in)

FENCING CHECKLIST

For wooden fencing, choose from the following:
- fencing panels
- closeboard fencing
- post-and-rail
- palisade
- chestnut paling

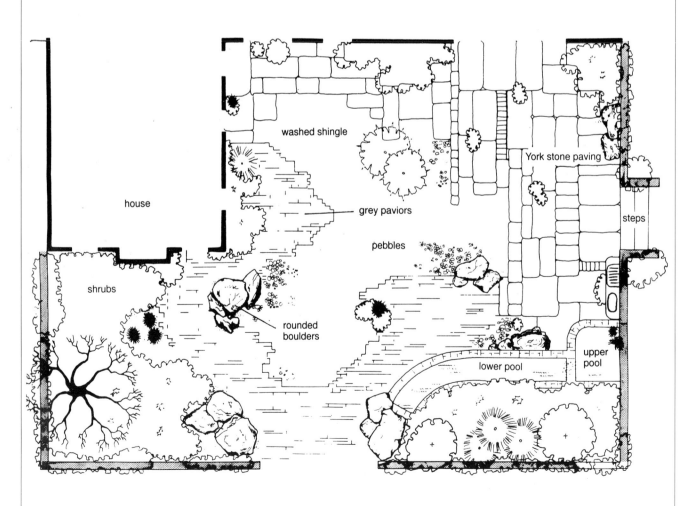

FIG 39 *Plan showing use of paving and boulders*

washed shingle

York stone paving

house

grey paviors

steps

pebbles

shrubs

rounded boulders

upper pool

lower pool

White palisade fencing, so often out of place, looks well here in this thatched cottage setting with flint and brick walls and piers. The gravel path is retained by granite setts and edged with Hidcote lavender.

ever, it is possible to make a more respectable edition by using the palings only, nailed directly on to a fence framework. This gives a rather pleasing, informal-looking fence and will be long lasting.

A visit to your local woodyard/ fencing specialist is recommended rather than settling for the standard products available in garden centres. They will also be prepared to make up fencing to your own requirements. You will find that, surprisingly, this does not inevitably work out more expensive than the standard panels.

Trellis

Trellis panels can be made up to any size of squares or diamonds. The standard panels generally available tend to be rather thin on the wood and 37 x 20mm (1^1/$_2$ x ^{3}/$_4$in) thickness of timber produces a far more substantial and satisfactory panel.

Trellis is used primarily for the support of climbing plants and, as light is available on both sides of the panel, your climbers will grow better at a lower level than on an equivalent fence panel. Again, the trellis should be good and substantial – trying to extract a mature climber from decayed trellis is not to be recommended. Even if you manage to get the old one off, the climber will still need to be supported and it will be difficult to reinstate a new panel. In many cases, cutting the climber back is necessary.

Trellis is easy to make yourself if you have the time. You will then be able to experiment with the size and shape of the divisions. At the top end of the market, there are now several firms specialising in trellis designs, both traditional and contemporary. With the advent of a wide range of coloured wood stains there is further scope for the more ambitious trellis designer.

Retaining Walls

Being a soft material and a natural one, wood is rarely out of place in the garden and can be considered as an alternative to nearly every 'hard' landscape surface. Logs may be used as retaining walls and either driven hard into the subsoil or set with concrete in a trench; be sure to purchase reasonably straight timbers that will butt well together for this purpose, or you may find your retaining wall leaks soil. Designers have used wood in this way to create the most exciting features, particularly suited to children's play areas. Wood of this quality and quantity is not cheap, however, so do not get too carried away unless you have a good budget.

STEPS

Steps are important in the garden, as the design and choice of materials will make a very profound impression on the feel of the garden as a whole.

Steps should be plenty wide enough, particularly if plants are to spill over the sides. As mentioned earlier, it is very easy to underestimate the number of steps required. Fig 40 shows what appears to be a totally satisfactory design, but the retaining wall is actually 1.5m (5ft) high and therefore requires 12 steps, so the effect on the design is that shown in Fig 41. A solution to this problem may be to divide the steps into two flights at 90° with a platform between them (Fig 42). This would also be more pleasant to walk up, having a 'break' in the journey. Alternatively, a complete rethink of the levels to create a less steep change by terracing may be the correct procedure. Fig 43 indicates the range of height and distance for treads and risers.

The choice of material must of course marry in with the adjacent materials. In an informal situation log steps might be ideal, in which case chestnut logs or tanalised softwood with the bark removed would be ideal. In a slightly more formal situation, railway sleepers or other heavy timber rails may be used as retainers in the path. Slices of log or tree trunk sections may also be used, but restricted to 'occasional use' steps only, as these are not for hurrying up and down, and can be slippery.

Brick steps give a greater sense of

STEPS CHECKLIST

Although essentially functional, a means of physically getting from one level to another, steps must be:
• easy to walk up and down
• elegant and not obtrusive
• sturdy and safe

---

permanence and unity where brickwork has been used in the paving design. These will need to be laid on edge to prevent their being dislodged. To achieve a height of 13cm (5in) for step risers, a tile insert can form an attractive detail. Where the steps are to be paved, the slab may extend beneath the brick riser and should extend over the front end of the riser below by 1½in (37mm). This will make a step look shallower and also nicer to walk on. Long flights of steps are best formed of concrete and then faced with brick and/or paving to avoid any possible cracking or sinkage.

SURFACES AND STONES
Paving
You cannot really afford to make a mistake when choosing paving. Paving materials alone are expensive and the labour of installation equally so.

As with walling materials, if you live in a natural stone area you prob-

---

ably cannot do better than to use the natural paving. If you live in a brick area, incorporate some brick to marry the paving to its surrounds, and perhaps break up a large expanse. Stone-flag paving is one of the most universally accepted aristocrats of paving, providing depth and subtle variation in colour. Due to its weight and availability, it is extremely expensive: however, you get what you pay for, and it will last more than a lifetime.

A cheaper way to buy natural stone is in smaller pieces to create a crazy-paving effect, but this is rather less impressive. It is, however, useful for curved paths and border edgings.

There are now a variety of imitation paving slabs available. In the early days there was nothing to commend them: now, however, there are some really extremely realistic slabs on the market, but shop around as there are still 'cheap and nasty' ones to be avoided. Do also consider slabs that are not pretending to be real stone. There are some good textured finishes, and even the most boring-looking grey slab can be enhanced by using other materials, particularly brick, to create a pattern that gives strength and interest to a paved area.

Bricks as paving on their own lend a very traditional feel to the garden. Due to their porous nature they also readily support the growth of moss,

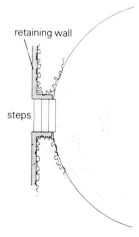

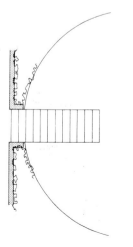

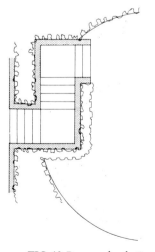

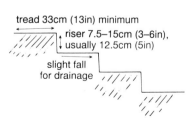

FIG 40 *Steps up on to a circular lawn: proposed design showing an inadequate number of steps*

FIG 41 *Number of steps actually needed*

FIG 42 *Proposed solution, using three flights of steps*

FIG 43 *Satisfactory dimensions for steps*

particularly in the joints between the bricks, whether cement-mortar pointed or not. Properly done, this will add years to the maturity of the garden.

You will need to choose brick that will withstand the frost, particularly where the bricks are being laid flat. There are also special brick paviors made for this purpose, if the colour brick you want is not available in a sufficiently hard standard brick. There are some lovely old-fashioned brick patterns – herringbone, basketweave and so on – make up your own pattern to add a little personality and interest. Another good use of brick paving is for curving paths or radiating around a garden ornament or even a tree.

There is now a wide range of interlocking paviors which are easy to lay and fairly hardwearing; these are excellent for driveways as an alternative to tarmac and come in many different colours. However, it is hard to beat the traditional materials such as granite setts, cobbles and grey stable-block paviors. These can be expensive, but used with other cheap materials will go a long way and add enormously to the charm of the garden.

Gravel
Gravel is both amenable and cheap, and offers considerable variety in shape and colour, and there are many possible uses for it in the garden.

If the correct grade is used, your garden plants can grow through the gravel but the weed seedlings will be unable to germinate on the dry, coarse surface – a sort of gravel mulch. This needs to be 20mm (3/4in) washed shingle, with the fine gravel and sand dust already removed.

Gravel can also be used as a path material, for which it is ideal, and traditionally as dug from the quarry is a mixture of aggregates that compact down to a hard surface. This surface, although functional, can look a little untidy and have a tendency to become dirty and muddy in wet weather. Thus, a thin blinding layer of the cleaner and neater-looking washed shingle can be spread on top (pea

---

SUCCESS WITH GRAVEL

Two important constructional points will ensure success with gravel paths:

• The shingle finishing layer (blinding) should be a very thin layer; too thickly spread and it will be difficult to walk on, will rut constantly and look untidy.

• If a hardcore or other larger stone base (such as limestone scalpings) has been used, this must have a finer blinding layer over it which has been well consolidated. This will avoid later problems of the layers mixing with constant use, and the larger stones working to the surface.

---

shingle (10mm /¹/3in) is usually used, but even this has a tendency to be trodden into the house).

As gravel is a loose material it will need to be contained adequately by brick or wooden edging. The bricks should be set in concrete and the wood should be tanalised planks.

Gravel (or shingle) is very useful as a linking surface to join other materials of different shapes and rigidity. A gravel path may merge from its formal boundaries to informal planting groups, and large pebbles, natural stone slabs and boulders associate particularly well with it and are used very effectively in oriental gardens.

Rocks and Boulders
The Japanese are the real experts in this field. Their art is the insight into and imitation of what is beautiful in the natural landscape, and the stones used therefore need to have a weathered, perhaps even water-worn, appearance. Unfortunately, such stones are difficult to purchase and expensive, as they need to be 'hand selected' from the natural landscape itself, usually many miles from your house. Quarried stone is certainly cheaper and available in all sizes, shapes and colours.

You will need to visit a stone merchant to appreciate fully the range and colours and, as every lorryload varies, select and order your stone at the time. Unfortunately, it is not often possible to select only the best stones from a load, and you will have to take the rough with the smooth. However, some of the most pleasant-looking rocks are merely outcrops emerging from the surrounding soil or vegetation, so only part of the stone need be visible, and thus only one or two good faces are important. If your stone is very angular and blocky or simply on the small side, carefully butting one stone to another to make the joints appear as a natural fault or crack will give the illusion of a much larger, more substantial stone.

It is important when forming the appearance of rock outcrops to imitate the natural rock strata and avoid creating one isolated rock patch. Positioning smaller and larger outcrops throughout a whole area of the garden will give a more harmonious and natural effect.

Rocks are hand movable up to about 250kg (5cwt), so ask for a range from 150–250kg (3–5cwt). However, it is well worth considering employing a specialist firm with the appropriate lifting equipment (or at least a team of suitably strong men) to enable you to use really large stones to lend a sense of permanence to a rock feature. As mentioned earlier, rockeries as such can go sadly wrong, and require a great deal of skill if they are to be successful.

GARDEN ORNAMENT
Furniture and Foibles
There is good money to be made in selling garden furniture, pots, statues and other such garden related hardware, and consequently there tends to be an overwhelming choice. Regrettably, however, you do need to sift through substantial quantities of poorly designed and cheaply made material to find anything that is likely to be suitable.

Perhaps the worst area in this respect is sculpture for the garden. For

Gravels of various colours and textures are separated by granite setts in the gravel garden by the pavilion at Preen Manor garden, Shropshire.

some unknown reason, the suppliers of garden sculpture seem to have the notion that we all want cherubs or gnomes. Where is the contemporary work that would blend into today's garden? With the advent of fibreglass resin-bond work it is perfectly possible to produce good statuary at relatively low prices.

Sculptures can be dramatic, particularly when used in silhouette against the skyline. They may be used as focal points in the garden and by virtue of their interest, inspire movement from one area to another. The historical pieces do, of course, have their place and can give a strong atmosphere and tranquillity to an area of the garden.

One area that has improved in recent years is that of terracotta, stone and fibreglass pots. There are some extremely elegant, often simply designed pots available. A nicely

grouped selection of pots can transform an area, particularly around the house and on the terrace, or down flights of steps, all of which give real scope for annual planting schemes. Unless you are absolutely sure that your pots are frostproof you will need to bring them in during the winter.

Tables, chairs and other garden furniture are very much a matter of personal taste, but as natural wood looks well in the garden, perhaps this should be the first choice. Unfortunately, well-designed wooden furniture still tends to be expensive, but hopefully this will improve, and with a searching there should be no problem in finding something suitable.

Ornamental Pools

Formal and informal pool designs are discussed in Chapter 2 – the informal pool can generally be larger – so the

first point to make here is that the visual design, technical detailing and choice of materials for a pool must all be carefully considered together and cannot be isolated. For instance, an intricate small-garden design with a high proportion of paving and walling will require a detailed pool design that is appropriate to the garden as a whole. Whether the design is formal or informal, though, areas suitable for bog plants and oxygenating plants must be included; appropriate plants are discussed on page 141. The three main waterproofing materials are looked at here.

Concrete and Cement-rendered Brick

Being rigid materials, the greatest problem with these is cracking. Usually this results from the subsoil base having moved and, thus stressing the rigid structure. Damage from freezing can also cause cracking. To avoid this problem, either design a dish-shaped section to allow free space for the expansion of ice or, where a vertical profile is being used, include an additional strengthening collar. If these cannot be provided, for example where the pool edge is a free standing wall, the only solution is to float wood or a similar material in the water during the winter period to divert the freezing ice force from the pond sides.

The advantages of concrete are limited to difficult shapes, compatibility with brickwork and, to a lesser extent, suitability for taking cascade pipework and fountain structures. It is essential to paint the rendered pool with a proprietary waterproofing paint as an additional precaution.

Flexible Liners
There are numerous lining materials now available which are ideal for informal pools, and particularly for larger areas where concrete would be too expensive and vulnerable to

cracking. They are also ideal for streams linking one pool to another. The lining should be laid on a 5cm (2in) minimum of builder's sand and ideally should be sandwiched between fibre matting to protect it from subsoil stones. Adding a little cement to the sand will also give strength at the edges of the pool.

There are, however, a few disadvantages to flexible liners which should be considered at the design stage. Unless the liner abuts a paved edge where it can run underneath, it may be visible at the edge of the pool. It will then need trailing plants such as Lesser periwinkle (*Vinca minor*), or Creeping Jenny (*Lysimachia nummularia*) or *Cotoneaster dammeri* to cover it successfully. Alternatively, the liner may be disguised by a layer of gravelly subsoil and rounded pebbles at the margins. Liners are also difficult to stick to other surfaces such as brick, although there are glue-type tapes which work satisfactorily on completely dry bricks. Unfortunately,

PUMP CHECKLIST

Choosing the size of a pump
Generally it is better to be over- rather than under-powered as it is always possible to turn a pump down. Working out accurately what size you need is far safer than guessing, and be prepared to spend a little money, as pumps are fairly expensive. One of the most common mistakes made when designing a circulating water system is to have the cascades too wide and the pump too small, the effect being of a dribble over the side of some large rock. Your supplier should be able to do the sums for you, given good information. He will need to know:
• The number and width of cascades
• Fountain display requirements
• Height from top to bottom pool
• Length of pipe required (distance from pump to outlet)
• Personal preference on flow over cascades (ie impressive and noisy or a gentle trickle)

A beach of waterworn pebbles enhances the informal garden pool at Denmans, Sussex while protecting and hiding the butyl pool liner.

CUT-AND-FILL

In order to achieve changes in level with the minimum of effort, consider the 'cut-and-fill' technique. Fig 44 shows how this system works. As a result of this soil moving, drainage may be necessary.

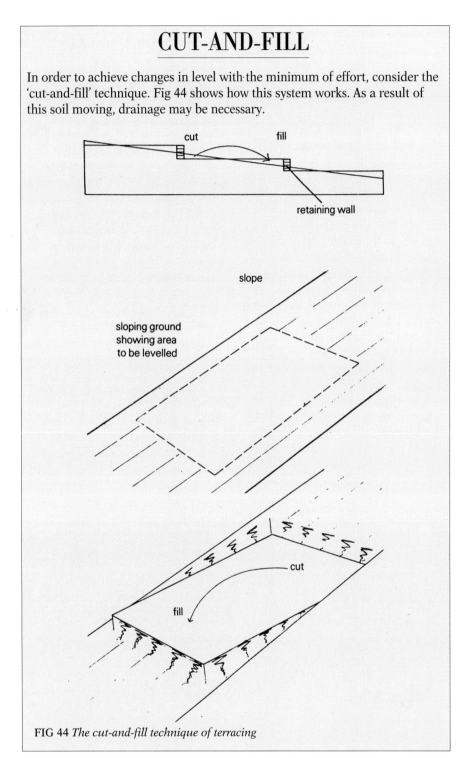

FIG 44 *The cut-and-fill technique of terracing*

Where rocks are to be used as a cascade feature, it is essential to take a liner underneath the rockwork, protected by a layer of waterproof concrete onto which the rocks are set, to retain any water leaking or soaking through the rockwork. All water will then be returned to the system.

Pumps, Fountains and Cascades
If you are going to have more than one pool with a cascade, the lower pool will need to be substantially larger than the upper pool in order to hold sufficient water to fill the system when running, without appearing empty and exposing the unsightly pool sides. The water in the upper pool(s) and stream(s) will rise by approximately 25mm (1/2in). A good depth is about 45–60cm (18–24in), but this will of course vary according to the pool size.

There are conflicting views on the best type of pump to use. Generally, submersible pumps are the easiest to install, most readily available and ideal for the small pool. Some would claim they are less reliable than the surface (or dry) pump. This unreliability is mainly due to the owner neglecting to clean the filter (which is in the bottom of the pool) and run the pump periodically through the winter period. A submersible pump should not be positioned directly on the bottom of the pool where the sediment will collect and block the filter, but ideally should be fitted in a separate chamber with easy access for cleaning.

Problems with a surface or dry pump are usually experienced when the pump chamber is located below ground, where flooding or simply condensation can damage the motor.

When considering a fountain display, bear in mind that the finer the jets, the more they will be prone to blocking. The bubble-type fountain displays are the best in this respect. There are, however, numerous types of fountain available and the choice is very much a matter of personal taste. The size of the display should, of course, be in scale with the pool. Do also bear in mind that in an exposed

bricks in this situation are usually wet or at least slightly damp.

There are two potential problems with lined ponds which can have an alarming effect. A pool liner may be forced up from the pool bottom to the surface. This can happen either where the existing water table rises during the winter period, or where there is organic matter in the subsoil beneath

the pool which rots, giving off methane gas bubbles. Neither problem arises frequently and both may be overcome by providing pipes as air vents or drains. It is best to avoid pipes passing through the liner. There are specially made bolted flanges to facilitate this; the only alternative is to have the pipework passing visibly over the liner.

position a fountain jet will easily be blown by the wind if it is too high or delicate.

Garden Lighting

As mentioned in Chapter 2, there is much to commend garden lighting. Surprisingly few lights are required and only low-power lamps – 100 watt is the maximum you are likely to need. The cabling should be installed at the earliest possible stage to avoid unnecessary disturbance later and should be put in by a qualified electrician, using armour cable and the necessary safety switches.

When deciding on the position of the lights, consider the main view points – living-room window, kitchen, and so on – and site the lamps at varying distances to highlight certain features. Ideally, the lights should have extra flex to allow you to move them to different plants as they come to their peak. Glare from the lights, or reflected glare from glossy foliage plants, may be a problem and again some consideration must be given to the positioning. If the garden is newly planted the lighting requirement will be less, but later needs must be anticipated and catered for in the location of power points for the developing planting.

Where large-scale lighting is required larger light units may be needed, in which case there are two alternative non-coloured lights that produce a different hue. Sodium gives a warm, if slightly artificial, orange light, while high-pressure mercury produces a most effective, almost ghostly silver light. Regretfully, neither can be produced as a small light unit for use in smaller gardens – ordinary coloured lamps do tend to detract from the garden's natural colouring.

For white light in the small garden, 100 watt spotlights are the most commonly used, although there are a variety of other units available, including low-voltage lights. Free-standing lamps, shaded lanterns and clear glass globes are all available, and are simply a matter of choice.

Soil mounding in a roadside situation in conjunction with evergreen shrub planting can help with screening and reduction of vehicle noise.

EARTHWORKS

Lawns

There are advantages and disadvantages to both turfing and seeding lawns, and it would be wrong to recommend one over the other. To a certain extent, price is an important consideration – seeding is certainly cheaper, while turf is variable in quality and price, the best being specialist seeded turf, which is sold in a number of grades, the next, good-quality or special meadow turf and, at the lower end, standard meadow turf.

If you want a good lawn without coarse grasses you should go for the specialist seeded turf but it is twice the price of good-quality meadow turf, which for most people is quite adequate. Standard meadow turf should generally be avoided, as it will contain a lot of coarse grasses and possibly other weeds – coarse grasses cannot be selectively killed, as there is no chemical that will distinguish one grass from another, and in this respect seeded turves are greatly superior.

Turfing has a considerable advantage if you have a poor stony soil, as a

LAWNS CHECKLIST

When creating a new lawn, the choice is between turfing, which
• is available in a range of qualities at varying prices
• is good on poor, stony soils
• can be laid at almost any time of year
• is relatively expensive
and seeding, which
• is relatively cheap
• gives you more control over the grasses which are included in your lawn
• will encourage dormant weed seeds to germinate
• must be carried out in late spring/early summer or late summer/early autumn

seeded area can take a while before developing sufficiently to smother the stones, but quite apart from the saving, sowing a lawn does guarantee that you have control of the grass species in the lawn. This can be particularly advantageous if you wish to have a lawn in a shaded area, or in an extremely wet or dry part of the garden. A seed merchant will be able to advise which mixture is the most suitable. You will find that some unwanted broadleaf weeds and coarse-grass seedlings will inevitably appear in your lawn, as there will be dormant seeds in your soil which will germinate at the same time as the sown grass. Most, however, will be annuals or tall perennials which will not survive regular grass mowing.

Turf may be laid almost throughout the year, with the exception of periods of drought or frozen ground. If you turf during the summer it will be essential to water the entire area regularly and thoroughly, as it will be prone to drying out and shrinking in the early period before rooting into the soil. When to sow seed is more critical. For best results, late spring/early summer will produce very quick germination, as will late summer/early autumn. At other times of year, when germination is either slow or, when very cold, completely

delayed, weed seeds, which can germinate at these lower temperatures, will compete with the grass when it starts into growth in the warmer weather.

Soil Mounding
Soil mounding and grading is one of those areas where subtlety and skill are essential for success. A relatively small rise in soil level will have a surprising effect, and often transform an otherwise flat garden: it is all too easy to have a load of soil delivered, rake it over a little, leave it 'as dumped' and expect it not to look like a burial mound! You need to try to copy nature and recreate it on a smaller scale in a garden. Soil mounding can greatly assist in screening and is instant. It can also reduce road noise and is particularly useful for establishing planting in areas that would otherwise be flat and poorly drained.

PLAN YOUR PLANTING

More detailed information on plants and specific combinations is given in Chapter 7. Here, the overall design is considered, and for this purpose it is assumed that you are planning a garden which is empty of planting.

Choosing which plants to include in your garden and preparing detailed planting plans is one of the most time-consuming planning operations. There are, after all, many plants to choose from and so many restraints: suitability of the soil, height, flower colours, spread, leaf shape, tolerance of shade, speed of growth and so on. Faced with a vacant garden one can easily be daunted and be tempted to go to the garden centre and pick up what happens to be looking good at the time. This is a grave mistake – you will still have to decide where to put the plants, and may discover that you haven't chosen the right plants for your purposes.

USING A SUITABILITY LIST

It is helpful first to write out a checklist of all your favourite plants that are suitable to include in the garden, or garden area, you are considering. *(Continued on page 58)*

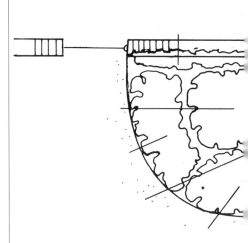

FIG 45 *Planting detail, using plants from list below*

SELECTION OF FAVOURITE PLANTS SUITABLE FOR THE AREA TO BE PLANTED

•Plants actually used in planting scheme

Sun-loving wall plants:
Campsis x *tagliabuana* 'Madame Galen'
•*Clematis* – in variety
•*Fremontodendron* 'California Glory'
Jasminum officinale
Roses – climbing
Solanum crispum 'Glasnevin'
•*Vitus coignetiae*
•Wisteria (white)

Medium and high planting for back of border:
•*Abelia* x *grandiflora*
•*Berberis* 'Goldilocks'
•*Ceanothus* 'Delight'
Deutzia x *hybrida* 'Strawberry Fields'
Hibiscus – in variety
Kolkwitzia amabilis 'Pink Cloud'
Phormium cookianum 'Tricolor'
•*Photinia* x *fraseri* 'Red Robin'
Pittosporum 'Garnettii'
x *Stranvinia* 'Redstart'
•*Syringa* – in variety

Shade-loving plants:
- •*Aucuba* – in variety
- *Bergenia* – in variety
- *Choisya ternata*
- •*Cotoneaster cochleatus*
- *Epimedium rubrum*
- *Euonymus fortunei* 'Emerald Gaiety'
- •*Euphorbia robbiae*
- *Geranium endressii* 'A.T. Johnson'
- •*Helleborus foetidus*
- *Hemerocallis* – in variety
- •*Hosta* – in variety
- •*Iris foetidissima*
- •*Lonicera periclymenum* 'Serotina'

- •*Mahonia japonica*
- *Philadelphus coronarius* 'Aurea'
- *Sarcococca hookerana digyna*
- •*Skimmia japonica* 'Fragrans'
- *Viburnum davidii*
- *Viburnum tinus* 'Eve Price'
- •*Vinca minor* – in variety

Low-growing sun-loving shrubs:
- •*Acanthus mollis latifolius*
- *Artemisia* 'Powis Castle'
- •*Caryopteris* x *clandonensis* 'Heavenly Blue'
- *Ceratostigma willmottianum*
- *Cistus dansereaui* 'Decumbens'

- •*Convolvulus cneorum*
- •*Cytisus purpureus* 'Atropurpurea'
- *Genista lydia*
- •*Hebe* 'Spenders Seedling'
- *Helianthemum* – in variety
- *Helichrysum italicum serotinum*
- *Indigofera heterantha*
- *Lavandula* – in variety
- •*Phlomis fruticosa*
- *Potentilla* 'Longacre'
- Roses – groundcover varieties
- *Ruta graveolens* 'Jackman's Blue'
- *Salvia officinalis* 'Purpureus'
- *Sedum spectabile* 'Brilliant'

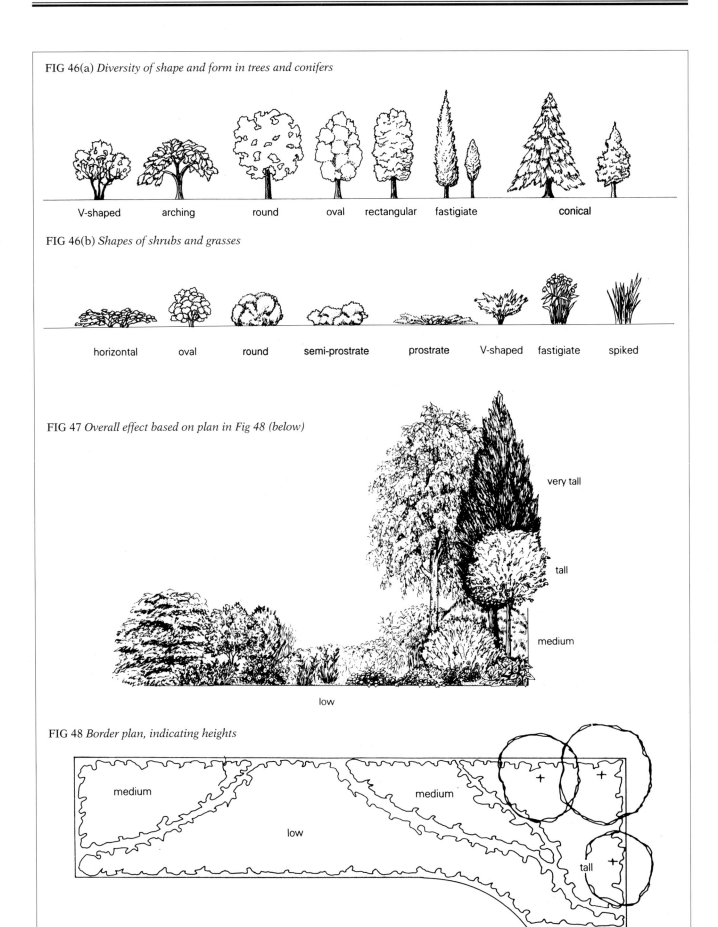

FIG 46(a) *Diversity of shape and form in trees and conifers*

V-shaped   arching   round   oval   rectangular   fastigiate   conical

FIG 46(b) *Shapes of shrubs and grasses*

horizontal   oval   round   semi-prostrate   prostrate   V-shaped   fastigiate   spiked

FIG 47 *Overall effect based on plan in Fig 48 (below)*

very tall

tall

medium

low

FIG 48 *Border plan, indicating heights*

medium

low

medium

tall

FIG 49

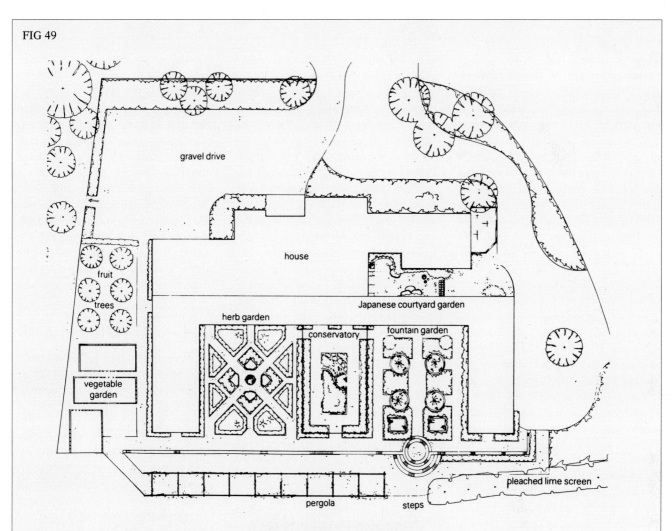

gravel drive

fruit

trees

house

Japanese courtyard garden

vegetable garden

herb garden

conservatory

fountain garden

pleached lime screen

pergola

steps

WALLED GARDEN

This project was particularly fascinating. It was part of a Victorian walled vegetable garden with potting sheds and three large greenhouses connected by a covered walkway. Planning permission was granted to convert the potting sheds into a single story house. The outer two greenhouses were converted into a small indoor swimming pool and two bedrooms. The central greenhouse was converted into a conservatory with a variety of tender plants, ponds and a waterfall.

The spaces between the greenhouses provided excellent sheltered, south-facing areas. A herb garden was proposed for one

and a fountain garden for the other. Both to include access paths.

To the south, two other properties built in the walled vegetable garden needed partial screening (the land sloped away and hence only the tops of the buildings were visible). A length of lime trees were planted for pleaching, along with a pergola to give instant screening and to form a pathway linking the semi-circular steps to the new vegetable garden.

To soften the walls of the former vegetable garden, now the property boundaries, marvellous opportunities presented themselves for a wide variety of climbing plants. Bold planting beds were formed for shrubs and perennials.

Other requirements were:
• adequate car parking and turning
• a small orchard area for trees on dwarf root-stocks
• vegetable plots – mainly for salad crops
• a solution to an uninspiring shaded area between the covered walkway and the house

The latter problem was resolved by the introduction of shingle, boulders and bold foliage plants (bamboos, Japanese maples, hostas,) in the style of a Japanese courtyard garden.

Looking down the length of this courtyard, a view to the east was achieved by making a circular hole through the garden wall – hence the lack of planting in this area.

Divide the list into trees, shrubs, herbaceous and groundcover plants. This 'suitability list' is often a very encouraging start. Remember to omit the obvious plants – such as acid-lovers if you have chalk, large trees if the garden is too small for them – and add more detailed constraints as you progress. The same exercise is equally valuable if you are planning just one border. This basic suitability list or 'pool' of plants to choose from can then be used to form the framework of your planting design.

DESIGNING BY HEIGHT

It might seem obvious that the height of the planting is important, and it is also a very good way to start on the positioning of your plants. For example, in a shrub border, before putting down any plant names draw a simple outline of the high and low areas as illustrated in Fig 48. This will enable you to get the essential frame-work correct and restrict the choice of plants within those areas of the border. At this stage you will also want to consider the shape and form of the plants and decide whether you wish to harmonise the planting or create a contrasting foliage effect.

DESIGNING BY COLOUR

The amount of vivid colour used in a garden is very much a personal choice. However, the following notes will help you to avoid an unplanned colour display and the possibility of a well-arranged planting scheme being ruined by one plant clashing with another and detracting from the scheme as a whole.

Firstly, there are some wonderful shades of green which can be very effective without including any colour at all. Grey foliage plants are also extremely useful, not only for their cool, tranquil effect, but also because adjacent colours become stronger by comparison. The repetition of some plants throughout the garden will also add real strength to a design – grey foliage is again particularly useful, while repeating a brightly coloured flower will also prevent it from

becoming an isolated focal point.

On specific colours, greens and reds together will tend to make colours appear much brighter. Red is a difficult colour to use as it tends to dominate. Similarly, pure white flowers are also difficult to blend with other plants as they tend to have a strong contrasting effect: off-white or cream is much easier. Some of the prettiest gardens are those where soft, subtle colouring has been used.

Although flowers and autumn colour can be planned to provide interest throughout most of the year, if you have the space it may be better to plan one border for one period of the year and another for another, rather than over-mix the flowering periods, resulting in the planting in one bed never looking really effective at any one time.

DESIGNING WITH GROUNDCOVER

When we think of plants that suppress weeds, we tend automatically to consider those plants generally termed 'groundcover' – plants that grow horizontally, spreading or creeping along the ground. However, when you are planning your planting design it is worth considering all those shrubs, large and small, that cast so much shade that weeds are unable to survive beneath them; *Cornus alba* varieties, *Viburnum plicatum* 'Mariesii', *Mahonia japonica*, *Prunus laurocerasus* 'Zabeliana', for example, all have this effect. These larger shrubs are in fact superior in many ways to the lower-growing groundcovers, in which larger perennial weeds occasionally develop, and a certain amount of weeding work is usually needed.

Having said this, the ground-smothering effect of the larger plants only develops when they are reaching maturity. The weed problem is at its worst at the start and it is therefore desirable to have a balance of ground-covers, planting quick-growing, low groundcover to be effective early on, such as *Euphorbia robbiae*, *Stachys olympica*, *Phuopsis* (*Crucianella*) *stylosa* and *Lamium maculatum* vari-

eties, some of which may die out naturally or simply be suppressed by the larger plants in due course.

PLANTING DENSITY

This is another difficult aspect of planting and one which tends to be dictated more by the garden owner's patience rather than rigid horticultural guidelines. All too often one sees gardens packed with plants: large shrubs 60cm (2ft) apart, trees only 2m (6ft) apart and so on, all to gain an instant effect. It is possible to do this satisfactorily, provided that those plants that will be retained in later years have been planned in their cor-

COURTYARD SCHEME

This scheme was commissioned by an hotel to create an attractive garden area for use by residents. A large expanse of paving was required for functions during the summer months. The hotel was a pleasant, old red-bricked building. To tie in with this and break the expanse of paving, bold panels of brick were incorporated in stretcher bond and basket-weave pattern. An existing tree formed a natural focal point and the opportunity for a tree seat. The formation of a series of formal pools and waterfalls were incorporated, with the centre pool wall being at sitting height. An old brick wall along the boundary provided an ideal opportunity for an open-sided pergola and climbers. There was a natural slope to the land, enabling the design to be on two levels to accommodate the waterfalls and steps. The entire area is enclosed, making the space very sheltered and pleasant.

rect positions and that you are prepared to remove the temporary plants when they start to compete with the main planting. A professional garden designer might plant out gardens aiming at a good effect within three to five years, and in many respects this is a very short period and open to some criticism.

Good maintenance is the key to the success of any garden (see Chapter 6). The real art lies in the knowledge of when to prune, when to move plants that are becoming too large and how to combine colours and shapes successfully. Also, the initial design structure must be right at the outset, with

Phuopsis (Crucianella) stylosa –
quick-growing summer-flowering groundcover for well drained soil.

FIG 50

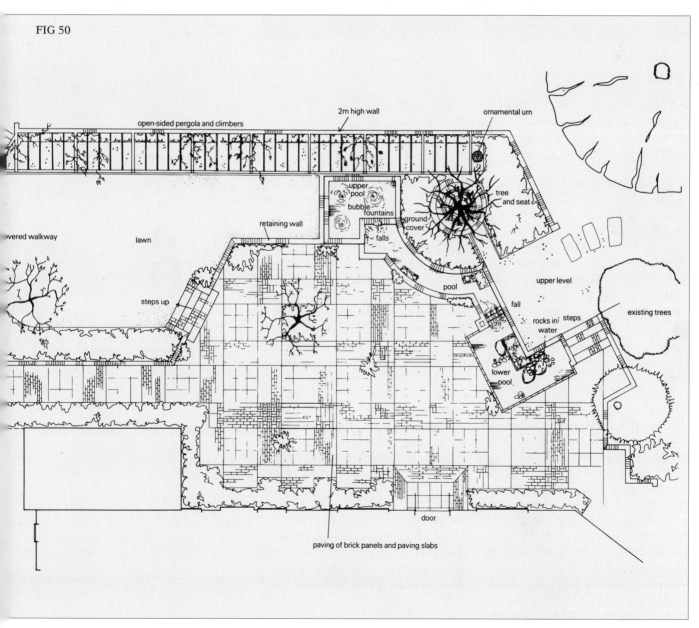

open-sided pergola and climbers

2m high wall

ornamental urn

upper pool

bubble fountains

tree and seat

ground cover

covered walkway

lawn

retaining wall

falls

pool

upper level

steps up

fall

rocks in water

steps

existing trees

lower pool

door

paving of brick panels and paving slabs

Sun-loving shrubs – buddleia, helichrysum, eleagnus, cistus, blend together in a well-drained garden.

the long-term and the short-lived plants in the right positions to avoid gaps initially, and to prevent these developing as the garden matures.

PLANT SELECTION
Finally, your planting design and choice of plants must not only survive but flourish in the garden if it is to look good. There is no point in nurturing a plant that in its wild state grows in moist, shady conditions and expecting it to look well in bright sunlight or in dry, unsuitable soil. Selecting those plants which will flourish in different situations – wet or dry, shady or exposed – is of vital importance and is discussed in detail in Chapter 7.

TRANSFERRING YOUR DESIGN TO THE GROUND

The joy of having prepared a well- and accurately planned garden as a scale drawing, is in setting out the reality on the ground. Ideally, you should have some setting out pegs 5cm sq x 30–45cm (2in sq x 12–18in), but garden canes are quite adequate at this stage. The simplest and most accurate way to set about the task of positioning the major points, and the corners of the main garden features, is

to follow the same principles used in undertaking the garden survey (Chapter 2), making a base line across the plot and measuring from various points along it.

Mark up a copy of your plan with the principal dimensions to save unnecessary time and possible mistakes. However well you have done your planning, when you come to measure it out on the ground, invariably something does not fit – even professionals cannot escape the inevitable unforeseen differences. Now is the time to take another look at the garden you have set out and be critical. Perhaps make some alterations where something is quite obviously wrong, but beware: have confidence in your design. Sometimes on initial setting out, areas can seem smaller or larger than they will actually appear when constructed and the planting has grown to give the vertical height and scale, but if it looks good on paper it will more than likely look good on completion.

The creation of the garden from this point is essentially a matter of craftsmanship and attention to good, sound constructional and planting techniques.
(Continued on page 69)

SUBURBAN BACK GARDEN

This garden already included a number of features, in particular some good mature trees, a shed, greenhouse and herb bed. In other respects, the area was quite lacking, being essentially a grass rectangle with narrow peripheral beds at the base of the boundary walls and fences. The main disadvantage of the garden was its north facing orientation. There was need to provide a south facing sitting area away from the shadow of the house.

Other requirements were:
• a pond
• plants of interest all year round
• a small vegetable garden and compost area

The main paved space was sited facing south-west, to gain the late afternoon/evening sun, and surrounded with a variety of planting. The planting and rose arches on the eastern boundary screened the the shed and the gap between the house and boundary fence. The informal pool, immediately adjacent to the terrace, was linked formally to the design of the brick and slab paving by a raised pool with waterfalls. The lower pool has a firm brick edging for ease of mowing and again visually linking its informal design to the terrace.

Planting details for Fig 51 (showing number of plants used)

1	5	*Hemerocallis* 'Pink Damask'
2	1	*Clematis viticella* 'Abundance'
3	1	*Skimmia japonica* 'Rubella'
4	1	*Mahonia japonica*
5	1	*Lonicera japonica* 'Repens'
6	5	*Molinia caerulea* 'Variegata'
7	1	*Skimmia japonica* 'Nymans'
8	5	*Epimedium x youngianum* 'Niveum'
9	5	*Alchemilla mollis*
10	1	*Philadelphus coronarius* 'Aureus'
11	3	*Hypericum x moseranum*
12	1	*Hedera colchica* 'Sulphur Heart'
13	1	*Parthenocissus henryana*
14	4	*Hydrangea serrata* 'Grayswood'
15	1	*Daphne cneorum*
16	7	*Epimedium x rubrum*
17	3	*Cornus alba* 'Elegantissima'
18	2	*Hedera helix* 'Harald'
19	3	*Juniperus squamata* 'Blue Carpet'
20	1	*Rose filipes* 'Kiftsgate'
21	2	*Berberis x ottawensis* 'Superba'
22	3	*Spiraea japonica* 'Candlelight'
23	3	*Aucuba japonica* 'Crotonifolia'
24	1	*Garrya elliptica* 'James Roof'
25	1	*Lonicera japonica* 'Halliana'
26	6	*Geranium endressii* 'Wargrave Pink'
27	5	*Waldsteinia ternata*

FIG 51

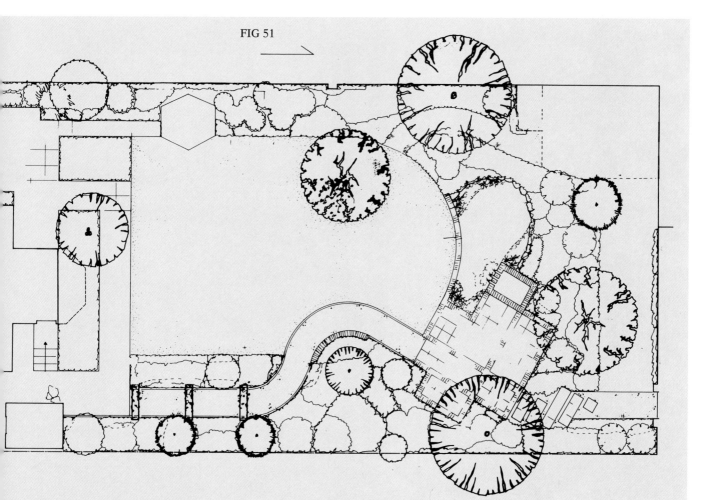

28 3 *Callicarpa bodinieri* 'Profusion'	58 5 *Iris pallida dalmatica* 'Variegata'
29 5 *Alchemilla mollis*	59 7 *Hemerocallis* 'Golden Chimes'
30 3 *Escallonia* 'Apple Blossom'	60 3 *Santolina chamaecyparissus*
31 5 *Bergenia* 'Silver Light'	61 3 *Helianthemum* 'The Bride'
32 1 *Amelanchier canadensis*	62 3 *Cytisus* x *kewensis*
33 5 *Vinca minor* 'Bowles Variety'	63 3 *Cistus* 'Silver Pink'
34 1 *Indigofera heterantha*	64 2 *Elaeagnus* x *ebbingei* 'Limelight'
35 1 *Cotoneaster* 'Gnom'	65 1 *Cotinus* 'Grace'
36 5 *Iris sibirica* 'Perry's Blue'	66 3 *Potentilla dahurica* 'Abbotswood'
37 3 *Potentilla* 'Primrose Beauty'	67 1 *Viburnum plicatum* 'Grandiflorum'
38 1 *Photinia* x *fraseri* 'Red Robin'	68 1 *Escallonia* 'Iveyi'
39 1 *Berberis temolaica*	69 5 *Euonymus fortunei* 'Emerald Gaiety'
40 1 *Magnolia stellata* 'Water Lily'	70 3 *Fuchsia magellanica* 'Versicolor'
41 5 *Acaena microphylla*	71 1 *Cotinus coggygria* 'Royal Purple'
42 5 *Euonymus fortunei* 'Emerald Gaiety'	72 3 *Helianthemum* 'Wisley Pink'
43 3 *Viburnum tinus* 'Gwenllian'	73 3 *Ajuga reptans* 'Atropurpurea'
44 5 *Agapanthus* Headbourne Hybrids	74 3 *Lavandula* 'Hidcote'
45 2 *Viburnum tinus* 'Eve Price'	75 1 *Rosa* 'Madame Alfred Carrière' (climber)
46 1 *Ceanothus* 'Cascade'	76 5 *Geranium* x *cantabrigiense*
47 15 *Cyclamen hederifolium*	77 5 *Rosa mundi*
48 1 *Kolkwitzia amabilis* 'Pink Cloud'	78 8 *Campanula portenschlagiana*
49 3 *Photinia glabra* 'Rubens'	79 3 *Heuchera* 'Palace Purple'
50 1 *Mahonia* x *media* 'Underway'	80 1 *Rosa* 'Dublin Bay' (climber)
51 1 *Pyracantha* 'Orange Glow'	81 3 *Ajuga reptans* 'Atropurpurea'
52 1 *Gleditsia triacanthos* 'Sunburst' (standard)	82 3 *Hebe brachysiphon* 'White Gem'
53 *Heuchera* 'Palace Purple' or 'Rachel'	83 5 *Festuca glauca*
54 3 *Fuchsia* 'Chillerton Beauty'	84 1 *Rosa* 'Handel' (climber)
55 5 *Stachys olympica* 'Silver Carpet'	85 1 Cherry 'Morello' (fan trained)
56 3 *Philadelphus* 'Manteau d'Hermine'	86 1 Apple Cox's Orange Pippin (espalier)
57 2 *Cotoneaster* 'Gnom'	87 1 Apple James Grieve (espalier)

THE INHERITED GARDEN

There was a time when the family home was lived in for a generation or more. Today, with a general increase in mobility, many people move houses several times within a few years. At every house move, therefore, we are inheriting not only a house, but also a garden.

The real difference between the move to the new house and the new garden is quite simple: people leave their personal possessions – the plants they have collected – in their gardens, and this can be a benefit, but also a major problem. There may be excellent features in the garden you have inherited but inevitably, also much you will wish to change.

First impressions of the garden you inherit are well worth jotting down: note your likes and dislikes at the earliest opportunity, otherwise you may become accustomed to your surroundings, accepting them as the norm, and you may miss the chance to make improvements.

It may be that you have had the garden for some time and have simply become bored and dissatisfied with it; this section also looks at ways of improving it.

CRITICISING YOUR GARDEN

Criticising your own garden can be a very useful exercise in establishing the important areas that could be improved. Unfortunately, it is not always easy to do. You may have a garden which is generally good, everyone tells you it is lovely, but you know somehow that it is not quite the garden you would like it to be. The problem lies in identifying exactly where improvements can be made.

Going through the lists of garden features in Chapter 2 may help identify any shortfalls, particularly with reference to other gardens that you have visited. Think about including definite features such as focal points, statues, terracotta pots, sundials and seats. Think too of the way you are using your garden. Is there sufficient room for sitting out and entertaining? Would you use your garden more if you could make space for different activities? Does the garden feel a little cramped, and would a greater feeling of space be an improvement? Creating the illusion of space can often be achieved by dividing the garden and restricting the view; surprisingly, an open, empty garden may appear smaller than it is, particularly if it is long and narrow. Given some divisions, restricting the view can give the impression that an extensive garden is just around the corner – even if it isn't. The eye is easily

deceived, using hedges, trellis or fences in a formal manner or, equally successfully, with informal shrub planting, provided the right plants are used to form a permanent, dense effect.

You may well have inherited a very basic old-style house- garden, like that shown in Fig 52 which really offers very little apart from its lawn as a play area, and a vegetable garden. Fig 53 shows the same plot incorporating the best of the existing features, but adding considerable interest and potential use for the owner. The same design principles have been used in amending this existing garden as would have been had you started

from scratch. You may find that your existing garden includes most of your requirements, but that their arrangement is poor – the sitting area too far from the house perhaps, or shaded for part of the day. Certainly, the area immediately adjacent to the house, particularly to the living room and the kitchen, should form a direct link to the garden. This is a critical area and you want to be able to look out of the house and be encouraged to venture out and use the garden.

We have mentioned the importance of considering the possible features to include in the garden, but discretion must be shown as it is quite easy to go too far. Is your garden

FIG 52 *Unimaginative, high-maintenance garden with narrow, peripheral planting beds and few features*

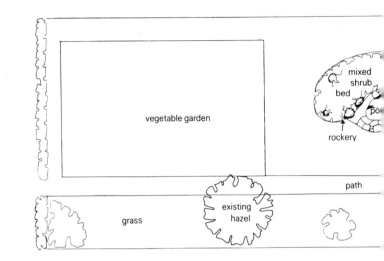

FIG 53 *The same plot, redesigned to create interest and be labour saving*

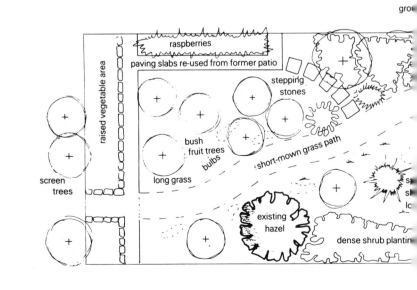

too fussy – are there just too many things in it, making it busy and restless? It may be that there are too many conflicting ideas: a formal pool and an informal pool, rockery, rose garden, heather garden and so on, which do not blend satisfactorily together. The overall theme must work, and perhaps some simplification would be beneficial.

If you are a keen gardener or plantsman you know how difficult it is *not* to buy plants when you see something interesting, and then you have the problem of finding where to put them. Over a period of time the garden can become cluttered and bitty, your original colour schemes become eroded, and a careful look and rearrangement of the plants is the only real solution.

Plants rarely stop growing. They may slow down in maturity, but they are always gradually striving to increase their coverage. Indeed, trees and shrubs have a tendency to grow larger than anticipated, and your garden will gradually become overgrown unless the appropriate action to maintain the garden in peak condition is taken on a regular basis. From time to time good positive criticism of how the planting has grown is necessary, followed by some substantial (even drastic) action and rearrangement, this can work wonders. Photographs of the garden taken a few years previously will help to identify the major changes. Living with the garden year in, year out, we tend not to notice these changes and photographs will immediately point them out.

There is just one further, and important, reason for any unhappiness with your garden – you may be bored with it. Why not make a change? There is no need to alter the whole garden, but why not try to come up with something new that no one has ever seen before? Brighten up that dull shady corner, move things around a bit. We do it inside our houses, why not outside?

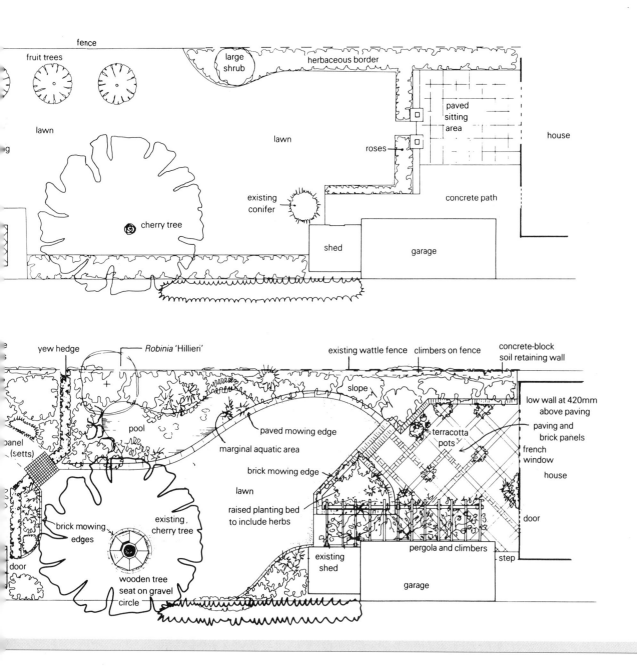

THE NEGLECTED WILDERNESS

The garden that has been neglected can be a real source of inspiration. Like beams and period details in a house, a garden too should have among the scrubby plants and weeds a few old trees and large shrubs to give the sense of character and maturity that only time can provide. Even an old tree stump could be furnished with climbers. The important thing to avoid is wading in with machete in hand ,desperate to tidy the place up a bit.

• First carry out a careful inspection of the plants to identify those that are important and if there are a number of them, label them with a hanging label, raffia or somthing similar. As mentioned earlier, when surveying the garden for replanting it is better to keep anything remotely suitable for retention at this stage.

• Some plants may be small enough to move and use elsewhere (see p15); these must also be labelled and this is best done in the summer, when the identification of the trees and shrubs is much easier – it is quite likely that there will be self-sown shrubs and trees such as buddleia, willow and birch, which are more difficult to distinguish from their garden varieties when dormant.

• If your garden, or part of it, is very heavily shaded by trees it may be necessary to remove some, but do bear in mind that good tree surgery can reduce the shading effect without losing the trees or affecting their beauty (see Chapter 6).

• Having labelled all the plants you wish to retain, then – and only then – is a ruthless frame of mind necessary to deal with the rest.

• Only too often you encounter the relatively recently planted garden that has been over planted and badly arranged, but is full of good young specimens, including perennials. In this case, make a note of all suitable plants for inclusion in a new planting scheme. However, be prepared to throw away or give to friends those plants that do not fit the scheme, as to retain them could be detrimental to the overall effect.

CASE STUDY

WORTHY SHRUBS

Very often, some very good or unusual shrubs will be either growing into each other or overshadowing one another, and will have to be sacrificed. You will need, therefore, to weigh up the merits of each, and particularly their lifespan. Every effort should be made to retain worthy mature (or maturing) shrubs that are widely spaced, to form the 'bones' of a new planting scheme. This is often possible by removing (and often resiting) several less desirable shrubs. The isolation of the exposed specimens will help to show their shape and form in contrast with their neighbours and the new planting. The mature shrubs will give the new planting scheme an instant effect which otherwise would not be possible.

FIG 54 *Two mature shrubs retained from an overgrown area, now isolated specimens:* Mahonia japonica *(left) and* Deutzia x hybrida *'Mont Rose'*

FIG 55 *The same mature shrubs effectively underplanted with ground-cover and shrubby and herbaceous foliage plants*

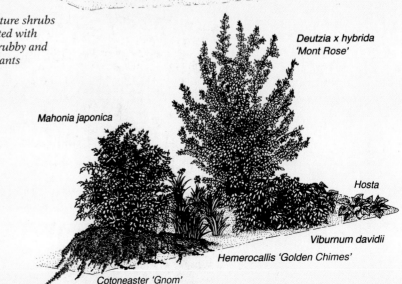

Deutzia x hybrida 'Mont Rose'

Mahonia japonica

Hosta

Viburnum davidii

Hemerocallis 'Golden Chimes'

Cotoneaster 'Gnom'

•PROBLEM SOLVER•

BOUNDARY PROBLEMS

Unfortunately, every garden owner seems to have problems with boundaries at one time or another. On moving into a new house and garden there is inevitably some form of conflict, often over ownership of the hedges: who cuts the top, and to what height? That aside, if you do inherit a garden that is overlooked, or you wish to screen an unsightly, more distant object, the right choice of planting can be a problem (see also pp 106–7).

• If you have a long, narrow garden, provided it is not too exposed and you do not wish to have a timber fence all the way round, consider the option of using plastic-coated chainlink fencing which, although unsightly when used on its own, it can be attractively planted with ivy. Use the *Hedera helix* varieties for hardiness and speed of growth, and to add a little colour, try some variegated varieties, such as 'Goldheart'. In this way, a very thin evergreen hedge can quickly be achieved without loss of space.

• Possibly the most common enquiry made to landscape designers or contractors is by the customer who wants to plant an instant tall evergreen screen to ensure privacy from their neighbours. The only sensible answer to this request used to be quite simply that it cannot be done – field-grown large evergreens move extremely badly, as they are committed to a full leaf exposure with transpiration all year, unlike deciduous plants, and are therefore prone to desiccation. However, the situation is changing fast, for within recent years an increasing range of large evergreens especially grown in big containers is becoming available. These trees are offered in sizes up to 4m (13ft) or more, to give immediate effect with the plant suffering little if any root disturbance in transplantation. An even wider range of semi-mature deciduous trees and shrubs is also available in large containers, making out-of-season planting possible. Deciduous trees up to 8m (25ft) are now container grown. The range of container-grown semi-mature deciduous shrubs is very large indeed, and includes Japanese maples and magnolias, which are often difficult to transplant successfully from the field.

CASE STUDIES

COMPROMISE

Where immediate effects are less important, a cheaper compromise would be to combine conifers, deciduous trees and evergreen shrubs. Plant a conifer hedge as a backcloth, with other shade-tolerant evergreens beneath the canopy of deciduous trees (see Fig 56). The scheme has the advantage that the conifer hedge itself is screened during the summer, and all year at low level. Semi-mature trees or evergreen shrubs could, of course, be used for part of this arrangement.

DISGUISE

You may have inherited a tall coniferous hedge in your garden, but although it does an admirable screening job you consider it to be forbidding, dark and ugly. If there is no space to screen with trees and shrubs (see above), try growing vigorous climbers into it. The Virginia Creeper (*Parthenocissus quinquefolia*) looks superb in the autumn with its brilliant red leaf colouring against the dark green conifer. Similarly in the spring, *Clematis montana*, or later in the summer *C. rehderiana*, and vigorous roses such as 'Kiftsgate' or 'Wedding Day', will look particularly effective. *Vitis coignetiae*, with its large, impressive leaves, will also rapidly scramble into a conifer hedge.

INSTANT AND LONG-TERM SOLUTIONS

On newer housing developments you are often faced with a garden already completely fenced in, looking extremely harsh and liable to remain so for a few years until the garden planting has developed. In these circumstances, choose a combination of bold shrub and hedge planting for long-term effect, interspersed with sections of fence clothed with quick-growing climbers. The secret is (a) to provide substantial training wires at the time of planting the climbers, ensuring that they are trained to cover the area required, and (b) to choose the right climbers for the aspect, particularly for their vigour (see Chapter 7). As standby plants for rapid growth, use evergreen honeysuckle *Lonicera japonica* 'Halliana' and Small-leaved Ivies *Hedera helix* varieties (many are variegated) for the bulk planting.

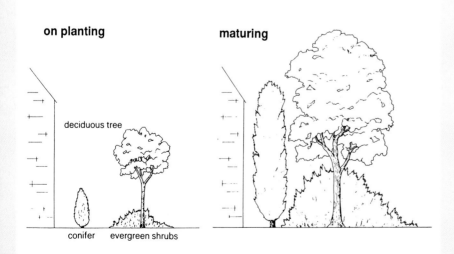

on planting   **maturing**

deciduous tree

conifer   evergreen shrubs

FIG 56 *Coniferous screen with deciduous trees and evergreen shrubs*

• PROBLEM SOLVER •

UNFORTUNATE PAVING

Everyone's taste in colour and materials is different. In the garden, one of the more expensive 'groundcovers' is paving. Quite frequently a problem crops up where a large expanse of paving has been laid by the previous owner, but it is either multi-coloured, bright pink, or has a poor finish to it, although maybe perfectly well laid and structurally very sound. It might even be tarmacadam or concrete. Rather than cart it all the way to the tip, there are some other options which might be considered.
• If the area is not to be the main sitting-out area, where tables and chairs are likely to be used, loose shingle could be spread over it to form an attractive and weed-free surface (it would require edging).
•Alternatively, the surface could first be sprayed with tar followed by a blinding of small pea shingle. Plants look particularly good spreading over gravel, and pockets could be excavated for additional planting within this surface.
•If you have inherited some reasonably good paving, which is not quite attractive enough for the main sitting area, consider lifting these and reusing the slabs, incorporating brick panels. Even if you do decide to re-pave the whole thing, the slabs could be used elsewhere, perhaps in the vegetable garden or, at worst, broken up as hardcore for use as foundations – this can even be a money saver.

•PROBLEM SOLVER•

A GARDEN OF WEEDS

Inevitably, when you inherit your garden you will be faced with a weed problem. What do you do with an herbaceous border that has reverted to weeds, apart perhaps from a few tough plants like golden rod (*Solidago*) which have themselves taken on the form of a weed and become a menace? The weeds will undoubtedly include all the worst enemies, such as ground elder, bindweed and the like.
• In these circumstances it will be impossible satisfactorily to dig out all the weed roots, and attempts to do so would be unnecessary, given the chemicals available. Even if there are some plants you would like to keep, their roots will be intertwined with weed roots and unless they are rare, or irreplaceable, it is usually best to sacrifice them in the clearance. Rare plants should be lifted (with weed root) and retained in a suitable corner situation (or container) to await propagation or replanting. The only solution to the border itself is to allow a full growing season and to spray the area repeatedly with chemicals such as glyphosate (see Chapter 6).
• Chemical weed control is likewise often essential where a rockery has become overgrown – rockeries are very difficult to keep weeded at the best of times. If the area of rock is too large, consider planting large ground-(and rock-) smothering plants that will also smother the weeds, for example *Juniperus squamata* 'Blue Carpet' or *J. horizontalis* varieties, *Cotoneaster dammeri* and many others (see Chapter 7). Before planting these subjects, however, the area should be sprayed with glyphosate to eliminate the weeds and allow these plants to establish.

•PROBLEM SOLVER•

PROBLEM PLANTS

If you discover that few of your plants are thriving in your inherited garden, the first possible cause that comes to mind is the soil. It may simply be very impoverished, it may be too wet and mostly clay, or dry, chalky and shallow (see Chapter 3 for details on how to improve your soil).
• Certainly, the poorly drained garden is a problem, and land drainage should be considered.
• For most other situations, the problems are usually those associated with an unsuitable choice of plants for the position. Sun-loving plants will not thrive in the shade and vice versa. However, for every situation there are groups of plants one can use: Chapter 7 provides details and lists of plants suitable for dry shady places, wet sites and hot, dry sites.
• There are also important maintenance considerations (see Chapter 6), such as the need to keep an adequate grass- and weed-free area around each newly planted tree if successful establishment and growth is to be achieved.

THE OVER-LARGE GARDEN

In the Victorian era, if you had a large garden you also had the money to support it. You would have had as many willing and inexpensive gardeners as were necessary. Today it is a different story and whether you like it or not, you must be a do-it-yourself enthusiast. Even a smaller garden can become a burden – circumstances can change and we may no longer have the time to spare, or as we get older we may not have enough energy to do the work.

• There are many quite simple alterations that can be made to make the garden more labour saving. Do also consider the possibility of a complete redesign; this could produce a very different garden, taking account of the new requirements and restrictions: the way you would plan the garden now may be very different from a few years ago (see Chapter 2). You may need to employ a landscaping firm to undertake the more major alterations, but the initial cost will be recovered in the long run by saving on employing labour to deal with the garden when it has got out of hand.

• The principal alterations could include reducing the total number of plants or features that need the most attention, ie those plants that need staking, tying and pruning, and hedges that need frequent trimming. Consider, therefore, doing away with rose beds, herbaceous borders and annual bedding areas. This does not mean that some of these subjects cannot be included, but that they should only be small groups or focal points of colour amid more permanent groundcover areas, both shrubby and herbaceous.

• Simplifying your planting into bold groups of one or two species or varieties rather than a mixed planting will reduce maintenance, though not to the extreme of the industrial-type planting we see in and around our towns – a compromise can be both labour-saving and effective.

• The shrubaceous border (see Chapter 7) could replace the herbaceous border or, if the herbaceous border is essential, it too can be made easier to maintain. A stone mowing edge could be added – aesthetically more pleasing and no edges to trim. As an additional aid, narrow paving may be used to divide the border into sections to give better access. The paving may not show during the summer as the plants spread.

• Reduce the area of short-mown lawn. Hours of valuable time and money can be lost to the lawn (see pp 98–9). With a ride-on mower, much of the short grass could be converted to longer grass areas, and spring bulbs and wild flowers could be added to the garden scene. Cutting will be required far less frequently. Bold planting of large shrub borders goes one step further in terms of reducing the maintenance in the long term (see pp 97–8). If your area of grass is small, consider replacing it with shingle (washed gravel) and selling the mower (see pp 86–87). If the lawn is large and converting it all to shingle would be too much, replacing just part of the area with gravel and planting would at least reduce the lawn area.

CASE STUDY

MOWING LAWNS

Many garden lawns, particularly those whose shape was never actually planned but resulted from the space that was left, will have difficult corners and slopes. Square corners are far from perfect; curves are much easier. If you can take the mower all round the perimeter of the lawn without stopping more than once or twice, this is ideal. Doing away with the corners and difficult slopes will mean more planted area, but if ground-smothering plants are used the maintenance will be reduced still further.

Strimming the edges is a tedious and lengthy job and the installation of a brick or paved mowing strip will save a lot of effort, as the mower cuts all the grass to the edges and plants which otherwise over-hang the grass are not damaged. This method is also excellent where grass abuts walls. The paving must be very slightly below the lawn surface to prevent the mower snagging. If the level is wrong the edging problem is back and the grass then needs to be edged to avoid hitting the paving! You might also consider enlarging the mowing edge, making it sufficiently wide to become a path.

INSPECTION COVERS

The newly built house and garden area you inherit may often be rather featureless, apart from the rubble and a fine collection of specially positioned inspection covers. They are invariably in the most inconvenient places and, at the time of your arrival, the focal points of the garden. There are several means of disguising these, depending upon their location and the proposed design of the garden.

• If an inspection cover occurs in an area which you would like to pave, there are specially made recessed lids available, and your paving can be cut to size and fit inside a frame. However, even these are still quite obviously visible as the inspection covers that they are.

• An alternative is actually to lay the paving over the inspection lid and leave it unpointed so that the slabs may be lifted. If necessary, you can often lower the lid by the removal of a layer of the bricks that support it.

• For other hard landscape areas, such as paths, inspection covers may be disguised by taking a shingle (washed gravel) path over them, but you must remember to make a note on your plan of their positions.

• Putting a garden ornament over the top is another possibility, but if the site is not ideal this tends to draw attention to the fact that there is a manhole cover beneath.

• If possible, the easiest solution is to incorporate the covers into planting areas (see pp 108–9).

THE STEEP GARDEN

It is lovely to have a magnificent view, but to do so might also involve inheriting a very steeply sloping garden, with its problems of maintenance and plant establishment.

• Wherever possible, terracing the garden will help enormously – a number of dwarf retaining walls will be less oppressive than high walls. Wood palisading is another option. However, these are both expensive and not always practical.

• On a slightly less steep slope, railway sleepers, if available, can be satisfactory, as their bulk holds them in place.

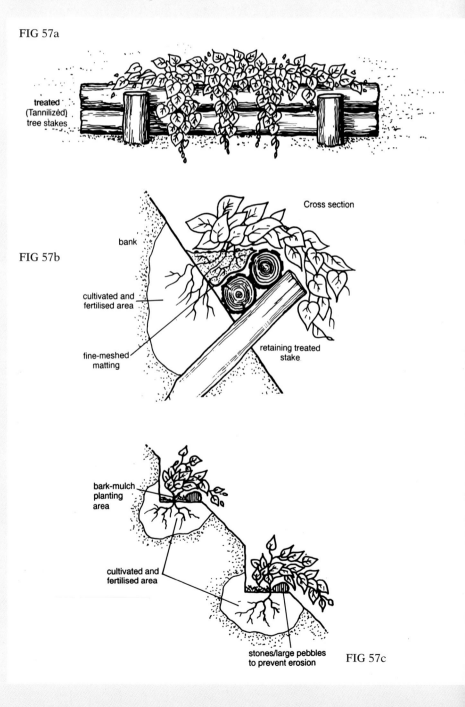

FIG 57a

treated (Tannilized) tree stakes

FIG 57b

Cross section

bank

cultivated and fertilised area

fine-meshed matting

retaining treated stake

bark-mulch planting area

cultivated and fertilised area

stones/large pebbles to prevent erosion   FIG 57c

Low growing and widespreading Genista Lydia is ideal for covering banks or difficult slopes. Its arching branches bear masses of broom-like flowers in early to mid-summer.

CASE STUDY

UNMOWABLE SLOPES
Chapter 7 gives details of how groundcover planting can be used instead of grass and which species are particularly effective. On an extremely steep slope, cultivating the soil may not be possible, and the L-shaped planting bays discussed in Chapter 7 may be difficult to achieve. Instead, use 1.8m (6ft) long treated tree stakes to make 1.2m (4ft) long planting bays, the points of the stakes being cut off to make the supporting pegs. To prevent the soil from being washed away a fine meshed matting or similar material should line the base and front side of the planting pocket (Fig 57). This method works well on steep banks in high rainfall areas or where frequent irrigation is possible. Fig 57c shows an alternative method, particularly useful for less steep banks in areas subject to droughts.

THE SMALLER GARDEN

A small garden, or garden space, is in many ways easier to plan than a larger one. The space restriction automatically rules out many features, enabling you to concentrate in more detail, and possibly greater imagination, on your chosen requirements. As the plants used in the small garden space are seen more closely, they gain an extra importance and interest: each individual leaf and its shape and texture is noticed rather than the overall shape of the plant alone. The effective use of contrasting foliage, such as hostas, grasses and bamboos, grouped together, can greatly enhance a small-garden planting scheme – floral colour may not, in fact, be of prime importance. Likewise, the hard landscape materials – bricks, paving slabs, cobbles and pebbles – can be treated almost as individuals.

One of the pitfalls when designing the small garden is trying to achieve too much, and including too many

SMALL GARDEN CHECKLIST

When planning a design for a small garden or garden space, do not:
• try to include too many features
• simply scale down a large garden
• try to provide an all-year-round floral display

features; a good, clear, but simple statement is likely to be more successful. By trying to include too much the scale can easily go wrong: you cannot scale down a larger garden into a small space, as the result would be both a visual and physical mistake. Paths still need to be a comfortable width to walk along and the spaces for chairs, table and people not too cramped – the principles of designing the small garden are exactly the same as for any size of garden.

An all-the-year-round floral colour display can be difficult to achieve. In very small gardens even to try to do so

Lavender and alchemilla frame the view across gravel and granite setts to the flowery urn focal point.

may be detrimental, resulting in a garden that is never effective at any one season. It is, therefore, better to get the overall structure of planting and foliage right and then concentrate on colour at certain times of the year. For summer, choose individual plants that have a long flowering season backed by compact evergreen shrubs to provide additional strength.

VEGETABLES
IN THE SMALLER GARDEN

It could be argued that, particularly where space is limited, there is little point in sacrificing ornamental flowering plants for vegetables and fruit which can easily be purchased from a shop. However, some fruit and vegetables are never better than straight from the garden, while others are unavailable in the shops.

When planning the vegetable areas, try to keep these small, avoiding big gaps when crops are harvested. Many vegetables are themselves ornamental, like the runner bean, which can be trained on a trellis, fence or pyramids made from bamboo canes tied together at the top. Other vegetables,

such as red lettuce or beetroot, can provide colour as well as food.

The herbs and vegetables could be surrounded by dwarf box or lavender as an edging, all making the vegetable garden more attractive, though adding considerably to the work involved. Bush fruit trees (grafted on dwarfing rootstocks), 'Ballerina' and espalier fruits, grown against a wall or fence, can be useful and effective, at the same time saving space. With careful planning all can be included in the design with the ornamental planting.

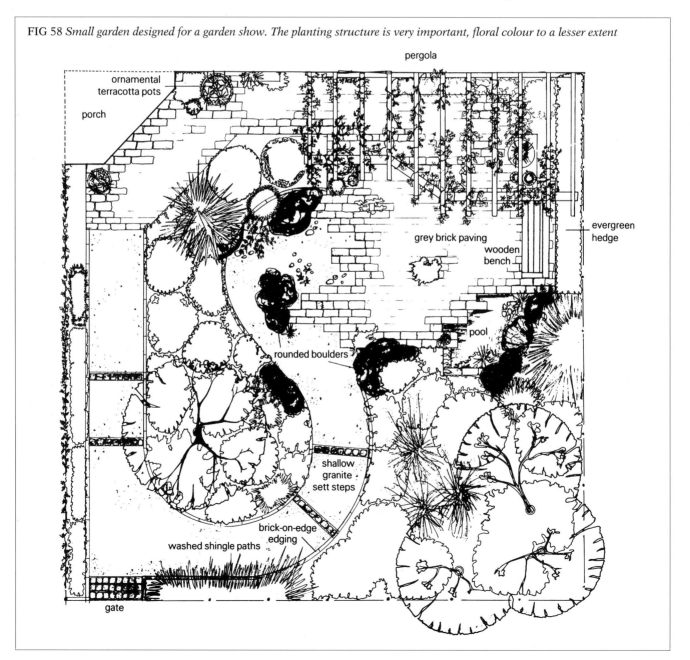

FIG 58 *Small garden designed for a garden show. The planting structure is very important, floral colour to a lesser extent*

pergola

ornamental
terracotta pots

porch

evergreen
hedge

grey brick paving

wooden
bench

pool

rounded boulders

shallow
granite
sett steps

brick-on-edge
edging

washed shingle paths

gate

Patio garden with pergola background, stable setts and gravel by Hillier Landscapes. (Designer Roderick Griffin.)

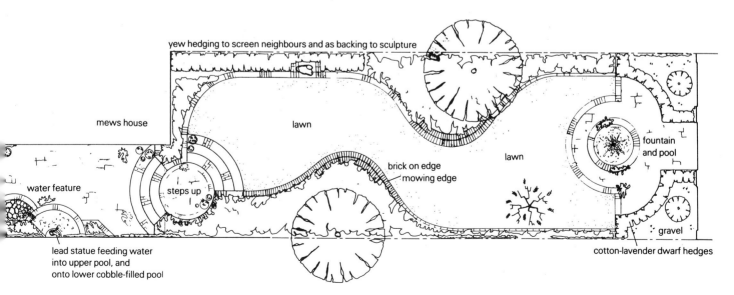

FIG 59 *Typical small city plot designed to be simple, effective and easily maintained*

CHAPTER 5

PLANTING YOUR GARDEN

To achieve the rapid and successful establishment of trees, shrubs and other garden plants, thorough and generous ground preparation is essential – this cannot be stressed too strongly.

Frequently, plants may be seen struggling to establish themselves slowly in inhospitable circumstances – a perimeter border which has for many years borne a jungle of scrub growth will be choked with the roots of the previous plants, even after clearance of top growth, and invariably stumps of trees or large shrubs which are left to regenerate will become major competition for new plants or, if dead, encourage the development of the dreaded honey fungus (*Armillaria*) on the rotting wood and the roots left in the ground. There is even greater competition for food and moisture in closely mown or rough grass areas: trees or shrubs introduced here with the minimum of preparation will take two or three times as long to establish – if they survive – owing to competition with the grass. Smaller shrubs, roses and herbaceous plants are unlikely to survive at all.

PREPARING THE GROUND

Ideally, in garden circumstances, the entire perimeter border, planting area or island bed should be dug to a depth of 45cm (1½ft).If chalk or gravel subsoil is encountered, it should be replaced, at least over the site of each tree or shrub, with good loamy topsoil. Roots and stumps of previous plantings should be removed in the course of this preparation. To help with large stumps, you can hire a stump-chipping machine which will reduce stumps of most sizes to saw-

dust, going below ground to a depth of up to 45cm (1½ft). These are now available in several sizes, from small hand-pushed models to tractor-mounted versions requiring generous access and room to manoeuvre.

In practice you can compromise, preparing borders of this nature, after clearance of stumps and as much root as possible, by a combination of rotovation to a depth of 20cm (9in) and hand-digging of corners or small areas missed by the rotovator.

Particularly on poor soils, individual sites for trees and shrubs within borders or cultivated areas should be further prepared for a minimum width of 1m (3ft) for shrubs, and 1.2m (4ft) for trees and larger shrubs; mix well-rotted farmyard manure, good compost and a slow-release fertiliser with the soil at the base of each 45cm (1½ft) excavation.

TURF OR ROUGH GRASS AREAS

Glyphosate weedkiller is most useful for killing off a turf area prior to rotovation or hand-digging. This herbicide, absorbed by green parts of the plant, is a non-residual type and is translocated back through the system of the plant to kill the roots as well as the top growth. Any glyphosate reaching the soil quickly becomes inactive and the ground is not rendered toxic to a subsequent crop. A month is necessary for the complete action of this weedkiller during the winter months or in times of low temperature, half this time being adequate during the warmer summer months. The land may then be successfully rotovated and hand-dug, with deeper preparations for trees and large shrubs, as already suggested. As it rots down, the dead turf adds

humus and root fibre to improve the texture and fertility of the soil.

When planting in isolated sites in turf or rough grass, or in any position where the whole area is not cultivated, sites should be not less than 1.2m (4ft) wide and cultivated to 0.6m (2ft) for each tree or large shrub, and 1m (3ft) wide and 45cm (1½ft) deep for smaller shrubs. In addition, break up the subsoil at the base of the hole. Unless planting is to take place immediately, it is wise to backfill prepared planting holes, particularly on clay or badly drained soils or in areas with a high water table, as in these conditions they will tend to fill with water and may remain very wet for several weeks especially in winter. Special pipe drainage from tree pits in clay soils may be necessary – individually dug holes can act as wells or soakaways and kill roots by drowning.

Indeed, the complete cultivation of border areas is strongly advised if at all possible – weaving between shrubs or small trees 1.2–4m (4–8ft) apart in an area of rough grass or lawn can be frustrating and time consuming for the weekend gardener, with limited time and an appreciation of unimpeded mowing! Furthermore, even with adequate preparation the grass remains (or reinvades the plant site) as serious competition, taking the lion's share of food and moisture from the soil in the vicinity; in addition, at some point trees and shrubs will suffer impact from the lawn mower, receiving damage to the base of their stems, which at best delays their establishment and at worst can kill them.

However, isolated, widely spaced trees or large shrub sites in lawn or rough grass areas must be accepted to

*Japanese maples (*Acer palmatum *cultivars) blend magnificently with many different hostas at the famous Savill Garden, Windsor. In the foreground is* Hosta fortunei *'Aurea marginata'. (For selections of Japanese maples, see pages 190–4 and Hosta pages 118–9.)*

some extent in most gardens, and here a generous cultivation area should be maintained around the site and kept free of grass and weeds for at least three years following planting.

Generally, small shrubs, roses and herbaceous plants in particular are demanding of nutrients and will quickly deteriorate without them. Well rotted farmyard manure is especially beneficial in the early stages, both as a source of nutrients and as a mulch, particularly when combined with peat or pulverised bark. Again, the best performance from roses and herbaceous plants will only be obtained on sites where there is deep and thorough cultivation in conjunction with generous manuring.

To sum up, the more thoroughly and diligently you prepare and maintain your borders and planting areas, the better will be the results in rapid establishment and good consistent growth in the following years.

BUYING PLANTS

Use the checklist to help you in selecting plants from the garden centre. If you are planning a border or area of your garden or have a professionally produced planting plan, it is a good idea to place an order with a nurseryman for plants not normally available container-grown from the garden centre. Such plants will normally be available between early autumn and late spring, dug from the open ground and rootballed or with roots protected by moist straw or similar material, with an outer cover of plastic or burlap. Allow at least four weeks for delivery, or three weeks for collection from the nursery premises. In the meantime, it is well worth preparing beds, borders or individual planting sites in advance, backfilling where necessary. Planting can then proceed with the minimum of delay on receipt of the plants.

PURCHASE CHECKLIST

At the garden centre, examine plants critically to ensure they are:
• new, fresh, vigorous stock, attractive to look at if not in flower, well furnished in the case of shrubs
• adequately moist, with not too many roots through the bottom of the pot
Reject:
• plants which show yellowing or diseased foliage or have premature leaf drop
• pot-bound plants or those in pots which are too small for the size of the plant or shrub they contain
Test:
• the weight of the plant – an exceptionally heavy pot may well be waterlogged and contain dead roots, while an unnaturally light pot may have a bone-dry centre.

HOW TO PLANT

Nursery stock, whether field grown (bareroot or rootballed in soil) or container grown, is produced today by most good nurserymen to exacting standards of size and quality. If correctly handled and planted, these plants have every chance of successful establishment.

BARE-ROOT TREES, SHRUBS AND ROSES

These should reach you individually wrapped, or with a number bundled together, with roots packed with moist straw or similar organic material and then enclosed in hessian or plastic film, which is secured to the stem of the plant or plants.

If weather conditions allow, plant within a few days of receipt – if delayed longer than about a week, temporary storage or 'laying-in' may be required (see below). If you are ready to proceed with planting, do not unpack the bundle until the hole or holes are ready to receive the plants, and certainly do not expose bare roots to cold winds – it doesn't take long to kill the fine root fibres so essential for quick establishment. As planting proceeds, use the damp packing material and hessian to cover roots after unpacking.

If possible, choose a fine, calm day when the soil is in a workable (friable) condition. Hole-out in the prepared site or area, at least 15cm (6in) greater than the width and depth of the root of the tree or shrub to be planted.

Feathered and standard trees will require a stake, ideally round, 5–7cm (2–3in) in diameter and treated with preservative. Position the stake after holing-out: it should be driven in with a large wooden mallet so that it is very firm in the subsoil. Recent research advocates the use of short stakes (say, 50–60cm (1¹/₂–2ft) above ground) used with a single purpose-made tree tie at the top of the stake, rather than taller stakes supporting the length of a standard stem (1.5m/5ft), as has long been the custom. The short-stake method stabilises the roots and lower part of the stem, allowing the remainder of the young trees to sway naturally in the wind and develop a strong wind-resistant trunk (Figs 60a–c). Larger heavy, extra heavy standard or semi-mature trees may require specialised staking or guying (see Figs 61 and 62).

Have on hand a wheelbarrow of suitable organic matter, such as coarse peat, pulverised bark or tree-planting compost. If the material contains no nutrients, as is the case with bark or peat, a compound or slow-release fertiliser can be mixed with the

FIG 60a *Correctly staked and secured tree, using the short-stake method. The buckle-type adjustable tie is at the very top of stake, with a nail to prevent it slipping down, and there is a weed-free or mulched area of at least 1m (3ft) in diameter*

compost to apply to the hole and around the roots of the tree or shrub when planting. This is particularly beneficial if the local soil is not of a fine, friable nature.

Before positioning the tree or shrub in the hole, trim off any damaged roots. If the shoot system seems large in comparison with the roots, some pruning of the top growth will encourage establishment of deciduous subjects by reducing the amount of top growth the roots have to support.

Planting is perhaps best carried out with an assistant to hold the tree or shrub at about the correct position in the hole so that, with backfilling, the soil level will be the same as the previous nursery soil mark on the stem. Initially, every effort should be made to spread the root system evenly so that it is not congested within the planting hole. Take great care not to position the plant too deeply or too shallowly. As a mixture of fine soil and compost, with fertiliser, is slowly backfilled, the assistant should agitate the plant gently up and down, to filter the fine soil and compost between the fibres of the roots. At the correct level, the plant should be well firmed in with the full weight of the body behind the heel. Further backfill to the soil mark on the stem and secure tree tie(s) where appropriate.

ROOTBALLED TREES, SHRUBS AND CONIFERS

These should be planted in a similar manner in the prepared border or planting site. First excavate a hole to an estimated correct depth, allowing for a finished level

to the nursery soil mark on the stem of the tree or shrub. If there is a depth of loose soil in the planting hole, light firming of this will be necessary before positioning the rootballed plant, in order to avoid settling or subsidence. Be careful to ensure that any budding or grafting union at the base of the stem of the tree is not buried. Such a union should normally be 5–6cm (2–2¹/₂in) above the finished soil level.

The soil-retaining material (usually hessian or plastic net) around the rootball should be removed with care, after positioning in the hole. With large, heavy rootballs, cut away the material from the top and sides of the rootball – if hessian (jute) or biodegradable plastic, it can remain under the rootball to rot down. Firm in thoroughly. Heavy, extra-heavy or semi-mature trees are often rootballed (or supplied in large containers) and will require staking or guying, particularly in exposed positions. Double staking with heavy-duty plastic or reinforced rubber hose or ties is a good method which avoids damage to roots by driving in stakes through the rootball or adjacent to the trunk (Fig 61). An alternative method for the largest specimens is the use of multiple wire or hawser guys (usually three), with tree branches protected by a rubber reinforced hose where contact is made (Fig 62). These guys ideally will require U-bolts top and bottom and turnbuckles on each guy, which will be secured at the base to a short stake of preserved wood 5 x 5cm (2 x 2in) wide and 60cm (2ft) long, driven at an angle towards the tree.

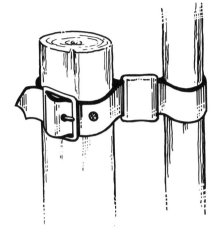

FIG 60b *Detail of tie, with nail through the belt into stake to prevent slipping*

FIG 60c *Badly staked tree. Wrongly positioned or slipping ties will result in a wound by the top of the stake; there should be a grass and weed-free area, ideally at least 1m (3ft) in diameter*

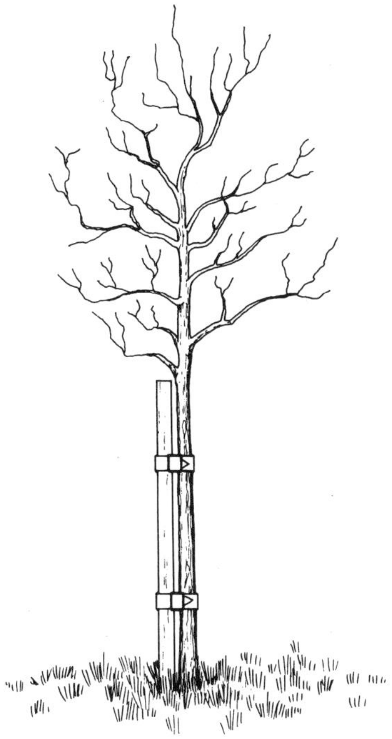

CONTAINER-GROWN NURSERY STOCK

Today a very wide range of trees, shrubs, conifers, roses, herbaceous plants, grasses, ferns and alpine or rock plants is available container or pot grown for planting the year round, though drought conditions in mid-summer and frost and snow in midwinter are best avoided. Such plants are grown in peat- or bark-based composts with nutrients added, which in a few months become exhausted.

It is very important to ensure when planting that there is a generous supply of fertile, fine topsoil, mixed on, say, a 50/50 basis with coarse peat or bark or a good planting compost, well laced with compound or slow-release fertiliser (if not present in the planting compost). The object of this generosity is to encourage the plant to root into the surrounding area and establish itself more rapidly – a mass of pure peat or bark surrounding the root of the container plant is as undesirable as is a planting site of unimproved local soil which may be clayish, gravelly or chalky.

It is equally important to ensure at all times of year that every container grown plant is adequately moist before it is placed in the ground – after handling a number of plants one soon realises that this or that specimen is unusually light in weight in comparison with others of the same size. The suspect container should be submerged in a bucket of water until air bubbles cease – it is not usually good enough simply to apply water from the top. If the centre of the rootball has become dry, the peat will remain dry following planting, even in winter, and eventually the plant will fail to establish and die. This is very important and is often neglected.

As with rootballed plants, firming of loose soil at the base of the planting hole may be necessary to avoid excessive settling. Remove or cut away the plastic container and examine the roots of the plant – a specimen in good condition should show a good proportion of active, usually white, roots on the surface. These should be gently teased away from the shape of the pot in order to encourage them to grow out into the surrounding prepared soil. If you find the plant to be excessively pot-bound or showing a large quantity of dead or dying inactive roots, reject it or put it aside to be exchanged. Firm the plant well into the ground and add a light covering of topsoil or compost. Water in and apply a mulch of pulverised bark, black polythene or coarse peat. As with rootballed trees, where necessary double staking will be appropriate for container-grown standard or feathered trees.

TEMPORARY STORAGE

The weather can be variable and unpredictable during the winter planting season. Nurserymen may despatch your order in good open weather conditions, but a lengthy period of frost and snow may well set in before planting is possible. Hardy bareroot and balled deciduous and evergreen trees and shrubs can usually be stored temporarily in barns, sheds or unheated garages. Slacken ties on shrubs (particularly evergreens) which are in bundles, but do not unpack at the root (unless known to be dry – in which event submerge the roots in water before repacking). Equally, good sheltered storage can often be found amid long-established rhododendrons or similar large evergreens. Straw, coarse bark, sawdust or similar materials can be used to prevent cold winds desiccating roots and freezing rootballs and containers. Stand container-grown plants upright, ideally on a soil, peat, sand or other absorbent surface, rather than on concrete or stone, and keep moist, but prevent from freezing, as suggested above for rootballed plants.

Perhaps due to building delays, flooding or other unusual causes, a planting area cannot be made ready for several weeks, even months, following receipt of your plants, and you will then need to 'lay-in' bare-root trees, shrubs (including roses) and balled evergreens. Take out a trench at least 30cm (1ft) deep in a sheltered, cultivated area, perhaps the vegetable garden, where there is good workable soil. Unpack the bundles and plant temporarily in the trench: space each shrub reasonably from its neighbour; spread the roots, filtering fine topsoil and peat between the root fibres (as with permanent planting); then 'heel-in' very firmly and finish off with fine soil to the nursery mark on the plant. Be careful to avoid leaving air pockets and water in thoroughly, particularly in late winter/early spring, when an upsurge of sap is due and the plant will rapidly desiccate without adequate water at the roots.

PLANTING

WHEN TO PLANT

The planting of most hardy subjects can be carried out safely at any time during open weather from mid-autumn to early spring in the case of deciduous open ground trees, shrubs and plants, and from early autumn to late spring for evergreen trees and shrubs, provided that proper and careful attention is given after planting. Ideally evergreens and conifers should be planted by the end of the year, or in mid to late spring, when desiccation of foliage is less likely. Open weather in the dead of winter is better for planting hardy subjects than a bad day in autumn or early spring. Hardy deciduous container- or pot-grown plants may be planted at any time, provided that watering is attended to and that the pot full of roots is thoroughly moist before planting, whatever the season. They should, however, never be planted when frozen.

There are many most desirable trees and shrubs, for instance from California and South America, which are borderline hardy in less hospitable climates and will be decidedly vulnerable to frosts and freezing winds while they are still small. For these, spring or late summer to early autumn planting is advised. Even then, temporary protection against spring frosts with polythene sheet, hessian or branches of conifers or evergreens positioned around the new plant is usually necessary, and again probably in the following winter if exceptionally severe weather is forecast. If spring planting is missed, establishing half-hardy subjects in late summer/early autumn has its advantages; with free rooting into warm soil the new plant becomes hardened and acclimatised, and better able to withstand the low temperatures of late autumn and the hard frosts of winter.

GETTING NEW PLANTS ESTABLISHED

PRUNING

Establishment of trees and shrubs, particularly those which are late planted as bare-root (open ground) stock larger than standard size or which are used in exposed situations, will be assisted by thinning or pruning back top growth by up to one-third. While you may perhaps be reluctant to do this, as the planted height of the tree is obviously influenced, this pruning often prevents substantial natural dieback or the failure of late-planted large nursery stock.

ROOT GROWTH

Plant roots have two main functions – to provide anchorage and support for the aerial portions of the tree, shrub or plant, and to extract nutrients and moisture from the ground and translocate these through the systems of the plant, thereby promoting establishment and growth. Most bare-rooted trees and shrubs suffer damage to their roots in the lifting and transplanting process and growth of new root is essential in order to ensure establishment in the new site.

As already advised, with trees planted at 1.5–1.8m (5–6ft) or more in height, stakes are necessary to stabilise the base of the stem and prevent the wrenching of existing roots in the

Rhododendron 'Curlew' prefers a shaded site (see page 203)

ground, with subsequent inhibition of new root formation. Furthermore, the ability to regenerate a new permanent root system, as opposed to a rather short-lived one able to absorb water and nutrients temporarily, depends very much on the particular tree involved; for instance, most poplars, willows and maples adapt well and rapidly regenerate good root systems, enabling them to be moved successfully as quite large trees. Other trees, notably birch, beech and oak, quickly lose their power to make permanent new roots.

Therefore, in addition to adequate firming at planting time, combined with stability of the root system by staking as necessary, we can give the new transplant the best possible chance by ensuring that there is adequate moisture in the vicinity of the roots from early spring onwards, and throughout the summer. This is best achieved by careful attention to watering, controlling the weeds which compete with transplants for food and moisture, and by applying suitable mulches to moist, weed-free soil over the root area.

WATERING

Watering-in following the planting of container-grown and bare-root trees, shrubs and conifers is a vital operation, particularly in the spring. A standard tree or large shrub or conifer will require at least one bucketful of water to settle the soil around the roots or rootball, and to ensure that there is adequate moisture present when the plant puts out its new roots with the advance of spring. If there is little rain, this should be repeated weekly during spring or early summer, when the plant demands the greatest amount of water. Overhead spraying with clear water in the evening following a warm day or periods of drying wind would also be beneficial.

MULCHING

A 5cm (2in) layer of an open-textured material applied to the root (cultivation) area of a tree, shrub or conifer can be of great value in conserving

moisture and reducing frequency of watering in times of drought. Coarse peat, half-rotted leaves, garden compost, well-rotted farmyard manure or a mixture of these are all useful as mulches.

A coarse grade of pulverised pine bark is effective as an open-textured and long-lasting mulch and has the added bonus of an attractive appearance. Bark is clean and easy to handle and allows convenient application of water and fertiliser to the root area of the plant, while discouraging the growth of weeds and repelling such troublesome garden pests as slugs and snails. However, avoid mulches which contain large wood chips: they are usually aesthetically unacceptable, and furthermore fungal problems may ensue, as well as excessive loss of nitrogen from the soil due to the slow rotting of the wood chips.

TREE PROTECTION
Tree Ties

Today's purpose-made tree ties undoubtedly provide an effective and efficient means of securing a tree to its stake – do not use string, rope or other materials. Modern rubber or plastic belting/buckle-type tree ties usually have a rubber or plastic spacer to separate the tree from the stake and prevent friction or damage to the stem. However, a tree tie must be correctly positioned; if only one is used on a short stake this should be at the very top – if positioned more than 5cm (2in) from the top of the stake and insufficiently tightened, the natural flexing of the head of the tree can result in a serious wound to the stem at the point of contact at the top of the stake. If this is allowed to persist, the head of the tree may well snap at this point. It is equally important to ensure

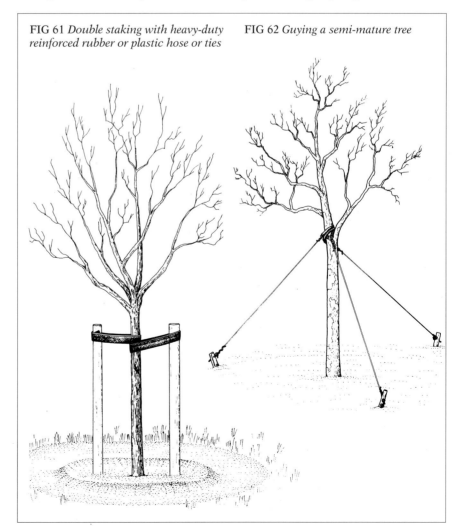

FIG 61 *Double staking with heavy-duty reinforced rubber or plastic hose or ties*

FIG 62 *Guying a semi-mature tree*

An attractive combination of trees and shrubs and mound-forming conifer (Thuja). *The flowering tree is* Cercis siliquastrum* *(Judas tree) all with plenty of growing space.*

that the tree tie – particularly the buckle type – is fixed to the stake by a single galvanised nail through the eye-hole usually provided, otherwise the buckle can slacken off and the tree tie drop down the stake, creating the situation described on p 74–5 (see Fig 60).

An essential aftercare task is the examination and adjustment of tree ties once or twice a year, and particularly before commencement of spring growth. Neglect of this simple routine can result in strangulation and serious damage to stems, or the breaking of the tree-tie belting.

Tree Guards
Protection against cattle, horses and sheep grazing in park land has traditionally been by means of heavy post and rail tree guards, ideally not less than 1.2m (4ft) square and up to 1.8m (6ft) in height. In such circumstances this type of protection remains the best method of preventing heavy animals damaging trees, conifers and shrubs by browsing, bark rubbing or stripping and by trampling of root areas – an important factor often overlooked.

Rabbits and hares, and to an increasing extent, deer, are often a problem in gardens in rural areas. The damage they do by browsing, bark-stripping and fraying and (in the case of rabbits) burrowing into the roots of newly planted trees, shrubs, roses and conifers is considerable. Fortunately, plastic-net tree guards in a variety of sizes have been developed in recent years which give a considerable measure of protection to young trees and plants against these animals. They are made from tough, light-degradable polyethylene with a mesh structure up to 25 x 35mm (1 x 1³/₈in), cut conveniently from a continuous length and rolled to various widths to protect a wide range of shrubs, tree transplants and conifers. The plastic mesh may be cut to various heights from 60cm (about 2¹/₂ft) to 2m (6ft). The guard thus formed is usually stapled to one or more rough-sawn or round wooden stakes, positioned to support it.

LABELLING

There are now a number of labelling systems available, and almost every one has some disadvantage as well as a number of advantages. Temporary labelling both outside and under glass is important, as this will detail not only the name of the plant but the record of seed sowing, cutting taking etc, and what is written should last at least several months.
• Temporary labels in seed pots or hung from the plant are usually plastic, 8–15cm (3–6in) long, and white or green, but could be wooden and of similar dimensions, painted white on one side. Names written with black pencil (2B) will last a reasonable length of time – longer on wood if used firmly pressed on to half-dry white undercoat paint. A waterproof marker pen can be reasonably non-fading as well as waterproof, but not necessarily permanent on all surfaces.
•Permanent labels are now available in metal (aluminium), laminated plastic and ceramic (stoneware). For aluminium, a special jig enables the punching of letters and numbers to form the lettering you require. These are certainly permanent, but not very beautiful. There are also labels made of anodised and etched aluminium, which may be written upon in ordinary pencil or chinagraph, the name lasting rather longer than on plastic or wood. You can also get engraved-to-order plastic laminate labels, in black with white lettering. These are most frequently seen in botanic gardens, arboreta, horticultural colleges etc, and can be hung or positioned on metal stems or wooden posts.

There are simple and inexpensive plastic labels available, with a hole at one end for hanging and pointed to insert in pots. These labels are of flexible white plastic, matt black on one side, and a metal stylus is provided to score or print the name in white on the black side. These labels are effective, reasonably permanent and unobtrusive in the garden, though easily dislodged or blown away if not attached to the plant.

Finally, there are also very attractive round or oval ceramic (stoneware) plant labels, 5–9cm (2–3¹/₂in) in diameter. The plant name is inscribed in black lettering and a stone/white glaze is applied before firing. There is a hole for the label to be hung if desired. Being stoneware they are very strong and, short of taking a hammer to them or dropping them from a great height on to a hard surface, they are almost indestructible. These labels are particularly attractive near the house in the vicinity of patios or pergolas, and are not expensive considering the work involved. Garden label suppliers are listed on page 220.

FIG 63 *Engraved plastic-laminate plant labels and ceramic (stoneware) labels*

Tree Shelters

For those planting trees in woodland circumstances or in exposed gardens, where they perhaps wish to establish choice or rare subjects available only as small plants less than 1m (3ft) high, consideration should be given to the use of plastic tree shelters. These vertical plastic tube structures, generally from 8–l5cm (3–6in) square, are used primarily to improve the survival, establishment and growth rate of young broadleaved tree transplants. Although not beautiful, the system seems to have proved successful so far, and its use is spreading; the trees rapidly produce a straight stem and are adequately protected from rabbits and deer and from exposure to wind while small, until growth reaches the top of the tube – usually 1.2m (4ft). Trees which are often very slow in growth and difficult to get through the baby stage (eg nothofagus, holly and oak) will benefit greatly.

WEED CONTROL

As stressed earlier, keeping planting sites and areas free of invading weeds and grass is of the greatest importance in the establishment and good growth of trees, shrubs, conifers and roses, and indeed of all cultivated plants. Starting with clean cultivated ground, free of perennial weed and weed roots such as dandelion, ground elder, couch, dock and so on, is essential – annual weed is relatively easy to deal with, and once an initial crop of annual weeds is removed, mulching with bark or a similar material, or with black polythene, is the best method of maintaining planting sites and areas free of competing weeds. Groundcover plants can further assist if planted into weed-free or mulched areas.

Black Polythene

Although often excluded from ornamental plantings on aesthetic grounds, medium-gauge black polythene sheeting has considerable value in weed control for up to three years among newly planted roses, shrubs, ornamental and fruit trees, as well as

bushes and hedging plants. In addition, it has the advantage of retaining moisture and promoting good growth and more reliable establishment of young plants.

Chemical Control

Chemical means of weed control these days are many, complicated and continually advancing. For the amateur, however, several products are now well established as reliable and effective, if sensibly and intelligently applied (see Chapter 6).

TOOLS AND EQUIPMENT

HAND TOOLS

The purchase of reliable, good-quality spades, forks, hoes, trowels and allied tools is a most sensible investment towards efficient and successful garden creation and maintenance. High-quality hand tools usually carry a five-year guarantee, and are well designed and a pleasure to handle and use. Often the business end is made of heat-treated carbon steel, the blades coated with epoxy-polyester for additional protection, or of high-grade stainless steel with wooden or lightweight aluminium shafts.

There are now ingenious multi-change ranges of clip-on tool heads used in conjunction with snap-lock aluminium handles up to 1.3m (4ft 3in) long to accommodate various hoes (draw and Dutch) and rakes (for seedbed preparation or lawn scarifying). It is also possible to fit a curved blade pruning saw to this length of shaft – most useful for pruning work in trees. A shorter T-handle system incorporates edging irons, lawn-edge trimmer, trowel, weeding fork etc. Such systems can be stored in the smallest of garden sheds, where space may be strictly limited. Good-quality secateurs and long-handled pruners or loppers are also essential for most gardens where shrubs, trees and fruit trees are grown.

MOTORISED EQUIPMENT

The owner of a larger garden will need some electric or motorised equipment.

Apart from lawn mowers, an electric hedge trimmer will be essential to supplement hand shears if hedges are extensive. The motorised strimmer is most useful for clearing around tree bases and removing herbage from difficult corners which are missed by the lawn mower. If trees abound, a smaller chainsaw is desirable, particularly if you have a woodburning stove to use the wood resulting from tree prunings – larger operations conducted by the local tree surgeon usually result in a heap of cord wood to be logged up. Great care should be exercised when using a chainsaw, as they can be lethal.

Larger lawns with surrounding deciduous trees may call for the use of a leaf sweeper (a wheeled vehicle which collects leaves into its hopper when pushed over lawns, paths or paved areas). Similarly, a powered cultivator reduces extensive hand-digging in vegetable gardens – or you may prefer to hire for this once-a-year operation. A wheeled fertiliser spreader is a useful device if you need to apply fertiliser or moss-killer evenly to a substantial lawn – but again, hiring is possible, even from the company who sell you the fertiliser or moss-killer dressings.

Lawn Mowers

Choose your lawn mower with care to suit the size and nature of the grass area it is likely to have to deal with and seek specialist advice, which is usually available from the vending company.

If you like to see traditional stripes on your lawn, you will require a cylinder mower, available in a number of sizes from about 50cm (l8in) to about 1m (36in) in width cut and powered by electricity or petrol engine.

If the finish is less important to you, a rotary-type machine will be appropriate, with a similar range of sizes and means of propulsion and usually a variable height of cut. Finally, the hover type so popular today enables you to mow informally in a variety of locations from odd corners to long grass areas, and particu-

*Persistent perennial weed – the ubiquitous ground elder or goutweed (*Aegopodium podagraria*) with creeping white roots should be thoroughly cleared before planting (see also Chapter 6).*

larly to deal efficiently with otherwise unmowable bank.

OTHER ESSENTIALS
Essential garden equipment should also include such items as a wheelbarrow (consider one of the newer 'ball barrows'); a knapsack or smaller pump-up type sprayer for weedkiller, insecticide or fungicide application (if you have several fruit trees, half or fully grown, a knapsack sprayer will be needed at least for winter wash spraying and probably at other times); unless the rainfall is heavy in your district, the knitted braided hosepipe (15-year guarantee) is a good investment, together with an oscillating sprinkler for lawn and vegetable-garden areas in particular. One or two watering cans

(usually plastic these days) and fitted with sensible roses, fine and coarse, will be necessary to transport water to patio containers, and for planting and maintaining newly-planted trees, shrubs, roses and so on.

The above items are essential for the reasonably efficient running of today's garden, whether small, medium or large.

In addition, a great many gadgets and labour-saving devices are available, usually from garden centres, designed to make life easier and gardening more pleasurable. These range from wooden clogs and gardeners' gloves to knee pads and aprons – the sort of items that make excellent birthday or Christmas presents for dedicated gardeners.

KEEPING RECORDS

If you have your own or a professionally produced garden plan, it will be worth keeping a garden record book in which to record changes, deaths, replacements, planting dates and so on.

Also, keep a record of seed sowing, noting dates of germination and potting on, and dates when cuttings were made and inserted – the source of seeds and cuttings is also worth noting, particularly if the plant is uncommon or rare.

When you visit gardens which are open to the public, it is worth taking a notebook in which to record plant associations or details of any particular planting scheme which impresses you.

CHAPTER 6

MAINTAINING YOUR GARDEN

In earlier chapters the emphasis was on making the most of the natural features of the garden through assessing the site, designing and planning, site preparation and the mechanics of planting. This chapter should be read in conjunction with the earlier ones at the design stage, but the main intention is to provide information on the management and maintenance of a garden from the point where the plans have been executed until the garden has matured and is ripe for redesigning.

WEED CONTROL

Weed control is quite simply the removal of unwanted plants. Generally, there are two reasons for removing weeds: firstly, because they are judged unsightly, and secondly, to remove competition for water and nutrients needed by the garden plants. A species may be a weed in one part of the garden and a plant in another and the best definition of a weed is a plant out of place. Aspects of weed control are discussed in Chapter 3, features on the biology of weeds and the need to remove competing vegetation on p 27. Methods of weed control include mechanical methods, herbicides and mulches discussed here. *(Continued on page 87)*

(Continued on page 87)

MAINTENANCE AND MANAGEMENT

There are two aspects of this stage. Maintenance includes the operations involved in keeping the garden, or a garden feature, in first-rate order, including:
• control of weeds
• application of fertilisers and feeding
• watering
• dealing with fungal or insect pests
• disposal of waste
• periodic activities such as pond cleaning and path maintenance
Maintenance is thus activity based.

Management involves the taking of decisions, such as:
• whether to employ time-saving ideas
• when to replace a shrub or tree, or to thin out overcrowded plants or divide herbaceous ones
• what grass-cutting policy and equipment to use
• aspects such as what pruning regime to use on shrubs
Management, therefore, is decision based.

However, these two aspects are closely inter-related and need to be considered together.

New young foliage of Acer pseudoplatanus *'Brilliantissimum'* is spectacular each spring and forms an eye-catching display. (See also page 129.)*

•PROBLEM SOLVER•
MECHANICAL WEED CONTROL

Mechanical methods of weed control include digging, hoeing, rotovating, cutting and pulling the weeds.

DIGGING
The soil is turned over and the weeds growing on the surface are buried where, deprived of sunlight, they should rot down and incorporate organic matter into the soil. Some perennial weeds with tap-roots (eg docks, dandelion) need digging out completely to prevent regeneration.

Disadvantages:
• Where there are weeds with perennial underground stems or rootstocks capable of making new growth such as couch grass, ground elder or bindweed, turning the soil over is unlikely to kill the weeds.
• Some weeds, like groundsel, are still capable of setting seeds even after being buried (although the seeds will not germinate until they are brought to the surface at some later stage).
• Existing weed seeds in the newly exposed soil surface will now be capable of germinating.
• Digging near to existing plants is likely to damage their root systems and reduce growth (although where the plants are making rampant vegetative growth, this might encourage flowering).

Advantages:
• Digging is a useful method for turning over the soil prior to planting and as a way to remove spot weeds like docks, but is limited in its value in an established bed or border.
• Where a perennial weed is present, a proportion of the weed's root or underground system can be removed by forking through the dug soil; this is unlikely to give satisfactory control, but will reduce the vigour of the weeds and make it easier to control them with a herbicide application to the new growth.

HOEING
The weeds are cut off at just below ground level.

Advantages:
• This can be very effective in dry weather, as the severed tops of the weeds wither and die.
• Hoeing can be a technique useful on bare conditions where perennial weeds are absent and as a therapeutic form of gardening, combining activity with a useful end product.

Disadvantages:
• In wet conditions, the weeds may be able to re-root into the soil. Also, in wet weather it may be difficult to hoe effectively, as the soil may cling to the hoe (stainless steel tools are much better in this respect).
• The frequent turning over of the top few centimetres of soil will continually expose new weed seeds to the right conditions for germination, and if a prolonged period follows when it is impossible or impractical to hoe, a healthy flush of weeds may develop.

ROTOVATING
A rotovator can be used as a hoe to keep the top few centimetres of the soil loose and friable and to chop up germinating seedlings and established weeds.

Advantages:
• Using a rotovator is less dependent upon weather conditions than using a hoe.
• It can be an effective method of weed control in specific situations where the plants are spaced so that a rotovator can be used between them.

Disadvantages:
• As with deep digging, too deep cultivation can restrict plant growth, and may accidentally damage the base of the plants.
• If the ground is sticky, rotovating can damage the soil structure. Rotovators should not be used where there are perennial weeds with under-ground stems and persistent roots (couch grass, bindweed, ground elder and Japanese knotweed), otherwise the effect will be to propagate and increase the incidence of these by spreading the live roots.

CUTTING
This is often advocated when establishing woodland, and certainly rampant weed growth can cause the death of plants by competition and by smothering.

Advantages:
Cutting woody weeds a few days prior to using a herbicide can reduce the quantity of herbicide needed.

Disadvantages:
• Research shows that cutting weeds, especially grasses, may actually increase the competition they put on the plants; this includes the close-mown grass near the base of a tree or shrub. In gardens the weeds should never be allowed to grow rampantly over plants and all plants will do better (newly planted trees and shrubs especially) with an area of at least 60cm (2ft) diameter, preferably 1.2m (4ft), that is kept free of all competing vegetation.

PULLING
• Pulling involves the removal by hand of individual weeds or groups of weeds.

Advantages:
• Pulling is useful where only the occasional weed is present, on intricate features such as a rockery, or where the weed is about to seed and other methods will entail the release of the seeds.
• It is often necessary where a weed has established closely in association with a valued plant or shrub.

Disadvantages:
• Pulling is not recommended on a large scale!

CHEMICAL WEED CONTROL

Herbicides are chemicals which can be very effective in controlling weeds and save much time and effort. However, when misused they can be a danger to the operator and kill off valuable plants; it is for these reasons that some people deprecate their use. If used with care, however, they are safe, effective and valuable tools in the garden. They must be stored safely, out of the reach of young children, and in many cases in a frost-free environment (as several are sold as formulations which will be altered and rendered ineffective by freezing). *They should only be used in accordance with the recommendations and application rate given on the label.*

Herbicides divide into two categories: contact herbicides and residual or persistent herbicides.

Contact herbicides:
• enter the plant by contact with the tissues, primarily leaves and shoots, on to which they are applied, and most require several hours without rain for effective penetration; also, there has to be sufficient foliage to take up a lethal dose of the herbicide
• are most useful during the spring, summer and autumn months
• are less effective against weeds with thick waxy cuticles, as found on many evergreens, or where the foliage is wilted due to drought conditions
• may either kill only the portion of the plant to which they are applied or may be moved, or translocated, through the plant to other tissues
• will have no lasting effect and will not kill the weeds which may start to germinate a few days after the herbicide is applied
• are most useful for clearing ground before planting and for spot treatment of weeds amongst established plants.

Care must be taken only to apply the herbicide to weeds, not to valued plants; this is especially important with translocated herbicides.

Residual or **persistent herbicides**:
• kill weeds following uptake from the soil, normally by the roots; they are applied to the soil surface and become bound into the soil
• are more or less insoluble in water and remain in the top few centimetres of the soil, persisting for a number of months
• can be used selectively to control germinating weeds, because the roots of established plants tend not to be in the very top few centimetres of the soil (except grasses), whereas nearly all germinating weeds initially root exclusively in this zone. Also, a germinating seedling is rather fragile, requiring less herbicide to kill it than an established plant. Persistence is a function of the quantity applied and of the rate of breakdown of the chemical in the soil
• should only be applied when soil conditions are suitable, ie the soil must be moist or adequate but not very heavy rain must follow application (a gentle watering will help in dry conditions)
• are rather slow in acting; some, however, can be applied to the soil during the winter period when the soil is generally moist
• function by creating a shallow surface layer of soil which contains the herbicide. Total weed control is only effective whilst the layer of treated soil is intact and any activity which breaks this layer will reduce the effectiveness of the herbicide
• are not compatible with pulling weeds or with hoeing and it is better to spot treat any weeds which develop with a contact herbicide.

If it is necessary to plant a shrub or tree into an area treated by a persistent herbicide within the likely period of its persistence, the top 10cm (4in) of soil should be removed from the planting pit and not used for backfilling. It is especially important not to bury treated soil while the herbicide is still active, as this will make it available to the roots even of plants which are normally tolerant to the product, and will also slow down the rate of breakdown of the herbicide.

METHODS OF APPLICATION
Several methods are available, each with some advantages and disadvantages. Most herbicides are applied as a water-based solution or suspension, usually either by a pressurised sprayer or from a watering can. Whatever equipment is used, it should be thoroughly washed out after use and made-up but unused batches of herbicide should not be kept; several formulations are corrosive if left in the equipment and others become ineffective.

Using a watering can tends to be rather imprecise and wasteful of the herbicide; however, it is a very convenient method for small-scale use and there is little risk, with care, of the herbicide drifting in the wind. If using a watering can for herbicides, it is sensible to keep one solely for this purpose; this removes the risk of killing plants because the can was not properly washed out. Using a pressurised sprayer is more economical of the herbicide but does require more care. Most pressure sprayers cannot be used when there is any appreciable wind, due to the risk of drift of the chemical.

Granular formulations of some herbicides are available. These can be applied by special devices, but within the garden the usual method is a glorified pepperpot. This is a small canister with holes in the top and the granules are shaken over the area of ground to be treated. The advantages of granular applications are that there is no risk of drifting and the herbicide can be placed through existing vegetation; any granules lodging in the foliage or shoots can be gently knocked to the ground, unlike water-based formulations where the herbicide will remain on the foliage of any plant.

Water-based applications can be used for both contact and persistent herbicides, but granules can only be used for persistent ones. Also, with granular formulations, the soil conditions must be suitable for the granules to break down and release the herbicide into the soil. This usually means it must be moist, but one commercial herbicide, which may become available for garden use, requires low soil temperatures for it to be bound into the soil and be persistent.

No herbicides will control all weeds with the same degree of efficiency. If a certain herbicide is used for a prolonged period, there is a tendency for a population of weeds with some resistance to that herbicide to develop. It is, therefore, a useful idea to alternate between herbicides or between methods of weed control.

WHAT TO APPLY?
The following notes are on a condensed selection of the herbicides available. Chemical names are given. In each case, the manufacturer's label recommendation must be consulted, both as regards use and safety considerations. Always take care to prevent herbicides reaching valued plants.

Weedout or **Clout** (*Alloxydim sodium*) is a contact herbicide which is grass specific, ie it only controls grasses. It does not harm other plants if used as recommended. Of grasses, it will kill a number of species, but vigorous ones like couch grass (*Agropyron repens*) are not killed but checked for the season of application. It is available as a water-based formulation which is applied in late spring or early summer before the grasses have made substantial growth. Its main use is to control grasses in areas of herbaceous plants, ground cover and amongst small shrubs.

Rootout or **Amcide** (*Ammonium sulphamate*) is a very effective herbicide for killing stumps and is easily translocated through the root system. It assists the decay of the stumps, as it degrades into an ammonia fertiliser, encouraging decay fungi. It can be used to control other plants and is available as water-soluble crystals.

Dalapon is a contact herbicide which will effectively control grasses. It is available either as a water-based formulation or as granules with Dichlobenil. It is used to kill couch and other grasses prior to cultivation and can be used with established shrubs but is less generally useful

than Glyphosate. When applied to clear ground, six to eight weeks should elapse before cultivation and twelve weeks before replanting. If used to kill grasses between existing shrubs, twelve rainfree hours are needed for uptake by the grasses and the foliage should not be sprayed to run-off, or the plants may be harmed by uptake from the soil.

Dichlobenil is a persistent herbicide applied in granular form. It is useful for controlling weeds in shrub beds and around trees. At the lower recommended dose rates, it will control germinating weeds and a number of established weeds. As the rate is increased, a greater range of weed species is controlled. At high rates, however, damage to plants is possible, particularly if the granules are allowed to lodge against the base of the stem. It is generally recommended that Dichlobenil should not be used on plants until they have been established for two years. It is usually applied in late winter/early spring when the soil is moist and it will then give season-long control.

Glyphosate is a contact herbicide which is translocated throughout the plant. It is very effective against grasses and many broadleaved weeds. It is applied to live foliage and absorbed into the plant, where it interferes with respiration. The rate of entry into the leaf is slow, and it is important that at least six hours without rain follow application, or it will be washed off. It is useful for killing weeds prior to cultivation and for spot treatment of weeds in shrub beds or around trees. Glyphosate is particularly useful for killing perennial weeds with underground rhizomes or grass areas. It is rather slow in action, taking from one to three weeks or so in summer to kill plants; consequently it is of little value against annual weeds, such as groundsel, as they can ripen viable seeds before the parent weed is killed; also, it will not prevent germination of the next crop of weeds. Spray must not be allowed to drift onto plants, as treating a small area of a susceptible species can kill or

damage the entire plant. If any accidental spraying of plants occurs, quickly wash the spray off the foliage or cut off the sprayed branch. On contact with the soil, it is quickly neutralised by the soil fauna. Follow instructions for applications.

Paraquat, often combined with **Diquat,** is a contact herbicide. It has a high mammalian toxicity. Nevertheless, provided the product is used in accordance with the manufacturer's label recommendations, it is a useful product. It is not translocated within the plant and therefore will not kill plants with extensive root systems. Its only real advantages over the much safer (to people) herbicide glyphosate are that it will kill weeds fairly quickly by disrupting photosynthesis and therefore can be used on annual weeds such as groundsel with some success, and it is quickly absorbed through the leaf cuticle, making it less susceptible to rain washing it off the foliage. As with glyphosate, it is quickly rendered ineffective on contact with the soil.

2,4-D and other **Lawn herbicides, (Mecoprop, Dichlorprop, Fenoprop** and **Dicamba),** are sold for the control or elimination of broadleaved weeds in lawns. These are all growth regulators. At the recommended dose rates, they do not adversely affect grasses but cause uncontrolled growth of broadleaved plants. Initially this shows as twisted and distorted leaves, followed by the death of the weed. Although usually sold as lawn herbicides, they can be used to kill broadleaved weeds in other places in the garden and 2,4-D is effective against bindweed. However, they can cause damage to all trees and shrubs, and 2,4-D is sold as part of a 'cocktail' of herbicides for the control of brushwood. 2,4-D is also volatile and in hot weather it can cause damage to nearby or overhead trees and shrubs.

A number of products are sold for the control of moss in lawns. These include lawn sand, which contains sulphate of iron and ammonium sulphate; these will also act as contact herbicides to broadleaved weeds.

•PROBLEM SOLVER•
MULCHING

A mulch is a layer of material covering the soil surface. Mulches are used to control weeds and moisture loss from the soil, to improve soil conditions, especially for certain plants, and to give a background against which some plants can be displayed. A mulch:

• prevents the loss of moisture from the underlying soil
• allows rainwater to percolate downwards
• smothers any weeds which germinate on the soil surface
• deprives other weed seeds of light, so keeping them dormant
• enables fertiliser in liquid or granular form to be applied.

Any seeds which germinate on the surface of the mulch can either be pulled or sprayed, whilst some mulching materials will provide little or no sustenance for the germinating weed.

Using a mulch is an attractive option where you do not wish to consider the use of herbicides, or where you want to restrict the use of herbicides. However, a mulch will also give a buffer layer around a plant, making the use of herbicides that much safer.

Mulches do not show footprints in the same way that bare earth does and therefore access paths for maintenance and for the enjoyment of plants are not needed with a thick organic mulch. However, with some materials birds and animals may scatter the mulch about whilst searching for worms.

APPLYING A MULCH
A mulch needs to let air be exchanged between the soil and the atmosphere, otherwise the soil beneath will become dead. Mulches should be put on to clean soil in a layer at least 5cm (2in) and preferably 10cm (4in) thick. Thinner layers, except for sheet mulches discussed below, are unlikely to achieve any improvement. The activity of earthworms and the decay

Bark-mulching is useful and effective as a buffer layer in this rose garden, allowing successful application of herbicides and fertilizer.

of organic mulches will slowly incorporate the lower layer into the soil, so the mulch will need to be topped up with an occasional topdressing; this is necessary even with gravel mulches, but not with many groundcover plants once these have covered the soil surface. Organic mulches can be used as a means of applying nutrients to a bed, either from the decay of the leafmould or from fertiliser added to the mulch.

With small plants, such as groundcover plants and heathers, care must be taken to ensure that the plants are not swamped by the mulch. Mulches which will heat up, such as grass mowings (which are generally unsuitable unless mixed with other materials, as they tend to form too dense a mat on their own), should not be built up into too deep a layer, and especially not close to the stem of plants, as the heat generated as they decompose may cause damage.

ORGANIC MULCHES
The commonest mulches are composed of organic materials like peat, pulverised conifer bark and leafmould. Organic mulches will last for one to three years for peat and leafmould to upwards of five years for pine bark. These are the best mulches for species such as rhododendron,

which naturally root into the surface layers of leafmould. Regular topdressing will retain a thick surface layer for these plants, and most mulching materials will also maintain the soil acidity. A thick organic mulch will keep the soil cool for these and other plants which prefer these conditions. Organic mulches are also beneficial for adding organic matter or humus to the soil, which is needed to keep the soil fauna and flora functioning well and recycling nutrients.

In shrub beds, fallen leaves can be left to add to the mulch. With the advent of chipping machines, brushwood and small branches, as well as leaves, can be chipped up and applied as a mulch, though care is needed in the use of mulches containing a high proportion of wood chippings (see p 77).

GRAVEL
Mulches can also be made from gravel. The grade of gravel used should be around 2cm (¾in) in diameter, or washed shingle. Gravel mulches can be very effective for displaying dwarf conifers and scree and

rockery plants. When first applied, they look rather stark, but the colour should soon mellow.

SHEET MULCHES

Sheet materials can also be used as mulches. The best material is 500-gauge black polythene, but bituminous roofing felt can also be used. The material needs to cut out all light, or weeds will germinate beneath it, partly negating the benefit of the mulch. Black polythene is often recommended for vegetable plots but can also be effectively used to hasten the establishment of woody plants; it is especially useful in out-of-the-way sites, which are easily neglected when it comes to watering and weed control, and where the unsightliness of the polythene is not an eyesore.

These materials, which are also available in purpose-made packs for trees and shrubs, will last for around three years before ultraviolet sunlight causes them to fail (at which stage they should be removed before they blow everywhere). They will control water loss better than other mulching materials, while there is normally sufficient space around the plants to permit rainwater to percolate and for the exchange of gases. Unlike the organic and gravel mulches, they heat up quickly and will give higher soil temperatures, making them very useful for plants which need to be encouraged to grow away in the spring, such as vegetables or strawberries.

Polythene sheeting can be held down using stones or clods of earth but it is much easier to bury the edge in the soil. A slit is made with a spade some 8–10cm (3–4in) in from the outline of the sheet; the spade is then used to push the edge of the sheet into this slit. When this is done on all four sides, the sheet should be held firmly in place, although some clods in the middle of a large sheet will help. If used around a newly planted tree, a slit should be made so that the sheet can be laid around the plant; ideally, the sheet used should be at least 1m (3ft) in diameter.

FERTILISERS, MANURES AND FEEDING

This section looks at whether additional nutrients should be provided as part of the management of a garden, and if so, how they should be made available to the plants.

SPECIFIC REQUIREMENTS

The nutrients needed by all plants, both major nutrients and trace elements, are discussed in Chapter 3. However, they are needed in different amounts by different plants, depending both upon species and the stage of growth. Rhododendrons, for instance, need calcium just like other plants, but they are adapted to situations where there is very little calcium available to them and the excess present in many soils acts as a poison and prevents their uptake of other nutrients. Again, species of hydrangea will grow on both acidic and alkaline soils, but it is only on naturally acidic soils that the best blue flowers are developed – this is because of the availability of aluminium ions at low soil pH (see p22) and their unavailability at higher pH. In both these examples, improvements in growth can be achieved by giving nutrients in a form adapted to let the plant absorb the necessary ingredients *despite* the soil pH. Some plants are sensitive to the quantity of a nutrient present in a soil. Rhododendron and members of the *Ericaceae* do not flourish on soils with high nitrogen levels; members of the *Proteaceae* (eg Embothrium) need soils with low levels of phosphate.

---

3 STEPS TO FEEDING YOUR GARDEN

When considering the feeding requirements of your garden, you will need to answer the following questions:
• What nutrients are needed by the plants?
• Are they already available in sufficient quantity in the soil?
• If they are not, what are the ways to provide them?

Plants grown for fruit effect will have a higher requirement for potassium and phosphorus than plants grown for foliage, when proportionately more nitrogen is needed. Feeding a plant grown for fruit, therefore, with a high-nitrogen fertiliser may result in vigorous vegetative growth but little or no fruit formation. Giving extra fertiliser may reduce the attractions of the plant. Where the beauty of the plant is in the large, bold foliage, as with an ailanthus or paulownia coppiced annually, nutrients are needed in good quantity for the best effect.

It is also important to consider where the nutrients in the soil are going. For example, where produce is being harvested from the site, either as fruit or vegetables, these often contain a disproportionate amount of the total nutrients in the plant. To maintain production, these nutrients should be replaced. Similarly, where leaves or mowings are being continually removed from a site, there is an outflow of nutrients which will need replacing. However, nutrients can also be 'lost' to the system by being tied up in permanent tissues, such as the woody bole of a tree.

HOW FERTILE IS YOUR SOIL?

The next step is to find out whether there are already sufficient nutrients available for the plants in the soil. It is possible to have the soil tested commercially by a number of firms, or alternatively small kits can be purchased. These will give an approximate indication of the relative fertility of the soil. Before using any figure or recommendation gained by soil testing, however, you should consider the types of plant you will be growing: the recommendations usually given with the soil-testing kits available in many garden centres are appropriate to most vegetable plots, but are too rich for shrub beds and many herbaceous plants.

Observation of plants growing on the site can be a very effective way to gauge the fertility of the soil. It requires a modicum of knowledge as

SOIL FERTILITY

The fertility of your soil can be judged by:
• having the soil tested
• observing plants already growing in your garden

to what the plant should look like, but comparison with the same plant in a neighbour's garden will go a long way towards helping you decide whether extra nutrients are needed. If the plants in your garden have much smaller leaves and poor fruit compared to others of the same form elsewhere, it is likely that yours are deficient in some nutrient (although you should first consider the possibility of a fungal infection to the roots). If, however, they are large, leafy and barren, it is likely that your plant is receiving too much nitrogen and either no fertiliser should be applied, or only potassium and phosphorus should be given. The simplest cases are where the plants are showing some deficiency symptom. These can be controlled by the addition of the appropriate fertiliser (see chapter 3).

Where there are no plants growing on the site, it is possible to obtain an indication of the fertility of the soil from observing weed species. For example, sheep's sorrel (*Rumex acetosella*) indicates a very acidic soil or surface layer, as does natural ling or heather (*Calluna vulgaris*); nettles indicate freely available nitrogen. These and other indications can be gained from reference to a wild flower book which gives details of the natural ecology of the weeds or wildflowers.

Most garden soils are not short of nutrients, although additional fertiliser given as a balanced feed at a low rate will often encourage better all-round growth. The main exceptions to this are where special groups of plants such as rhododendron are being grown, and on very acidic or alkaline sites, where nutrient availability may be affected by the pH (see p 22). Lime can be used to raise the pH and sulphur to lower it.

FEEDING YOUR SOIL

There are several ways in which nutrients can be applied to a soil or plant; these include mulches (see pp 86–87), manures and chemical or artificial fertilisers.

MANURES

These are made from waste products, either from the composting of garden refuse or from animal droppings mixed with straw. Spent mushroom compost or spent hops are also available. Farmyard manure is a messy material, but a number of products are available where the manure has been dried and made more convenient to handle. Manures are variable in the quantity of nutrients they contain and should not be used in too generous a layer at one time. For a well-rotted farmyard manure or garden compost, a layer from 2–5cm (1–2in) thick should be spread over the soil surface, except for plants which are gross feeders, such as asparagus or roses, which will tolerate up to 10cm (4in).

With most plants, it is important to use well-rotted manures; raw or fresh manures can cause three sets of problems:
• There may be an excess of ammonia in raw manures such as pig slurry and chicken waste which will damage roots or poison the soil
• Where there is fresh organic matter present, such as straw, the soil bacteria which break this down into humus will use nitrogen and other nutrients from the soil and cause a short-term deficiency
• Where the manure has not been properly composted and has not reached a sufficient temperature to kill any weed seeds present, they will germinate, giving a beautiful flush of weeds!

However, manures are useful for adding organic matter or humus to the soil, which assists the natural processes working for soil fertility.

ARTIFICIAL FERTILISERS

These do not have the drawbacks of being particularly messy or smelly, but they do not add humus to the soil and it is much easier to damage the plants by adding too much. Also, artificial fertilisers will have the effect of either making the soil more acidic (usually) or more alkaline (less often), depending upon how the fertilisers are formulated. This can be used to advantage: for example, where the soil pH is slightly too high for the optimum growth of plants (such as roses), the use of ammonium sulphate formulations to provide nitrogen will tend to make the soil more acidic. In other circumstances, such as where cabbages are being grown, the use of lime may be needed to restore the pH.

Most artificial fertilisers are sold as balanced formulations containing a range of the major nutrients and described as, eg 12:9:8, showing that the fertiliser will give 12 parts of nitrogen (N) (either as ammonium or nitrate – this is given on the label), 9 parts of phosphorus (P) and 8 parts of potassium (K) per unit applied. It is possible to purchase the ingredients singly. Formulations giving trace elements are also available.

There are several different ways to apply artificial fertilisers:
• Granular fertilisers should be spread evenly over the soil at a rate of around 50–60gm per square metre (2oz per square yard). This should only be carried out when the soil is moist and generally should be applied in the spring. If the soil is dry, the fertiliser will not enter it and may either scorch the plants or be washed away next time it rains. With granular fertilisers which are applied in the autumn, there is likely to be a considerable loss of nutrients due to leaching; applications at this time of the year should average one-third of the above figure. Formulations giving a slow or controlled release of the nutrients are available, and allow a larger initial application with little risk of either scorching or leaching. These are particularly valuable when planting trees and shrubs, as they encourage establishment and ensure sustained growth.
• Fertilisers can also be applied in liquid solution. There are advantages in that the nutrients are in a form immediately usable by the plant (in fact, they can be given direct to the foliage as a foliar application) and there is a much lower risk of loss of nutrients from leaching. The drawback is that it is less easy to know precisely how much is being given. However, this should not be much of a problem where the liquid feed is given as part of a regular watering regime. Diluters are available which will give an appropriate solution when used with a garden hose and a small reservoir of fertiliser.

WATERING

Water is an essential ingredient in plant growth and must be available to the plant in adequate quantity: emergency watering in midsummer may keep the plant alive until next year but will not create an effective display, and the need for it may result in poor growth, flower and fruit the following season as well.

The time to ensure that there is sufficient water available for plant growth is *before* a shortage develops. The first action in preventing plants from dying due to lack of water is good planting practice and the control of water loss, either directly from the soil or by competing weeds. Weed control and effective mulches will go a long way towards achieving this objective.

There are occasions where watering will be needed. These are with newly planted stock, especially container-grown trees and shrubs planted in leaf during the spring or growing season, and when there is a very dry summer.

EFFECTIVE WATERING

When watering an area, give a good soaking once a week or fortnight rather than a light application every day or so. The heavy application will rewet the soil, leaving a reserve of moisture in the soil which can be tapped by the plant over the coming days. This will encourage the roots to spread into the soil and exploit it to the full. Applying water little and often will not adequately wet the soil, and the lower portion will remain dry whilst the surface layer is regularly wetted. The effect of this will be to prevent the roots growing into the lower soil, restricting them to the top portion; when the regular watering is omitted for any reason, the plant will quickly exhaust the reserves and wither. There is little risk of overwatering a plant in the open ground with a weekly watering (although it is a very real threat to plants in pots or tubs).

In high summer, the potential weekly loss of water from a square

WATERING CHECKLIST

For effective and efficient watering:
• do not water little and often
• give a good soaking less frequently
• use a sprinkler where possible
• water in the late afternoon or overnight
• a hosepipe at gentle pressure is more effective for individual plants than a watering can
• pay special attention to newly planted stock
• use a seep hose in dry areas of the garden

metre (yard) of ground is equivalent to a layer approximately 2.5cm (1in) in depth, or 91 litres (20 gallons). This is the amount which should be given each week during these months to replace water lost by evaporation through the plant's foliage or from the soil surface. During late spring and late summer the corresponding figures are 68 litres (15 gallons) per square metre (yard), and 45 litres (10 gallons) respectively. In practice, the soil will retain a reserve of moisture, and with established plantings the above volumes of water need not be given for the first week or two when there has been no rain. Also, with some plants, a slight shortage during late summer may encourage flower-bud initiation.

The best way to provide water is by a sprinkler system. The oscillating models will give a better and more even coverage than the rotatory versions. Late afternoon or overnight are the best times to apply water, as there is no risk of the foliage of sensitive plants being scorched and the cooler temperatures will result in less loss from evaporation. A rain gauge is useful for measuring the volume of water applied, or for recording the weekly rainfall total. Individual plants can be watered with a watering can, but this will involve several fillings to give sufficient water; a hosepipe at a *gentle pressure* is more effective for individual plants.

Newly planted stock can need extra attention. This is especially so during the winter period with container-grown evergreens – they can dry out during cold, dry periods – and with container-grown shrubs planted when in full leaf. Here the plant has been receiving regular watering during the time in the nursery or garden centre and the volume of compost around the roots is unlikely to keep the plant healthy for more than a few days or so in the absence of watering. Such newly planted stock will need extra watering, probably every second or third day for the first fortnight, and then reduced to a weekly or fortnightly watering as above. In these circumstances, the extra waterings are intended not to re-wet the soil in the potential rooting area but to moisten the compost around the plant's roots whilst they extend out into the soil; 9 litres (2 gallons) from a watering can (with a weekly full watering) should be appropriate (see also p 77).

In known dry areas of the garden – under walls or near hedges or the roots of large trees – a seep hose can be invaluable for applying water, particularly to newly planted stock, and for slowly wetting dust-dry soil, which will often not absorb water applied conventionally from hosepipe or sprinkler. The seep hose, which is usually supplied in short lengths, is perforated to allow water to percolate slowly, and is laid on the surface of the soil between shrubs or plants.

PEST AND DISEASE CONTROL

Individual gardeners adopt differing approaches to pests and diseases ranging from the *laissez-faire* attitude of enjoying the natural history aspects of bugs and fungi, to a scorched-earth policy of total elimination. Fortunately, with ornamental plants only the occasional pest or disease becomes a serious problem.

When using chemical methods to control any pest or disease, it is important to follow the recommendations given under herbicides on pp 84–85,

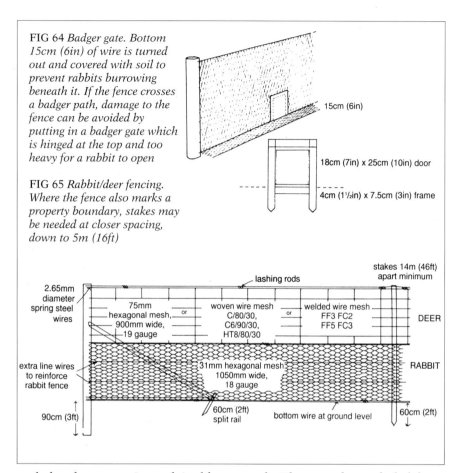

FIG 64 *Badger gate. Bottom 15cm (6in) of wire is turned out and covered with soil to prevent rabbits burrowing beneath it. If the fence crosses a badger path, damage to the fence can be avoided by putting in a badger gate which is hinged at the top and too heavy for a rabbit to open*

FIG 65 *Rabbit/deer fencing. Where the fence also marks a property boundary, stakes may be needed at closer spacing, down to 5m (16ft)*

and also the precautions advised by the manufacturer of the product. A bewildering variety of chemicals is available, though a number are regularly withdrawn after only a few years on the market on safety or environmental grounds, while others are restricted to professional use only. Some of the books and leaflets listed in Further Reading will help you keep up to date with what is available and make an informed choice.

ANIMAL PESTS

Deer, rabbits and similar animals may be very attractive but can cause considerable damage in a garden. The best method for limiting damage is to fence them out; other techniques, such as shooting, are rarely practical within a garden! Chemical repellents are not totally effective and are rather unsightly. However, where fencing is not feasible, they may be useful.

Rabbits can cause damage by eating or bark-stripping small trees and any new shoots, and also by burrowing to eat roots of newly planted

stock. They can be excluded by a fence. This should be constructed, as shown in Fig 65, using wire netting with a mesh size of 3cm (1¼in) and a height of 1m (3ft 3in). The lower 15cm (6in) should be buried facing outwards, which will reduce the risk of rabbits burrowing in from outside. The wire will need to supported by a stake every 3–4m (10–13ft).

In country areas, deer cause damage by either eating the foliage or using trees and large shrubs as rubbing posts to remove velvet from the antlers or for territory marking. Although they can damage a wide range of plants, those most affected include bedding roses, where the young shoots are a choice delicacy. An option, therefore, is to avoid the use of such plants or to enclose the rose garden, rather than the entire garden, within a deer-proof fence. To be effective, a deer-proof fence must totally enclose the protected area, and this may be aesthetically unacceptable. Depending upon species , the height of the fence will need to be from 1.2m

(4ft) (roe deer) to 2m (6½ft) (red or fallow deer), although it can also serve as a boundary fence (see Fig 65). The use of electric fencing similar to that used by farmers to control sheep or cattle may be successful against deer in some garden circumstances. Badgers can cause serious damage to deer and rabbit fences and badger gates can be constructed where a problem is found to exist, as shown in Fig 64.

Other animals, such as squirrels and birds, can be troublesome, but are difficult to exclude, except from vegetable frames and fruit cages.

CARING FOR YOUR PLANTS

TREE MAINTENANCE
Tree maintenance consists of removing stakes and ties, as well as some tree surgery, such as removing damaged or diseased branches or controlling growth. Aspects of pruning for fruit production are not considered in this book.

Removing Stakes and Ties
Staking and tying a tree is discussed in detail in Chapter 5. A stake is only needed to hold the young tree's roots in place whilst it becomes established; a stout stake should not be used to support the crown of a tree, as this leads to delayed thickening of the stem, and frequently to disaster during strong winds (if support of the stem is needed, a bamboo cane will provide it). If the tree has been carefully planted and weed growth controlled, the function of holding the roots firm should no longer be needed after the second winter, although in very exposed locations, a further year may be necessary.

Spring is the best time to remove a stake and tie. At this season the tree will be making active root growth, and when it first comes into leaf it will only carry a small crop of leaves; during the summer it will strengthen the trunk and should be capable of withstanding the autumn gales. If the stake is removed in late summer, the quantity of foliage will be much larger and there is a risk of the tree being damaged by late summer or early autumn gales before the stem has adjusted to the change. If removing a stake at other times of the year, it is a wise precaution to thin out the crown of the tree to reduce the area of foliage. When removing a stake, it is usually better to saw it off at ground level; this risks the stake rotting away and possibly infecting the tree, but the disturbance which will follow the forced removal of a stake will usually cause more harm.

With fast-growing trees, it is important to check that the tie is not constricting the stem, or the stake rubbing against it. The tie, or top tie if more than one has been employed, should always be within 3cm (1½in) of the top of the stake so that there is no prospect of the tree rubbing against it and causing a wound. Secure the tie to the stake with a nail to prevent it slipping downwards. Plastic tree ties usually expand safely in the warm temperatures of summer and only rarely cause constriction of the stem, but webbing based ties can be far more damaging and should be loosened as the tree grows.

Tree Surgery
The purpose of tree surgery is to prolong the safe life of a tree and to control its development. The following is intended to give an outline of tree surgery relating to small trees. When it comes to work in large trees, the reader is strongly advised to consult a professional arboricultural consultant or employ a qualified tree surgeon (see Useful Addresses, p220).

Practical tree surgery in the garden will involve removing branches which are unhealthy or create a poor branch structure, and controlling the growth of trees so that they give the best return for the space they occupy.

Diseased and damaged branches should be removed because they can lead to further disease and dieback of branches. Where two branches rub against each other, the bark at the point of contact will be damaged, per-

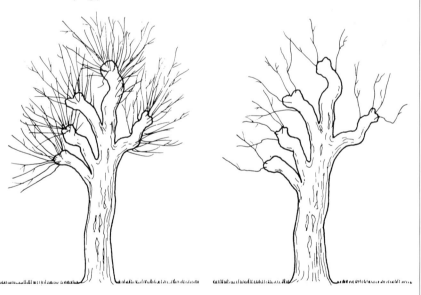

FIG 66 *A hornbeam before and after thinning to remove dead, diseased or damaged branches and to reduce density. Foliage will develop more evenly the following spring*

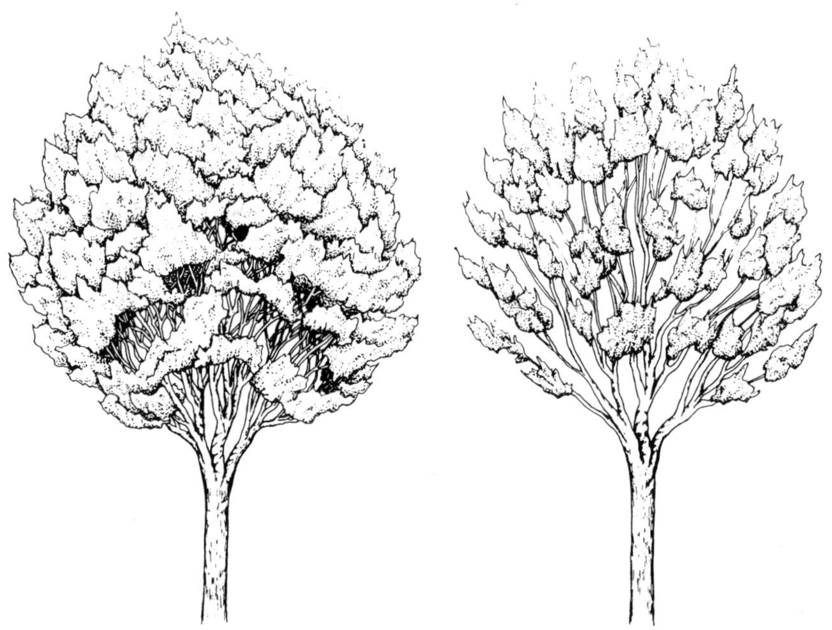

FIG 67 *The dense mass of regrowth from pollarding may appear acceptable during the summer but is ugly in winter and will lead to decay at the cuts. Reducing the number of regrowth shoots (right) may reduce the density of foliage and shade, but is still very ugly*

mitting the entry of decay fungi, and in a strong wind one may snap off at this point which acts as a fulcrum. It is also sensible to remove branches which cross from one side of the crown to the other, as if left they will create a tangled mass of branches.

Dead branches should always be removed. If they are left, there is the risk of decay fungi entering the tree but, more seriously, they will fall to the ground at some time and could cause injury or damage.

Trees will often grow larger or denser than originally intended, or a large growing tree will have been planted where there is insufficient space for its full development. In these circumstances, there are several ways to control the growth of a tree. None is as satisfactory as having the right tree for the site but, as replacing a tree involves a loss of amenity until the new tree grows, pruning is often preferable.

The traditional approach of lopping off the branches, giving a pollarded tree, is *not* the solution. This causes the tree to grow very vigorously from the cut surfaces and the new growths will quickly become as large as the original, often casting an even denser shade. If the process is repeated, decay soon sets into the cut surfaces, making the new growths unsafe.

Where the shade cast by a tree is too dense, the effective solution is to thin out the crown of the tree This involves removing a proportion of the branches whilst retaining the present natural outline. As none of the branches are cut back hard, the amount of regrowth is much less, therefore the tree takes longer to become as dense as it was originally (Fig 67).

TREES AND THE LAW

Trees impose a legal liability upon their owners. This is part of the same requirement that you are responsible for any damage caused through your negligence by something you have brought onto your land and then allowed to 'escape'. Inspect all the trees in your garden at least once a year, checking for broken, dead or diseased branches which may fall down and cause injury or damage, and signs of weakness, such as fungal bodies arising from the stem or directly from the roots.

If a tree grows over the boundary of a property, it may cause a nuisance and to avoid problems you should negotiate with your neighbour over what action to take.

Trees may be subject to a tree preservation order or be in a conservation area, which means that local authorities must be consulted before any pruning or felling is carried out. Exceptions include when the tree is obviously unsafe. See Reading List for more information.

MAINTAINING SHRUBS

The maintenance of shrubs involves keeping the plants and the ground around them in good order – by weed control and fertiliser applications – and controlling the growth so that the optimum pleasure is obtained from the bed or individual specimen plant.

Methods for controlling the growth will vary depending upon species and location. Most shrubs do not need annual pruning, but many will be more attractive for it. The purpose and consequences of the pruning need to be considered before the plants are cut back.

Pruning for Health

This involves the removal of dead, damaged or overcrowded shoots. In this way, potentially damaging decay fungi which gain entry to weak shoots can be prevented from invading the healthy ones, and the number of places where damaging insects can hide can be reduced. This aspect of pruning includes prompt action to remove a dying shoot which shows during the growing season.

CASE STUDY

THINNING OR LOPPING ?

The difference between lopping and thinning out a tree can be illustrated for sycamore (*Acer pseudoplatanus*). On its own, this will ultimately make a tree as much as 20m (65ft) tall, but from approximately 10m (33ft) high the rate of upward growth of a tree in the open slows down markedly as it starts to flower and seed. If a 15m (49ft) tree is lopped back to 10m (33ft), it will regrow at the rate of a metre a year for several years, until it is 15–18m (49–59ft) tall; only then will it start to flower and fruit, but by this time it is larger and casting a denser shade than a tree which was thinned out when 15m (49ft) tall. The thinned tree will continue to flower and fruit, and consequently grow only slowly. Where a tree is spreading too wide, its spread can be reduced by 'drop-crotching' or crown reduction. This involves retaining the present natural shape but on a smaller crown. The process is similar to thinning. Long extending branches are cut back to a crotch or side branch, and because there is live foliage beyond the point of cutting there is little dense regrowth.

FIG 68 *Drop-crotching to reduce the spread without altering basic appearance*

HOW TO REMOVE A BRANCH

When removing a branch for any reason, the aim should be to cut it so that natural healing is assisted. A tree lays down a system of defence barriers which prevent the entry of decay fungi. If these are breached, decay is more likely and healing slowed.

Normally, at the base of a branch there is a natural swelling or collar. This is closer to the stem on the top side and further out on the lower side. This collar shows up more clearly in some species, such as whitebeam (*Sorbus aria*). The objective is to cut just outside the line of this collar. Where there is no obvious collar, the cut should still be made at the angle shown in the diagram. This will involve making a cut nearly at right angles or transversely across the branch, and therefore the area of exposed wood will be less than if the branch is cut off flush with the stem.

If the branch to be removed is a large one, ie over 5cm (2in) thick, it should be removed in two stages involving three cuts. The first cut is an under-cut some 30cm (12in) from the collar and penetrating approximately one-quarter to one-third of the way through the branch. This cut is designed to prevent the branch tearing back down the stem when it is cut through. The second cut is made just beyond the first cut and removes the branch. The stub is then removed in a third cut just outside the collar.

The tree will cover the cut surface by making callus growth from the cambium tissue – the layer of actively growing cells between the wood and the bark by which all radial growth is made. Protecting this layer of cells from drying out will hasten callusing. However, research has shown that treating the central part of the cut surface with a tree paint can hasten decay. The recommendation, therefore, is to apply a protective treatment, either latex, bitumastic or any water-repellent material which does not harm plant tissues (eg vaseline or lanolin) to the zone around the cambium layer and to leave the central part of the wound untreated. If this sounds too complex, it is better to leave the wound open to the air than to cover the entire surface

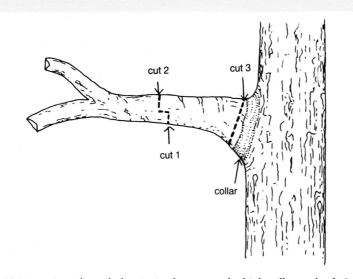

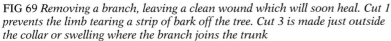

FIG 69 *Removing a branch, leaving a clean wound which will soon heal. Cut 1 prevents the limb tearing a strip of bark off the tree. Cut 3 is made just outside the collar or swelling where the branch joins the trunk*

WHY PRUNE?

The purpose of pruning is to:
• control the shape of the plant
• increase the beauty or quality of the flowers, fruit, foliage or bark
• remove diseased or potentially disease-carrying portions

When cutting out diseased material, always make the cuts into sound or healthy wood well beneath the infected portion; ensure no brown stain is present in the remaining wood. Diseased wood should be promptly burnt. With some diseases, such as Fireblight and Dutch elm disease, the organism responsible is likely to have penetrated some distance below the obvious signs, and removal of the branch from its point of origin is advised. When cutting diseased shoots, it is good practice to sterilise the knife or secateurs used by wiping them on a rag soaked in methylated spirits, ideally after each cut. This will reduce the chance of transferring the cause of the infection to a new branch or plant next time the tool is used.

Controlling or Reshaping
Many of the more vigorous shrubs will grow into small trees or in time become very wide-spreading. They therefore need pruning to keep them within the space allotted or to rejuvenate an old plant.

The technique for reducing the spread of a shrub is similar to that for trees in that too great a reduction will lead to excessive regrowth, defeating the objective. If a branch extends too far in one direction, it can either be reduced to a suitable crotch (see Fig 68) or should be removed from the base. Indiscriminate hacking back will usually give a mediocre result of a tangled mass of leafy new shoots.

An overgrown shrub can be rejuvenated by cutting it back either to ground level or to low down on the stem. Most, but not all, plants will coppice or regrow after this treatment

FIG 70 *Pruning cuts on a shrub or rose*

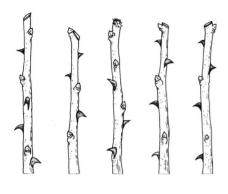

and will make very useful plants in less time than if a new specimen is planted. Subjects where this is a useful technique include lilac (*Syringa*) and mock orange (*Philadelphus*) but it can also be used on overgrown plants of buddleia, holly, hazel, yew and other similar large shrubs . The dense mass of new shoots produced as a result of this treatment will require selective thinning in order that a smaller number of well-spaced, strong shoots are retained to form a balanced, compact but shapely shrub for the future. This system will not work on conifers (there are rare exceptions) and many evergreen shrubs do not respond that well; hebes and camellias, for instance, may sometimes fail to regrow. If a large shrub is in poor health, cutting it back may rejuvenate it, but where the plant is diseased, perhaps at the roots, it will often fail.

Suckers

These are a natural feature of many shrubs, but in species which are propagated by grafting on to a rootstock there will frequently be growths from the rootstock. If they are left, they will often be more vigorous than the choice plant and swamp it. Suckers should be removed from the lower stem or root system where they originate; cutting them off at soil level will only encourage their proliferation. The simplest method is to force a spade gently down between the stem and the suckers and then pull the sucker with one hand and lever the spade away from the stem with the other.

Variegated Plants

These will often produce patches where there is no variegation, just plain green foliage. As with suckers, these must be removed – even whole branches – before they dominate and ruin the plant.

Pruning for Attractiveness

There are several different ways to prune shrubs to enhance performance. The variations between the techniques of pruning are primarily related to the season or timing of the operation and the type of wood on which the desirable characteristics of the plant are displayed.

Which technique is appropriate depends upon the growth characteristics of the particular shrub and also upon what is desired of it: similar plants in one genus may require very different pruning regimes to flower to best effect, eg different buddleia and clematis. The first requirement is to know which species you have and when it will flower. If you are not familiar with a plant in a newly acquired garden, it often pays to wait and see what it does before pruning.

Shrubs for Late Summer and Autumn Effect

The simplest group of shrubs to prune are those which flower in late summer on the current season's growths, such as *Buddleia davidii*, caryopteris, *Clematis tangutica*, *C. jackmanii*, fuchsia, hypericum and indigofera.

Shrubs for late summer/autumn effect –
Disanthus cercidifolius*, medium-sized shrub for acid soils – here contrast with the yellow autumn leaves of a young birch.*

Shrubs for winter effect – the yellow berries of Cotoneaster *'Rothschildianus'*, effective against the evergreen foliage, usually persist into late winter (see page 176).*

*Shrubs for Spring
and Early Summer Effect*

Many plants flowering in the early part of the season, usually up to mid-summer, do so from flowerbuds laid down during the previous summer. Examples are *Buddleia alternifolia, B. globosa, Clematis montana*, and species and rambler roses. With these, it is disastrous to prune them hard in late winter, as all the coming season's flowers will be cut off. Instead they should be pruned as soon as flowering has finished, removing the shoots which have just flowered so that vigorous young shoots can replace them and develop next year's flowers. Pruning of these plants should not be severe. Also, with several plants, for example *Rosa* species and *Berberis* x *stenophylla*, the fruits are an attractive part of the display, and this aspect will be lost by heavy pruning.

Similar to the above group are many shrubs which, while flowering on the previous year's growth, produce most flowers on short spur

The bark and tree-disc path to Prunus serrula* *is flanked by forget-me-not and yellow epimedium with* Prunus sargentii *(right) at Beth Chatto Gardens, Essex.*

These plants can be cut back to old wood in late winter or early spring, and most will give larger or more strongly coloured flowers than if left unpruned. All the flowering plants in this group will give a display without pruning and this will be earlier in the season than on pruned plants, although the plant's habit may not be as attractive.

Shrubs for Winter Effect

Plants grown for the effect of the winter bark of one-year-old twigs, such as *Cornus alba, Rubus cockburnianus* and *Salix alba* 'Britzensis' ('Chermesina'), or for bold summer foliage, such as coppiced plants of ailanthus, paulownia and *Cornus alba* 'Elegantissima', produce longer and more brightly coloured twigs or larger leaves if cut back hard in late winter.

HOW TO PRUNE SHRUBS

Pruning cuts should be made just above a bud. The cut should be at a slightly oblique angle across the stem; start level with the bud but on the opposite side. The cut should be close to the bud, but not so close that it is damaged. Cuts should be clean, and crushing of the twig should be avoided. The diagram shows examples of correct and incorrect pruning cuts.

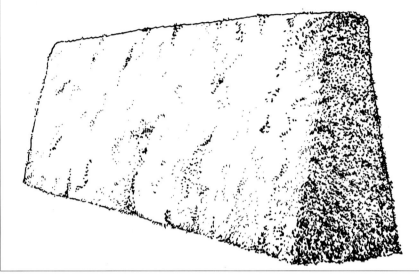

FIG 71 *Correct profile for a durable hedge, furnished to ground level*

Popular flowering shrubs, for example Philadelphus *'Sybille'* *and* Weigela florida *'Variegata',* * (above) respond to a three-year pruning cycle (see pages 95–6).*

growths off two-year-old shoots. Examples include deutzia, forsythia, kolkwitzia, philadelphus, ribes and weigela. In these plants, the pruning needs to be carried out on a three-year cycle. Immediately after flowering, the three-year-old shoots are removed and the current year's shoots selected to replace them; this will usually involve thinning out the number of current and previous and one-year-old shoots.

Evergreens
Many smaller evergreen plants do not respond to any pruning or are rather touchy. These include plants such as cistus, which can only be pruned when young. Brooms, such as cytisus, genista and spartium, and most conifers, such as chamaecyparis and x cupressocyparis, can only be cut back into wood which is still green; if you cut into old wood, the plant will die back. These plants can only practically be pruned to retain a shape.

Tools
Pruning cuts can be made using a variety of tools. The most effective is a sharp pruning knife, but this needs skilled handling for best results. Most pruning is carried out using secateurs. The best models are the scissor type, in which a sharp cutting blade is drawn across the edge of a non-moving or static blade; the static blade can cause slight compression of the plant tissues, so it should be positioned against the portion of shoot to be discarded. Anvil secateurs are the other type, in which a sharp blade compresses the twig against an anvil. This type causes more damage to the twig but will tackle thicker shoots and the damage is generally acceptable.

CLIPPING FORMAL HEDGES

PLANT TYPE		WHEN TO CLIP	REMARKS
Vigorous:	*Crataegus monogyna* (hawthorn) *Ligustrum ovalifolium* (privet) *Lonicera nitida*	Every four to six weeks during the growing season	Vigorous species need frequent trimming if neatness and formality are to be maintained. Box is less vigorous
Dwarf:	*Buxus sempervirens* (box)	Once in spring, once late summer/ early autumn	
Slower-growing:	*Carpinus betulus* (hornbeam) *Fagus sylvatica* (beech) etc	Once in mid-to late summer	In certain seasons, a late flush of growth may need removing
Conifers:	*Taxus baccata* (yew) *Thuja plicata* (western red cedar) etc	Once in late summer/ early autumn	If clipped earlier, late flushes of growth not may ripen before autumn frosts
Evergreens:	*Ilex aquifolium* (holly) *Prunus laurocerasus* (cherry laurel) etc	Once in late summer/ early autumn	

WARNING

Yew (*Taxus baccata*) and common or cherry laurel (*Prunus laurocerasus*) are poisonous if ingested. This applies to all parts, and particularly the seeds and berries.

Pruning saws and long-handled pruners are useful for shoots of greater diameter.

MAINTAINING HEDGES

Maintaining a hedge is largely a matter of correct cutting or trimming; however, fertilising to maintain vigour should not be forgotten where a large quantity of foliage is removed each year.

Hedges can be either formal or informal. Informal hedges, such as a boundary or partition planting of *Rosa rugosa* or *Potentilla fruticosa*, do not require clipping so much as periodic pruning to restrain the shape of the hedge. *Rosa rugosa* should be cut back nearly to ground level in early spring, as this species flowers on the current season's growth, but the potentilla requires only a minimum of pruning , as it flowers mainly on the previous season's growth.

With a formal hedge, the objective should be to keep it fully furnished to the ground, achieved by making the base wider than the top (Fig 71). This will allow light to reach the lower part of the hedge and also help it withstand the elements, especially wind and snow. Too many hedges are the reverse – much broader at the top and bare at the base.

CLIPPING FORMAL HEDGES

Hedges can be clipped using powered hedge trimmers or shears and these tools are satisfactory for most hedging plants. However, for large-leafed evergreens, such as laurel (*Prunus laurocerasus*), secateurs should be used: hedge trimmers will cut or mangle many leaves, which will remain as an eyesore on the hedge for many months.

Newly planted shrubs like the familiar Forsythia intermedia *'Spectabilis'* benefit from bark mulching to help with weed control and hasten establishment.*

MAINTAINING HERBACEOUS BORDERS

Apart from general aspects of gardening, such as weed control and fertilising, maintaining an herbaceous border involves dividing the plants every few years to maintain their vigour, staking the lankier sorts and usually cutting the plants down to ground level in autumn.

Weed Control

Many herbaceous plants will act as effective forms of groundcover and swamp most weeds. The first essential, therefore, is that the border is free of persistent perennial weeds from the time of planting, as it is easier to keep difficult weeds out than to eradicate them when they are established amongst the roots of a perennial plant. Glyphosate in both liquid and gel form for spot treatment by spraying or painting on to the foliage of weeds (see p 85) is useful. Where woody weeds, such as bramble or sycamore seedlings, become estab-

lished, these can be removed with a spade or fork they can be cut down and new growth can be treated with glyphosate gel. The application of a mulch, such as pulverised bark, between the crowns of the herbaceous plants can greatly assist in keeping the bed weed-free.

Supporting Plants

Many of the taller growing herbaceous plants will need supporting, otherwise windy weather is likely to see them broken or bent. An individual stake or cane is appropriate for the tall single stems of delphiniums and hollyhocks. For plants which make a mass of stems to a metre or so, a 'cage' is more suitable. This can be made from string stretched around three or four bamboo canes, or be a plastic- or wire-mesh cylinder which is placed around the crown before growth starts in the spring; another alternative is to use peasticks – pieces of branched brushwood. Yet another effective system consists in stretching a plastic or rope

One of the best of all herbaceous groundcover plants to associate with shrubs – Geranium endressii *A.T. Johnson* (see page 127).*

net with 15cm (6in) square mesh supported by short posts up to 60cm (2ft) above ground level, which will support the herbaceous stems as they grow through it. Whichever form of staking is applied, provided it is the correct height for the plant, ie 20–50cm (8–20in) shorter than the average height of the plant, growth before flowering will soon hide the supporting structure.

Cutting Back

After the plants have died back in late autumn, the dead portions can be cut off and added to the rubbish tip or compost heap. Any woody weeds can also be removed at this stage and a mulch or manure dressing applied in the spring. There is no need to rush into cutting back the dying foliage as it can often be attractive, even when brown or covered with hoar frost in winter.

Dividing Plants

Many herbaceous plants will grow very vigorously once well established. If left alone, they will tend to suppress each other and the quality of the flowers will deteriorate. Most plants in the herbaceous border will make a

better display if they are lifted once every three years during the dormant season. The older and weaker parts of the plants are discarded and the vigorous young portions replanted at the initial spacing. This will also allow any perennial weeds which are establishing themselves in the bed to be removed, or sprayed, and for compost or manure to be worked into the soil. It is also an opportunity to control the spread of the more rampant members of the border.

'Shrubaceous' Borders

Herbaceous borders are often considered a dying form of gardening, as they are prone to invading weeds such as ground elder, require a large input of labour to give good (spectacular) results and are featureless over the winter period. There is a trend now to combine herbaceous plants and shrubs together in 'shrubaceous' borders; the plants suitable for these associations are discussed further in Chapter 7. They need to be fairly vigorous species, such as alchemilla, dicentra, geranium, hellebore, hosta, hemerocallis, pulmonaria and waldsteinia, with widely spaced compact *(Continued on page 100)*

LOOKING AFTER YOUR LAWN

The following suggestions are intended for situations where the grass areas are for family play or to set off the surrounding planting, rather than where a perfect lawn is intended. Many books give detailed prescriptions for making and maintaining perfect lawns – if that is what you want.

MOWING

Close-mown Lawns

Mowers cut either by a revolving cylinder or a rotating blade. Cylinder mowers are better where a neat effect is required and the grass cuttings are removed from the site, whereas rotary mowers are faster and will tackle longer grass or wetter conditions. Mowers are discussed in more detail in Chapter 5. Mowing has a pronounced effect both upon the appearance and the composition of the lawn. When the grass is actively growing in early summer, it may need cutting every week or ten days. At this season, the maximum length of time it can safely be left, if a lawn effect is required, is a fortnight. At the beginning and the end of the growing season, and usually during dry periods from midsummer on, the grass will not need such frequent cutting and a fortnightly cycle should be adopted.

The frequency and height of cutting will determine the species of grass and other plants present.

• Where the cut is made close to the soil surface, only plants able to grow from the base will survive and flourish; this will include certain species of grass but also plants such as plantain, daisies and moss.

• If the grass is cut longer, other species of grass can survive, whilst daisies may gradually disappear.

• Very close mowing, ie with the blades set at only 15mm (^{5}/8in) or less above ground level, will tend to induce a larger crop of weeds and moss.

• The optimum for weed control and

general durability under the influence of children is to set the mower blades at 20–25mm (3/4–1in). Also, where the grass grows this long, the frequency of cutting needed to maintain an attractive appearance is reduced.

Meadow Lawns!
Lawns do not *have* to be cut closely and frequently. In the right circumstances, very attractive meadow lawns can be created by only cutting the grass two or three times a year. In a meadow, wild flowers can flower and seed if the area is only cut periodically; with intensive mowing, these plants are soon eliminated or reduced to sterile plants.

If you wish to grow a variety of such plants, giving a succession of flowering times throughout the summer, the different areas must be cut at different times, correlated with the flowering and fruiting season of the meadow herbs present. With bulbs, such as daffodils or snake's-head fritillary, the area must not be cut until early summer, or the bulbs are unlikely to flower satisfactorily the next year and will not naturalise. With flowers such as vetches, cranesbills or wild orchids, an early cut no later than mid-spring can be given to tidy up the area, with the next cut in late summer or early autumn. Avoid cutting at different seasons in following years, as this will hinder the development of a flora suited to one particular mowing regime.

Apart from the attractions of the meadow flowers, meadow lawns require substantially less effort to maintain! They will look attractive and cared-for if a half-metre-wide strip is regularly cut around the edges and close-mown access paths are formed if space permits.

FEEDING
This is necessary to maintain a heavily used or frequently mown lawn in good order. The regular removal of the mowings means an effective loss of nutrients and these need replacing if the grass is to flourish.

A wide variety of fertilisers are sold specifically formulated for use on lawns. Two different types are often used: an autumn feed, with relatively more phosphorus and potassium to nitrogen, is given to promote healthy growth prior to the ravages of winter, while in the spring a heavier application of a formulation with more nitrogen is used.

Where a meadow lawn is intended, little or no feeding should be given. Most of the attractive wild flowers prefer a lower level of nutrients and are swamped by grasses where too much fertiliser is applied. In these situations, the removal of the periodic mowings will gradually alter the nutrient status of the ground in favour of the meadow plants.

AERATION
Where worms are controlled or where the soil gets trampled and compacted, such as by the playing of games, aeration will be necessary. This will relieve compaction and improve both the drainage of moisture through the soil and the oxygen available to plant roots. A compacted lawn will take a long time to dry out following rain and the grass will grow much less well, tending to look scraggy.

Aeration can be carried out using several different tools. The simplest is a fork, which is pushed into the ground and lifted slightly, to create a space around the prongs. Mechanical tools which will perform the same function are available. Some of these make holes in the turf with a solid tine, as with the fork, or have a blade which makes a narrow slit. These methods work effectively, although they compress the soil as the tine is inserted. A more effective technique is to extract a core of turf and soil using a machine with hollow tines. Because these remove a core of soil, they cause less additional compaction, which is relieved as the soil expands to fill the space left by the removal of the core. The cores can either be left to weather down (as happens to earthworm casts) or removed and grit brushed into the holes to give a long-term improvement in drainage. Aeration should be carried out from late autumn into winter and the lawn not used immediately after treatment.

Where earthworms are not present in quantity, there is often a build-up of organic matter on the soil surface from the roots of grasses or old mowings. This can harbour disease and make mowing difficult. It can be removed either using a spring-time rake or a machine designed for the purpose. The ideal time for this operation is either in the autumn or after the first cut in spring.

WEED AND MOSS CONTROL
In a lawn, weed control will consist of removing unwanted weeds, such as daisies or moss. Lawn herbicides are invaluable in removing certain weeds. However, any respite gained may only be temporary, especially if some aspect of management is favouring the weed at the expense of the grass; for example, raising the height of mowing will act against daisies.

Moss can be a particularly troublesome weed to control. Moss killers will give some respite but several other things should be done at the same time to achieve any lasting effect. Moss will flourish where the soil is permanently damp, such as when it is shaded for much of the day, or drainage is poor; it will also grow better where either the soil pH is low or the nutrient status is low. The complete cure, therefore, involves killing the moss with a suitable herbicide and removing the remains from the soil using a spring-time rake; feeding the grass with an appropriate fertiliser and raising the pH if necessary; improving the natural drainage by aerating the soil; and, if practical, reducing the shading of the lawn. Consider planting shade-tolerant groundcover plants in the shadiest areas where it is doubtful that grass will ever be very satisfactory.

MAINTAINING PATHS

Weeds need controlling on paths for two reasons:

• They are unsightly
• They will cause damage to the path materials

Existing weeds should be killed using a herbicide such as glyphosate, which is sprayed on to the exposed foliage and is translocated into the root system. With many weeds, one application is sufficient, but with some, such as bindweed, dock and creeping thistle, several applications may be needed to achieve control. Longer-lasting control can be achieved by the careful use of sodium chlorate, but may be moved laterally by rain and will damage surrounding plants and lawn margins.

Slimy growths of algae on paving stones can be very dangerous, although it does not cause any damage to the path itself. They will form wherever the path remains damp, such as when shaded by tall vegetation or buildings. If the former is the cause, redesigning the garden can reduce the problem. Slimes can be controlled by washing the path with phenol- or chlorine-based disinfectants.

and controllable shrubs or shrub roses. These should be chosen to blend with the herbaceous plants and give structure year-round.

MAINTAINING GROUNDCOVER
Groundcover plants make a close and dense layer of vegetation over the soil surface, preventing weeds from becoming established. Initially, weed-free ground is essential, as the plants will take a couple of seasons to cover the ground fully and will not suppress established perennial weeds, such as couch grass, coltsfoot or thistle.

Groundcover plants include shrubby species, such as *Rubus tri-*

color, *Vinca minor* and *Hedera helix* cultivars, which remain green all winter, and herbaceous plants, such as hostas and hardy geraniums. The annual maintenance is slightly different for the two groups.

Herbaceous Groundcover
Herbaceous plants should have the dead tops removed after they have died down, in late autumn or over the winter. Any woody weeds, such as brambles, should be dug out at the same time; any regrowth should be painted with glyphosate gel in early summer. Any bare patches, perhaps where plants have died, should be replanted at the same time using surplus plants from another area after refertilising the soil.

Shrubby Groundcover
Woody groundcover plants will benefit from a periodic trim. With most, this should be carried out in early spring and the plants will quickly recover the ground. It does not need to be an annual operation. Plants like heathers will benefit from the old flower-heads being removed after flowering – in autumn for the summer-flowering ones, and in late spring for the winter-flowering heathers. Some woody groundcover plants also tend to spread outside the confines of their allotted space and will need regular cutting. This is particularly so with vigorous plants like *Rubus tricolor*, which makes long growths to 2m (6½ft) in a season and will tip layer the ends of the shoots.

Some groundcover plants, such as *Hypericum calycinum* and *Vinca major* will spread by underground root suckers, and the perimeter of the area may need to be dug once a year to prevent spread.

Groundcover will benefit from the occasional feed, but apart from herbaceous plants, should not need mulching once established, as the natural leaf litter is usually left *in situ*. Many forms of groundcover and particularly those mentioned above, will last ten to fifteen years before needing to be replanted or divided.

RECYCLING GARDEN WASTE

Any human activity seems to generate an inordinate quantity of waste material, and gardening is no exception. Most of the waste will be in the form of organic matter, such as clippings and mowings, but poly-bags and chemical containers will also feature. Inorganic waste should be placed in the rubbish bin, but much organic matter can be usefully recycled to the benefit of the garden.

The prime method for recycling waste is through the compost heap. Here the material is rotted down by soil bacteria and turned into manure. As the material is put on to the compost heap, it should be

CARING FOR YOUR POND

Once a pond is established, its maintenance will involve three aspects: protecting the fish, controlling weed growth, and preventing other plant debris from entering the pond.

PROTECTING FISH
The main threats to fish come from cats and herons. These can be controlled in several ways. At the design stage, the pond can be built so that the water level is 25cm (10in) below the bank level. This will make it difficult for these predators to fish effectively, but can look unsightly – as if the pond has a leak! Completely covering the pond with wire netting will largely prevent predation, but makes a mockery of having fish in the first place; in such circumstances, more pleasure can be derived from a fish-free pond, enjoying the effect and appearance of the water and wildlife such as dragon and damsel flies. A more

chopped as small as possible and mixed up. The addition of a nitrogen fertiliser, such as ammonium sulphate or one of the compost starters available from garden centres, will hasten the decay process and enrich the compost. The material in the heap should be moist but not wet and the heap will need protecting from rain.

Heat from the decomposition process should raise the compost to a temperature which will kill weed seeds. The outer few centimetres of the heap will not become as hot, and to avoid putting weed-ridden compost on the soil the heap should be turned, or the outer layers can be put aside and used to start the next batch. The time taken to make usable compost will vary from three or so months during the summer to six months or more over winter.

Lawn mowings are generally too small and dense to make good compost on their own, but if mixed with leaves or straw will have the right consistency.

Garden waste can be chopped using an electrical shredder, which will make materials such as twiggy prunings suitable for inclusion in the compost heap, or as a mulching material for immediate use on shrub beds.

Not all organic waste is suitable for recycling. Diseased portions of plants, along with soil containing a disease organism such as honey fungus, should either be burnt or dispatched to the rubbish bin or local civic amenities tip.

A bonfire is a useful method of getting rid of woody or diseased material but should only be used for waste which cannot conveniently be dis-

posed of in other ways. They should be positioned so that smoke does not blow over the fence or across a road – a neighbour's bonfire can be a source of irritation and dispute. Letting the waste material dry out will reduce the amount of smoke created, as will an efficient, hot fire. Care must also be taken to ensure that flames from a bonfire do not damage plant foliage, nor sparks fly off and set light to your neighbour's thatched cottage or damage a polythene greenhouse. Material such as leaves should never be burnt. Apart from creating too much smoke, this is a waste of a useful mulching or composting material. Also, plastics and used chemical cartons should not be burnt, as they may release poisonous compounds.

effective method of reducing feline and heron predation is a strand of strong fishing wire stretched approximately 25cm (10in) above water level and within 15cm (6in) of the edge. A single strand is effective against herons, but where cats are a problem, several strands may be needed. From a distance, the wire will not be obtrusive.

The most effective way to safeguard the fish is to make the pond as large as practical and to use marginal plants to distance the edge from the open water; this will also allow a wider range of fish to be kept and plants to be grown. Larger ponds will involve using a polymer sheeting material or concrete to make the pond, as preformed ponds are usually too small. However, remember that claws can damage sheeting materials and these need protecting by a layer of mud or rounded pebbles at vulnerable points or to form a small beach. Pond construction is discussed in Chapter 4.

CONTROLLING WEED GROWTH
Vigorous aquatic growth needs controlling to prevent it swamping the

pond. This will apply to marginal plants, submerged oxygenating weed and water-lilies. Fast growing aquatic weeds will need to be controlled as they become too rampant, but marginal plants and lilies are better controlled in autumn or early spring, ie after or before new growth is made, as the appearance of the pond will be temporarily affected. In each case, the excess growth should be removed. Plants from the actively extending end of the clump should be used to replace any bare areas. With water lilies, 15cm (6in) long tips of the rhizomes should be kept and repotted and the older woody parts discarded.

Algae will often turn the pond rather green and murky in early summer. This is a natural process and normally the water clears after a few weeks, although where there are many fish or the pond is small, this may take some time. An appropriate number of submerged aquatics (oxygenators) will help to speed clearance (see Chapter 7). Avoid introducing fish to a new pond until oxygenators and wildlife are well established.

PLANT DEBRIS
The pond should be kept free, as much as possible, from falling leaves and other debris. As these decompose, they will absorb oxygen and cause the water to turn stagnant and foul. This is especially a problem where small ponds are situated close to trees and shrubs. Most ponds, however, will accumulate some leaves and debris, and it will usually be necessary to clean out the pond every third year or so. This should be an early spring job, before the plants have started into growth. Take care not to destroy the larvae of damsel and dragon flies and transfer the fish, weeds, and so on into a temporary tank whilst emptying the pond.

POND CHECKLIST
Pond Maintenance involves:
• protecting the fish
• controlling weed growth
• preventing plant debris entering the pond

CHAPTER 7

CHOOSING PLANTS

SOIL TYPE

Of prime consideration when selecting plants for your design is the soil type in your garden, particularly whether it is acid – below pH 6.5 – or alkaline or limy/chalky – above pH 7.0.

ACID OR ALKALINE?

At around pH 7.0, usually known as neutral, certain shrubs or trees which are usually associated with acid soil will perform reasonably well, though perhaps not growing as large or living as long as they would on soil of lower pH. Here we might include *Hamamelis* (witch hazel), *Cytisus* (brooms), winter-flowering heathers (*Erica carnea* cultivars), certain magnolias, *Castanea* (sweet chestnut) and *Eucryphia*, among a few others frequently planted.

Most trees, shrubs and plants which grow satisfactorily on an alkaline or chalky soil will perform equally well on a neutral or acid soil.

It makes good sense to avoid choosing plants unsuited to your soil, particularly the larger trees and shrubs which are important to the structure or design of the garden. The plant lists, and other references in this book, state whether plants are lime-hating (calcifuge). Principal examples of lime-hating plants are members of the *Ericaceae* (with the notable exception of *Arbutus*) such as rhododendrons and azaleas, heathers (*Calluna, Erica, Daboecia*), *Kalmia, Leucothoe, Pernettya* (now *Gaultheria*) and *Vaccinium*; regrettably, we must also include here camellias, which in nature grow on peaty or sandy soils.

Lime-hating trees, unfortunately for those on chalky soils, include such beauties as *Halesia* (snowdrop tree), *Liquidambar* and *Nyssa* (tupelo).

In addition, there are several lime-tolerant trees and shrubs normally grown for their autumn leaf colour which are not recommended on chalk and limestone soils because their autumn leaves often shrivel or turn brown instead of displaying the vivid hues of orange or scarlet that they would on acid soil. Particularly guilty are *Acer davidii* and *A. rufinerve* (snakebark maples), and *A. rubrum* (Canadian maple) *Cercidiphyllum japonicum*, the kadsura tree, but this tendency can vary from garden to garden within the same district. However, it is a comfort for those who garden on limy soil that *Sorbus*
(Continued on page 104)

On pages 144-150, schemes have been provided for focal-point plantings to give effect for much of the year. The ideas can be extended if space permits to furnish larger borders or small 'theme' compartments within the garden.

Schemes A to D assume that background evergreen shrubs or a hedge are present (or can be planted), and can be adapted for most aspects in sun or semi-shade. Here the planting is confined to dwarf, medium or large shrubs in association with low-growing groundcovering plants, both shrubby and herbaceous, in a sequence of colour combinations. All shrubs, trees, conifers and plants suggested are * (AGM 1993) with very few exceptions.

Schemes E and F include shrubs with bold, large or heavily lobed leaves, providing interesting shapes and textures. For a focal point by patio or island-bed planting, up-

FOCAL POINT PLANTINGS

right (fastigiate) trees or conifers may be cleverly contrasted with mound-forming or pendulous forms of evergreen or deciduous flowering shrubs and conifers. To these may be added a careful blend of ground-covering herbaceous perennials and ornamental grasses.

Scheme G proposes the use of shrubs and small trees, giving exceptional displays of autumn colour of leaf and berry, together with significant spring and summer flower. Effective shrubby or herbaceous groundcovers are included; alternatives for alkaline gardens are suggested where acid soil (lime-hating) shrubs (A) are named in this arrangement.

Scheme H blends winter-bark effects with variegated foliage and

interesting groundcovers, to give colour at most seasons. Bulbs can be used to advantage in both of these schemes, particularly in association with hostas and many of the lower-growing groundcovers.

Key to Planting Schemes

HP	Hardy perennial
HHP	Half-hardy perennial
DS	Dwarf shrub (30–60cm/1–2ft)
SS	Small shrub (1–1.5m/3–5ft)
MS	Medium shrub (1.5–3m/3–10ft)
LS	Large shrub (over 3m/l0ft)
ST	Small tree (eventual height 4.5–9m/15–30ft)
MT	Medium tree (eventual height 10–18m/33–60ft)
LT	Large tree (eventual height over 18m/60ft)
GC	Suitable for use as groundcover
E	Evergreen

•PROBLEM SOLVER•
RAISED BEDS FOR LIME-HATERS

Although it is frequently stressed that plants unsuited to the soil of your garden should be avoided, people who have grown up with rhododendrons and azaleas since childhood are sometimes reluctant to relinquish them in their new gardens in chalk or limestone districts. If you really must grow such lime-haters in a chalk garden, you can build a properly sealed-off raised and retained bed, fill it with a few cubic metres of special peaty, lime-free compost, and grow a few of the smaller, more compact rhododendrons – such little gems as *R. calostrotum*, 'Gigha', *R. yakushimanum*, 'Bluebird', 'Jenny', 'Curlew' and 'Princess Anne', to name but a few of the many suitable ones now available.

The bed will dry out less in summer if it experiences shade for at least part of the day, and can often form a focal point of colour and interest from the house. Heathers for flower and foliage at all seasons can be added as groundcover, while other small calcifuge plants, like the delicious *Gentiana sinoörnata* or one of its hybrids, would extend the season with spectacular autumn flowers.

Usually in chalk or limestone districts the public water supply is alkaline too; a white deposit on leaves is proof of this. In such localities it is worth installing one or more waterbutts to catch rainwater for use on the lime-haters in your raised bed.

A semi-shaded site is preferable for evergreens, rhododendrons and pieris. Heathers (*Erica* and *Calluna*) should be well clipped after flowering to maintain a compact shape.

Retaining walls for the bed should be 30–60cm (1–2ft) high and built of natural walling stone (sandstone or granite is best). Peat blocks, if available, are also very suitable. Seal off alkaline soil with 5cm (2in) of sand and then a sheet of polythene, perforated for drainage. Infill with 15cm (6in) of coarse, lime-free drainage material before adding at least 30cm (1ft) of lime-free, peaty compost. Small rocks may be positioned between the plants if desired. Draping alpine plants such as phlox, aubretia, helianthemum, thymes and so on may be planted into the wall during construction. Low-growing groundcovers should be sited about 30cm (1ft) apart between the specimen shrubs.

This arrangement, without sealing off, can also be used for lime-tolerant dwarf conifers and shrubs with low-growing groundcover plants (thyme, campanula, phlox, etc) and dwarf bulbs. Any well-drained, fertile soil is appropriate.

FIG 72 *Plan for a raised bed*

Specimen Shrubs
1 *Rhododendron yakushimanum* 'Koichiro Wada' (pink opening white, mid-late)
2 *Rhododendron* 'Princess Anne' or 'Curlew' (yellow, mid)
3 *Rhododendron* 'Moerheim' (violet-blue, early) or 'Elizabeth Hobbie' (scarlet translucent, early)
4 *Pieris japonica* 'Little Heath'

Groundcover Plants
a *Lithodora diffusa* 'Grace Ward' (white)
b *Gentiana sino-ornata*
c *Erica carnea* 'Foxhollow'
d *Gaultheria procumbens*
e *Erica cinerea* 'Stephen Davis'
f *Calluna vulgaris* 'Kinlochruel' (double white) or 'Robert Chapman' (bronze leaves)
g *Vaccinium vitis-idaea* 'Koralle'
h *Calluna vulgaris* 'J.H. Hamilton' or 'Mullion'
i *Phlox* 'Chattahoochee'
j *Erica carnea* 'Myretown Ruby'
k *Daboecia cantabrica* 'Waley's Red'

sargentiana, most of the sumachs (*Rhus*), many deciduous berberis, and *Euonymus alatus* and *E. europaeus* colour reliably and brilliantly in the autumn on the poorest of shallow soil over chalk.

Herbaceous and alpine plants for display and for groundcover are generally less troublesome over soil, but among the calcifuge plants commonly found in gardens are certain autumn-flowering gentians, lupins and meconopsis. On the other hand, white- or grey-foliaged plants and sub-shrubs which secrete chalk from glands on their leaves, such as dianthus (pinks and carnations), encrusted saxifrages and gypsophila seem happier on an alkaline soil; so do lavenders, artemisias, santolinas, osteospermums (*Dimorphotheca*), cistus and helianthemums, perhaps because of the sharp drainage the chalk soil affords.

DRAINAGE

Other problems are encountered with light, sandy, free-draining soils and heavy, badly drained, often clay soils, which become hopelessly wet in winter and hard baked and cracking in summer.

Free-draining Soil

While a large number of trees, shrubs and plants will adapt to an amazingly wide spectrum of soil conditions, some shallow-rooted subjects will suffer in severe summer droughts on light sandy soil, but survive on shallow well-drained soil over chalk – in spite of its limitations in other respects, the moisture stored in the porous chalk can prove a life-saver.

In milder districts and in many coastal areas, shrubs and trees with grey foliage do well in very porous soils. Many of them, like *Cistus*, *Elaeagnus*, *Halimium*, *Phlomis*, rosemary, lavender, *Artemisia*, and so on, are Mediterranean in origin.

Moist Situations

Few plants, trees or shrubs are tolerant of permanently badly drained or waterlogged situations. In these con-

ditions, it is worth organising some form of drainage (see p 23) and then digging in copious quantities of humus, farmyard manure or other bulky organic material in an effort to improve texture and aeration. River or waterside situations are different, however, and are suitable for several trees and shrubs that one normally finds in such circumstances, such as willows (*Salix*) in both shrubby and tree form – a large, diverse and fascinating genus – alder (*Alnus*), dogwood (*Cornus*), sea buckthorn (*Hippophaë*) and tamarisk (*Tamarix*).

Testing your Soil

Unless you wish to grow vegetables or fruit extensively, expert comprehensive soil testing and analysis is superfluous. The presence of sand, peat, chalk or limestone is usually fairly obvious, but in borderline cases, and there are many, use an inexpensive soil-testing kit to determine the pH of your soil. Also, note the plants in nearby countryside: if heather or bracken, or in wooded areas the 'wild' rhododendron, *R. ponticum*, are growing there, the soil will be acid. Wild clematis (old man's beard) in the hedges usually indicates an alkaline soil, as does the presence of native shrubs of chalk downland, particularly yew, box, wayfaring tree and spindleberry.

PLANT HEIGHT AND SPREAD

As important in the long term as the selection of plants that suit your soil is the careful consideration of their likely ultimate size, particularly with trees and larger shrubs – everything always grows bigger than you expect.

There may be a tendency today to treat a small garden as you might a room, 'redecorating' or refurnishing it after eight or ten years, a task often carried out anyway if the property changes hands. Nevertheless, we all have some responsibility when we contribute major items, such as trees, to the local landscape – whether rural, urban or suburban – to ensure that they are suited to their surroundings

and will go on providing a framework for the garden for many years. We may not live long enough to see a tree in maturity or we may move on to another garden, but someone will have to face any problem our tree may cause, such as blocked drains from invading roots, impoverished garden soil, damage to house foundations, exclusion of light from the windows, heavy shading of the garden, or even merely the blocking of gutters with copious quantities of autumn leaves. Had a smaller tree been selected or a more appropriate site chosen, perhaps none of these problems would have arisen.

In urban gardens, many of us have inherited difficulties caused by planting carried out by our predecessors a hundred or more years ago, when few trees other than forest species of ultimate large size were available. The noble stature of such trees as oak, beech, lime, even sycamore, are still much admired and valued by architects today as part of the urban scene, but they bring their problems. In ordinary gardens it is better not to plant these major trees, which are best suited to parkland or a few really spacious gardens, where there is room for them to grow to their full stature without being heavily pruned or lopped, with the loss of their natural grace and beauty. Where such trees exist, some compromise may be reached by having a few branches removed, the heads thinned and shaped, and crowns lifted – work for a skilled tree surgeon with the technical know-how, sophisticated equipment and an artistic eye.

Today there are many delightful small trees to choose from, and we can keep to those with an eventual height of say 4.5–9m (15–30ft), or at most to medium-size trees with an eventual height of 10–18m (33–60ft), in small gardens in urban areas, and particularly near buildings.

For such important plantings, make a careful study of ultimate sizes, spread and shape when considering how the trees are to be placed and spaced. In later years it may be better to remove every other tree (or to suggest doing this to those who buy your property) rather than rely on heavy pruning or lopping, which so spoils the natural form and beauty of individual specimens. Most garden trees, such as cherries (*Prunus*), ornamental crab (*Malus*), rowan and whitebeam (*Sorbus*), and thorns (*Crataegus*), should be spaced at least 6–8m (20–26ft) apart. With sensible planting of a variety of medium to large shrubs in between them, trees at this spacing should have adequate room to develop shape and form.

CLIMATE

Most gardeners in temperate climates, and particularly those who are plantsmen or collectors, will wish to include some plants from Mediterranean countries, Australia, New Zealand, western America and South America in their gardens, and in many areas they will overwinter successfully – in most years. Such plants provide diversity and richness in our gardens, and it is a pity to exclude them solely on the grounds that they cannot be guaranteed hardy in a particular climate. With well-considered siting and good drainage, the possibilities are remarkable. Certainly it would be a shame to be without such shrubs as *Ceanothus*, *Pittosporum*, *Cistus* and *Hebe*, *Phlomis* and *Helichrysum*, although severe winters will take a toll on them in exposed areas.

For important focal points reserved for a permanent specimen tree or shrub, however, choose a species known to be hardy in your area. When borderline-hardy shrubs which are well established do succumb in a severe winter, it is usually only after they have given five or ten years of good service, and replacement plants will usually develop with amazing speed if the stump and roots of the dead plant are removed and the site thoroughly cultivated and manured. Remember that a great many borderline plants will survive and do well even in cold areas if they are given the protection of a warm wall and nearby sheltering evergreens.

Pittosporum tenuifolium *'Tom Thumb' requires careful siting to avoid winter damage but is well worth the effort.*

Particularly for new plantings, additional protection with straw, leaves and hessian or plastic covers can be given in hard spells. You should be prepared to go to this trouble for several winters until the plant is thoroughly established and has reached a reasonable size. Plastic or hessian covers are best used during the period when the most severe weather can be expected. In new gardens in exposed areas, it is worth delaying planting tender or borderline-hardy subjects until you have successfully established some hardy evergreens for shelter (see pp 106–7). *(Continued on page 112)*

•PROBLEM SOLVER•
PLANTS FOR SCREENING

Plants can rapidly screen off undesirable objects, such as distant pylons, the neighbour's washing, nearby tin sheds, distant or not-so-distant housing which has mushroomed seemingly overnight, or that specially annoying focal point on which one's eye often settles – the neighbour's second-storey window which overlooks your lounge and patio! Well chosen, these screening plants, albeit with some gentle pruning and shaping, need never outgrow their situation and can also be most attractive in the garden scene.

Avoid conifers that will ultimately become forest-size (*Thuya*, *Cupressus* and *Chamaecyparis*), all too soon blocking sunshine, endangering roofs and becoming too tall to clip or restrain – or being ruined by splaying after a heavy snowfall.

SUBSTANTIAL BOUNDARY SCREENING
Busy roads and railways need solid, heavy-leaved, dense and evergreen screening to help with sound as well as vision blocking. Cultivars of the broad-leaved holly (*Ilex* x *altaclerensis*) and *Viburnum rhytidophyllum* with elephant-ear leaves, form tall (3–4.5m/10–15ft) large-leaved evergreens effective in flower and berry. Also frequently planted as a substantial evergreen screen are the common and Portuguese laurels (*Prunus laurocerasus* and *P. lusitanica*); the latter has greater tolerance of most soils, including shallow chalk and greater resistance to disease. The geographic form for the Azores Islands, *P. lusitanica azorica*, is especially good, with rapid growth, handsome reddish young leaves and an arching habit. *P. laurocerasus* leaves and berries are toxic if ingested. Alternatively, as a welcome substitute for the overplanted Leyland cypress, try an excellent, dense, close-growing, bright green cypress needing little clipping, *Chamaecyparis lawsoniana* 'Green Hedger'.

COMPACT MEDIUM-HEIGHT SCREENING
For this, choose hardy evergreen shrubs which are known to adapt well as hedge plants and may ultimately grow satisfactorily to 2.5–4m (8–12ft). Often a height of 3.5–4.5m (12–15ft) is adequate for screening; there is no point in using taller plants, which must block some of the sunshine reaching your garden. If you have enough room, large-growing cotoneasters, which are evergreen (or semi-evergreen), are ideal for such low-level screening; they also provide good spring flowers and spectacular autumn berries in yellow, red or pink. *Cotoneaster* 'Cornubia', 'Pink Champagne', 'John Waterer' or 'Rothschildianus' are all fast-growing with arching branches. They will spread as wide as they grow high, 3–4.5m (10–15ft), but their beauty is lost if they are heavily pruned, so space them as widely as possible for best results.

> **Useful Screening Plants**
> *Aucuba japonica* cultivars
> *Cotoneaster lacteus*
> *C. sternianus*
> *C. serotinus* (*glaucophyllus vestitus*)
> *Elaeagnus* x *ebbingei*
> *E.* x *ebbingei* 'Limelight'
> *E. macrophylla*
> *Hebe salicifolius*
> *Osmanthus* x *Osmarea burkwoodii*
> *Pyracantha* (disease-resistant varieties)
> *Viburnum* 'Pragense'
> See Chapter 8 for most descriptions.

The remarkably hardy Hebe salicifolia *makes an excellent dense evergreen hedge, flowering spectacularly in summer. It can reach at least 2.5cm (8ft) and is very suitable for boundaries in town gardens.*

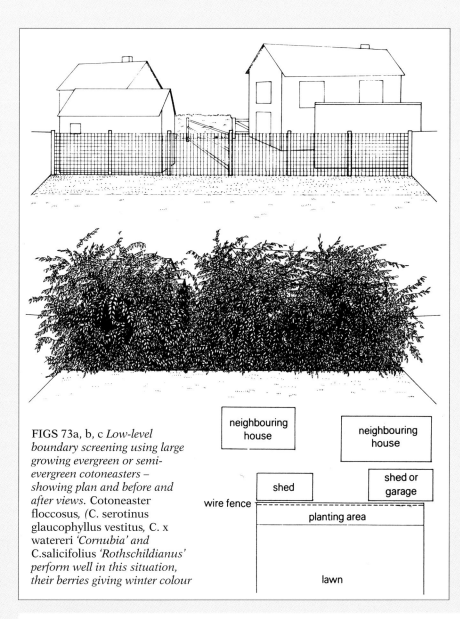

FIGS 73a, b, c *Low-level boundary screening using large growing evergreen or semi-evergreen cotoneasters – showing plan and before and after views.* Cotoneaster floccosus, *(C. serotinus glaucophyllus vestitus, C. x watereri 'Cornubia'* and C.salicifolius *'Rothschildianus' perform well in this situation, their berries giving winter colour*

CASE STUDY

EVERGREEN SCREEN

The ubiquitous Leyland cypress (x *Cupressocyparis leylandii*) is useful as a temporary screen, and is clippable to form a dense evergreen hedge to any reasonable size above 2.4m (8ft), but it is also very demanding of space and will impoverish the soil, particularly if unrestricted. Plant it in association with other slower-growing screening plants which in the course of time will take over, however, and the Leyland cypress can later be reduced to hedge size or even removed in some cases. *Thuja plicata* 'Fastigiata' is both neater and more adaptable to regular clipping although slower in growth. A most attractive evergreen screening plant to try – at least 1.8m (6ft) away from your Leyland cypress planting – is the rapid-growing and strikingly variegated *Rhamnus alaterna* 'Argenteovariegata', which will reach up to 3m (10ft) in sheltered garden conditions. It will also appreciate the shelter of the cypress and look well against it. In cold or exposed districts use *Ilex aquifolium* 'Argenteomarginata', which is hardier and gives a similar effect, but is slower growing. In pleasing contrast, suitably spaced off, add *Cryptomeria japonica* 'Elegans', a conifer whose juvenile growth assumes a red-bronze hue in the winter. This handsome conifer can reach 6m (18^{1}/2ft) or more (but watch for splaying in snow). Scots pine (*Pinus sylvestris*) is slow growing but forms a charming small tree if its growth is stopped at 3.6m (12ft) or 4.6m (15ft), making an elegant spreading head of arching evergreen branches. Extra large container-grown specimens are often available from specialist nurserymen for immediate effect.

FIG 74 *Evergreen screen giving interest of shape and form, with variegated and colour changing foliage*

FIG 75 *Plan view of Fig 74*

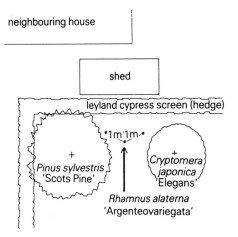

•PROBLEM SOLVER•

SCREENING INSPECTION COVERS

Another type of screen planting, usually low, is needed in most gardens – the covering of at least one metal drain-inspection cover, usually about 50x60cm (1¹/₂x2ft) or more, while leaving it still accessible when need the arises.

If a septic tank of the latest 'giant bottle' type has been installed there is little restriction over planting, but with the older type involving large concrete tanks at or just below ground level, it is necessary to ensure that there is enough depth of soil – ideally at least 30cm (1ft) – to support suitable shrubs. With older installations that do not have modern plastic piping, it is also vital to avoid water-seeking species, such as willows and dogwoods, as their roots will inevitably find faults or cracks in the pipes and may quickly block them. These conspicuous metal covers can frequently be incorporated into border areas, which may be suitably curved to include them. If left isolated near the borders, these covers can be both an eyesore and an impediment to mowing.

Euonymus fortunei 'Emerald 'n Gold'*, evergreen and variegated, where low growth is required.

CASE STUDY

ISLAND BEDS

If a cover is well isolated in the lawn area, then an island bed is usually possible. Make it any reasonable size so as to incorporate the cover and shrubs which provide a focal point of colour and interest. Relatively low-growing shrubs or conifers which are both evergreen and of spreading and dense habit, but not armed with prickles (avoid berberis, pyracantha and holly in particular) are suitable. Sometimes a group of three to five plants of one variety of prostrate juniper or cotoneaster will screen a cluster of two or three covers.

A more generous planting area would allow the grouping of several varieties of shrubs to produce a focal point of interest at all seasons. Hardy evergreen shrubs and conifers of low, spreading habit are appropriate for this – and remember that ivies can creep as well as climb!

The lists suggest some plants suitable for all fertile soils and for most situations in sun or semi-shade. Hardy evergreen shrubs of compact but taller growth are suitable if the site allows.

Low-growing Shrubs
(predominantly evergreen)
Cotoneaster cochleatus
Cotoneaster conspicuus decorus
C. integrifolium (microphyllus)
C. salicifolius 'Gnom'
C. 'Coral Beauty'
Euonymus fortunei 'Coloratus', 'Emerald Gaiety' and 'Emerald 'n Gold'
Hebe 'Marjorie' and 'Mrs Winder'
H. pinguifolia 'Pagei' and 'Sutherlandii'
Hedera helix 'Little Diamond', 'Ivalace'
Mahonia japonica
Phlomis fruticosa
Prunus laurocerasus 'Otto Luyken'
Senecio 'Sunshine'

Taller Shrubs
(for flower, foliage and berry all year)
Cotoneaster floccosus
Elaeagnus x *ebbingei* 'Limelight' and 'Gilt Edge'
Escallonia 'Donard Radiance'
Lonicera nitida 'Baggesen's Gold'
Osmanthus x *burkwoodii*
Viburnum tinus 'Eve Price'

Conifers (see Fig 77)
Juniperus horizontalis 'Wiltonii'
J. Sabina 'No Tam Blight' ('New Blue')
J. squamata 'Blue Carpet'
J. x *media* 'Mordigan Gold' and 'Old Gold'
Microbiota decussata (related to juniper)
Pinus mugo pumilio
Taxus baccata 'Repens Aurea'

In Shaded Areas
Buxus microphylla
B. sempervirens
Hedera colchica 'Dentata Variegata'
H. helix 'Hibernica' and 'Goldchild'
Mahonia aquifolium 'Apollo'
Pachysandra terminalis and 'Variegata'
Prunus laurocerasus 'Zabeliana'
Sarcococca confusa

In Heavily Shaded Areas
Aucuba japonica cultivars
Danaë racemosa
Euonymus japonica 'Latifolius Albomarginatus'
Skimmia japonica cultivars

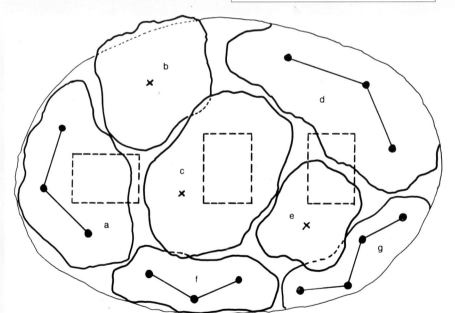

FIG 76 *Screening a septic tank cover. Use dwarf to medium evergreen shrubs to form a feature of colour and year-round interest of flower, berry and grey or variegated foliage, while keeping the covers reasonably accessible. This scheme is for sun or semi-shade in all fertile soils*

a 3 *Lonicera nitida* 'Baggesen's Gold'
b 1 *Viburnum tinus* 'Eve Price' or 2 *V. davidii*
c 2 *Cotoneaster floccosus* or *lacteus*
d 3 *Senecio* 'Sunshine' (greyi Hort.)
e 1 *Elaeagnus* x *ebbingei* 'Limelight' or 'Gilt Edge'
f 3 *Euonymus fortunei* 'Emerald Gaiety'
g 4 *Euonymus fortunei* 'Emerald 'n' Gold' or *Hebe pinguifolia* 'Pagei'

FIG 77 *Screening of inspection cover using prostrate junipers. Among others,* Juniperus x media *'Old Gold' or* sabina *'No Tam Blight' ('New Blue') are ideal for this task: they do not get too large, and they leave access to the inspection cover and for grass cutting*

•PROBLEM SOLVER•

PLANTS FOR DIFFICULT BANKS

Steep, unmowable banks are frequently a problem, though groundcovering and mound-forming shrubs can be used with advantage to clothe them in an attractive and labour-saving manner. Assuming at least 22cm (9in) of reasonably good top soil is present, often covered with coarse grass, it is best to kill off the grass with the translocating herbicide glyphosate. Remove the dead grass, leaving the roots intact, and the bank is then ready to prepare for planting.

PLANTING METHOD

Plant into the base of 'L'-shaped level stations cut into the bank. The more generously the sites are prepared, the better establishment and growth will be. Rain or irrigation water draining down the banks should run into the L-shaped station and into the roots of new plants rather than running to waste down the bank. This method is particularly useful in areas of low rainfall, or where summer droughts are experienced. A bark, pebble or gravel mulch to each planting site will further assist establishment and good growth, retained, if necessary, by small pieces of stone (Fig 57c, p 68).

USING INVASIVE SPECIES

Species frequently used on banks are the invasive *Hypericum calycinum* (Rose of Sharon), *Cerastium tomentosum* (snow-in-summer), *Rubus tricolor*, *Vinca major* (greater periwinkle) and *Hedera helix* 'Hibernica' (Irish ivy). On acid soils heathers or *Gaultheria shallon* may be used. Either of these can be planted at three to five per square metre, or yard, and will quickly colonise to form solid and impenetrable planting, often inhibiting growth or smothering any newly planted small tree or shrub associated with it. Such a planting is undoubtedly low maintenance and useful on path sides and in areas which are visually less important.

SHRUBS AND CONIFERS FOR BANKS
Shrubs

Artemisia 'Powis Castle'
Choisya ternata and *ternata* 'Sundance'
Cotoneaster floccosus
C. nanshan
C. 'Coral Beauty'
Cytisus praecox 'Allgold'
Genista hispanica
G. lydia
Hebe albicans and cultivars
H. pimeleoides 'Quicksilver'
H. rakaiensis
H. 'Spender's Seedling'
Potentilla cultivars, particularly 'Elizabeth', 'Tangerine', 'Eastleigh Cream' and 'Abbotswood'
Rosmarinus officinalis 'Severn Sea'

Shrub roses

Mound-forming and ground-covering shrub roses include *Raubritter* x *paulii*, 'Max Graf', 'Red Max Graf', 'Bonica', 'Rosy Cushion', 'Pheasant', 'Swany', *wichuraiana* (semi-evergreen)and many others.

    Taller shrub roses with arching branches include: *R. rubrifolia*, 'Canary Bird', 'Fritz Nobis', 'Gypsy Boy' and 'Macrantha'.

    Many others will adapt to this task. This list is more intended to point you in the right direction.

Specimen conifers

(‡ = leaves/berries/seeds poisonous if eaten)
Juniperus chinensis 'Pfitzeriana' and other cultivars
J. 'Grey Owl'
J. squamata 'Blue Carpet'
Picea pungens 'Procumbens'
Pinus mugo pumilio
Taxus baccata 'Repens Aurea' or 'Repandans'‡

Dwarf and medium-size specimen shrubs (• = particularly tolerant of shade;
‡ = leaves/berries/seeds poisonous if eaten)
Acer palmatum 'Dissectum' and cultivars•
Buxus sempervirens•
Ceanothus thyrsiflorus 'Repens'
Cistus corbariensis
Cotoneaster horizontalis
Prunus laurocerasus 'Otto Luyken'•‡ and 'Zabeliana'•‡
Pyracantha 'Soleil D'Or' and 'Golden Dome'
Senecio 'Sunshine'
Skimmia confusa 'Kew Green' (male)•
Viburnum tinus and cultivars

FIG 78

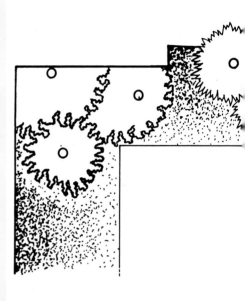

FIG 79

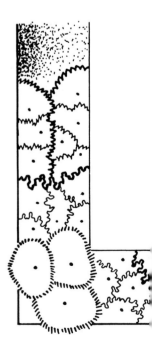

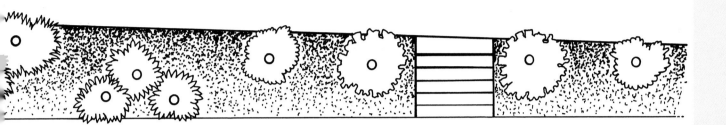

CASE STUDY

PROMINENT BANKS

In prominent situations – say, the banks
surrounding a disused tennis lawn or a swimming
pool – a varied planting is needed, perhaps
associating groups of shrubs of similar character
and vigour at a wider spacing of 50cm–1m
(1½–3ft) – varying with the size and strength of
the shrub – to furnish the bank completely.

Some useful hardy shrubs and shrub roses for
this task are given in the lists (left), suitable for
sun or semi-shade in all fertile soils. In most
cases, unless the areas involved are very small,
groups of three of a kind or more are
recommended. It is possible to build up plantings
of colour and effect throughout the year.

Sometimes it is possible to part-mow a bank
from the top with a hover-type mower. In this
case, groups or focal points of planting can be
introduced at 2–3m (6–10ft) or more apart with
mown grass between. Conifers and dwarf to
medium-size shrubs particularly useful for this
specimen style of planting are also given in the
list.

FIG 78 *Plants for a difficult corner of a lawn tennis court, an arrangement
with part-mowing between widely spaced shrubs in a shady area. Any
fertile well-drained soil:*
a *Pyracantha* 'Soleil D'Or' or 'Orange Glow'
b *Prunus laurocerasus* 'Zabeliana' or 'Otto Luyken'
c *Photinia davidiana* 'Pallette' *or Pyracantha* 'Sparkler'
d *Buxus sempervirens* or *Skimmia confusa* 'Kew Green'
e *Acer palmatum* 'Dissectum' or 'Dissectum Crimson Queen'

FIG 79 *Complete coverage of a difficult corner bank with a variety of shrubs
for year-round effect, in a sunny or semi-shaded situation:*
a *Cotoneaster dammeri*
b *Artemisia* 'Powis Castle'
c Groundcover rose 'Red Max Graf' or 'Fiona'
d *Potentilla fruticosa* 'Tilford Cream' or *dahurica* 'Abbotswood'
e *Ceanothus thyrsiflorus repens*
f Groundcover rose *wichuraiana* or 'Swany'
g *Genista hispanica*
h *Hebe pimeleoides* 'Quicksilver'
i *Hebe recurva* 'Boughton Silver'
j *Hypericum moseranum*
k Groundcover rose 'Bonica' or 'Max Graf'
l *Potentilla* 'Elizabeth' or 'Longacre'
m *Cotoneaster* 'Gnom' or 'Coral Beauty'
n *Senecio* 'Sunshine' or *Juniperus* 'Grey Owl'

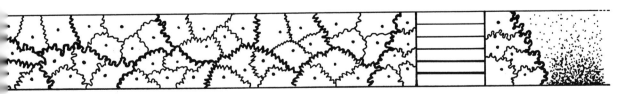

'SHRUBACEOUS' BORDERS AND ISLAND BEDS

Shrubaceous association in a shady situation – Golden elder (Sambucus racemosa 'Plumosa Aurea') with late-summer flowering Anemone x hybrida 'Queen Charlotte'* (see also page 116).

We seem at last to be moving away from the conventional herbaceous border so popular in the 1920s and 1930s and so labour intensive, with its choice of plants requiring staking, tying and frequent lifting and splitting and replanting. Gardeners must be thankful for the 'shrubaceous' border – produced by a sensible system of planting using widely spaced predominantly evergreen shrubs of various shapes and sizes but naturally compact or controllable by pruning; these specimens should be associated with a carefully chosen infill of mainly dwarf or medium height herbaceous perennials, which are either groundcovering or self-supporting and largely of easy culture once established.

By using shrubs to give 'bones' or a more natural and permanent structure, with interest in all seasons through flowers, foliage and berries, shrubaceous planting offers another dimension that is lacking from the conventional herbaceous border,

traditionally cut down annually in autumn 'to tidy the garden' for the winter. Instead, we introduce carefully chosen specimens, often evergreen shrubs, widely spaced to show their natural character and elegance and adding year-round interest of leaf, flower and often berry. Herbaceous plants chosen to associate with them should combine beauty of flower and foliage with reasonable permanence and ease of maintenance.

Circumstances frequently seem to dictate that borders are located on garden boundaries and backed by a wall, fence or hedge. But why not a shrubaceous island bed, introducing a few carefully chosen shrubs or conifers to the excellent herbaceous island bed?

USING HARDY PERENNIALS
Of the multitude of hardy herbaceous perennials available, some are more suitable than others to associate with shrubs or even shrubby trees to form

an important constituent of the shrubaceous border. To qualify, they should be reasonably hardy and long-lived once established, thereupon requiring the minimum of attention; while lifting, splitting and replanting will not be entirely eliminated, plants requiring frequent division or propagation should be avoided in such a planting, where the accent is on low maintenance. One might think that this will rule out a host of old favourites, but this is not so; indeed, they are often favourites because they have good constitutions and have persisted well, frequently in circumstances of neglect. A worthwhile hardy herbaceous perennial should have reasonable vigour and good ground covering potential, but not be invasive.

Ideally, plants should be selected both for a satisfactory blend of flower and foliage, and for their height and spread in relation to the specimen shrubs which are an important part of the border. Such specimens should be planted as large as possible and, assuming all planting is carried out at the same time in a prepared area, at least 60cm (2ft) distant from vigorous herbaceous plantings, as these mature quickly and will tend to swamp or inhibit the shrubs' growth. While most herbaceous plants will be relatively low growing, occasional variations in height or accent points in the foreground or middle distance are

usually necessary – aconitum, kniphofia and delphinium are typical plants for such situations.

Most herbaceous perennials should be grouped in threes or fives of a kind, 30–45cm (12–8in) apart each way within the group. It is worth having island beds and borders prepared well in advance (see Chapter 5). Incorporation of well-rotted farmyard manure and a slow-release fertiliser

will ensure rapid establishment and good growth.

The planting should be easily maintained and should provide colour and interest at all seasons. Any discrepancies in arrangement are easily adjusted in the next planting season, or even beforehand during the growing season if the ground is consistently moist, as is often the case in cooler climates.

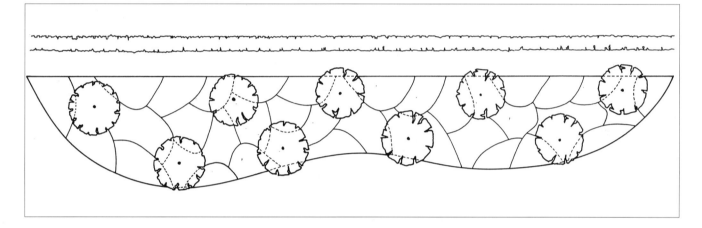

SHRUBACEOUS BORDERS

The plans given here illustrate a suggested shape and planting for shrubaceous borders and a shrubaceous island bed, with planting to give a year-round effect on all fertile soils, whether acid or alkaline. (Acid soil is essential if rhododendrons are included.)

The borders in Figs 80 and 81 are designed to cover an area up to approximately 20 x 2–2.5m (60 x 6–8ft) but are adaptable to smaller or larger areas. Site herbaceous plants at 30–45cm (1–1¹/2ft) apart within groups of three to five plants of a kind and spaced off at least 45–60cm (1¹/2–2ft) from the base of newly planted shrubs. Some adjustment or thinning of herbaceous plants and pruning and shaping of shrubs may be necessary as the plants grow to maturity, the herbaceous plants maturing more quickly. Avoid closer planting of the shrubs.

FIG 80 OPEN SUNNY SHRUBACEOUS BORDER
Shrubs (* = evergreen)
*S1   *Viburnum tinus* 'Gwenllian' or 'Eve Price'
*S2   *Yucca filamentosa* 'Bright Edge' or 'Variegata'
S3   Shrub Rose 'Erfurt'
*S4   *Daphne retusa* or x *burkwoodii*
*S5   *Ceanothus* 'Puget Blue' or *Eucryphia glutinosa*
*S6   *Hebe pimeleoides* 'Quicksilver', 'Red Edge' or 'Pewter Dome'
S7   *Rosa moyesii* 'Geranium'
S8   *Magnolia stellata* 'Water Lily'
*S9   *Elaeagnus* x *ebbingei* 'Gilt Edge'

Herbaceous perennials
h1   *Euphorbia polychroma*
h2   *Geranium endressii* 'A.T. Johnson' or 'Wargrave Pink'

h3   *Crocosmia* 'Lucifer'
h4   *Santolina pinnata* 'Edward Bowles'
h5   *Helianthemum* 'Wisley Pink' or 'Firedragon'
h6   *Kniphofia caulescens* or 'Shining Sceptre'
h7   *Delphinium* 'Summer Skies' or 'Blue Fountains'
h8   *Gypsophila* 'Rosy Veil'
h9   *Aster novae-angliae* 'Alma Potschke'
h10   *Hemerocallis* 'Pink Damask' or 'Stafford'
h11   *Lythrum salicaria* 'Firecandle'
h12   *Stipa calamagrostis* (grass)
h13   *Geranium* 'Johnson's Blue'
h14   *Salvia nemerosa* 'Superba'
h15   *Lysimachia punctata*
h16   *Nepeta* 'Six Hill Giant'
h17   *Alchemilla mollis*
h18   *Agapanthus* 'Headbourne Hybrids' or 'Lilliput'
h19   *Aster* x *frikartii* Mönch
h20   *Hemerocallis* 'Golden Chimes'
h21   *Aster novi-belgii* Little Pink Beauty'
h22   *Polygonum campanulatum* or *bistorta* 'Superbum'
h23   *Helictotrichon sempervirens* (grass)
h24   *Geranium* 'Ann Folkard' or *macrorrhizum* 'Ingwersen's Variety'
h25   *Delphinium* 'Lamartine'
h26   *Achillea* 'Moonshine' or *filipendula* 'Coronation Gold'
h27   *Euphorbia griffithii* 'Fireglow'
h28   *Rudbeckia fulgida* 'Goldsturm'
h29   *Iris pallida dalmatica* 'Variegata'
h30   *Aster amellus* 'King George'
h31   *Kniphofia* 'Bressingham Hybrids'
h32   *Lavandula* 'Hidcote Variety'
h33   *Ruta graveolens* 'Jackman's Blue'

FIG 81 **SHADED SHRUBACEOUS BORDER**

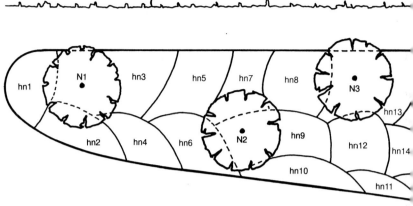

Shrubs (• = evergreen)
- •N1 *Rhododendron yakushimanum* 'Koichira Wada' (or *Ilex aquifolium* 'Golden Milkboy')
- N2 *Hydrangea* 'Preziosa' (or 'Geoffrey Chadbund')
- N3 *Acer palmatum* 'Bloodgood'
- •N4 *Berberis verruculosa*
- •N5 *Cotoneaster lacteus* (or *Sambucus racemosa* 'Plumosa Aurea')
- N6 *Weigela praecox* 'Variegata' (or 'Rubidor')
- •N7 *Daphne bholua* 'Jacqueline Postill'
- N8 *Acer palmatum* 'Dissectum'
- •N9 *Mahonia japonica*
- •N10 *Rhododendron* 'Winsome' (or *Viburnum* x *burkwoodii* 'Anne Russell')

Herbaceous perennials
- hn1 *Alchemilla mollis*
- hn2 *Geranium wallichianum* 'Buxton's Variety' (or 'Johnson's Blue')
- hn3 *Astilbe* 'Bressingham Beauty'
- hn4 *Bergenia* 'Ballawley'
- hn5 *Anemone hybrida* 'Queen Charlotte'
- hn6 *Hosta* 'August Moon' (or *fortunei* 'Aurea')
- hn7 *Campanula latifolia* 'Brantwood' (or 'Gloaming')
- hn8 *Kirengeshoma palmata*
- hn9 *Helleborus foetidus*
- hn10 *Brunnera macrophylla* 'Variegata' (or *macrophylla*)
- hn11 *Ajuga reptans* 'Burgundy Glow'
- hn12 *Aconitum septentrionalis* 'Ivorine'
- hn13 *Lysimachia clethroides*
- hn14 *Paeonia* 'Sarah Bernhardt'
- hn15 *Dicentra eximia* 'Alba' (or 'Luxurians')
- hn16 *Phlox paniculata* 'White Admiral'
- hn17 *Astilbe taquetii* 'Superba'
- hn18 *Hosta* 'Royal Standard'
- hn19 *Lamium* 'Beacon Silver' (or *Pulmonaria saccharata* 'Pink Dawn')
- hn20 *Epimedium rubrum*
- hn21 *Liriope muscari*
- hn22 *Astrantia major* 'Sunningdale Variegated'
- hn23 *Astilbe* 'Irrlicht'
- hn24 *Phlox maculata* 'Alpha' (or 'Omega')
- hn25 *Campanula lactiflora* 'Prichard's Variety'
- hn26 *Bergenia* 'Silverlight'
- hn27 *Hosta undulata*
- hn28 *Helleborus orientalis*
- hn29 *Rodgersia aesculifolia* (or *podophylla*)
- hn30 *Paeonia* 'Karl Rosenfield'
- hn31 *Aconitum* 'Bressingham Spire'
- hn32 *Cimicifuga ramosa* 'Atropurpurea' (or *racemosa*)
- hn33 *Phlox paniculata* 'Starfire'
- hn34 *Anemone hybrida* 'White Queen'
- hn35 *Helleborus lividus* 'Corsicus'
- hn36 *Campanula alliariifolia* 'Ivory Bells'
- hn37 *Astilbe* 'Fire' (or 'Fanal')
- hn38 *Hosta* 'Halcyon' (or 'Elegans')
- hn39 *Epimedium* x *warleyense* (or *perralderanum*)
- hn40 *Gentiana asclepiadea*

FIG 82 **SHRUBACEOUS ISLAND BED**
Dwarf and slow growing conifers; dwarf compact shrubs and herbaceous ground cover plants for all fertile soils, in an open, but not exposed situation. Viewed from all sides the island bed is more effective if mounded up to 15cm (6in) proud of surrounding lawns.

Conifers
- C1 *Chamaecyparis lawsoniana* 'Pygmaea Argentea'
- C2 *Pinus mugo* 'Ophir' or *parviflora* 'Adcock's Dwarf'
- C3 *Juniperus communis* 'Hibernica' (or 'Sentinel')

Shrubs
- S1 *Ceanothus* 'Blue Mound' (or *thyrsiflorus repens*)
- S2 *Viburnum davidii*
- S3 *Berberis thunbergii* 'Harlequin' (or 'Rose Glow')
- S4 *Daphne* x *mantensiana* 'Manten' (or *tangutica*)

Herbaceous perennials and groundcover
- hi1 *Geranium* 'Ann Folkard' (or *sanguineum lancastriense*)
- hi2 *Artemisia maritima canescens*
- hi3 *Sedum* 'Autumn Joy'
- hi4 *Hakonechloa macra* 'Albo-aurea' (grass)
- hi5 *Aster* (dwarf) *novi-belgii* 'Audrey'
- hi6 *Lavandula spica* 'Rosea'
- hi7 *Paeonia officinalis* 'Alba Plena' (or 'Rosea Plena')
- hi8 *Ruta graveolens* 'Jackman's Blue'
- hi9 *Helianthemum* 'Jubilee'
- hi10 *Helianthemum* 'Mrs C. W. Earle'
- hi11 *Salvia nemerosa* 'Lubeca'
- hi12 *Gypsophila* 'Rosy Veil'
- hi13 *Iris pallida dalmatica* 'Variegata'
- hi14 *Lavandula spica* 'Hidcote' (or 'Munstead')
- hi15 *Euphorbia polychroma*
- h16 *Santolina chamaecyparissus nana* (*corsica*)
- hi17 *Stachys macrantha*
- hi18 *Vinca minor* 'La Grave' (or 'Gertrude Jekyll')
- hi19 *Waldsteinia ternata*
- hi20 *Molinia caerulea* 'Variegata' (grass)
- hi21 *Helianthemum* 'Wisley Primrose'
- hi22 *Persicaria vaccinifolium*

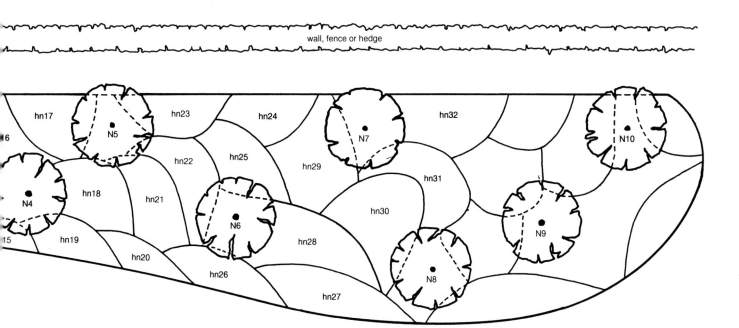

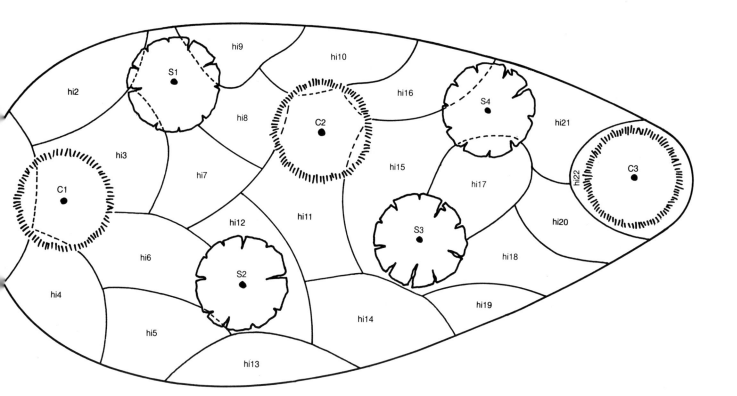

CHOOSING HARDY PERENNIALS FOR SHRUBACEOUS PLANTINGS

Even within the necessary limitations, there are plenty of hardy herbaceous perennials – indeed almost too many – to choose from, and certainly enough to satisfy most tastes. Unless otherwise noted, all those listed below are tolerant of a wide range of fertile soils, whether acid or alkaline (limy). Good drainage will help with the overwintering of less hardy or short-lived subjects.

Plants marked with an asterisk* have been accorded an Award of Garden Merit 1993 (see p152. All are hardy (H4) unless otherwise marked).

Achillea 'Moonshine* (H3) A yarrow with year-round silver filigree foliage and large flat heads of clear yellow flowers effective from mid- to late summer and invaluable for drying for winter decoration. 60cm (2¹/2ft). 'Gold Plate' is taller, has green filigree foliage and large dense heads of golden flowers, retaining their colour well when cut and dried. l–1.5m (3¹/2–5ft).

Aconitum septentrionalis *'Ivorine'*.

Aconitum (Monkshood)   Spiky, easily grown plants effective in summer, with delphinium-like hooded flowers. 'Bressingham Spire'* (violet-blue) and *A.* x *bicolor** and *septentrionalis* 'Ivorine' (ivory white) are excellent. About 90cm (3ft). The sap and all parts of *Aconitum* (species and cultivars) can be irritant on contact or poisonous if ingested.

Agapanthus   The hardy Headbourne Hybrids are superb for their umbels of china or violet blue, late summer and autumn flowers. A well-drained site is necessary. Select good forms if you can – buy when in flower from a garden centre or nursery. 60cm–1m (2–3ft). A large white-flowered variety, *A. campanulatus* 'Albus', is less often seen, well worth acquiring and hardy, and 'Lilliput' dwarf and deep blue.

Ajuga   Forms or cultivars of our native bugle (*A. reptans*) make excellent groundcover, particularly in moist conditions. 'Atropurpurea'* has bronze-purple leaves; 'Burgundy Glow'* has purple leaves becoming wine-red as the season advances, and edged with cream and pink. Both 15cm (6in).

Alchemilla mollis* (Lady's mantle)   A popular clump-forming plant with large round, pleated, soft hairy leaves and greenish-yellow flowers in summer. Blends well with *Nepeta* (catmint) or blue hardy *Geranium*. Succeeds everywhere. 25–30cm (10–12in).

Aster novae-angliae *'Alma Potschke'**.

Anemone x *hybrida*   Useful late summer and autumn flowering members of the large anemone family, usually referred to as Japanese anemones. They have large saucer-shaped white or pink single or semi-double flowers, particularly 'Bressingham Glow', semi-double rose-red, 35–50cm (1–1¹/2ft); 'Queen Charlotte'*, single pink, 60cm (2ft); 'Honorine Jobert'*, large single white, about 1m (3–3¹/2ft).

Artemisia maritima f. *canescens*   A beautiful and non-invasive form of our native wormwood, making low mounds of silver filigree. 25–30cm (10–12in).

Aster   Of this large genus of daisy-flowered plants the well-known Michaelmas daisies are the most common. Regrettably, they are often marred by mildew and can be unreliable in their performance, though some of the smaller, dwarf hybrids are rewarding. Instead, try the compact disease-free *amellus* cultivars, notably 'King George'*, brilliant ultramarine blue, 60cm (2ft) and the very beautiful hybrid x *frikartii* 'Mönch'*, with large peacock-blue flowers with orange centres, 80cm (2¹/2ft). Cultivars of *A. novae-angliae* are also disease-free and distinct in habit and foliage, particularly the new 'Alma Potschke'*, a compact newcomer with startling salmon-rose flowers on branching heads, about

1m (3ft). Among dwarf Michaelmas daisies, *A. novii-belgii* 'Audrey', mauve-blue, 30cm (1ft) and 'Little Pink Beauty', 40cm (16in), are particularly good value.

Astilbe   The herbaceous spiraeas, with their conspicuous, brightly coloured plumes contribute a brilliant display in mid- to late summer; deep moist soil will produce the best results. Good cultivars are 'Bressingham Beauty', deep rich pink, about 1m (3ft); 'Fanal'*, a long-flowering red, 60cm (2ft) and 'Bridal Veil'*, snowy-white, 50cm (about 1¹/2ft).

Astrantia major (Masterwort)   A vigorous, easy plant for semi-shade, with attractive, long-lasting pale green flowers, usually tinted pink or red, 60cm (2ft). *A. major* 'Sunningdale Variegated'* is a beautifully marked selection of this species, its handsome lobed leaves conspicuously splashed with cream and yellow, the typical umbels of flower following as a bonus later in the summer, as the variegation ages to green.

Bergenia   An indispensable plant for shrubaceous planting with roundish, leathery evergreen leaves and winter or early spring flowers. An adaptable plant for shade. There are some first-class hybrids of German origin, including 'Ballawley' ('Delbees'), with leaves attractively tinted red in winter and bright pink flowers in early to mid-spring, about 30cm (1ft); 'Evening Glow' ('Abendglut'), with copper-coloured winter leaves and deep crimson-purple flowers in late spring, 30cm (1ft); and 'Silverlight'* ('Silberlicht'), white-flowered, aging to pink, 30cm (1ft).

Brunnera macrophylla (*Anchusa myosotidi-flora*)   Best described as a large-leaved perennial forget-me-not, useful as groundcover and very pretty in late spring and early summer with its bright blue flowers. There is a scarce form 'Hadspen Cream'* with leaves broadly margined creamy-white, which is well worth seeking out. Shelter from cold wind is desirable. 50cm (1¹/2ft).

Campanula   Of the large family of bell-flowers there are several appropriate for planting in shrubaceous borders and island beds, notably *alliarifolia* 'Ivory Bells'. Particularly tolerant of shade, it

Astrantia major '*Sunningdale Variegated*'*.

has rosettes of soft, hairy grey-green heart-shaped leaves, from which come arching stems of creamy-white flowers, effective for a long period from early to late summer. *C. lactiflora* is taller, but also useful in this setting. Its flowers can be variable in colour and the best forms usually available are 'Prichard's Variety'*, violet-blue, and 'Loddon Anna'*, soft lilac-pink. Both 1.2–1.5m (4–5ft). *C. latifolia* is a form of the giant bellflower, very striking, with stout erect stems and large pendulous flowers, particularly 'Alba' (white) and 'Brantwood' (violet-purple), both 1.2m (4ft). Both *lactiflora* and *latifolia* cultivars are useful to give height between shrub specimens.

Crocosmia   Exciting and effective montbretia-like plants with spiky or sword-like leaves and summer flowers in startling shades of red, orange and yellow. Newer hybrids include 'Lucifer'* – a brilliant large orange-red, robust in growth to about 1m (3ft); 'Emily McKenzie', with deep orange flowers with mahogany-coloured throat, 60cm (2–2¹/2ft) and 'Solfaterre'* (H3), orange-yellow, 60cm (2–2¹/2ft). Protect corms from hard frost.

Delphiniums   Can also be used to good advantage, particularly the dainty Belladonna hybrids, generally shorter and with smaller flowers than the more conventional large-flowered hybrids. Seed-raised plants of varieties like 'Cliveden

Beauty,' single, 1m (3ft); 'Lamartine', violet-blue, 1.5m (5ft), and 'Summer Skies', sky blue, 1.5m (5ft), may show some variation in flower, but usually within acceptable limits. Vegetatively propagated cultivars of delphinium are scarce today in nurseries, and some of the old named varieties are becoming conservation items for collectors or connoisseurs. The sap and all parts of Delphinium (species and cultivars) can be irritant on contact and poisonous if eaten.

Dicentra (*Dielytra*) (Dutchman's breeches or Bleeding hearts)   Excellent in shady situations, providing dainty, fern-like, usually glaucous foliage. The shape of the flowers gives this plant its common name. *D. formosa* (*eximia*) 'Alba', 25cm (10in) tall, has white flowers and 'Luxuriant'*, 30cm (1ft) tall, deep rose flowers on graceful stems. The larger, taller *spectabilis**, while striking in flower, has the disadvantage of dying down after flowering and leaving a hole in the border! There is also a choice white variety, *spectabilis* 'Alba'*.

Epimedium (Barrenwort or Bishop's hat)   The latter name refers to the delightful flowers of this excellent groundcover plant, its flowers daintily poised on slender stems with the young leaves in spring, while the foliage remains as pleasing groundcover, adding a bonus of autumn tint. Among a number of species and hybrids the following are particularly rewarding: *perralderianum*, an Algerian species with bright yellow flowers carried in arching sprays and glossy green leaves with prickly edges, 25cm (10in); x *rubrum**, with crimson flowers and good autumn leaf colour, 30cm (1ft); x *warleyense*, a lovely and distinct hybrid with coppery-red flowers, 25cm (10in), and particularly the doyenne of the genus, x *youngianum* 'Niveum'*, a very beautiful little plant with bronze young leaves and glistening white flowers, on slender stems, 15cm (6in).

Euphorbia　Of the many spurges, the following two are appropriate for the shrubaceous border and are usually readily available: *polychroma** (*epithymoides*) produces bright yellow bracts in early spring, forming mounds 45cm (1¹/2ft) in height; *amydaloides* var. *robbiae** (Mrs Robb's spurge) is mildly invasive, but excellent groundcover, with dark evergreen rosettes on erect stems and bright yellow flowerheads, up to 45–50cm (about 1¹/2ft). E. *griffithii* 'Fireglow' is perhaps the most colourful of the hardier spurges, quickly forming large clumps up to 80cm–1m (about 3ft) high, surmounted in late spring with brilliant flame-coloured bracts contrasting well with the bright green foliage, while *E.g.* 'Dixter'* has darker foliage.

Gentiana　We usually think of gentians as low-growing mountain plants, but *asclepiadea**, the willow gentian, is an admirable plant for the shrubaceous border, with graceful arching stems and clusters of gentian-blue flowers in the axils of the leaves in late summer. There is a white form, 'Alba'. Both reach 60cm (about 2ft).

Geranium (Cranesbill)　The true hardy geraniums are among the most colourful and useful of groundcover plants, and associate magnificently with shrubs, beautiful in both leaf and flower in sun or shade – even dry shade. Among the best and most perpetual are 'Ann Folkard', golden-yellow foliage and large, black-eyed, magenta flowers, 30cm (12in); *endressii* 'Wargrave Pink'*, silvery pink, 45cm (1¹/2ft); 'Johnson's Blue'*, with

deeply cut foliage and clouds of bright blue flowers throughout the summer; and *macrorrhizum* 'Ingwersen's Variety'*, aromatic foliage, neat compact habit and shell-pink flowers from late spring to midsummer, 35cm (14in). There is also a white-flowered form, *G.m.* 'Album'*. Finally, there is the popular *wallichianum* 'Buxton's Variety'* (H3–4) with beautiful cup-shaped, violet-purple flowers with a white eye, from midsummer to early autumn. About 30cm (1ft) and slightly tender until fully established.

Gypsophila paniculata 'Rosy Veil'*　Essentially a plant for well-drained sunny positions, where it will form excellent groundcover. The mounds of grey foliage are covered throughout the summer with dainty double pink flowers and are as useful for cutting as the flowers of its taller relatives. About 30cm (1ft).

Helianthemum (Sun rose or Rock rose)　Strictly a dwarf groundcovering shrub, these have always been considered with herbaceous perennials and are indispensable sun-loving groundcover plants for the foreground of a well-drained border or island bed. A small plant will rapidly make a 60cm (2ft) wide mound or more of green or grey-green evergreen foliage, often completely covered in summer with brilliant, usually saucer-shaped flowers, in a remarkable range of colours. There are one or two good double forms. As a genus they are not long lived, but clipping when flowering is over to maintain a compact habit will keep them going for some years. They are excellent value. Some of the best cultivars are H. *nummularium* 'Amy Baring'*, clear orange, compact; H. 'Firedragon'* ('Mrs Clay'), orange-flame; 'Jubilee'*, double primrose yellow; 'Mrs C. W. Earle'*, double scarlet; 'Rhodanthe Carneum', pale pink with orange base and silvery-grey foliage; and 'Wisley Primrose'* and 'Wisley Pink' with single flowers and grey foliage.

Helleborus　A group of magnificent shade-loving, early-flowering plants which include the well-known Christmas rose, (H. *niger**) with pure white saucer-shaped flowers from early winter to early spring, 30cm (1ft), and the Lenten Rose (*orientalis*), usually available in a mixture of

colours from white and crimson to purple with delightful spotting and flecking, the cup-shaped blooms hanging on stems of up to 45cm (1¹/2ft) from midwinter to early spring. H. *foetidus* is a most rewarding plant, significant throughout winter, with panicles of green, purple-tipped nodding blooms above mounds of deeply cut evergreen leaves, 60cm (2ft). Equally evergreen, the Corsican hellebore H. *lividus corsicus** (*argutifolius*) forms clumps of leathery and spiny glaucous leaves, copper-tinted when young; apple-green, saucer-shaped flowers are produced in quantity in late winter and early spring. This is an outstanding plant. Both *foetidus* and *lividus corsicus* make an important contribution to the winter garden scene. The sap of all species and cultivars of *Helleborus* can be irritant on contact.

Hemerocallis (Day lily)　A clump-forming, long-lived herbaceous perennial, useful early in the year for its distinctive clumps of graceful, fresh green, arching leaves and during summer for its long succession of trumpet flowers borne in clusters. Prefers moist soil. Hybridists, particularly in the USA, have worked extensively on this genus; among the many cultivars available are four distinct and outstanding varieties, 'Golden Chimes'*, deep yellow, 60cm (2ft); 'Pink Damask'*, reflexed deep pink flowers, 60–75cm (2–3ft); 'Stafford', deep crimson with greenish-yellow throat, 60–75cm (2–3ft); and 'Stella d'Oro'*, dwarf and neat, with a long season of golden flowers.

Hosta (Plantain lily)　Considered by many to be the most handsome and desirable of all herbaceous plants, offering superb arching leaves in summer and erect stems of pendulous tubular or trumpet-shaped flowers from midsummer to autumn. Hostas will thrive in any fertile soil in sun or shade, provided it is moist. There has been great interest in recent years in Britain and the USA in selecting and breeding interesting new cultivars. The late Eric Smith, Hillier's herbaceous propagator in the 1950s and early 60s, bred a number of new hybrids involving the late-flowering species H. *tardiflora* and contributing in no small measure to the popularity of the genus. Some of his hybrids are now being extensively propagated, and specialist societies promote the genus enthusiastically. Among the many species and hybrids commercially available, the following are particularly outstanding: 'August Moon', a USA introduction, with large, golden-yellow leaves which hold their colour well throughout the summer, even in a sunny situation; flowers are pale mauve, 60cm (2ft); *crispula**, although now scarce remains one of the choicest and most elegant of variegated species; 'Elegans'* (sieboldiana 'Elegans') has some of the largest leaves of any hosta, corrugated and silvery-grey, 60cm (2ft); *fortunei* 'Albopicta'* is most striking in late spring and early summer, when its clumps of broad oval leaves are bright yellow with a contrasting green edge; the flowers are lilac in mid- to late summer, 50–60cm (1¹/2–2ft); 'Frances Williams'* is an outstanding cultivar, in effect 'Elegans' with unusual beige-yellow variegation and mauve flowers from early to late summer, up to 1m (3ft); *lancifolia** is quite distinct with small clumps of narrow, shining deep-green leaves and quantities of lilac or violet flowers from midsummer to early autumn – a splendid contrast with the larger-leaved species; 'Royal Standard'* is a hybrid of *plantaginea*, with pale green, prominently veined leaves and scented white tubular flowers in late summer and autumn; 'Thomas Hogg' has deep green leaves with broad creamy-white margins and remains one of the most reliable variegated varieties; the flowers are deep lilac in early to mid-summer, 60cm (2ft); var. *undulata** produces neat clumps of leaves with wavy margins and prominent central white variegation; 'Halcyon*' is an Eric Smith *tardiana* hybrid, forming mounds of bright silvery-grey leaves of good substance and deep lilac flowers in mid- to late summer, 45cm (1¹/2ft); *ventricosa* 'Variegata'* is one of the best and most handsome of all variegated hostas, with large, shining, heart-shaped leaves generously edged with gold; unusual deep-blue flowers are produced in mid- to late summer, about 60–90cm (2–3ft).

Note that slugs and snails will cause great damage to the hairless, unprotected leaves of hostas. Wage war with slug and snail pellets, and liquid slug killer, if you wish to enjoy your hostas at their best. These pests are most active in moist, warm, summer weather.

You can have the best of both worlds by associating hostas with some of the best daffodil varieties, which can be planted in groups on the fringes of the clumps. After they have performed in the early spring, the dying foliage of the daffodils is soon covered by the arching leaves of the hostas.

Iris   Of this large and diverse genus a select few species and varieties are particularly useful and effective in shrubaceous borders, *I. foetidissima*, (Gladwyn iris) is remarkably shade tolerant. Its evergreen leaves and showy scarlet seeds in winter compensate well for its dingy lilac-blue flowers; its cultivar 'Variegata' has leaves longitudinally striped creamy white; both reach 60–75cm (2–2¹/2ft); *pallida* Argentea/Variegata' is a very striking plant throughout the growing season, its blue-grey sword-like leaves generously striped creamy white; *p.* 'Aurea Variegata' is a scarcer plant with golden variegated leaves; both have excellent large mid-blue flowers, well worthy of a sunny, well-drained focal point; *unguicularis** (*stylosa*) the lavender-blue, winter-flowering Algerian iris, is well known and indispensable for a hot, dry, sunny position; its cultivar 'Mary Barnard' is a violet-purple, free-flowering form worth seeking out. The sap from leaves, seeds and rhizomes of most *Iris* species and cultivars can be irritant on contact or poisonous if eaten.

Kirengeshoma palmata*   A typical native of Japan, its elegant palmate foliage is reminiscent of the Japanese maple. Prefers a moist and shaded situation. In late summer and autumn, tubular, waxy, canary-yellow bellflowers appear poised on stems up to about 1m (3ft).

Kniphofia (*Tritoma*) (Red hot poker or Torch lily)   Of great value as an accent point in foreground or middle distance, and to provide a bold effect. In some species the yucca-like foliage is evergreen or near evergreen. *K. caulescens** (H3–4), with bicolor flowers, of buff-yellow and salmon-red in early summer set against broad, glaucous foliage is a distinct and worthwhile species, about 1m (3ft); a delightful dwarf species *galpinii** (H3–4) is invaluable for its late, saffron-orange flowers produced in early to mid-autumn amid grass-like foliage, 60–75cm (2–2¹/2ft) – regrettably, the correctly named plant is now scarce in cultivation* (H3–4) *triangularis* is usually offered as a near substitute. An ever-changing range of named hybrids in many shades and combinations of yellow, scarlet and orange is offered today by nurserymen. 'Samuel's

Kniphofia caulescens*. *Though often variable in leaf, this hardy evergreen species usually produces the bicolour flowerheads at midsummer.*

Key: * = AGM 1993   H4 = Hardy   H3 = Hardy in mild areas   H2 = Requires protection   H1 = Usually a greenhouse plant

Sensation'*, vivid scarlet, 1–5m (5ft); 'Little Maid'* (H3–4), yellow shading to ivory-white, 60–75cm (2–2¹/2ft); and 'Shining Sceptre', golden orange, 1m (3ft), are excellent new varieties.

Lamium (Deadnettle)   Excellent ground-cover. *L. maculatum* (Spotted deadnettle) has a prominent central white stripe to its leaves and pink-purple flowers in late spring; it can be invasive and may require some controlling. 'Beacon Silver', with smaller, bright silvery leaves with narrow green margins and pink flowers, is much less invasive and no more than 10cm (4in), while 'White Nancy'* is an excellent newcomer with white flowers freely produced.

Lavandula   A familiar and much-loved garden plant, lavender makes excellent dwarf hedges and associates well with stonework and rose plantings, and can also be used effectively in groups in the foreground of shrubaceous borders or island beds. Essentially a maritime plant, it succeeds almost anywhere in well-drained conditions and an open sunny site. All species and varieties are aro-

matic, and there is now some variation in colour and habit. In addition to the familiar *angustifolia* (*spica*), the old English lavender, notable cultivars are 'Alba', with narrow grey-green leaves and white flowers on erect stems in early summer, about 1m (3ft); 'Hidcote'* ('Nana Atropurpurea'), perhaps the most pop-ular, and certainly the most compact form, with narrow grey-green leaves and dense violet spikes, 60cm (2ft); 'Munstead', which can best be described as a compact dwarf form of the old English lavender, producing typical lavender-blue flowers in midsummer; and to complete the colour range, a neat, com-pact, narrow-leaved form 'Rosea', with lavender-pink flowers in midsummer, 60cm (2ft). *L. vera,** the Dutch lavender, has distinctly broader grey leaves with lavender-blue flowers and is of robust growth, up to about 1m (3ft). A striking and worthy newcomer to commerce is L. *stoechas* subsp. *pedunculata** ('Papillon') (H3), a form of the French lavender with 'butterfly-wing' petals emerging from the top of the purple flower spikes in early to midsummer; very aromatic, 1m (3ft).

Lavandula stoechas *subsp.* pedunculata*(H3) *('Papillon').*

Liriope muscari*   A shade-tolerant member of the lily family, making clumps of arching, evergreen grass-like foliage. Grape-hyacinth-like violet-purple spikes of bell-shaped flowers appear as late as early to mid-autumn. A useful and unusual groundcover plant worthy of wider use. 45cm (1¹/2ft).

Lysimachia (Loosestrife)   Excellent ground-cover and a spectacular flowering plant. *L. clethroides** forms clumps of graceful arching stems terminating in racemes of white clethra-like flowers from mid-summer to early autumn; the long, wil-lowy, leaves tint well in the autumn, about 1m (3ft); *nummularia* (Creeping Jenny) makes most useful low ground-cover in shady places or on moist banks. A familiar cottage-garden plant, its bright yellow flowers show up well against the dark green leaves. There is also a yellow-leaved form, 'Aurea'*, 5cm (2in); *punctata* is taller and very conspicuous, with whorls of bright yellow flowers in mid- to late summer. It associates well with *Lythrum*, enjoying moist border or waterside conditions; 1m (3ft).

Lythrum (Purple loosestrife)   Selected forms make showy border plants and are excellent by water. *L. salicaria* 'Firecandle'* produces spikes of bright rose-red in mid- to late summer, 1.5m (5ft). A more dwarf plant, *virgatum* 'Rose Queen' has bright rose-purple flowers, not usually exceeding 60cm (2ft).

Nepeta x *faassenii* (Catmint) (H3)   A familiar and invaluable edging and groundcovering plant, up to 30cm (1ft) high, with aromatic grey foliage and spikes of lavender-mauve flowers produced from late spring to early autumn. 'Six Hills Giant' is slightly taller, 60cm (2ft), and hardier. Associates well with *Alchemilla mollis* and is best in a sunny, well-drained position; spring planting is recommended.

Ophiopogon planiscapus 'Nigrescens'*   Distinct and unusual as low-growing groundcover, with blackish-purple evergreen leaves in grass-like tufts, small white flowers in late summer and then black berries. Adaptable to sunshine or shade. 10cm (4in). Slow growing.

Pachysandra terminalis   A most useful evergreen, shrubby, carpeting plant. Toothed leaves are clustered at stem tips, and small whitish flowers are produced in late winter to early spring. 'Variegata'* is the form with silver-variegated leaves. Both about 15cm (6in) high, they make reliable, if slow, groundcover in shade.

Paeonia   Paeonies are much-loved and long-lived garden plants for sunshine and semi-shade. Established clumps produce spectacular double or single flowers from the end of spring until midsummer. The foliage often tints crimson in autumn. Among the many varieties usually available, the following are particularly notable for their large scented blooms: 'Bowl of Beauty'*, large semi-double, deep pink with creamy centre; 'Duchesse de Nemours'*, double cream, fading white, fragrant blooms; 'Felix Crousse'*, double, deep crimson; 'Sarah Bernhardt'*, apple-blossom pink, double. The old-fashioned cottage garden paeonies, so reliable and

spectacular in flower each year, are regrettably not scented. Choose from officinalis 'Alba Plena', double white; 'Rosea Plena'*, double pink; and 'Rubra Plena'*, double, deep crimson, all reaching about 75cm (2¹/2ft). *P. peregrina* (*lobata*) 'Sunshine'* is distinct with large, single salmon-orange flowers in late spring, 75cm (2¹/2ft).

Phlox   The border phlox, with their wide range of colours, are among the most desirable of plants, particularly for moist semi-shade, producing fragrant blooms from midsummer to early autumn. Regrettably, they are not without problems, and sometimes are not the easiest plants to establish. Check before buying that container-grown plants do not bear signs of eelworm infection – usually evident in poor brittle growth and puckered, distorted leaves. Excellent, well-tried varieties still commercially available include: *maculata* 'Alpha'*, with tapering spikes of pink flowers, 60–75cm (2–2¹/2ft) and the following *paniculata* (*decussata*) varieties: 'Dodo Hanbury Forbes'*, clear pink, 1m (3ft); 'Harlequin' with leaves variegated creamy-white and violet flowers which contrast well, 1m (3ft); 'Marlborough', compact habit and purple flowers, 1m (3ft); 'Prince of Orange'*, large orange panicles, 60cm (2ft); 'Sandringham', large pink flowers with darker centre, 75cm (2¹/2ft); 'Brigadier'*, perhaps the best red available, about 1m (3ft); and 'White Admiral'*, the best white variety , 75cm (2¹/2ft).

Polygonatum x *hybridum* (Solomon's seal)   A familiar and invaluable plant for the shadiest of conditions under trees, with white, hanging, bell-like flowers in spring and graceful arching stems, up to 75cm (2¹/2ft) tall, and clothed with pointed ovate leaves.

Persicaria (*Polygonum*)   A large and varied genus containing many weedy plants of no horticultural value, as well as a number of rampant plants suitable for waterside and naturalising. Hardy species particularly appropriate for shrubaceous borders include *bistorta* 'Superbum'*, a compact large-flowered form of the wild bistort, producing long cylindrical spikes of bright pink flowers in midsummer and

again in early autumn, 60cm (2ft); *campanulatum*, mildly invasive, but controllable and well worthy of a border position, with grey-green pointed leaves and pale pink flowers over an extended period in summer, 1m (3ft); *vacciniifolium**, which forms mats of wiry trailing stems, conspicuous well into the autumn, with spikes of bright pink flowers; 15cm (6in), and excellent low groundcover.

Potentilla   Although many people think of potentillas as shrubs, there are a number of worthy herbaceous species and cultivars which make excellent, showy, free-flowering groundcover, notably *nepalensis* 'Miss Willmott*', with sprawling masses of strawberry-like foliage and carmine-pink flowers throughout the summer, 30–50cm (1–1¹/2ft) and 'Gibson's Scarlet'*, with large, single vivid red flowers and a similar habit, 50cm (1¹/2ft).

Pulmonaria (Lungwort)   A most attractive and useful spring-flowering, shade-tolerant groundcover plant. *P. angustifolia** has gentian-blue hanging bells and associates well with the common primrose, 15–25cm (6–10in); *rubra** is vigorous and reliable, with excellent soft red flowers, 25cm (10in); *saccharata* has white marbled foliage and flowers of variable colour from pink to blue; *s.* 'Pink Dawn', has been selected for its distinct flower colour, 25cm (10in). Forms of *saccharata* showing exceptional silvery leaf variation are worth seeking out and can be most effective in shady areas – one has been named 'Argentea'*. Pulmonarias are useful in dry shade.

Rodgersia   Handsome plants for moist soil in sun or shade, notable as much for their distinct and variable foliage as for their complementary spikes of white or pink flowers, produced in early to midsummer. They associate well with waterside plantings: *aesculifolia** has horse chestnut-like leaves and white flowers, 1.2m (4ft); *pinnata* 'Superba'* has bronze-tinted pinnate leaves and clear pink flowers, 75cm–1m (2¹/2–3ft); *tabularis* is very distinct, with flat, parasol-like pale leaves and spikes of creamy-white flowers, 60–75cm (2–2¹/2ft).

Rudbeckia (Cone flower or Black-eyed Susan)   Easy and effective border plants, particularly *fulgida* 'Goldsturm'* *(sulli-*

Stachys macrantha 'Robusta'* – an
excellent, vigorous and showy groundcover
plant and form of a British native

vantii 'Goldsturm'), a fine plant with stiff stems and masses of golden, black-centred daisy flowers with pointed petals from midsummer to early autumn, 75cm (2¹/2ft).

Ruta graveolens 'Jackman's Blue'* A much improved selected form of the long-cultivated medicinal herb rue. Bright yellow flowers contrast well with the glaucous blue, much-divided foliage, which is pungently aromatic when touched. Prune back in the spring to maintain a compact habit (60cm/2ft) – but be sure to wear gloves, as contact with sap or foliage can cause a serious skin rash.

Salvia The hardier herbaceous and sub-shrubby species of sage are among the most effective groundcovering and decorative plants for the border. They include the common sage, *officinalis*, with aromatic grey-green foliage and blue-purple flowers, much valued as a pot herb. Several cultivars have variegated or coloured leaves, particularly 'Icterina'* (H3–4), variegated green and gold, 'Purpurascens'*, with stems and leaves suffused purple; and 'Tricolor' (H3), of more compact habit and less robust growth, its leaves splashed with creamy-white and suffused purple and pink; all up to 60cm (2ft). *S. nemorosa* 'Lubecca' ('Compacta') has dense spikes of rich purple flowers in the summer (a compact form of an old border favourite), 50–60cm (1¹/2–2ft).

Santolina (Cotton lavender) Invaluable, dense, low-growing evergreen shrubs with usually grey foliage and dainty, button-like yellow flowers. They associate well with sages and lavenders and are best in a dry, sunny situation. *S. chamaecyparissus* (*incana*) has densely woolly, silver-hued foliage and lemon-yellow flowers, 50–60cm (1¹/2–2ft); the Corsican form of this, *S. c. nana** (*corsica*), is distinctly more compact, about 30cm (1ft); *pinnata* subsp. *neapolitana** has less dense finely divided grey-green foliage and primrose yellow flowers, 60cm (2ft); *rosmarinifolia* 'Primrose Gem'* has a dense, rounded habit with vivid green leaves, contrasting well with lemon-yellow flowers, 60cm (2ft).

Sedum Most of the smaller-leaved species of this large family are suited to the rock garden, but larger-leaved kinds make good border plants for sunny situations, their late summer and autumn flowers attractive to butterflies and bees. Among the best available are 'Autumn Joy'*, with large, long-lasting salmon-pink flowers, bronze tinted in autumn, about 50cm (1¹/2ft) and 'Ruby Glow'*, a first-class plant of lax habit with deep ruby-red flowers looking good against the blue-grey foliage in autumn, about 25cm (10in).

Smilacina racemosa A handsome plant, its foliage reminiscent of Solomon's seal and liking similar shady conditions. Distinct in its panicles of creamy-white flowers in late spring and early summer, 60cm (2ft).

Stachys Several species make excellent groundcover, notably *macrantha* 'Robusta'*, a vigorous and effective groundcover plant with broadly ovate, downy leaves and large rosy-violet hooded flowers in spiked whorls in late spring and early summer, excellent with old-fashioned roses and worthy of wider planting, 50cm (1¹/2ft). The more familiar *olympica* (*lanata* – Lamb's ears) has silvery-grey felt-like leaves, and spikes of purple-pink flowers in midsummer. The non-flowering form 'Silver Carpet', 10–20cm (4–8in) is the best form to plant for effective grey groundcover in dry, sunny situations.

*Tiarella cordifolia** (Foam flower) Excellent groundcover in shady places and not invasive. Spikes of white flowers in feathery masses are produced in late spring and early summer, 25cm (10in).

Vinca (Periwinkle) Popular, much planted, trailing evergreens which thrive in sun or shade. While *major* (Greater periwinkle), is a rampant grower suitable for unsightly banks, its variegated form 'Variegata'* ('Elegantissima') is less invasive and has brightly margined creamy-white leaves. Both have bright blue flowers from late spring to early autumn, and reach about 50cm (1¹/2ft). *V. minor* (Lesser periwinkle), makes neat and pleasing groundcover and is much smaller and more prostrate. Of a number of cultivars the following are particularly rewarding in flower. 'La Grave'* ('Bowles Variety'), single azure-blue; 'Gertrude Jekyll'*, with glistening white flowers, well worthy of the name it bears; and 'Variegata' with leaves marginally-variegated creamy-white, and blue flowers.

Waldsteinia ternata A most useful low and effective carpeting plant of the strawberry family. Neat carpets of trifoliate hairy leaves persist well; bright yellow flowers in the spring make a pleasing contrast. Sun or semi-shade. 10cm (4in).

PLANTS FOR SPECIAL FEATURES

This section has been designed to help you select plants for a variety of different garden situations. It includes as many as possible of the plants which have been accorded an Award of Garden Merit 1993, indicated (as elsewhere) by an asterisk* (see p152 for further details). Unless otherwise indicated, all plants in the lists are hardy (H4). (See p 116.)

COURTYARDS, TERRACES AND PATIOS

Most gardens today have a sitting area, sometimes no more than a few concrete slabs, catching the sun for most of the day. More favoured gardens have a patio or terrace of patterned paving, perhaps relieved with areas of brick and gravel. A few people are proud possessors of a courtyard, paved with natural stone, where there may be areas of warm sunshine or cool shade and shelter from the wind.

The design and construction of these desirable features are discussed elsewhere (see pp 42–51). Here, suitable plants are recommended to complement such areas: shrubs, shrub roses, associated herbaceous plants and, perhaps, a tree to delight the eye and provide colour and interest at all seasons when viewed from the house. Scent of flower and foliage is very important, while the ultimate shape, size and vigour of shrubs and plants must be considered in order to create an interesting and effective blend. Of course, many of the essentially hardy, compact or smaller-growing subjects considered in Chapter 8, and in the lists of shrubs and plants for shrubaceous borders, are equally appropriate here, but in these sheltered walled areas against the house, we can – with a good chance of more permanent success – grow a considerable range of borderline hardy shrubs, plants and climbers which may not be possible elsewhere in the garden.

Sunny house wall border – Cytisus battandieri *with compact form 'Yellow Tail' (inset);* Cistus x purpureus* *(bottom left) and* Helichrysum italicum* *– grey leaves yellow flowers (under window).*

When planting, it is worth ensuring that there is good drainage and adequate space to accommodate the wall shrubs and plants you wish to grow. A well-prepared border is best given as much width as can be spared, and is so much better than removing a single slab.

Paved areas invite the use of tubs, pots, urns and similar ornamental containers. While these are frequently used for annuals for spring or summer display, permanent planting is certainly possible, but should be carefully chosen – variegated evergreens, some of which can be clipped to any reasonable shape and size, are good choices.

The following is a carefully considered selection of suitable plants to choose from, including some newer introductions – there are, of course, many more possibilities.

CLIMBERS FOR SUN

Climbing or pillar roses can provide scented and perpetual or recurrent flower where there is adequate height or space between windows. Particularly good value are:

. . . .

'Aloha' Deep rose-pink, perpetual.
'Dublin Bay'* Recurrent, double, deep red.
'Iceberg' The climbing version* of perhaps the most popular white rose.
'Maigold'* Vigorous, early, gold with a bronze sheen.

. . . .

Clematis will often blend in well with roses and live happily with them, particularly the less vigorous large-flowered hybrids, for example 'Henryi'*, creamy-white with two periods of flower, and 'Hagley Hybrid', soft shell-pink from early summer to early autumn. Some of the species could also be included, notably:

. . . .

C. *alpina* 'Frances Rivis'* Blue with white centre; 'Ruby', purple-pink intermittently through summer. *macropetala* 'Lagoon'* The best deep blue form of this double-flowered species; 'Markham's Pink'* a

Key: * = AGM 1993   H4 = Hardy   H3 = Hardy in mild areas   H2 = Requires protection   H1 = Usually a greenhouse plant

delightful form, the lantern-like pink flowers in spring are followed by attractive seed heads. *montana* 'Tetrarose'* A superb hybrid of compact, strong growth, lilac-rose flowers and bronze spring foliage. *rehderiana** Delightful cowslip-scented pale yellow bell flowers in late summer and autumn.

CLIMBERS FOR SHADE
Honeysuckles (*Lonicera*) can provide good coverage and satisfying fragrance, particularly:

Lonicera x *americana** Pale to deep yellow with purple tint in early to midsummer. *periclymenum* 'Graham Thomas'* A superb selection of the common woodbine. Regrettably, not all honeysuckles are as fragrant as this one, flowering from late spring until autumn.

Variegated ivies which are self-clinging are also excellent:

Hedera canariensis 'Gloire de Marengo* (H3) has silver-grey-white/variegated foliage. *H. colchica* 'Dentata Variegata'*, creamy-yellow marginal variegation to the large leaves, while variegated forms of the common ivy (*H. helix*) can be most effective for smaller areas. 'Glacier'* (H3–4), has silvery-grey leaves with a white margin, and 'Goldchild'* (H3–4), which has yellow margined leaves.

All ivies have sap which can be irritant on contact.

WALL SHRUBS FOR SUN AND SHADE
As space permits, wall shrubs trained to trellis or wire and suitably pruned are of good value as background shrubs – dwarf planting is seen to good advantage against them. Consider particularly:

Ceanothus arboreus 'Trewithen Blue'* (H3) (E) Large leaves and deep blue spring flowers make this a superb wall shrub. *Cytisus battandieri** (Moroccan broom) (E) Justifiably popular and an excellent wall shrub, with pineapple-scented cone-shaped clusters of yellow flowers, seen well against the silky grey foliage in

midsummer. The scarce cultivar 'Yellow Tail' has extra-long spikes and a more compact habit. Best in a sunny site. *Euonymus fortunei* 'Silver Queen'* (E) (Sh) Provides striking creamy marginal variegation year-round and with some initial help is self-supporting. *Pyracantha* 'Soleil d'Or' (E) (Sh) With orange-yellow fruits, this firethorn is free-fruiting. *Robinia hispida* 'Macrophylla' The large-leaved form of rose acacia is best grown against a sunny wall, where its brittle branches can be well supported. Clusters of rose-pink pea flowers are spectacular midsummer. *Solanum crispum* 'Glasnevin'* (H3) (Semi-E) An easy climber for sunny fence or wall, yellow-centred purple-blue flowers are produced generously through summer and autumn.

SHRUBS
The following is a shortlist of some of the most desirable shrubs for patios and courtyards, most of them dwarf, mound-forming or of compact habit. Do not plant too closely and consider the ultimate size of the shrub, even allowing for some pruning.

Many familiar plants, for example, *Cistus* x *purpureus*, *Convolvulus cneorum*, *Daphne* x *burkwoodii*, *Euonymus fortunei*, 'Emerald Gaiety' or one of the many hebes, will fulfil the useful function of covering unsightly, leggy stems if set at the base of climbing rose or clematis. The climbers, particularly clematis, will also appreciate the shading of their roots and lower stems and respond with enhanced performance.

Abelia Particularly *chinensis*, 'Edward Goucher' and x *grandiflora*. (Semi-E) *Abeliophyllum distichum*. *Acer palmatum* (Japanese maples) 'Crimson Queen'* and 'Butterfly'*; *A. shirasawanum* (*japonicum*) 'Aureum'* (Sh); 'Dissectum' cultivars. (Sh)(T) (See Chapter 8.) *Camellia* Among the multitude of varieties available, outstanding are *japonica* 'Adolphe Audusson'*, blood-red with prominent golden stamens; x *williamsii*

Camellia x williamsii 'Donation' is still perhaps the most reliable, spectacular and readily available camellia, adaptable for wall, border or tub culture.*

'E. T. R. Carlyon'*, a good late-flowering semi-double to double pure white, and 'Donation'*, silvery-pink, beautifully veined semi-double. Bushy upright habit (A) (T) (E) (Sh) *Ceanothus* 'Blue Mound'* (H3) (E) *Choisya ternata**; *t.* 'Sundance'* (H3); and 'Aztec Pearl'* (E) *Cistus* (Sun rose) Particularly x *aguilari* 'Maculatus'* (H3), 'Peggy Sammons'* (H3), x *purpureus** (H3), and x *skanbergii** (H3) (E). Good drainage essential. *Convolvulus cneorum** (H3) One of the finest grey-foliaged plants for a patio. (E) *Daphne* Many of the species and cultivars, and particularly *bholua* 'Jacqueline Postill'*, x *burkwoodii**, *cneorum** and cultivars, *collina**, x *mantensiana* 'Manten', *odora* 'Aureomarginata', *retusa**. All (E) except x *burkwoodii* (Semi-E) *Euonymus* Several species and cultivars, particularly the following, which are adaptable to sunshine or shade and will climb a low wall: *fortunei* 'Emerald Gaiety'*, 'Emerald 'n' Gold'*, 'Silver Queen'*. (T) (E) *Fabiana imbricata* 'Violacea'* (H3) (E) *Fuchsia* Many hardy cultivars, particularly 'Chillerton Beauty', 'Lady Thumb', 'Lena', 'Mdme Cornellisen', 'Versicolor', 'Prosperity' and 'Tom Thumb'. All * (H3). (T) (Sh) x *Fatshedera lizei** (H2–3). (Sh) (E)

(Sh) = Shady site desirable   (A) = Acid soil essential   (E) = Evergreen   (T) = Good for tub or container

Fuchsia *'Prosperity'** is one of the few near-hardy double-flowered fuchsias and is upright and vigorous.

x *Halimiocistus wintonensis* and 'Merristwood Cream', and *Halimium ocymoides*. All * (H3). (E)

Hebe   Many species and cultivars, particularly *albicans**, and its new cultivar 'Red Edge'*; 'Blue Clouds'* (H3,) flowering from early summer to early winter; *colensoi* 'Glauca'; *cupressoides* 'Boughton Dome'* (H3–4) x *franciscana* 'Variegata'* (H2); 'Great Orme'* (H3); *pimeleoides* 'Quicksilver'*; *recurva* 'Boughton Silver'* (H3); *parvifolia angustifolia** ('Spender's Seedling'). (E) (T).

Hedera   Including some ivies relatively new to commerce – mound-forming, some variegated and some quite different: 'Pedata' ('Caenwoodiana'), 'Ivalace', 'Little Diamond' (H3–4), 'Manda's Crested'*. All * (Sh) (T) (E).

Helichrysum   Particularly *italicum** (H3) and *splendidum**. (E)

Hydrangea   Many species and cultivars. Some exciting and compact newcomers include *arborescens* 'Annabelle'*, 'Ayesha'*, *involucrata* 'Hortensis'*; in the hortensia group, 'Ami Pasquier'* and 'Madame Emile Moullière'*; in the lacecap group, the unique 'Geoffrey

Chadbund'*, a remarkable light red unaffected by differing soils; 'Blue Ware' and 'Tricolor'* as much for its variegated leaves as for its flower; *paniculata* 'Praecox'* for midsummer flower and 'Tardiva' with its stiff erect spikes in mid-autumn; *aspera* subsp. *sargentiana** and 'Villosa' for bold foliage; and *serrata* 'Preziosa'* for rose-pink flowers in quantity and purple-tinted leaves and stems. (Sh) (T)

Hypericum   Of the many St John's Worts, very rewarding and less frequently planted are x *cyathiflorum* 'Gold Cup', with its arching branches, and *kouytchense**, with bright red fruits.

Mimulus aurantiacus* (H2–3) (Shrubby musk). (E)

Myrtus (E)   Particularly the new *luma* 'Glanleam Gold' (H3) and *communis* subsp. *tarentina** (H3). (T) (E)

Nandina domestica* (H3) and 'Nana Purpurea' (E)

Ozothamnus ledifolius* and *rosmarinifolius* 'Silver Jubilee'* (H3). (E) (T)

Paeonia suffruticosa (Moutain tree paeony) Superb varieties are available, double or semi-double in pink, red and white.

Perovskia atriplicifolia 'Blue Spire'*.

Philadelphus (Mock orange)   Particularly 'Belle Etoile*', 'Manteau d'Hermine'*, 'Sybille'* and *coronarius* 'Variegatus'*.

Phlomis (E) *chrysophylla** (H3), *fruticosa**, *italica*.

Phormium (New Zealand flax)   Many exciting forms with highly coloured and variegated leaves, which have been introduced recently from New Zealand. The larger ones are excellent in the patio border, while weaker growers make excellent tub or container plants: take care that they do not become frozen in winter in a container – they can be put in the garage or cold greenhouse for the hardest weather period. Among the best are *cookianum* 'Cream Delight'* (H3), 'Tricolor'* (H3–4), 'Dazzler', 'Maori Sunrise', 'Sundowner'* (H3) (T) and *tenax* 'Variegata'* (H3–4). (E)

Photinia x *fraseri* 'Red Robin'*. Red young shoots on all soils. (E)

Phygelius   Hillier's Peter Dummer has produced a range of exciting new hybrids. Outstanding are x *rectus* 'Salmon Leap', 'Devil's Tears', 'Moonraker' and 'Winchester Fanfare', all making excellent patio plants. (E)

Pieris   Particularly 'Flaming Silver'* and 'Forest Flame'*; *japonica* 'Little Heath'*, a new compact and bushy plant with white margined leaves and coppery young growth; *j*. 'White Rim'* ('Variegata') and 'Valley Valentine'. All * (A) (T) (E)

Phygelius x rectus *'Winchester Fanfare'* – the first and still among the best of Hillier propagator Peter Dummer's renowned hybrids.

Key: * = AGM 1993   H4 = Hardy   H3 = Hardy in mild areas   H2 = Requires protection   H1 = Usually a greenhouse plant

Potentilla fruticosa 'Tangerine' keeps its flower colour best in semi-shade.*

Pittosporum   Well worth a carefully chosen sheltered site; *eugenoides* 'Variegatum', 'Garnettii', *tenuifolium*, wonderful for screening and clippable, *t.* 'Tom Thumb' and *t.* 'Warnham Gold'. All * (H3). (T) (E)

Potentilla   Of the many available, try particularly *arbuscula* 'Beesii'*, *fruticosa* 'Daydawn'*, 'Elizabeth'*, 'Red Ace'* (Sh), 'Tangerine'* (Sh), and 'Tilford Cream'*.

*Prunus tenell*a 'Fire Hill'* and 'Dwarf Russian Almond'.

Punica granatum 'Nana' (Dwarf pomegranate) (H3). (T)

Rhaphiolepis x *delacourii* 'Coates' Crimson' (H3). Leathery-leaved dwarf with summer flowers. (E) (T)

Rhamnus alaterna 'Argenteovariegata'*. Fast growing variegated evergreen – clippable. (E)

Rhododendron (including *Azalea*)   Among the multitude of species and cultivars available today, particularly of note for compact dwarf growth, interesting leaf and reliable flower are: calostrotum 'Gigha', *dauricum* 'Midwinter', and the incomparable, irresistible *yakushimanum* 'Koichiro Wada'. Among the hybrids are 'Brocade', 'Curlew', 'Elizabeth Hobbie', 'Golden Torch' and 'Winsome'. There is also a large range of dwarf evergreen Japanese azaleas to choose from; particularly good are: 'Blaauw's Pink', 'Kure-no-yuki', 'Rosebud' and 'Vuyk's Scarlet'. All * (A) (Sh) (T) (E)

Rosmarinus officinalis   'Severn Sea'* and 'Benenden'* (H3). (T) (E)

Skimmia japonica cultivars. (E) (T) (Sh)

Sarcococca hookeriana var. *humilis*. Scented winter flowers, gloosy leaves, black berries. (E) (T) (Sh)

Spiraea japonica   'Goldflame', 'Shiburi', ('Shirobana') ,and 'Nana' ('Alpina'). All * (Sh)

Viburnum davidii, x *juddii* and *tinus* 'Eve Price'. All * (Sh)

Yucca (E) Excellent variegated cultivars include *filamentosa* 'Bright Edge'* and *flaccida* 'Golden Sword'*. Both (H3). (T)

Zenobia pulverulenta   Little-known shrub with aniseed-scented white blooms in pendulous clusters in spring and bloomy, grey-blue leaves and young shoots. Worthy of wider planting. Acid soil required. (A) (Sh) (Semi-E)

....

ROSES

Roses, particularly shrub roses, including old-fashioned, bourbon, china and hybrid musk, are invaluable for flower and fragrance near the house. Some of the best and most compact and free-flowering, in a variety of colours, include:

....

Species roses and their hybrids
chinensis 'Mutabilis'* (H3–4), *gallica* 'Versicolor'*, (Rosa Mundi), *moyesii* 'Geranium'* and *rugosa* 'Fru Dagmar Hastrup'*.

Bourbon roses   'Boule de Neige', 'Gipsy Boy'* and 'Zéphirine Drouhin'*.

Hybrid musk roses   'Ballerina'*, 'Buff

Beauty'*, 'Felicia'*, 'Penelope'*.

Modern shrub roses   'Blanc Double de Coubert'*, 'Golden Wings'*, the excellent new 'Graham Thomas'*, 'Marguerite Hilling'*, and 'Marjorie Fair' (red with white eye), and 'Scarlet Fire'* ('Schlarlachglut').

Old-fashioned roses   So desirable for their scent: 'Charles de Mills'*, 'Fantin Latour'*, 'Maiden's Blush', 'Madame Hardy'* and 'Shailer's White Moss'*.

English roses   Exciting new compact roses combining the scent and flower shape of the best of the old roses with the colour range and continuous flowering of some modern cultivars: 'Abraham Darby', 'Fisherman's Friend', 'Mary Rose' and 'Winchester Cathedral' are particularly recommended.

Patio roses   Bred with this setting in mind, these are neat, compact and disease free, usually with groundcovering potential, and marvellous in the foreground and in association with grey-foliage shrubs like lavender, *Santolina* and *Helianthemum*. Try particularly: 'Elegant Pearl', single creamy-white; 'Gentle Touch'*, pale pink hybrid tea blooms in clusters and Rose of the Year 1986; 'Robin Redbreast', dark red with white eye, bushy and spreading, and 'Sweet Magic'*, double golden-orange, joint Rose of the Year, 1987.

Groundcover Rose 'Nozomi' is a reliable performer, adaptable and versatile; excellent for slopes, low walls. Try it in a tub but do not forget to feed it!*

(Sh) = Shady site desirable   (A) = Acid soil essential   (E) = Evergreen   (T) = Good for tub or container

Groundcovering and mound-forming roses   These free-flowering roses are often listed confusingly under ramblers or modern shrub roses; particularly notable and reliable are 'Bonica'*, rose pink, recurrent, cupped blooms, mound-forming, slowly to about 75cm (2¹/₂ft); 'The Fairy'*, a delightful groundcovering rose with small shiny leaves and sprays of rose-pink flowers from midsummer until late autumn; 'Little White Pet'*, double white, mound-forming, to 60cm (2ft); 'Nozomi'*, single pearly pink, prostrate arching growth; 'Rosy Cushion'*, vigorous, large single pink flowers with ivory centres, to 1m (3ft); 'Suma'*, a miniature climber or groundcover, ruby-red with yellow stamens.

....

HERBACEOUS PERENNIALS
Below are listed some good companions to 'live-in' with your shrubs and roses – again, many of those listed under plants for shrubaceous borders (see pp116–22) are equally appropriate, so included here are those which are less hardy or require the shelter afforded by patio areas.

....

Acaena (New Zealand burr)   The grey-green *buchananii* and the bronze-leaved *microphylla**, with its startling red, spiny burrs, make excellent carpeting or paving plants. 5cm (2in).

*Acanthus spinosus**   The 'architect's plant' fits well in these conditions.

Agapanthus (Lily of the Nile)   Particularly the hardier though variable Headbourne Hybrids; good, named cultivars are now becoming available, notably 'Loch Hope'*, 'Isis' and 'Lilliput' (All H3). Excellent in tubs or containers.

*Alchemilla mollis** (Lady's mantle)   Needs no introduction.

Anemone x *hybrida* (Japanese anemone)   Excellent for late summer and autumn effect, and long lived. Particularly good are 'Honorine Jobert'* (white) and 'Queen Charlotte'* (pink)

Artemisia absinthium 'Lambrook Silver'   Associates well with shrub roses.

Campanula alliarifolia 'Ivory Bells'   Shade tolerant, and looks good with shrub roses, as does the taller *lactiflora* 'Prichard's Variety'*, its rich blue flowers reaching about 1m (3ft).

Carex hachÿoeonsis (*morrowii*) 'Evergold'*   Strikingly variegated and does well in moist semi-shade.

*Crambe cordifolia**   One of those bold plants grown as much for its foliage effect as its huge panicles of white gypsophila-like flowers in summer. Up to 2m (6ft).

Crinum   Well sited in deep soil in a sunny border, *C.* x *powellii** is permanent and beautiful with its pale-pink trumpet flowers, excellent for flower arranging.

Crocosmia   Although montbretia-like, this has large sword-like leaves and sprays of trumpet flowers in vivid colours in summer and autumn. Notable varieties are 'Lucifer'* (flame red), 'Solfaterre' * (H3) (lemon yellow) and *masonicorum** (H3) (scarlet).

Dianthus   Most gardeners would not be without the well-loved pinks of our cottage gardens. The Cheddar pink *gratianopolitanus** (*caesius*), with fragrant single pink flowers in late spring and early summer, is gardenworthy, as is x *allwoodii* 'Doris'*, a perpetual-flowering double shell-pink, and 'Mrs Sinkins', the common fragrant double white, invaluable for edging paved areas.

Diascia   Some of this spectacular group of plants from the highlands of South Africa are proving reasonably hardy in well-drained, sunny conditions. They can be brilliant *en masse* in varying shades of pink. A number of species and cultivars are available and, as yet, names may be a little confused, but all are excellent value. Particularly distinct are 'Ruby Field'* (H3–4), which produces a long succession of pale pink, lipped flowers rising from ground-hugging mats of green leaves, to about 25cm (10in), while *rigescens** (H3) is taller and more vigorous, possibly less hardy and has spikes of soft pink flowers, in arching sprays, continuous from early summer to mid-autumn.

Dicentra (*Dielytra*) (Dutchman's breeches or Bleeding heart)   All are beautiful and happy in shady spots, notably 'Langtrees'* and 'Luxuriant'*.

Dictamnus albus   The burning bush, a beautiful and unusual plant, is so called because the inflammable oil exuded by glands on the flower stalks will ignite on warm summer evenings. The type plant has white flowers, and *purpureus** (*fraxinella*) purple or rose-red. 60cm (2ft).

Dierama pulcherrima   The wand flower has graceful arching stems carrying hanging bells of pink or white trumpet-shaped flowers in summer. Up to 1.2m (4ft).

Dimorphotheca (Cape marigold or Star of the veldt)   See *Osteospermum*.

Euphorbia   The hardier members of the spurge family are superb plants for patio or courtyard in sun or semi-shade, particularly *epithymoides** (*polychroma*), a mound-forming plant with bright yellow bracts in early spring, about 50cm (1¹/₂ft); and *characias* subsp. *wulfenii**, a handsome evergreen, shrubby spurge with glaucous blue foliage and large heads of buff or greenish-yellow flowers in spring and early summer, 1.2m (4ft). Sap from all parts of most species can be irritant on contact or poisonous if ingested.

Geranium   The cranesbills fit in excellently with courtyard and patio planting in sun or shade, notably x *oxonianum* 'A. T. Johnson'*, silvery-pink; *macrorrhizum* 'Album' (white) and 'Ingwersen's Variety'* (shell pink), 35cm (14in); and 'Johnson's Blue'*, 50cm (1¹/₂ft), particularly fine in association with shrub roses.

Hellebores and *Hostas*   Equally at home here as they are in shaded shrubaceous borders and moist situations.

*Kirengeshoma palmata**   With its nodding, waxy, pale yellow bells in autumn and maple-like palmate leaves, this requires a moist, shady situation. 1m (3ft).

Lamium maculatum 'Beacon Silver' gives excellent low, silver-variegated groundcover; 'White Nancy'* has white flowers, freely produced.

Lavatera 'Rosea'* (*olbia* 'Rosea') (Tree mallow)   Spectacular throughout summer, with its large pink hollyhock-type flowers and grey downy leaves. A sunny situation and plenty of space is required. 2m (6ft) tall by 1m (3ft) wide. 'Barnsley'*(H3–4), which has pale pink flowers with a cherry-red eye, is now very popular.

*Liriope muscari**   Evergreen grass-like foliage and purple flower spikes in autumn. 50cm (1¹/₂ft).

Nepeta x *faassenii*   Catmint is as useful here as *Alchemilla mollis*, with which it associates well.

*Nerine bowdenii** (H3–4)   The nerines are South African bulbous plants for the base of warm walls, producing welcome and beautiful pink lily-like trumpets from early to late autumn. 'Fenwick's Variety' is the best form. They are a magnificent and permanent planting, and look well with grey groundcover, such as *Helianthemum* 'Wisley Primrose'*, *Stachys byzantina* (*olympica*) 'Silver Carpet', or *Acaena buchananii*.

Oenothera missouriensis* (H3–4)   The prostrate evening primrose with large, fragrant, soft yellow blooms throughout summer. 25cm (10in). 'Fireworks'* is taller, with golden-yellow summer flowers and basal rosettes of multicoloured leaves in the spring. 35cm (14in).

Ophiopogon planiscapus 'Nigrescens.'*   The blackish-purple leaves are unique and ideal in patio areas.

Origanum vulgare (Marjoram)   In particular 'Aureum'*, the golden-leaved form of the herb, bright and aromatic, goes well in paved areas. About 25cm (10in). *O.* 'Herrenhausen'* is an excellent introduction, reliable, long-lived, violet flowers with purple bracts summer and autumn. Well drained site. 60cm (2ft).

Osteospermum (*Dimorphotheca*) (Cape marigold or Star of the veldt)   There are a number of distinct and showy species and cultivars, which are excellent value in full sun on a well-drained soil; winter protection may be necessary for some. They also make superb pot or container plants. *O. jucundum barbariae** (H3–4) has aromatic foliage and unique pink daisy flowers with burnished bronze reverses; *ecklonis* 'Prostratum'* (H3–4), white above and purple beneath, is subshrubby and excellent. About 60cm (2ft).

Penstemon   Easy, sun-loving plants, producing large quantities of tubular foxglove-like flowers throughout summer. Very rewarding are the dainty 'Evelyn'* (H3–4), with fine, pale green foliage and pink, red-flushed flowers, 'Garnet', a larger grower with brilliant wine-red blooms throughout the summer, about 50cm (1¹/2ft), and 'Hidcote Pink'* (H3).

Potentilla   The herbaceous varieties, particularly *nepalensis* 'Miss Willmott'* (pink), and 'William Rollison'* (orange), are appropriate here.

Pulmonaria saccharata (Lungwort) and

cultivars   Excellent in a shady spot.

Rudbeckia fulgida 'Goldsturm'* (Black-eyed Susan)   A sun lover.

Salvia officinalis (Common sage)   The species, and its cultivars 'Icterina'* (H3–4) (variegated) and 'Purpurascens'* (purple-leaved).

Santolina chamaecyparissus* (Lavender cotton)   A good grey plant with fine filigree foliage. Also its dwarf variety *Nana*.

Scabiosa   Particularly the Caucasian *S. caucasica* 'Clive Greaves'* and its white form 'Miss Willmott'*, both superb for cutting, look well in patio areas among the shrubs and shrub roses. Less commonly seen, *S. rumelica* (*Knautia macedonica*) is well worth a place, with its deep, rich crimson flowers throughout the summer. These scabious all reach about 60cm (2ft).

Schizostylis coccinea   Although mildly invasive, this is an invaluable autumn-flowering plant, with gladiolus-like flowers throughout the autumn. 'Major'* is a fine, large-flowered crimson form, and 'Mrs Hegarty' a clear rose-pink. 50-60cm (1¹/2-2ft).

Stachys olympica 'Silver Carpet'   The non-flowering version of the silvery-grey 'Lamb's ears'. 10-20cm (4-6in).

Thymus   The thymes are excellent in paved areas; try particularly some selected forms of the chalk downland plant *praecox* (*serpyllum*), which are transformed into sheets of colour throughout the summer; 'Albus'*, the white-flowered form; 'Coccineus'*, rich crimson; and the grey-leaved 'Pink Chintz'*, with shell-pink flowers, 2.5cm (about 1in); 'Porlock' is essentially a dense, low, hummocky shrub to about 25cm (10in), covered in pink flowers in late spring and early summer. All thymes are aromatic and forms of the lemon thyme, x *citriodorus*, and the common thyme, *vulgaris*, are both favourite flavouring herbs; *vulgaris* 'Aureus' has bright yellow foliage and x *citriodorus* 'Silver Queen'* has effective white variegation, 25cm (10in).

Verbascum (Mullein)   Handsome in foliage and flower and, although not long-lived, self-sown seedlings appear pleasantly in unexpected places. Most have handsome large leaves, particularly *bombyciferum**

('Broussa'), white woolly leaves and yellow flowers; 'Gainsborough'*, canary-yellow spikes; and 'Pink Domino'*, rose-pink with a darker centre. All 1–1.2m (3–4ft) or more and effective, spiking up between shrubs or in sunny paved areas.

Veronica (Speedwell)   These are the herbaceous rather than shrubby veronicas (for these, see *Hebe*). Of the many species and cultivars, perhaps the most rewarding for courtyard and patio is *teucrium* 'Crater Lake Blue'*, a reliable plant with long spikes of vivid ultramarine blue throughout the summer, 30cm (1ft).

Waldsteinia ternata   An excellent, neat evergreen carpeting plant with golden-yellow flowers in spring.

Penstemon 'Hidcote Pink'* is vigorous and very free-flowering and is widely available.

(Sh) = Shady site desirable   (A) = Acid soil essential   (E) = Evergreen   (Std) = Standard   (F) = Upright/fastigiate habit

HARDY ORNAMENTAL GRASSES AND FERNS

These are assured of suitable homes in courtyards and patios. Of those described in Chapter 8, the following grasses are appropriate:

....

For sunny situations:

Festuca glauca
Helictotrichon sempervirens
Stipa calamagrostis
*S. gigantea**

....

For shadier situations:

Hakonechloa macra 'Aureola'* ('Albo-aurea')
Milium effusum 'Aureum'* (Bowles' golden grass)
Molinia caerulea 'Variegata'*

....

Most smaller-growing ferns can be effectively sited where they can enjoy a cool, moist root-run, perhaps in a shady courtyard or patio, notably:

....

*Adiantum pedatum** (Maidenhair fern)
Can be successful in a draught-free, moist and shady area
*Athyrium felix-femina** (Lady fern)
*Blechnum spicant** (Hard fern)
Phyllitis (*Scolopendrium*) (Hart's tongue)
Polystichum setiferum 'Plumoso-divisilobum'* (Soft shield fern)
Particularly magnificent in a paved setting

....

SMALL TREES AND SHRUBS

A small tree in a patio or courtyard is often a necessity for shade or desirable as an effective and important focal point. Many of the larger shrubs reach proportions of small trees, and some may be pruned or tailored to fit quite small areas.

Those suitable, and available, come in two groups. The first group comprises those with a straight standard stem, usually 1.5–2m (5–6ft), and small-formed head of branches. Some varieties are 'topwork grafted' on the stem of another variety, in order to make an effective standard tree (Std) more quickly. Such specimens should be carefully staked and the graft protected until the growth of new tissue has made the union strong. Suckers from the stem or base or in the vicinity of the graft union should be removed immediately. Many of the trees in this group form weeping or semi-weeping specimens and a few are of fastigiate or upright growth (F). Here are a few examples.

....

Acer palmatum 'Dissectum'* and cultivars. (Std)
Acer platanoides 'Globosum' A compact form of Norway maple; also *pseudoplatanus* 'Brilliantissimum'* (Std)
Caragana arborescens 'Lorbergii' An elegant form of the Pea Tree with narrow grass-like foliage
Cotoneaster 'Hybridus Pendulus' and Gnom' (Std) (E)
Malus 'Red Jade' and 'Royal Beauty'
Morus alba 'Pendula' (Weeping white mulberry)
Prunus 'Amanogawa' (F); 'Cheal's Weeping'*; and *yedoensis* 'Shidare Yoshino'
Robinia x *slavinii* 'Hillieri'*
Salix caprea 'Kilmarnock'* (Weeping Kilmarnock willow); *purpurea* 'Pendula'* (Weeping purple osier) (Std)

....

A number of the smaller-growing species and cultivars of rowan make excellent small, compact trees, particularly:

....

Sorbus aucuparia 'Fastigiata' (F). *cashmiriana**, with white fruits; 'Joseph Rock'* (F), with amber fruits; and *vilmorinii**, with rose-red fruits and an elegant foliage and habit.

....

The second group of small trees for patios comprises plants which may slowly reach the proportions of a large multi-stemmed shrub or small shrubby tree. Many have the advantage of being evergreen and reveal great diversity of habit, foliage and flower. However, they are frequently slow in growth and are rarely supplied above 1m (3ft) in height; they will consequently take some years to become effective as a small specimen or shrubby tree. They are less frequently planted, but none the less desirable for that specially important site. Here is a select list of likely candidates:

Acer palmatum 'Bloodgood'*, 'Osakazuki'*, 'Seir yu'* and 'Ribesifolium'.
Aesculus pavia 'Atrosanguinea'.
Albizia julibrissin 'Rosea'* (H3).
Aralia elata and 'Variegata'*.
Arbutus unedo 'Rubra'*. (E).
Cornus 'Eddie's White Wonder'* and 'Norman Hadden'*. (A) (Semi-E).
Cotinus 'Grace'*.
Embothrium coccineum 'Norquinco Form'* (H3) (Chilean fire bush). (A) (E).
Eucalyptus panciflora subsp. *niphophila** (Snow gum). (E).
*Genista aetnensis** (Mount Etna broom).
Halesia monticola var. *vestita** (Snowdrop tree). (A).
*Hoheria glabrata** and 'Glory of Amlwch'*(H3). (Semi-E).
Magnolia species and cultivars, particularly 'Heaven Scent'* (A) x *loebneri* 'Leonard Messel'*; *salicifolia* *sieboldii** 'Susan'* (A) and *wilsonii**.
Ptelea trifoliata 'Aurea'*.

....

WEEPING STANDARD AND STANDARD ROSES

A weeping standard rose can be used to make an effective and colourful formal specimen in the smallest of paved areas. It may require training on special 'umbrellas', which are usually available from good garden centres. Weeping standard roses are usually 'topwork grafted' and suckers below the graft point should be removed immediately. Some of the old favourites are frequently available, and some new cultivars are being tried with success. Some are less weeping than others, however, and tend to make neat, ball-headed specimens, so inspect before you buy! The following selection gives a wide range of colour:

....

'Bonica'*   Rose-pink, recurrent.
'Canary Bird'   A long-established favourite, bright yellow with fern-like leaves.
'Crimson Shower'*.
'Emily Gray'   Double, deep yellow.
'The Fairy'*   Double rose pink.
'Little White Pet'*   Double white pompoms.
'Marjorie Fair'*   Red with a white eye.
'Sanders White Rambler'*.

Key: * = AGM 1993   H4 = Hardy   H3 = Hardy in mild areas   H2 = Requires protection   H1 = Usually a greenhouse plant

DRY GARDENING

If you have a sun-trap area in your garden, you will be able to try growing a wide range of conifers, shrubs and herbaceous plants from the Mediterranean, California, South Africa, Australasia and similar areas where hot, dry conditions are experienced. Sharp drainage is of the utmost importance, particularly if these plants are to overwinter satisfactorily in a cooler climate. A mulch of gravel will make a pleasing and weed-free finish, the plants benefiting from the cool root-run this affords.

SMALL TREES

Depending upon the area involved, you may not need more than three or four widely-spaced shrubby trees, and a choice might be made from any of the following:

. . . .

Arbutus x *andrachnoides** (Grecian strawberry tree). (E)

Caragana arborescens 'Lorbergii'*   A form of the Pea Tree with narrow leaflets.

Cercis canadensis 'Forest Pansy'*; *siliquastrum** (Judas tree).

Colutea arborescens (Bladder senna) Bright yellow flowers and bronze-coloured inflated seed pods together all summer. A large shrub which can reach almost tree-like proportions.

Pittosporum 'Garnetti'* (H3)   The grey-green leaves are margined white and are pink tinted in winter. Perhaps the most reliable of the evergreen and variegated pittosporums.

Quercus suber (Cork oak)   Grows satisfactorily in warmer areas and will be the envy of your friends and neighbours.

Rhamnus alaterna 'Argenteovariegata'* One of the best of all variegated evergreen shrubs. Fast-growing.

Robinia slavinii 'Hillieri'*   For its elegant habit and pink summer flowers.

Sophora tetraptera 'Grandiflora'* (H3)   The best form of the New Zealand Kowhai could be used if your garden is very sheltered or has a warm wall.

. . . .

CONIFERS

The following make large upright shrubs or small trees:

Cupressus macrocarpa 'Gold Crest'* (H3) or 'Golden Pillar'; *sempervirens* 'Green Pencil' and 'Swaine's Golden'* (H3). (E)

Ginkgo biloba* (Maidenhair Tree)   A deciduous and unique conifer, which has a narrow conical form 'Tremonia', worthy of a place in the dry garden and worth seeking out.

Juniperus chinensis 'Obelisk'*; *communis* 'Hibernica'* (Irish Juniper); *scopulorum* 'Blue Heaven'*. (E)

Pinus sylvestris 'Fastigiata'   A unique upright form of the Scots pine. (E)

Taxus baccata 'Fastigiata'* (Irish yew). (E)

. . . .

To complement these, one or more evergreen conifers of more spreading or rounded habit could be chosen:

. . . .

Cedrus libani 'Sargentii'.

Cryptomeria japonica 'Bandai-sugi'*.

Juniperus x *media* 'Blaauw'* or 'Old Gold'.

Pinus parviflora 'Adcock's Dwarf'*.

Taxus baccata 'Semperaurea'*.

. . . .

COMPACT SHRUBS

Dwarf to large shrubs which are likely to do well in these circumstances include:

Arbutus unedo 'Rubra'. (E)

Artemisia 'Powis Castle'* (H3–4). (E)

Atriplex halimus. (Semi-E)

Buddleia   In considerable variety, particularly: alternifolia 'Argentea'; *davidii* 'Harlequin'; 'Lochinch'* (H3–4) and x *weyerana* 'Sungold'*.

Carpenteria californica* (H3). (E)

Caryopteris x *clandonensis* 'Heavenly Blue'*.

Cassinia fulvida and *vauvilliersii albida* (E).

Ceanothus 'Blue Mound'* (H3). (E) ; 'Gloire de Versailles'*.

Ceratostigma willmottianum * (H3–4).

Choisya ternata* and *t*. 'Sundance'* (H3); 'Aztec Pearl'*. (E)

Cistus aguilari 'Maculatus'*; *populifolius lasiocalyx**; *pulverulentus** and x *skanbergii**. All (H3). (E)

Clerodendrum trichotomum var. *fargesii* Late-summer flower and blue autumn fruits.

Convolvulus cneorum* (H3). (E)

Cytisus (broom)   Many species and varieties, notably: *nigricans, praecox* 'Allgold'*; 'Minstead'* (white-tinged lilac).

Daphne   Particularly *bholua* 'Jacqueline Postill'* (H3); x *mantensiana* 'Manten' and *tangutica**. (E)

Dorycnium hirsutum*. (E)

Indigofera heterantha* (gerardiana) *an elegant small late summer flowering shrub.*

(Sh) = Shady site desirable   (A) = Acid soil essential   (E) = Evergreen

Genista aetnensis (Mount Etna broom).

Helichrysum italicum* (H3) and *splendidum** (H3). (E)

Hibiscus syriacus cultivars, notably: 'Blue Bird'*; 'Diana'*, single white; 'Hinomaru', anemone-centred, pink with cerise centre; 'Woodbridge'*, rose pink with a carmine eye.

Indigofera heterantha (gerardiana)*.

Olearia x *scilloniensis** (H3). (E)

Perovskia atriplicifolia 'Blue Spire'*.

Phlomis 'Edward Bowles' and *italica** (H3). (E)

Phormium tenax* and *cookianum** (H3) and cultivars.

Romneya coulteri* (Californian tree poppy).

Tamarix ramosissima 'Rubra'* (late summer/autumn flower) and *tetrandra** (spring flower).

Yucca filamentosa* and *f.* 'Bright Edge' (H3)

. . . .

SUBSHRUBS AND HERBACEOUS GROUNDCOVER

These will blend together to make the type of *maquis* growth so familiar in Mediterranean areas. Besides the familiar lavender, rosemary, santolina and sage (salvia), you could include:

Acaena (New Zealand burr).

Acanthus (Architect's plant).

Agapanthus 'Headbourne Hybrids; *campanulatus* 'Albus'.

Artemisia absinthium 'Lambrook Silver'*, *maritima f. canescens*.

Ballota pseudodictamnus* (H3–4).

Diascia From the highlands of South Africa. Excellent value in full sun.

Eryngium (Sea holly), *alpinum** and *giganteum**.

Euphorbia Particularly: *characias* subsp. *wulfenii**, *griffithii* 'Fireglow' and *epithymoides** (*polychroma*).

Hypericum olympicum 'Grandiflorum'.

Nepeta species and cultivars.

Osteospermum species and cultivars.

Penstemon 'Evelyn'* and 'Garnet'*.

Sedum 'Ruby Glow'* and 'Autumn Joy'*.

Stachys olympica.

Zauschneria (Californian fuchsia), *californica* 'Dublin' (H3).

. . . .

ORNAMENTAL GRASSES

As many enjoy a sunny well-drained situation they should be included, particularly:

Festuca glauca,'Blaufuchs'*

Helictotrichon sempervirens*

Stipa calamagrostis and *gigantea**.

Helichrysum italicum *subsp.* serotinum, *the curry plant with* Erigeron karvinskianus (mucronatus).

BULBS

Many bulbous plants naturalise well in such circumstances.

. . . .

Allium (Ornamental onion) Many species, some rather invasive. Acceptable for this purpose are: *christophii** (*albo-pilosum*); *moly** (Golden garlic); *rosenbachianum*; and *siculum*.

Anemone blanda* and cultivars.

Fritillaria These do well in these conditions, notably the well-known *imperialis* (Crown imperial;) *acmopetala**; *pallidiflora**; and *pyrenaica**.

Galtonia viridiflora* (*candicans*) Hanging white bells, useful for summer flower.

Nerine bowdenii* (H3–4) Spectacular heads of pink flowers, useful for cutting up to late autumn.

Tulip species and cultivars.

. . . .

There are many other possibilities and a specialist bulb grower should be consulted.

•PROBLEM SOLVER•

DRY SHADE

Shade induced by a dense canopy of large trees, such as beech, is one of the most difficult situations to cope with in the garden – the situation is made worse by the invading roots of the trees causing the shade, and inevitably there is drought which is difficult to contend with. Sometimes efforts are made to seal off roots by means of plastic sheeting or corrugated iron inserted in the ground, but it remains a difficult circumstance in which to garden successfully.

Mahonia aquifolium 'Apollo'* is tolerant of dry shade.

TREES, SHRUBS AND GROUNDCOVER

There are a number of tough ever-green shrubs that will grow even in these circumstances. *Aucuba japonica* and its variegated cultivars will slowly reach 2m each way (6 x 6ft). Generally lower growing, *Mahonia aquifolium* and its cultivar 'Apollo'* will produce bright yellow flowers in spring to enliven the gloom. Less commonly seen and amazingly tolerant of dry shade is the Alexandrian laurel, *Danae racemosa**, and *Ruscus aculeatus* (Butcher's broom), with its curious dark green, spiky leaves. Large red berries are borne by female or her-maphrodite forms.

Shrubby evergreen groundcover is catered for by many of the ivy species and cultivars, particularly *Hedera colchica* 'Dentata Variegata'*, with its large broad leaves generously mar-gined yellow. Although slow, *Pachysandra terminalis** and its varie-gated form are reliable here. *Vinca* (Periwinkle), both *major* and *minor*, makes effective groundcover in shade, but will take longer to establish in very dry conditions. *V. minor* is the neater of the two. One of the most satisfac-tory shrubby groundcovers in dry shade is *Hedera helix hibernica** (Irish ivy), with its bright, shining leaves and dense, permanent cover. *Ilex aquifolium** (Common holly), *Taxus baccata** (Yew) and *Buxus semper-virens** (Box), and many of their culti-vars, once established will be effective and tolerant in dry shade situations.

HERBACEOUS PERENNIALS

Really successful herbaceous plants which are long lived in this situation are few. Perhaps the most responsive and certainly the most rampant is the variegated form of 'Yellow archangel', *Lamiastrum galeobdolon* 'Variegatum'; not only is this luxuriant in growth, but it is a very beautiful plant under the shade of trees, where its bright silver leaf variegation and yellow deadnettle flowers show up well. Amazingly tolerant and also very beautiful is the hardy *Geranium macr-orrhizum* 'Ingwersen's Variety'*. Other species seem less successful and per-manent. Many of the epimediums will colonise quite well, notably *E. per-ralderianum* and x *rubrum**. Once established, *Euphorbia amygdaloides* var. *robbiae** (Mrs Robb's spurge) seems to perform quite well, and the clump-forming Gladwyn iris, *Iris foe-tidissima*, and its variegated form will provide welcome evergreen clumps of dark, shining leaves; its seed pods, which open in the autumn to display bright orange seeds are a delight for flower arrangers, but the dull mauve, veined flowers of early summer scarcely show up in the gloom.

Lamiastrum galeobdolen *'Variegatum' is beautiful if rampant even in dry shade under trees.*

Key: (B) = Suitable for boundary planting   (E) = Evergreen

HEDGES

Screen planting in particular was discussed earlier in this chapter (see pp 106-7). Undoubtedly hedge or boundary planting and screening are functional and are closely linked. In most gardens it is necessary to define a boundary and very often in the interests of privacy it needs to be dense, evergreen, and of a minimum height to achieve the screening required. A boundary hedge may also need to be reasonably proof against the unauthorised entry of people or animals, such as dogs and farm stock. Rabbits and deer are an increasing problem, and special fencing is necessary here in addition to the boundary hedge (see p 90).

Hedges, whether formal or informal, should be composed of plants which respond satisfactorily to clipping or pruning – once mature, the majority of hedges only require an annual clipping to ensure the necessary density of their growth (see Chapter 6). Hedges need not, however, be dull and functional – they can be beautiful in flower, foliage and berry, and the range of plants adaptable for this purpose is remarkable. This includes forest trees, such as beech (*Fagus sylvatica*), hornbeam (*Carpinus betulus*) and the evergreen holm oak (*Quercus ilex*); among conifers, the ubiquitous Leyland cypress (x *Cupressocyparis leylandii*) forms the fastest-growing evergreen tall hedge or screen; pines, such as *Pinus nigra* (Austrian pine) and *sylvestris* (Scots pine) make beautiful and functional evergreen screens; and Western Red Cedar (*Thuja plicata* and *T. p.* 'Fastigiata') responds well to clipping. Yew (*Taxus baccata*), perhaps not so slow in growth as generally supposed, is one of the finest of all evergreens for formal hedges within the garden, or on the boundary in urban areas (unless near grazing cattle, horses or other animals – it should not be forgotten that yew leaves, stems and particularly seeds within the attractive fruits are poisonous if swallowed), while equally effective and faster in

growth is *T.* x *media* 'Hicksii'*, a very hardy, free-fruiting hybrid (*cuspidata* x *baccata*) with wider, glossy, spine-tipped leaves, worthy of wider recognition and planting.

A wide range of shrubs, both evergreen and deciduous, will make flowering and berrying hedges within the garden and on the boundary – from dwarf hedges of lavender and rosemary to taller hedges of berberis, cotoneaster, pyracantha, rhododendron, roses – both species and hybrids – tamarix and viburnum, but avoid the straggly *Lonicera nitida* other than as a low hedge (as a very fast-growing substitute for box), when it will require a great deal of clipping.

PREPARATION OF GROUND AND PLANTING

Hedges are usually permanent features in the garden and the site they occupy should be well prepared, cultivated to a depth of 50cm (1½ft) and, ideally, a width of 60cm–1m (2–3ft). Well-rotted farmyard manure should be dug into the base of the trench before backfilling, allowing for settlement before planting.

Open-ground, loose-rooted deciduous hedge plants, such as thorn, beech and hornbeam, are best planted in the autumn, and certainly before the end of winter. Many hedge plants are container grown these days, which certainly allows flexibility in planting times. A balanced, preferably slow-release fertiliser, should be added at planting to the root area of the hedge, which should then be mulched with bark or well-rotted leaves. Attention to watering in the first and second springs following planting is essential, particularly with loose-rooted (open ground) transplants.

The spacing for most subjects is 50–60cm (1½–2ft). A slightly wider hedge is possible if a staggered planting arrangement is adopted; for taller informal screens, plant in a staggered arrangement, 1–1.5m (3–5ft) apart.

RECOMMENDED HEDGE PLANTS

In the following list of recommended

trees and shrubs for hedging or screening, those followed by (B) are particularly appropriate for boundary planting.

*Acer campestre** (Field maple)   Excellent for rustic or tapestry hedges involving thorn, blackthorn, holly, etc. Bright red young shoots and golden autumn colour. (B)

Beech   See *Fagus sylvatica*.

Berberis   All are spiny, many are evergreen. Particularly gardenworthy are: x *frikartii* 'Telstar'* (E), a splendid newcomer forming an impenetrable hedge; x *media* 'Red Jewel'* (Semi-E), with dense, spiny leaves turning purple-red in autumn, and a sport of x media 'Parkjuwel'* (Semi-E); x *stenophylla** (B) (E), superb as an informal hedge of arching habit, orange-yellow flowers in spring; *thunbergii**, with neat compact habit, bright green leaves, rich red autumn colour; *thunbergii* 'Red Chief'*, a selection of *thunbergii* 'Atropurpurea' with deep purple foliage and arching habit; *thunbergii* 'Atropurpurea Nana'*, making an excellent dwarf hedge to about 50cm (1½ft), purple foliage throughout the growing season; *verruculosa** (E), a fine hedge plant, with lustrous green leaves white beneath, flowers golden yellow.

Blackthorn   See *Prunus spinosa*.

*Buxus sempervirens**   The traditional box of small to medium-size hedges, of dense habit when clipped. (B) (E) 'Suffruticosa'* is the dwarf compact form for formal hedges and parterres.

*Carpinus betulus** (Hornbeam)   Excellent for formal hedges or boundary planting. (B)

Chamaecyparis lawsoniana (B) (E) (Lawson cypress)   Variable from seed; for a trimmed hedge it is better to plant a good proven cultivar such as 'Pembury Blue'*, silver-grey, or 'Green Hedger'*. (B) (E)

Cotoneaster   Of many possibilities, the following are particularly recommended: *sternianus** (B) (E), with small sage-green leaves silvery-white beneath and abundant orange fruits in autumn; *lacteus** (E), a denser evergreen hedge, with oval leaves grey beneath and late-ripening red fruits which frequently last until the New Year; *serotinus* (B) (E), with rounded leathery leaves, abundant flowers in midsummer and red berries through the winter; and *simonsii** (Semi-E), with a very upright habit and masses of scarlet fruits (B).

Crataegus monogyna (Quickthorn, Hawthorn or May) (B)   The commonest and most reliable of hedges or screens for all soils, but keep well clipped to reduce the risk of fireblight.

x *Cupressocyparis leylandii* (Leyland cypress) Much planted, extremely fast-growing hybrid cypress. Excellent tall hedge or screen for exposed gardens. Improved golden forms are now available, including: 'Gold Rider'*, a bright yellow resistant to burning in full sun, and 'Robinson's Gold'*, with yellow foliage, turning golden-bronze in the spring. Tapestry hedges, green and gold, make a pleasing variation. (B) (E)

Escallonia   Many species and cultivars make good evergreen hedges in coastal areas, with abundant flower in summer and autumn. Hardier, reliable sorts include: 'Apple Blossom'*, 'Crimson Spire'*, 'Donard Radiance'*, 'Donard Seedling'; *rubra**. (B) (E)

*Fagus sylvatica** (Beech)   A very popular hedging or screening plant. When clipped as a hedge it retains its russet brown leaves throughout the winter. The purple form (purpurea group), though scarcer, is also good for hedging. (B)

Hebe x *franciscana* 'Blue Gem'* (H3)   An excellent dense, low hedge of rounded leaves, particularly recommended for seaside gardens. The hardier 'Spender's Seedling'* produces white flowers over several months. (E)

Ilex x *altaclerensis* (Broad-leaved holly) and cultivars   These make excellent taller hedges and screens. *I. aquifolium** (Common holly) is one of the best and densest of all evergreen hedges; stockproof and impenetrable, it may be used formally or informally. (B) (E)

Laurel   See *Prunus lusitanica*.

Laurustinus   See *Viburnum tinus*.

Lavandula angustifolia (Lavender)   A popular low aromatic hedge for sunny situations, eg as edgings to borders of shrub roses, particularly 'Hidcote'* or 'Munstead Dwarf'. (E)

Ligustrum ovalifolium (Privet)   Perhaps the commonest of all garden hedge plants, and easily managed. Long-established

hedges tend to be vulnerable to honey fungus; *ovalifolium* 'Aureum'* (Golden privet) is well known and much loved. (B) (E)

Lonicera nitida   There are several forms of the shrubby honeysuckle: 'Ernest Wilson' with its tiny leaves, makes a neat, very low hedge, almost a substitute for box, but needs clipping many times during the summer. It becomes leggy and unsatisfactory if grown above 1.2–1.5m (4–5ft) but the golden form, 'Baggesen's Gold'*, is as worthy in its way as golden privet. (E)

Olearia   For coastal areas in particular and sheltered gardens inland, the 'Daisy bushes' are excellent value, particularly *macrodonta* 'Major'* (H3) (New Zealand holly), with grey silvery leaves. (E) (B)

*Pinus nigra** (Austrian pine) and *sylvestris* (Scots pine) make excellent medium to tall boundary screens up to 3–5m (9–16ft), while *mugo* var. *pumilo**, a vigorous dwarf form of the mountain pine, makes a low and attractive screen up to 2m (6ft). (B) (E)

Pittosporum   Not reliably hardy inland, but a magnificent and fast-growing shrub for the boundary or within the garden, particularly in coastal districts: *tenuifolium** (H3), with its wavy margined grey-green leaves, can be blended with several of its cultivars like 'Irene Paterson'* (H3), 'Purpureum' and 'Warnham Gold'* (H3) to give an attractive tapestry effect. (B) (E)

Potentilla   Several cultivars make excellent low, flowering hedges, particularly: 'Elizabeth'*, mid-yellow; 'Daydawn'*, peach-pink; 'Goldfinger'*, deep yellow; and 'Primrose Beauty'*, pale yellow, grey-green foliage. Excellent to border the vegetable garden.

Prunus   This large family, which includes cherry laurel and the flowering cherries, has a number of trees or shrubby trees which adapt well as hedges, particularly: x *cistena*, the purple-leaved 'Sand cherry' with white flowers in spring and rich red with foliage, making a good low hedge; *laurocerasus** (Cherry laurel) (B) (E), large, long, glossy leaves and excellent as a tall, dense screen; and *lusitanica** (Portuguese laurel) (B) (E), the best of the laurels, with dark green leathery and purple-tinted leaves and white flower

spikes in early summer, excellent on chalk and alkaline soils. Several of its varieties are equally useful as hedge plants, notably: subsp. *azorica**, (H3–4) 'Myrtifolia' and 'Variegata'; *spinosa* (Blackthorn or sloe) (B), a familiar and much-loved hedge plant with small white flowers on bare branches in early spring and bloomy black fruits (sloes) in the autumn. A dense, spiny, impenetrable hedge.

Pyracantha (Firethorn)   Makes impenetrable prickly hedges, with spring flower and autumn/winter berries. It is best to plant scab- and fireblight-resistant cultivars such as rogersiana 'Flava'* (yellow-fruited); *P.* 'Orange Glow*' (orange-red berries); or 'Teton', with strong vertical growth and orange fruits. (B) (E)

*Quercus ilex** (Holm or evergreen oak) Makes an excellent hedge or taller screen inland or on the coast, where it resists salt-laden gales. (B) (E)

Rhododendron ponticum   Suitable as a large-scale, bushy informal boundary hedge of medium to large size, denser than laurel and with pale purple flowers in early summer; for acid soil only. (A) (B) (E)

Rosa   Many of the shrub roses make excellent hedges, some with an extended season of flower plus heps in the autumn, particularly: 'Canary Bird'*, bright yellow and fern-like foliage; *eglanteria** (rubiginosa) (Sweet briar or eglantine); and *rugosa*, a very reliable hedge with recurrent flowers. The following cultivars are particularly good: *rugosa* 'Alba'*; r. 'Fru Dagmar Hastrup'*; r. 'Roseriae de L'Haÿ'* and r. 'Rubra'*. Hybrid musk roses of bushy habit are nearly perpetual flowering; excellent are: 'Cornelia'*, coppery-pink; 'Felicia'*, salmon-pink and 'Penelope'*, shell pink. Other hybrids particularly suitable include: 'Stanwell Perpetual', blush-white with greyish foliage, and 'Schneezwerg'*, perpetual white flowers with orange heps.

Rosmarinus officinalis (Rosemary)   This favourite aromatic shrub has two forms excellent for hedging: *officinalis* 'Fastigiatus' or 'Miss Jessup's Upright'*, which is vigorous and erect, and 'Severn Sea'*, low-growing and with arching branches and brilliant blue flowers. This

(Sh) = Shady site desirable   (A) = Acid soil essential   (E) = Evergreen   (B) = Suitable for boundary planting

makes an excellent evergreen hedge to border the vegetable garden without shading the crops. (E)

Taxus baccata (English yew)   Perhaps the best all-round evergreen hedge plant for formal purposes within the garden. It can be very long-lived, but likes a well-drained site in sun or shade; excellent on chalk. Leaves and seeds are poisonous if ingested. Equally worthy is the hybrid . x *media* 'Hicksii'*, broadly columnar in habit and a little faster in growth. (E)

Thuya plicata (*lobbii*) (Western red cedar)

A fast-growing conifer with fresh green foliage, pineapple-scented when crushed. Suitable when clipped as a formal hedge or as a tall screen. 'Fastigiata'* is a narrow columnar form most appropriate for tall formal hedges. (B) (E)

Viburnum tinus (E)   One of the most popular evergreen winter-flowering hedges, good in coastal districts and towns. 'Eve Price'*, with pink, scented flowers and carmine buds, has a neat compact habit.

Yew   See *Taxus baccata*.

Hybrid musk rose 'Penelope', deservedly the most popular hybrid musk by reason of its neat habit and freedom of flower, makes an excellent scented hedge.*

Key: * = AGM 1993   H4 = Hardy   H3 = Hardy in mild areas   H2 = Requires protection   H1 = Usually a greenhouse plant

WALLS, FENCES AND FRAMES

Boundary walls and fences, and walls of houses and outbuildings, frequently require beautifying; often there are unsightly pipes or large unbroken areas of brick to screen. This provides an opportunity to grow many of the more spectacular flowering shrubs and climbers of borderline hardiness which may not

be possible away from the warmth and shelter of a wall, particularly in cold districts.

You should endeavour to choose wall shrubs or climbers appropriate to the area to be covered – almost everything is likely to get bigger than you think and some restriction will be necessary, but extensive pruning may reduce flowering potential. With a two- or three-storey house where the space between the windows is not likely to be great, usually between

1–2m (3–6ft), a wall shrub, climber or climbing rose adaptable to such narrow confines should be considered. For instance, on a warm wall *Fremontodendron* 'California Glory' or, in very mild areas, *Acacia dealbata* could be considered; a wisteria is frequently trained up a narrow area to fan out above and between the windows. Suitable supporting wires strained through vine eyes, or trellis on batten, should be installed to cover the required area.

Take the aspect of the wall into account when making your choice, and do not plant too closely, generally speaking, 2–2.5m (6–8ft) apart is about right. Here is a selection according to aspect.

....

HIGH, SUNNY WALLS AND FENCES
Climbers
Actinidia kolomikta*.

Campis x *tagliabuana* 'Madame Galen'*.

Clematis Particularly large-flowered hybrids x *jackmanii**, 'Huldine', 'Niobe'* and 'Perle d'Azur'*.

Jasminum officinale* and cultivars.

Passiflora caerulea* (H3) (Passion flower). (E)

Roses Climbing species and cultivars, notably: *Rosa banksiae* 'Lutea'*; *brunonii* 'La Mortola; and stronger growing cultivars, particularly: 'Easlea's Golden Rambler'*; 'Mermaid'* (H3–4), large yellow single (E); 'Madame Gregoire Staechelin'*, large, rich deep pink; 'Souvenir de Claudius Denoyel'*, large double crimson, recurrent. Many produce fragrant flowers.

Schisandra grandiflora 'Rubriflora'.

Solanum crispum 'Glasnevin'* (H3). (Semi-E)

Trachelospermum jasminoides (E) and *j.* 'Variegata'. Both * (H2–3) (E)

Wisteria sinensis* and cultivars.

....

Wall shrubs
Abutilon vitifolium 'Veronica Tennant'* (H3). (E)

Acacia baileyana and *dealbata* (Mimosa). Both * (H2). (E)

Buddleia colvilei 'Kewensis' and *crispa*.

Ceanothus 'Puget Blue'*. (E)

Escallonia *x* iveyi* *(H3) – a vigorous hybrid – can be kept compact by pruning. The handsome glossy leaves set off the white late summer flowers.*

(Sh) = Shady site desirable   (A) = Acid soil essential   (E) = Evergreen

Trachelospermum asiaticum* *(H3) is scented and will self-cling to a low (or high) sunny wall.*

*Cytisus battandieri**.

Escallonia 'Iveyi'* (H3). (E)

Fremontodendron 'California Glory'* (H3).
A magnificent shrub with large golden
mallow flowers all summer. But take care
when handling or pruning – loose down
or felt on the leaves and stems can be very
irritant to skin and eyes, or if inhaled. (E)

Magnolia grandiflora and cultivars flowering
at a relatively early age, such as
'Exmouth'* and 'Goliath'* which, with
generous cultivation, may flower within 8
or 10 years of planting. This is the classic
evergreen wall shrub for the two- or
three-storey house, but does require 2–3m
(6–10ft) of width to make effective growth
and display its large, long, rusty-backed
leaves and immense, highly scented
cream-coloured flowers, produced
throughout the summer. (E)

Sophora tetraptera 'Grandiflora'* (H3).

. . . .

HIGH, SHADY WALLS AND FENCES

Many of these are equally good on
sunny walls.

Climbers

Akebia quinata. (E)

Berberidopsis corallina. (E)

Clematis viticella cultivars, notably 'Madame
Julia Correvon'*, 'Polish Spirit'*, 'Bill

Mackenzie'* and *rehderiana**.

Hedera colchica and cultivars.* (E)

Hedera helix cultivars*. (E)

*Hydrangea petiolaris**.

Lonicera (Honeysuckle)   Most species and
cultivars, particularly *L. japonica*
'Halliana'* (E), *periclymenum* 'Belgica'*
and *tragophylla**.

Parthenocissus   Particularly *henryana**;
*quinquefolia** and *tricuspidata* 'Veitchii'*.

Pileostegia viburnoides. (E)

Roses   Several climbing and rambler roses
perform well on shady walls and fences,
particularly: 'Aloha', 'Crimson Shower'*,
'Golden Showers'*, 'Gloire de Dijon'*,
'Maigold'*, 'Madame Alfred Carrière'*,
'New Dawn'* and 'Parade'*.

Schizophragma hydrangeoides and
*integrifolina**. *Vitis* (ornamental vines),
particularly 'Brant'*, *coignetiae**, and
vinifera 'Purpurea'*.

. . . .

Wall Shrubs

Azara microphylla (H3). (E)

Camellia x *williamsii* and cultivars, notably:
'Anticipation'*; 'Donation'*. 'E. T. R.
Carlyon'*. Not on walls that get morning
sun. (A) (E)

Chaenomeles japonica and cultivars,
particularly 'Crimson & Gold'* and
'Knaphill Scarlet'*.

Crinodendron (*Tricuspidaria*) *hookerianum**
(H3). (A) (E)

Drimys winteri. (E)

*Eriobotrya japonica** (H3) (Loquat). (E)

Garrya elliptica 'James Roof'. (E)

Kerria japonica 'Pleniflora'*.

Pyracantha   Choose disease-resistant
species and cultivars (See p 134). (E)

Rhamnus alaterna 'Argenteovariegata'*. (E)

. . . .

For bungalows or one-storey structures, garage walls and garden fences,
wall shrubs and climbers of less
vigour are required. Vigorous
climbing roses and vines like
Parthenocissus quinquefolia (Virginia
creeper) will grow into gutterings and
under roof tiles or slates, and heavy
and continual pruning will be necessary to restrict them. Some climbers
and wall shrubs of moderate growth
are included in the list below; some
are also suitable for balustrades, low
dividing walls within the garden or
positions under windows.

. . . .

LOWER, SUNNY WALLS

Climbers

Clematis alpina 'Francis Rivis'* and
macropetala 'Markham's Pink'*; *tangutica*;
'Aureolin';* *viticella* 'Alba Luxurians'*;
'Royal Velours'* and 'Venosa Volacea'*.

*Eccremocarpus scaber** (H3).

*Trachelospermum asiaticum**. (H2–3) (E)

Vitis vinifera 'Incana' and 'Purpurea'* (H2–3).

. . . .

Wall shrubs

Abelia 'Edward Goucher'* (E) and
schumannii.

Lippia citriodora (*Aloysia triphylla*) (Lemon-
scented verbena).

Callistemon citrinus 'Splendens'* (H1–3),
*linearis** (H3) and *salignus** (H3) (Bottle
brush). (E)

Ceanothus   Several evergreen cultivars are
suitable. Try *thyrsiflorus* var. *repens** (H3)
and 'Blue Mound'.* (H3). (E)

Cistus x *skanbergii** (H3) and
x *corbariensis** (E).

*Coronilla valentina glauca** (H2–3) and *C.v.*
'Citrina'* (H3). (E).

Corokia cotoneaster.

*Pittosporum tenuifolium** (H3) and
cultivars. (E)

Hebe x *franciscana* 'Variegata'* (H2) and
*hulkeana** (H3). (E)

Key: * = AGM 1993   H4 = Hardy   H3 = Hardy in mild areas   H2 = Requires protection   H1 = Usually a greenhouse plant

LOWER SHADY WALLS
Climbers

Clematis species and cultivars, particularly *cirrhosa balearica** (E) (Fern-leaved clematis); *montana* 'Tetrarose'*; and large-flowered hybrid 'Nelly Moser'*.

Hedera helix variegated cultivars, particularly 'Adam'; 'Goldchild'* (H3–4), 'Ivalace'* and 'Tricolor' ('Marginata Elegantissima'). (E)

Lonicera japonica 'Aureoreticulata'* (Evergreen honeysuckle.) (E)

Lonicera periclymenum 'Graham Thomas'* or 'Serotina'*.

Wall shrubs

Chaenomeles (Japonica)   Particularly 'Nicoline'* and 'Pink Lady'*.

Daphne odora 'Aureomarginata'. (E)

Euonymus fortunei 'Emerald 'n' Gold'*; 'Silver Queen'*. (E)

Hebe cupressoides 'Boughton Dome'* (H3–4). (E)

Hydrangea arborescens 'Annabelle'* and *serrata* 'Preziosa'*.

*Hypericum kouytchense**.

*Jasminum nudiflorum** (Winter jasmine).

Ribes sanguineum 'Brocklebankii'*.

PERGOLA BEAMS

Pergolas constructed of well-preserved rustic poles or sawn timber, the uprights set 2–3m (6–9ft) apart, make delightful features in the garden and good accommodation for the more vigorous climbers, which often need considerable restriction on house walls and fences. It is usually sufficient to site a vigorous climber, such as wisteria or vitis, at every other upright; then, with well-prepared sites, growth will be adequate to cover roof beams and make a canopy of foliage and flower. Less vigorous, more upright growing climbers are frequently adaptable to furnish the uprights in between (see below).

Climbers

The following are vigorous climbers, particularly suitable for pergola roof beams, which may need wire between to afford adequate support:

Actinidia chinensis (Chinese gooseberry Kiwi fruit) (male and female).

Aristolochia macrophylla.

*Celastrus orbiculatus** (hermaphrodite form).

Clematis montana f. *grandiflora**and *C.* 'Bill MacKenzie'*.

Humulus lupulus 'Aureus'* (Golden hop).

*Vitis coignetiae**.

*Wisteria sinensis** and cultivars.

PERGOLA UPRIGHTS, TRIPODS AND ARCHES
Climbers

There are a number of climbers of moderate growth, particularly clematis, climbing roses, honeysuckles and ornamental vines, which are particularly useful for furnishing the uprights of pergolas, rather than the roof beams. Such plants also do useful duty on rustic tripods in shrubaceous borders or elsewhere in the garden, and on the many rustic or plastic-covered wire archways that are used today.

Do not forget to add a small mound-forming shrub, such as potentilla, hydrangea, hardy fuchsia, cistus or phlomis, or perhaps a group of hostas, at the base of pergola pole or tripod – this not only looks better, but provides a cool root-run for the climber, particularly clematis. Try:

Clematis: *alpina* and *macropetala* cultivars; *viticella* 'Polish Spirit'*, and the large-flowered hybrids such as 'Comtesse de Bouchaud'*, rose pink; 'Huldine', pearly white; 'Niobe'*, the best red; 'Perle d'Azur'*, the best light blue.

Climbing roses, including: 'Aloha', 'Climbing Iceberg'*, 'Dublin Bay'*, Climbing Pom-Pom de Paris', 'Zephirine Drouhin'* (Bourbon).

Vines, including: *Vitis vinifera* 'Incana' and 'Purpurea'*.

Scented honeysuckles: *Lonicera periclymenum* 'Graham Thomas'*; *L. japonica* 'Aureoreticulata* (E), with net-variegated leaves.

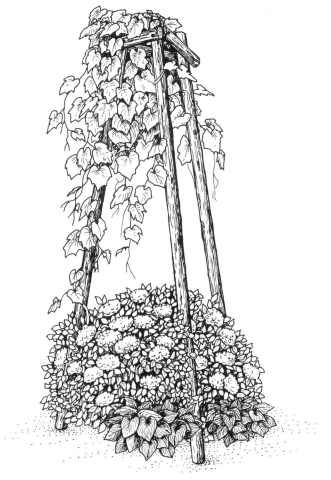

FIG 83 *Vine climbing a rustic tripod, with hydrangea and hostas at base*

(Sh) = Shady site desirable   (A) = Acid soil essential   (E) = Evergreen

ROCK GARDENS

Rock gardens remain popular as features in the modern garden and in public places. For devotees of the alpine plant, a well designed and constructed garden with bold pieces of preferably local stone is essential to accommodate and display a wide range of these plants, including dwarf bulbs, dwarf and slow-growing conifers and dwarf, mound-forming or prostrate shrubs.

Alpine gardening is a vast subject, and one of the world's largest horticultural societies, The Alpine Garden Society, exists to further the knowledge of alpine plants and to encourage their cultivation. Here we must regrettably confine ourselves to recommending dwarf and slow-growing conifers, dwarf shrubs and easy, reliable groundcovering plants to 'live in' with them in a rock-garden environment.

Most well-drained garden soils, with the addition of sand, grit and peat or leafmould, if heavy, are quite

suitable for general rock garden planting of this nature, though more specialised conditions are required for many of the high-altitude alpines and rarities. It is, however, essential to ensure that the soil or compost is free of perennial weeds, particularly ground elder and bindweed, which, if entrenched under rocks, will be extremely difficult to eradicate. Although frustrating for most gardeners, it is worth allowing the summer months to elapse after constructing a rock garden, in order to remove crops of weed and any perennial weed root before planting in the autumn or the following spring. After planting, a stone-chipping mulch will be both attractive and in keeping, and the plants will appreciate the cool root-run. Varying sizes of gravels and pebbles are available which simulate scree conditions.

Dwarf and slow-growing conifers and dwarf shrubs should be widely spaced, at least 1.5–2m (4½–6ft) apart. Most will get larger than you think, and the beauty of their shape and

form is lost if they are not well separated from neighbours.

Groundcovering alpine plants help to set them off and to complete the scene, but can be depressed to some extent by the growth of the conifers and shrubs.

DWARF AND SLOW-GROWING CONIFERS

There is now a very large range of these available. All are evergreen and make miniature spires, mounds, sprawls and carpets of blue, grey, green, silver or variegated foliage. Dwarf shrubs, many of which are evergreen, again display a diversity of shape and form, colour of foliage and flower. The following is a small selection from the many available:

. . . .

Chamaecyparis lawsoniana 'Ellwood's Pillar'; 'Pygmaea Argentea'*; 'Summer Snow'; *obtusa* 'Nana Aurea'*; and *pisifera* 'Golden Mop'*.

Cryptomeria japonica 'Vilmoriniana'*.

Juniperus communis 'Compressa'*; *horizontalis* 'Wiltonii'*; *procumbens*

Daphne cneorum* *a classic scented evergreen and the easiest daphne for general rock garden planting is more readily available than its cultivars*
(see page 178).

Geranium sanguineum *striatum** (lancastriense) – *a very garden-worthy British native with a long flowering season (see below).*

'Nana'*; and *squamata* 'Blue Star'*.

Picea mariana 'Nana'*.

Pinus parviflora 'Adcock's Dwarf'* and *sylvestris* 'Beauvronensis'*.

Thuya plicata 'Stoneham Gold'*.

Tsuga canadensis 'Jeddeloh'* and 'Prostrata'.

. . . .

DWARF SHRUBS

Again, the choice is very large. Neat, compact, 'trimmable' growth is important, as is generous spacing. Select from:

. . . .

Anthyllis hermanniae.

Berberis thunbergii 'Atropurpurea Nana'*.

Ceanothus 'Blue Mound '*. (E)

Cytisus x *beanii**.

Daphne species and cultivars, particularly: collina*; *cneorum* 'Eximia'*; *mantensiana* 'Manten'; x *napolitana**; and *retusa**. (E)

Fuchsia 'Tom Thumb'* (H3).

*Halimium ocymoides** (H3). (E)

Hebe cupressoides 'Boughton Dome'* (H3–4); *pimeleoides* 'Quicksilver'*. (E)

Lavandula angustifolia 'Nana Alba'. (E)

Nandina domestica 'Nana Purpurea'. (E)

*Parahebe catarractae** (H3). (E)

Potentilla arbuscula 'Beesii'*.

Rhododendron 'Curlew'*; *impeditum**; 'Elisabeth Hobbie'*; *yakushimanum* 'Koichiro Wada'* (some shade desirable). (A) (E)

Spiraea japonica 'Nana'*.

. . . .

COMPACT, GROUNDCOVERING ROCK PLANTS OR ALPINES

Generally, site these in groups of three or more of a kind, 20–30cm (8–12in) apart, grouped between shrubs and conifers and to furnish crevices between the rocks. Heathers (*Erica, Calluna, Daboecia*) are also useful for this task, although acid soil is essential for all but *Erica carnea* and its cultivars. Most garden centres offer a good range of rock plants, and the following might make a basic and reliable collection to give effect throughout the growing season:

. . . .

*Acaena microphylla**.

Ajuga reptans 'Burgundy Glow'*.

Arabis ferdinandi-coburgii 'Variegata'*.

Armeria maritima 'Vindictive'* (Thrift).

Aubretia in variety.

*Campanula carpatica** and cultivars; *C. portenschlagiana* (*muralis*) and 'Birch Hybrid'*.

*Dianthus deltoides** and cultivars.

Diascia 'Ruby Field'* (H3–4) and *rigescens** (H3).

*Dryas octopetala**.

*Gentiana septemfida**.

*Geranium dalmaticum** and *sanguineum striatum** (*lancastriense*).

Gypsophila repens 'Dorothy Teacher'*.

Helianthemum in variety. (E)

Lithospermum diffusum 'Heavenly Blue'. (A)

Persicaria (*Polygonum*) *vacciniifolia**.

Phlox douglasii and *P. subulata* cultivars.

*Pulsatilla vulgaris** and cultivars (Pasque flower).

Saxifraga (mossy) 'Pixie' and 'Sanguinea Superba'*. (E)

Thymus citriodorus 'Aureus'*; 'Porlock'; *praecox* (*serpyllum*) 'Coccineus'*; *t.* 'Pink Chintz'*.

*Veronica prostrata** (*rupestris*).

*Viola cornuta** and *c.* 'Alba'*.

(Sh) = Shady site desirable   (A) = Acid soil essential   (E) = Evergreen

WATER GARDENS

Chapter 4 discussed the siting, design and construction of pools, so let's look now at the planting.

WATER LILIES

Assuming that the water feature is in an open situation, hardy water lilies can be installed with every chance of success, particularly if the water warms up well in summer and is still. The use of a fountain will reduce the space available for the successful culture of water lilies. Specialists in this field today have a wide range of *Nymphaea* (water lilies) available in a variety of colours and sizes. Select according to the depth of water – it is possible to grow delightful small water lilies in a very few inches of water and, at the other end of the scale, some of the large and vigorous growers will cover several square metres of a lake. However, most requirements are met by the following varieties, which can be conveniently termed 'small growers' with a surface spread of leaves and flowers of approximately 60cm (2ft).

....

Nymphaea odorata 'Alba', white cup-shaped, scented flowers; *odorata* 'Turicensis' has soft, scented, rose-coloured flowers with elongated petals; *alba* 'Froebelii' is one of the best and most free-flowering red for small ponds; and *pygmaea* 'Helvola'*, with tiny flowers of sulphur yellow – a superb miniature for a large bowl or tub, or the smallest of ponds.

....

For larger pools, the following water lilies have a surface spread of about 1m (3ft):

....

Nymphaea 'Gonnere'* – goblet-shaped flowers of pure white; *odorata* 'W. B. Shaw' produces scented shell-pink flowers of good size, held well above the surface of the water; 'James Brydon'* is one of the most popular, with rich carmine-pink flowers with a silvery sheen, succeeding in semi-shady situations where many would fail; 'Marliacea Chromatella'*, perhaps the most reliable yellow-flowered water lily, the blooms

looking good against the marbled leaves and remaining open in the evening; and 'Escarboucle'*, perhaps the finest of all red water lilies and very free flowering.

....

SUBMERGED OXYGENATING PLANTS

These are an essential part of the planting of a pool or lake; together with water lilies, the oxygenators help to reduce the incidence of algae (blanket weed) which is often so troublesome when establishing new ponds. Furthermore, a good supply of oxygenating weed helps to starve the algae of nutrients and reduce the incidence of cloudy or soupy water.

Oxygenating plants should be installed at the rate of one per 60sq cm (2sq ft), for pools of up to 9sq m (100sq ft). They are usually supplied in bunches of unrooted stems with a small lead weight attached to cause them to sink. They establish more readily, however, if planted in coarse gravel or sand, perhaps retained by bricks on the pond bottom. Alternatively a plastic seed tray or small purpose-made planting crate will accommodate five or six bunches. Soil can be used but tends to discolour the water.

Introducing fish too early in the life of the pond is often a mistake, as they may dislodge or consume oxygenating plants in the absence of other food. At least a month should elapse after planting before the introduction of fish, and then the insectivorous golden orfe is to be preferred.

Good submerged oxygenating plants include:

....

Callitriche verna (Water starwort).
Ceratophyllum demersum (Water hornwort).
Elodea densa.
Hottonia palustris (Water violet).
Potamogeton crispus.
Ranunculus aquatilis (Water buttercup) Masses of small white flowers on the surface.
Stratiotes aloides (Water soldier) An unusual and interesting native oxygenator, with spiky leaves like pineapple tops, rising to the surface only to produce their curious white flowers.

MARGINAL TREES AND SHRUBS

In naturally moist soil and where there is adequate space, there are a number of small or medium sized (usually deciduous) trees and conifers which can be effective if well spaced to allow for their ultimate growth. Large-growing willows, like *Salix* x *sepulcralis* 'Chrysocoma' and most poplars, should be reserved for wide areas and not used near ponds in small gardens, where they will rapidly reach a large size and need removing or heavy pollarding. There are also many suitable shrubs which can be seen to good advantage if well spaced between trees and associating marginal aquatic plants. Winter bark effects from shrubby willow (*Salix*) and dogwood (*Cornus*) can be particularly striking.

TREES FOR SMALLER PONDS

Alnus glutinosa (Alder) 'Imperialis'*, with finely cut foliage.
Amelanchier 'Ballerina'* (Snowy mespilus).
Betula pendula* (Silver birch) and 'Dalecarlica'* (Swedish birch).
Populus tremula 'Pendula' (Weeping aspen).
Salix (Willow)   The smaller-growing tree species, notably: *alba* 'Sericea'*; *caprea* 'Kilmarnock'* (Kilmarnock willow); *daphnoides* 'Aglaia'* (Violet willow); x *sepulcralis* x 'Erythroflexuosa', twisted leaves and pendulous, contorted stems; *pentandra* (Bay willow) and *purpurea* 'Pendula'* (Weeping purple osier).

....

Among conifers:
Taxodium ascendens 'Nutans'*.

....

TREES FOR LARGE PONDS AND LAKES

Alnus cordata* (Italian alder) and *glutinosa* (Common alder).
Betula papyrifera (Paper-bark birch); *nigra** (River birch) and *utilis* 'Jermyns'*.
Populus   Particularly *alba* 'Pyramidalis'; *canescens* 'Macrophylla'; 'Eugenei'; x *canadensis* 'Serotina Aurea'*; *tremula** (Aspen).
Quercus palustris* (Pin oak).
Salix (Willow)   Larger growers, notably *alba* (White willow); x *rubens* 'Basfordiana'*; *alba* 'Caerulea' (Cricket-bat willow); x *sepulchalis* 'Chrysocoma'*

Key: * = AGM 1993   H4 = Hardy   H3 = Hardy in mild areas   H2 = Requires protection   H1 = Usually a greenhouse plant

(Weeping willow); *fragilis* (Crack willow); *babylonica* (*matsudana*) (Pekin willow) and its cultivars 'Pendula' and 'Tortuosa'*.

Among conifers:

*Metasequoia glyptostroboides** (Dawn redwood) and cultivars.

*Taxodium distichum** (Swamp cypress).

WATERSIDE SHRUBS

Any of the following enjoy moist conditions and blend well near water. Some are less commonly seen and worthy of wider planting.

Andromeda polifolia 'Macrophylla'* (Bog rosemary). (A) (E)

Cornus alba and cultivars. For variegated foliage: 'Aurea'; 'Elegantissima'*; 'Spaethii'*; 'Variegata'. For winter bark effects: *alba* 'Sibirica'*; *stolonifera* 'Flaviramea'*.

*Hippophaë rhamnoides** (Sea buckthorn).

Ledum groenlandicum (Labrador tea) and *palustre* (Wild rosemary). (A) (E)

Lindera benzoin (Spice bush) and *obtusiloba**. (A)

Myrica gale (Sweet gale or Bog myrtle). (A)

Neillia thibetica (*longiracemosa*).

Physocarpus opulifolius (ninebark) and cultivars, including 'Dart's Gold'*.

Salix   There are many suitable shrubby species of this diverse and fascinating genus, notably: *alba* 'Britzensis'* and 'Vitellina'*, when stooled, for red and bright yellow winter-bark effects; *elaeagnos** (hoary willow); *fargesii*; *hastata* 'Wehrhahnii'*; *helvetica**; *lanata**; *purpurea* 'Gracilis'; *repens argentea**.

Bamboos:

Arundinaria.

Phyllostachys.

Sasa.

(See Chapter 8 for details).

MARGINAL AQUATIC PLANTS

These add greatly to the character, interest and completeness of a pool. Many are adaptable from several inches of shallow water to permanently damp soil. Planting instructions and depth of water are normally noted on plant labels supplied by nurserymen or garden centres. Some first-class marginal aquatics include:

Acorus calamus 'Variegatus'   A striking variegated plant with iris-like leaves, striped cream and gold. About 60cm (2ft).

Alisma plantago-aquatica (Water plantain) Large plantain-like leaves and whorls of pale pink flowers on branched stems. 60cm (2ft).

*Butomus umbellatus** (Flowering rush) A beautiful wild plant with triangular rush-like leaves and rose-pink flowers. 75cm (2¹/2ft).

Caltha palustris (Marsh marigold or kingcup)   A well-known wild plant. The double-flowered form 'Flore Pleno'* is more compact and a good garden plant. 30cm (1ft).

Glyceria maxima 'Variegata' (*aquatica* 'Variegata')   One of the most conspicuous of variegated grasses, it adapts to moist soil or shallow water. 60cm (2ft).

Iris kaempferi   (Japanese clematis iris) One of the many irises associated with waterside conditions. It is spectacular in

Houttuynia cordata 'Chamaeleon' is a spectacular and versatile newcomer which can be used as a shaded patio container plant. It is equally good in moist soil or as a marginal aquatic if contained – it tends to ramble!*

(Sh) = Shady site desirable   (A) = Acid soil essential   (E) = Evergreen

summer with varying shades and combinations of blue, purple and white flowers of clematis-like shape. Acid soil preferred, 60cm (2ft); Iris *laevigata** will produce a similar effect and flowers of deep blue; it is tolerant of all soils. 60cm (2ft).

*Lysichiton americanum** A striking plant with large yellow spathes, typical of the arum family, produced in mid-spring. Large, lush green leaves follow the flowers. There is also a white-flowered species, *camtschatcensis**.

Mentha aquatica (Water mint) Helps to keep the water pure and clear. It has sweet-smelling, bronze-purple foliage and clusters of deep lilac flowers. 30–45cm (1–1¹/2ft).

*Pontederia cordata** (Pickerel weed) Handsome spikes of blue flowers in summer and autumn. 45–60cm (1¹/2–2ft).

Ranunculus lingua 'Grandiflorus' (Great spearwort) A handsome plant with large lanceolate leaves and yellow buttercup flowers. 60cm–1m (2–3ft).

Sagittaria (Arrowhead) Unusual leaves which give the plant its name, and the species *S. sagittifolia* has whorls of white, purple-centred, three-petalled flowers in summer. 30–45cm (1–1¹/2ft).

Scirpus tabernaemontani (Bulrush) There are two interesting forms of moderate growth and suitable for ponds: 'Albescens', a tall plant with green and white variegated stems, 1m (3ft), and 'Zebrinus', with zebra stripes of green and white, about 1m (3ft).

Sparganium ramosum (Bur-reed) An unusual, branched plant, most interesting when clothed with the green spiky fruits which follow its heads of yellow flower. About 1m (3ft).

Typha (Reed-mace or False bulrush) The charming dwarf species *minima*, with grass-like leaves and small brown pokers, is the best plant for the smaller pool. The giant reed-mace, *latifolia*, erroneously known as bulrush, can be a very invasive plant which, unless restrained, will colonise large areas of pond or lake.

Veronica beccabunga (Brooklime) is an interesting, fleshy plant with bright blue flowers. 15cm (6in).

*Zantedeschia aethiopica** (H3) (Arum lily) An African species, which will usually survive colder winters if given at least 15cm (6in) of water over its crown. Alternatively, if pot grown, it can be housed under cold glass for the winter. It makes a striking contribution to the beauty of the pond margin, with its large white spathes and large leaves. 'Crowborough' is a hardier form with smaller spathes and leaves.

PLANTING POOL PLANTS

Late spring and early summer are the most sensible times to move and re-establish aquatic plants, both water lilies and marginals. They move best when coming into active growth and when the water is warming up for summer. The planting season can continue into late summer if necessary, but no later than this, as establishment will not be complete before the water cools and winter closes in.

Today, plastic tubs and purpose-made baskets with perforated sides provide an ideal method of accommodating water lilies and marginal aquatics in the concrete, fibreglass or butyl rubber-lined pool. In natural ponds, these containers can also be used to restrict the growth of water lilies and some marginal plants where necessary, and stockades composed of preserved (tanalised) wooden posts or half posts driven into the bed of the natural pond will restrict the advance of the more invasive marginal aquatics. Such treatment also provides a neat finish to the edge of a natural pond or island in a pond.

The standard water-lily basket is 30 x 30 x 20cm (12 x 12 x 8in) with tapering sides. Unless set in mud at the bottom of the pond or surrounded by two or three courses of bricks on the bottom of the pool, it will tend to be top heavy and fall over. Good medium to heavy garden soil, with the addition of chopped turf, is a good mixture to use. Peaty, sandy or chalky soil should be avoided, as should soil-less compost or farmyard manure or fertilisers, which will all tend to encourage the growth of algae and excessive growth of vigorous marginals and oxygenators.

Containers for marginals in artificial pools are often accommodated on a shelf around the edge. Here again, the commercial plastic planting crate, usually of smaller size and perhaps 15cm (6in) deep with tapering sides, will need support with bricks, unless a broad-based edition is available – perhaps in time manufacturers will learn!

WATERSIDE HERBACEOUS PLANTS

There are many herbaceous plants suitable for the soil adjoining natural pools, which will take an overflow or be naturally moist by capillary action or from a stream feeding the pool. Here, as space allows, you can accommodate such impressive specimens as:

Astilbe 'Bridal Veil', 'Fanal' and 'Rheinland'. (All *).

*Filipendula purpurea**

Gunnera manicata Gigantic rhubarb-like leaves, 2m (6¹/2ft) or more across on prickly stalks.

Hemerocallis 'Golden Chimes', 'Pink Damask' and 'Stella D'Oro'. (All *).

Hosta crispula 'Halcyon', 'Royal Standard' and 'Wide Brim'. (All *).

Lysimachia punctata (Yellow loosestrife).

*Lythrum salicaria** (Purple loosestrife) 'Firecandle'.

*Osmunda regalis** The distinguished Royal Fern.

Peltyphyllum peltatum Umbrella-like leaves, pink flowers preceding the foliage in mid-spring.

Rodgersia pinnata 'Superba'* and *aesculifolium**

It is also possible to naturalise a considerable range of moisture-loving candelabra primulas which, if happy, will increase and colonise, particularly *Primula beesiana, bulleyana*, denticulata*, florindae*, japonica* and vialii**.

Spectacular planting can still be enjoyed by those possessing a natural pool, where the surrounding soil is moist. Regrettably, artificial pools of concrete, fibreglass or butyl rubber are sealed off from the local soil, which may be dry and unsuitable for such plants unless a specially moist area can be contrived.

PLANT GROUPING FOR EFFECT

Plant groupings can achieve year-round impact of colour, shape, form and texture if carefully planned – foliage, flower, berry, even winter bark can be effective. The great range of shrubs available, evergreen and deciduous, extends from low groundcovers to tall screeners. Conifers offer a bewildering if beautiful range of sizes, shapes and textures and, with few exceptions, are evergreen, evergrey, evergold – or even everbronze or everpurple! Variegation in deciduous and evergreen trees and shrubs and conifers can create satisfying and eye-catching effects too, particularly when used as a focal point.

It must be stressed, that it is most important to take account of the likely ultimate growth (as well as suitability for your soil) of the trees, shrubs and conifers chosen. Even allowing for pruning where this is desirable, these 'bones' of the garden scene should be well spaced to allow for their development, thereby achieving the impact they can create. Large-growing shrubs are often planted within 0.3m–0.6m (1–2ft) of one another or of a less vigorous shrub, because their foliage may happen to blend, or perhaps the owner has seen them arranged like this at a flower show. Unfortunately, the stronger will quickly engulf the weaker and if they both survive neither can develop satisfactorily.

Space garden trees or medium-height conifers at least 4–6m (12–20ft) apart; dwarf, medium or large shrubs should be 1.5–2.5m (5–8ft) or more apart. Ultimate growth is often greater than you imagine, particularly on heavy loams or clay. Between the trees and shrubs can be grown a fascinating range of associated planting, both shrubby and herbaceous, generally of a groundcovering nature. As well as low-growing shrubs, long-lived herbaceous perennials can be used, together with ornamental grasses, ferns and prostrate or mound-forming shrub roses and low-spreading conifers; site them

A splendid tall vigorous Cotinus *'Grace'* may be kept compact by formative pruning while young. The large purple leaves turn scarlet in autumn. (A Peter Dummer hybrid.)*

0.3–1m (1–3ft) apart each way, often in groups of three or more of a kind, in order to ensure rapid coverage – closer for herbaceous plants, grasses and ferns, and wider apart for roses and conifers.

Within the limits of soil, aspect and sensible spacing, the possibilities are infinite, and the year-round interest, variety and artistic satisfaction that can be achieved from such a planting is boundless. However, in your planning do take account of colour blending as well as the vigour of your plants. Pleasing colour blends or contrasts are equally desirable when you arrange the groundcovers; these should be of sim-

ilar vigour in order that weaker growers are not swamped or overrun by more lusty neighbours. Be warned, however: it is easy to be bitten by the 'plantsman's bug' and to collect a great number of individually beautiful and interesting plants and shrubs, packing them in (often too closely) and rapidly making a formless mini-jungle. (But it's fun!). Most of the plants used in the following schemes were awarded Award of Garden Merit 1993 (see p152). (See p102 for Key to Planting Schemes.)

PLANTING SCHEME A

Red and purple with silver and grey foliage, sun or semi-shade. To be used in association with pale yellow, white, pale blue or pink flowers.

. . . .

Shrubs

Olearia macrodonta 'Major'	LS E (A1)
Cotinus coggygria 'Royal Purple' or 'Grace'	LS (A2)
Cornus alba 'Elegantissima'	MS (A3)
Senecio 'Sunshine or *Artemisia* 'Powis Castle'	SSE (A4)

Herbaceous perennials and groundcovers

Alchemilla mollis	HP (AS)
Geranium endressii 'A. T. Johnson' or 'Wargrave Pink'	HP (A6)
Hosta 'Elegans' or 'Frances Williams'	HP (A7)
Campanula lactiflora 'Prichard's Variety' or *alliarifolia* 'Ivory Bells	HP (A8)
Hemerocallis 'Golden Chimes' or *Helleborus argutifolius (corsicus)*	HP (A9)

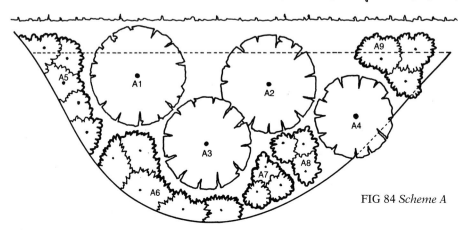

FIG 84 *Scheme A*

PLANTING SCHEME B

Golden or yellow and bronze or copper-tinted foliage.

Associate with yellow, orange or red flowers.

. . . .

Shrubs

Sambucus racemosa 'Plumosa Aurea'
or 'Sutherland'   LS (Bl)
Berberis thunbergii 'Red Chief' (SS)
or *Rosa rubrifolia* (*glauca*)   MS (B2)
Choisya ternata 'Sundance'   SS E (B3)
Physocarpus opulifolius 'Dart's Gold' SS (B4)
Euphorbia epithymoides (*polychroma*)
or *palustris*   HP (B5)

. . . .

Herbaceous perennials and groundcovers

Bergenia 'Evening Glow'
or *cordifolia* 'Purpurea'   HP E (B6)
Epimedium rubrum   HP E (B7)
Crocosmia 'Lucifer'   HP (B8)
Euonymus fortunei 'Emerald 'n' Gold'
                                               DS E (B9)

. . . .

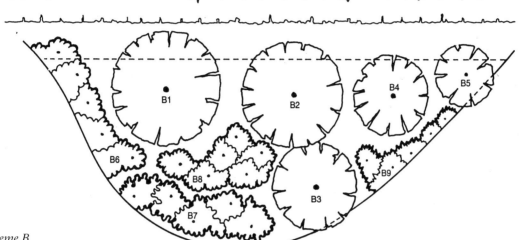

FIG 85 *Scheme B*

Choisya ternata *'Sundance'*(H3) is a striking form of Mexican orange blossom. The golden foliage is consistent throughout the year. Best sited in semi-shade.

Weigela florida *'Variegata'* underplanted with* Geranium endressii *'Wargrave Pink'*.*

Dicentra formosa *'Luxuriant'* – one of the best of new dicentra hybrids.*

PLANTING SCHEME C

Silver- and gold-variegated foliage. This is evergreen and deciduous and will go well with white, pink or blue flowers.

. . . .

Shrubs

Cornus alternifolia 'Argentea'	LS/ST (Cl)
or *Aralia elata* 'Variegata'	LS/ST
Elaeagnus x *ebbingei* 'Gilt Edge'	
or 'Limelight'	LS E (C2)
Weigela florida 'Variegata'	SS/MS (C3)
Rhamnus alaterna	
'Argenteovariegata'	LS E (C4)

Herbaceous perennials and groundcovers

Dicentra formosa 'Langtrees'	
or 'Luxuriant'	HP (C5)
Hosta crispula or *undulata*	HP (C6)
Geranium 'Johnson's Blue'	
or *endressi* 'Wargrave Pink'	HP (C7)
Campanula 'Burghaltii' or *persicifolia*	
'Telham Beauty'	HP(C8)

. . . .

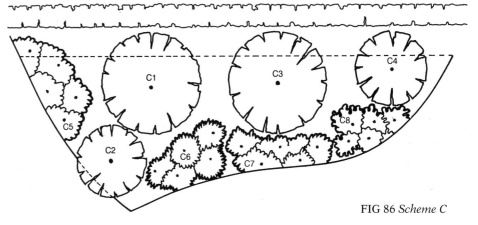

FIG 86 *Scheme C*

PLANTING SCHEME D

Shades of green and pale yellow leaves for shaded areas. To be associated with white, pale yellow or blue flowers.

....

Shrubs

Aucuba japonica 'Crotonifolia'
or *Euonymus japonicus* 'Marieke'
(or 'Ovatus Aureus')   LS E (Dl)
Viburnum opulus 'Sterile' or *plicatum*
'Lanarth'   MS (D2)
Danae racemosa   DS E (D3)

FIG 87 *Scheme D*

Herbaceous perennials and groundcovers

Gentiana asclepiadea   HP (D4)
Polygonatum x *hybridum*
(Solomon's seal)   HP (DS)
Vinca major 'Variegata'   HP E (D6)
Hosta fortunei 'Aurea'
or 'Honeybells'   HP (D7)
Kirengeshoma palmata   HP (D8)
Hakonechloa macra 'Aureola' ('Albo-aurea')
or *Milium effusum* 'Aureum'
(Bowles' golden grass)   HP (D9)
Helleborus argutifolius (corsicus)
                 HP E (D10)

PLANTING SCHEME E

Foliage shape and texture for an open sunny situation and well-drained soil.

....

Shrubs and conifers

Phlomis 'Edward Bowles'   SS E (E1)
Juniperus communis 'Hibernica'
          (conifer) LS E (E2)
Phormium tenax 'Purpureum'
or 'Variegatum'   MS E (E3)
Photinia 'Red Robin'   MS E (E4)
Thuja occidentalis 'Rheingold'
          (conifer) E (E5)
Aralia elata   LS (E6)
Modern shrub rose 'Heritage'
or 'Mary Rose'   SS (E7)
Cryptomeria japonica
'Elegans Nana'   (conifer) DS E (E8)
Juniperus squamata 'Blue Star'
or 'Blue Carpet'   (conifer) DS E (E9)
Shrub rose 'Rosy Cushion'
or 'Little White Pet'   DS (E10)

....

Herbaceous perennials and groundcovers

Waldsteinia ternata   HP (E11)
Agapanthus 'Headbourne Hybrids'
or 'Lilliput'   HP (E12)
Shrub rose 'Red Max Graf'
or 'Suma'   GC (E13)
Acanthus spinosus   HP (E14)
Helianthemum 'Wisley Pink'
or 'Mrs Clay' ('Firedragon') GC E (E15)
Penstemon 'Garnet'   HP (E16)
Santolina chamaecyparissus 'Nana'
(var. *corsica*)   GC E (E17)
Alchemilla mollis   HP (E18)
Geranium macrorrhizum
'Ingwersen's Variety'   GC E (E19)
Cotoneaster dammeri
or 'Gnom'   GC E (E20)
Erica carnea 'Ann Sparkes'
or 'Foxhollow'   GC E (E21)

....

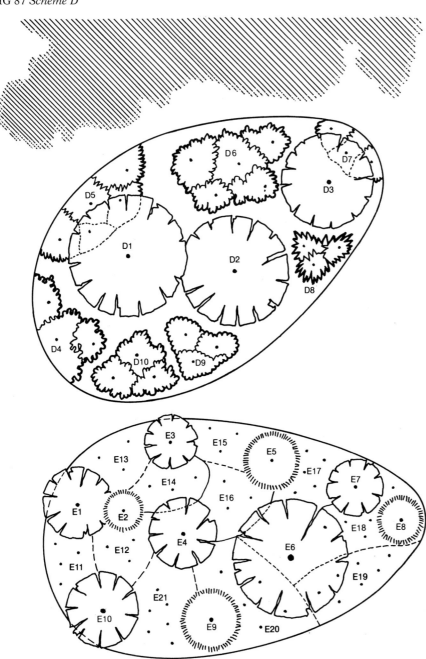

FIG 88 *Scheme E*

PLANTING SCHEME F

Foliage shape and texture for a semi-shaded position and well-drained soil.

. . . .

Shrubs

Hydrangea paniculata 'Tardiva'	MS (F1)
Rhododendron macabeanum (A) or *Ilex* x	
altaclerensis 'Lawsoniana'	LS/ST E (F2)
Hydrangea aspera or *villosa*	MS (F3)
Acer japonicum 'Aconitifolium'	
or 'Vitifolium'	LS (F4)
x *Fatshedera lizei*	MS E (F5)

Herbaceous perennials and ground covers

Ophiopogon planiscapus	
'Nigrescens'	HP (F6)
Hosta fortunei 'Aureo-marginata'	HP (F7)
Hedera helix 'Manda's Crested'	GC E (F8)
Rodgersia pinnata 'Superba'	HP (F9)
Cimicifuga ramosa	
'Atropurpurea'	HP (F10)
Euphorbia polychroma (epithymoides)	
	HP (F11)
Anemone x *hybrida*	
'Queen Charlotte'	HP (F12)
Athyrium felix-femina	(fern) (F13)
Hosta fortunei 'Albopicta'	
or *Undulata*	HP (F14)
Bergenia 'Silberlicht'	HP (F15)
Polystichum setiferum	
'Plumoso-divisilobum'	(fern) (F16)
Hakonechloa macra 'Aureola'	
('Albo-aurea')	(grass) (F17)

. . . .

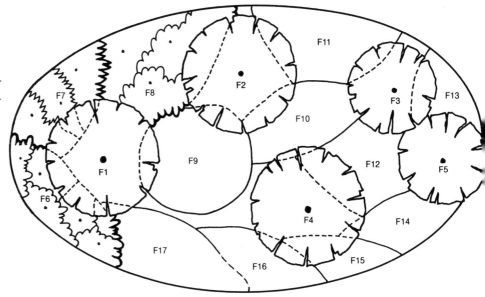

FIG 89 *Scheme F*

Euphorbia polychroma* *produces flowers in spring and the leaves turn scarlet in autumn before falling.*

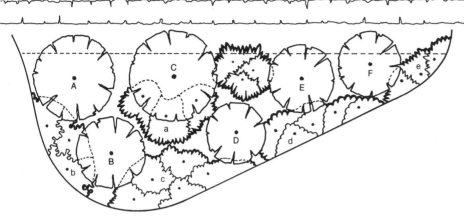

FIG 90 *Scheme G*

PLANTING SCHEME G

Autumn foliage and berries combined with spring and summer flowers.

. . . .

Shrubs/Trees

Disanthus cercidifolius (A)	
or *Rhus glabra* 'Laciniata'	MS (A)
Euonymus alatus	MS (B)
Prunus 'Spire'	
or *Photinia villosa*	ST (C)
Berberis x *media* 'Parkjuweel'	
or 'Red Jewel'	SS (Semi E) (D)
Fothergilla major (A)	
or *Hamamelis vernalis* 'Sandra'	MS (E)
Prunus glandulosa 'Alba Plena'	SS (F)

Groundcovers – shrubby and herbaceous

Cotoneaster conspicuus 'Decorus'	DS E
or *C.*'Gnom'	DS E (a)
Hosta 'Elegans'	
or 'Frances Williams'	HP (b)
Polygonum affine 'Donald Lowndes'	HP (c)
Bergenia *cordifolia* 'Purpurea'	
or 'Bressingham Ruby'	HP E (d)
Hosta undulata	HP (e)

. . . .

Fothergilla major* *in its autumn cloak and there are white flower clusters in early spring.*

PLANTING SCHEME H

Shrubs/small trees with winter bark effects, for sun or semi-shade. Some variegated foliage, plus groundcovers and ferns with interesting foliage and flower.

. . . .

Shrubs/small trees

Acer griseum (Paper-bark maple) or *davidii*
(Snakebark maple)   ST (A)
Rubus cockburnianus   MS (B)
Cornus alba 'Elegantissima'‡   MS (C)
Euonymus fortunei 'Emerald Gaiety'
or 'Emerald 'n' Gold'   SS E (D)
Cornus stolonifera 'Flaviramea'‡
or 'White Gold'‡   MS (E)
(‡ Stool/coppice periodically to maintain
compact habit and brightly coloured shoots)

Groundcovers and ferns

Hosta lancifolia   HP (a)
Hosta fortunei 'Albo picta'
or 'Wide Brim'   HP (b)
Lamium maculatum 'Beacon Silver'
or 'White Nancy'   HP (c)
Ajuga reptans 'Burgundy Glow'   HP (d)
Alchemilla mollis   HP (e)
Osmunda regalis or *Onoclea sensibilis*
    (fern) (f)
Vinca major 'Variegata'   GC (E) (g)

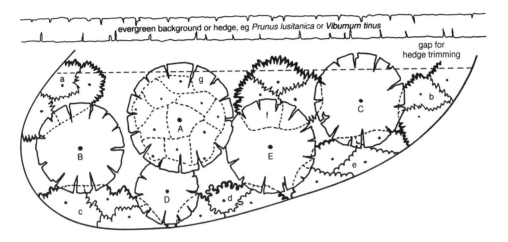

FIG 91 *Scheme H*

CHAPTER 8

PLANTS FOR PERSONAL COLLECTIONS

To some, a garden is a setting, whether for playing games or eating barbecues, or for showing off the property to popular acclaim. Others think that anyone can design an attractive layout (or at least try to) but that gardening is a question of using and enjoying plants. Of course, both views have their limitations: a plantsman's collection may be too specialised to be beautiful, just as a functional landscape may be unwelcoming.

Earlier chapters concentrated on 'technical' considerations: subjects like how to plan the garden, the act of planting, shrub maintenance, and which colours of plants associate to best effect. This section is not primarily concerned with these aspects; instead, its starting point is the sheer enjoyment which can be gained from taking a passionate interest in plants.

WHY DEVELOP A PERSONAL COLLECTION?

A personal plant collection can add that extra zest to gardening which comes from having something which few other people possess. Many of the plant genera or groupings discussed in the following pages, such as roses or clematis, include some very popular, everyday items, but the knowledge that 96 per cent of all gardens contain hybrid tea or floribunda roses removes some of the impetus to grow them! After all, who really wants to be like everyone else? There are of course, many more rose cultivars available than just hybrid teas and floribundas (now strictly known as 'large-flowered' and 'cluster-flowered' roses respectively). These, as well as the attractive species and old-fash-

ioned roses, provide an extra dimension to rose growing.

A personal collection is rewarding for the information it provides. Nearly every subject becomes more interesting as you learn more about it. Growing the common plants in any genus means growing those which nurserymen have selected, and the range of suitable plants available is so large that no nursery can offer a complete list. Most of the plants in general circulation in the nursery trade are good and reliable examples of their species, but there are often many equally good forms or related species which are not commonly available. Sometimes this is because they are old varieties, no longer in fashion, sometimes they are too new and have not caught the eye of the right exponent of their group of plants.

Many of the commonest plants have been selected for their instant appeal, but where they gain in brilliance of colour or size of blooms is frequently matched by a loss of beauty and subtlety. Get to know a group of plants and you soon appreciate the potential of a wider range of forms, and can marvel at the beauty offered by foliage, flower, fruit and habit.

Each of the following plant profiles gives an overview of one genus of plants, such as clematis, or a special group of plants, like grasses and bamboos. Each of the genera selected (and many have sadly had to be omitted for reasons of space) contains not only a number of well-known and common species or cultivars, but also a number of uncommon but desirable ones, offering a range of characteristics or uses beyond those employed in the

CONSERVING PLANTS

In recent years there has been a remarkable rise in plant conservation groups. In Britain, for example, the National Council for the Conservation of Plants and Gardens (NCCPG) has instituted a system of National Plant Collections – in 1992 there were more than 550 collections available for inspection. The main tasks of the National Collection holders are to conserve stocks of garden plants otherwise threatened with loss or extinction, and to encourage propagation and availability of a wider range of worthy garden plants. This chapter offers a selection of plant profiles to encourage you to build up a personal collection of effective and gardenworthy trees, shrubs and plants to suit your garden, soil and locality, as well as your taste.

'average' garden. All are, or should shortly be, available commercially, albeit with a little searching. Within the profiles, the main features of the genus or group are highlighted for instant reference, while practical matters such as particular planting or pruning requirements are included where appropriate.

The aim of this chapter is to help in broadening your outlook and to encourage the development of a specialised interest in building a unique collection to give your garden a truly individual identity.

AWARD OF GARDEN MERIT 1993 (AGM 1993)

Subjects for this award are recommended to the Council of the Royal Horticultural Society on the basis of their assessment as *Valuable Garden Plants* suitable for gardens of all sizes from the smallest to the largest.

The plant so awarded should be:
• excellent for ordinary garden decoration or use in the open or under protection, according to hardiness
• of good constitution
• available in the horticultural trade.

The plant should not be:
• particularly susceptible to any pest or disease
• a subject requiring highly specialised growing conditions
• subject to an unreasonable degree of reversion.

During 1992 the RHS Committees reassessed all plants to which the AGM award had already been granted and made further recommendations. We have included these latest recommendations in the book, denoted by an asterisk * following the name, both here in the lists of recommended plants and elsewhere.

The RHS has also included a hardiness rating for each plant awarded; adopting the system formerly confined to rhododendrons and azaleas (H1–H4). Most of the awarded plants mentioned here are considered 'hardy' (H4). Where this is *not* the case we have included the rating after the asterisk [eg, *(H3)] (apart from rhododendrons and azaleas where all ratings are given).

The RHS will be reviewing and updating their Award of Garden Merit recommendations regularly.

BERBERIS AND MAHONIA

INSTANT REFERENCE

• BERBERIS: Well-barbed species make excellent hedges; often prolific masses of flower in yellow and orange shades, plus range of foliage colours and some with good berries.

• MAHONIA: Good architectural plants; flower racemes in winter and spring in shades of yellow, often fragrant; large, pinnate leaves.

• Dwarf to large shrubs
• Evergreen and deciduous
• Upright or low and spreading
• Most soils
• Hardy

Between them these shrubs offer the garden a wide range of extremely handsome and useful plants, and are so closely related botanically that they are grouped together here. The major difference between the two is that mahonias are thornless (apart from the leaf-edges) and have larger, pinnate foliage; both range from low, spreading shrubs to large, upright ones.

MAKING A CHOICE
Dwarf Growers
Many berberis are low growing and ideal as small, mainly evergreen, ground-smothering shrubs. *B.* x *frikartii* 'Amstelveen'* is shade tolerant and has dark, glossy green and spiny leaves which are glaucous beneath and carried on drooping shoots to form a dense, compact mound. *B.* x *interposita* 'Wallich's Purple' forms a dense, round mound of arching stems, the young leaves attractively bronze-red. In both of these the yellow spring flowers look particularly good against the dark foliage. *B.* x *stenophylla* 'Corallina Compacta'* forms a dwarf shrub, growing to little more than 30cm (1ft), with coral-red buds opening to yellow. It makes an excellent rock-garden shrub.

Among dwarf and low-growing mahonias, *M. aquifolium* 'Apollo' is a particularly good, spreading variety with deep golden-yellow flowers, an improvement on the type species – the Oregon Grape – which tends to be rather straggly in growth. Other distinct and worthy cultivars of this species are 'Atropurpurea', with red-purple leaves during winter and spring, and 'Moseri', most notable for its bronze-red young leaves, later turning green.

Mahonia nervosa has conspicuous racemes of flowers in late spring set off by the lustrous leaves, which turn scarlet in winter, but avoid this species on shallow, chalky soil.

Foliage and Flower
Although generally small in size of flower, berberis produce them in prolific masses, and none more so than the commonly planted evergreen *Berberis* x *stenophylla** and its many forms. Often used to make a hedge,

Berberis thunbergii in autumn with the fruit seen against leaves which change from green through yellow to scarlet (see page 154).

Berberis thunbergii *'Red Chief'* makes a small shrub with arching branches. Its red stems and purple leaves are eye-catching throughout the growing season.*

the plant is magnificent when in full flower; to avoid removing flowers it is important only to clip the hedge during early summer, following flowering. The excellent new cultivar 'Claret Cascade' has its flowers flushed red and young foliage tinted purple. The dwarf-growing variety 'Coccinea' has crimson buds that open orange. *Berberis darwinii**, an orange-flowered species worthy of its distinguished discoverer Charles Darwin, is also spectacular in flower and is often used for hedging. *B. linearifolia* 'Jewel' has conspicuous flowers, scarlet in bud and opening to bright orange, complementing the narrow, glossy dark green leaves. *B. valdiviana* grows to 3m (10ft) or more, making a handsome, large and stately evergreen, its long drooping racemes of saffron-yellow flowers looking good in spring against the leathery, polished dark green leaves. A hybrid of this species with *B. darwinii* has been named 'Goldilocks'*

and combines the best attributes of its distinguished parents, making a large, vigorous shrub with arching, upright branches. The dark, glossy green leaves show off the deep golden-yellow flowers, which hang in red-stalked clusters for a good period in spring. Talented Hillier propagator, Peter Dummer, created this hybrid in 1978.

The larger flower racemes of mahonias are often equally spectacular, notably those of *M. japonica**, which ranks among the most distinguished of evergreen shrubs hardy in the northern hemisphere. This very shade-tolerant species forms a magnificent shrub, with deep green, pinnate leaves and long, drooping racemes of fragrant, lemon-yellow flowers produced as the weather allows from late autumn to early spring. There are also a number of superb hybrids of this species with *M. lomariifolia*, flowering mainly in late autumn and early winter and known

collectively as *M.* x *media*. They all have excellent architectural leaves and make spectacular winter-flowering plants of both upright and lax habit. Of particular note are 'Lionel Fortescue'* with long, upright racemes; 'Charity'*, perhaps the best known and most widely planted of this group, forming a large shrub of stately, upright habit with long and spreading flower racemes; and 'Underway', which has similar flowering qualities and a relatively compact habit, very appropriate for the small garden. In a well-drained, sunny site, *M. trifoliolata* var. *glauca* makes a striking medium-sized shrub with conspicuously veined, spiny and glaucous leaflets that set off the clusters of spring flowers and the red-currant-like berries which follow.

Coloured Foliage Effects
While the mahonias already mentioned provide some marvellously architectural effects in the garden, many smaller-leafed berberis provide a wide range of foliage colour, particularly the deciduous species, which colour well in the autumn. There are, however, forms with purple-red foliage throughout the summer, notably the large-growing *B.* x *ottawensis* 'Superba'*, which forms a vigorous, medium to large shrub displaying rich purple foliage, yellow spring flowers and red autumn berries. In similar vein is *B. thunbergii* 'Atropurpurea' and its very much dwarfed form 'Atropurpurea Nana'*, the latter reaching only about 45cm (1¹/₂ft). Other selected forms of *B. thunbergii** include 'Red Chief'*; 'Helmond Pillar' of narrow, upright habit and rich purple foliage; and 'Rose Glow'*, its purple young leaves mottled silver-pink. In marked contrast, the cultivar *B. thunbergii* 'Aurea' has yellow leaves becoming pale green by late summer and requiring a semi-shaded site to avoid sun scorch. The excellent semi-evergreen small shrub *B.* x *media* 'Parkjuweel'* has almost spineless leaves which colour very richly in the autumn, often remaining until the following spring. *Berberis*

temolaica is a beautiful species forming a vigorous medium-sized shrub. It is unusual in having glaucous foliage of a delightful grey-blue tint, particularly effective in spring in combination with its delicate, pale primrose flowers.

Berries and Autumn Leaf Colour

Among the best berberis combining these attributes are the following deciduous hybrids and species, which generally make excellent small or dwarf shrubs for the garden. 'Bountiful' has clusters of coral-red berries on arching branches; *B. georgei* is particularly effective, with good crops of crimson berries in pendulous clusters, often persisting into the new year; and 'Rubrostilla'* is a most impressive autumn plant, with translucent coral-red berries and unfailing autumn leaf colour. As already mentioned, *Berberis thunbergii** colours particularly well in autumn, as do most of its cultivars. The purple-leaved forms often change to claret or scarlet as autumn approaches, notably 'Red Pillar', with its upright habit and red-purple leaves

turning bright scarlet, and 'Kobold', a very free-fruiting dwarf form of dense, rounded habit.

Evergreen Hedges and Screens

Of the evergreen berberis species there are some handsome and well-barbed species which make excellent dense and impenetrable hedges, ideal for deterring invasion from next door's dogs and children. Perhaps the best of these is *B. gagnepainii*, a tough, dark, dense hedging plant with narrow leaves and blue-black bloomy berries in the autumn. *B. julianae* is ideal as a tall hedging or screening plant of dense, erect habit. It is extremely hardy and very spiny, and the leaves are copper tinted when young. *B. sanguinea* 'Panlanensis' is ideal for smaller hedges to about 1m (3ft); of very neat growth, its tiny leaves are sea-green in colour and fine toothed. *B. verruculosa** is ideal for a dense hedge up to 1.5m (5ft). The small, glossy dark green leaves are white beneath, displaying the solitary golden-yellow flowers to good effect. It is very neat and compact, if slow growing.

BETULA (BIRCHES)

INSTANT REFERENCE

- Small to large trees
- Deciduous
- Upright, rounded or weeping
- Beautiful barks (smooth or peeling), spring catkins, attractive leaves and autumn colour
- Most well-drained soils, but dislike heavy clays or shallow soils over chalk
- Hardy
- Very attractive specimen trees

Silver birch (*Betula pendula*) is one of the most common trees planted in gardens and can make a delightful specimen. It is renowned for its silvery-white bark, upright habit with graceful pendulous branches, and a light, open crown of diamond-shaped leaves which turn yellow in autumn. Other birches include shrubs – not just trees – which compare favourably with it in foliage, bark and autumn colour although, to be honest, none has the grace of habit of the best individuals of silver birch. However, other types are worthy of serious consideration, especially where you have room for more than one tree, or where every other garden in the vicinity contains a monotony of silver birches!

Birches are normally considered medium to large trees, and most of the species and cultivars will grow to 10–15m (33–50ft), some to 25–30m (80–100ft) if conditions are absolutely perfect. However, they do not all grow as large – some are not even a metre tall – and there are birches suited to most gardens.

The attractive features of birches include their bark (surely their strongest contribution), foliage, especially in autumn dress, and catkins in early spring. The seeds are also a valued food source for several birds, such as redpolls, siskins and tits. Barks range from the brilliant white of

Mahonia x media 'Lionel Fortescue' magnificent at all times for its evergreen architectural leaves and in late autumn/early winter for its upright flower racemes (see page 153).*

Within a few years of planting, Betula nigra*, the River birch from USA, develops wonderful shaggy brown/black bark which is a feature throughout the year. A fine waterside tree.*

demand than many other trees. They can be safely used closer to buildings on shrinkable clay subsoils than most other trees, although it is always desirable not to plant them closer than a distance of at least half their ultimate height from the dwelling.

Birches are intolerant of shade and need an open position if they are to flourish. Also, although they cast a relatively light and dappled shade, they compete effectively with other plants for soil moisture and nutrients and do not make good overstorey trees. They are best planted where the bark and habit can be enjoyed, not to provide overhead shelter (although they give excellent side shelter) except for dappled shade over a sitting area.

Practical Matters
SOIL
Birches are fairly fast-growing trees, and will grow well on most soils, the main exception being heavy clays, although they do not flourish on shallow soils over chalk. They are very much at home on sandy, well-drained soils. Brown birch (*B. pubescens*) naturally grows on damp sites but is scarcely worth planting in a garden. Birches do not tolerate periods of drought and on sharply-draining soils watering is desirable in dry summers.

PLANTING
The roots tend to be rather coarse and widespread, and birches can be more difficult to move and establish than many other trees. Smaller trees are easier to move and more reliable; they will also grow away more rapidly than larger trees. The important considerations for successful establishment are to ensure that the plants are of good quality and that they are not allowed to dry out either before or after planting.

PRUNING
Birches will bleed if cut during the late-spring period, at which time pruning should be avoided.

PESTS AND DISEASES
Birches are not usually affected by

Paper and Jacquemont birches at one extreme, to the mahogany bark of Himalayan birch at the other, with the silver white of silver birch somewhere in the middle. The bark may also be tight and smooth, as in silver birch, or peel off in large sheets, as with Chinese red-bark birch. The leaves are usually light green and small, but in Monarch birch they are large and lime-like (to 17cm–6½in). The catkins open in early spring before the leaves and, when fully expanded, the male catkins can be around 15cm (6in) long (in *B. jacquemontii* 'Jermyns').

Birches have a lower water

serious insect or fungal pests although, like most trees, diseases such as honey fungus can kill them. Old trees are soon decayed by the birch polypore fungus, but in any case they are not long-lived trees, 50 years being a good life. They form associations with soil fungi, and fruit bodies of these fungi (eg the fly agaric toadstool) are often found around the trees, especially on sandy soils.

MAKING A CHOICE
White-bark Birches
B. pendula* (Silver birch) is, as already mentioned, the most common birch in gardens. The species shows some variability in habit and general quality: at its best it is almost unsurpassable, but poor individuals on sites where the soil is too heavy may have little to recommend them. It also tends to grow too large for many situations, often attaining a height of 20m (70ft). *B.p.* 'Crispa'* ('Dalecarlica' of the horticultural trade, not the true Swedish cut-leaf clone) is an excellent form. The habit is upright with only light branching, on which are carried long pendulous branchlets; the leaves are deeply and attractively cut. 'Fastigiata' has a crown which is narrow at the base but broadens above, with erect, sinuous branches. It may be suitable for sites where space is limited; however, it has none of the grace and charm of other selections and is of curiosity value only. 'Tristis'* is a graceful form with a narrow, erect habit and long hanging curtains of branchlets. 'Crispa' ('Darlecarlica'), 'Fastigiata' and 'Tristis' will make tall trees. 'Purpurea' is a form with leaves which are deep purple. Because it has the characteristic open crown of silver birch it can look lost except against a strongly contrasting background, such as a golden cypress. 'Youngii'* has pendulous branches and branchlets, forming a mound of weeping foliage. It only slowly (if at all) grows taller than the height to which it is trained, but will spread 5–8m (16–26ft) in diameter. It is a useful weeping tree for a small garden.

B. pubescens (White, Downy or Brown birch) is the second native tree birch. It tolerates damper situations than silver birch and is a longer-lived and larger-growing tree, but lacks the graceful charm of silver birch. The twigs are downy, whilst the bark is frequently dull brown on young trees and white or off-white on older ones.

B. papyrifera (Paper birch) has smooth bark which peels in thin paper-like layers, hence its common name. Another is Canoe-bark birch – the framework of the original Canadian canoes was covered by sheets of its bark. The bark colour is often a vivid white, much more so than in silver birch, with a creamy, pink or pale orange hue. The habit is rather stiff, making a small to medium tree with an open, rounded crown. *B.p.* var. *kenaica* is one of several varieties; it has a creamy-white to reddish-brown bark.

B. szechuanica (Sichuan birch), also known as *B. platyphylla* var. *szechuanica*, has a rather gaunt aspect to the rounded crown. The leaves are heart-shaped or rhombic in outline, dark green above and rather glaucous beneath; they are relatively large and carried well spaced on the branches. The striking feature of this tree is the chalky whiteness of the bark. It has such a generous coating of betulin, the waxy compound which gives many birches their white bark, that it can be rubbed off like whitewash or chalk from a blackboard.

B. ermanii (Erman Birch) is grown for its bark, which in young trees is a good white colour, becoming creamy-white with a pink or orange tinge and strongly peeling in old trees. Erman birch makes a medium-sized tree with neat leaves which turn a good golden yellow in autumn. 'Grayswood Hill'* is a selection with striking white bark and good golden-yellow autumn colour. *B.* 'Fetisowii' is a hybrid of Polish origin. It forms a narrow erect tree and develops a chalky-white peeling bark. *B. utilis* var. *jacquemontii** (Jacquemont birch) is perhaps the best known white-barked birch apart from silver birch. It makes an admirable small to medium tree

with a really bright, smooth yet peeling bark which is exceptionally white. The crown is upright, becoming rounded in older trees, and the leaves turn a good golden colour in the autumn. This plant can be very attractive if used to create an avenue along a drive – the white bark will shine out in a ghostly way in the car headlights – or where garden lighting is contemplated. Botanically it is part of the wide-ranging Himalayan birch, which extends from Afghanistan to western China, though Jacquemont birch is restricted to the western Himalayas from central Nepal to north-west India. The forms from further east have bark which is bright pink, mahogany or coppery brown and peels in large, thin sheets, giving a kaleidoscope of differing colours when the sun shines through bark which is still partly attached. As with all trees with a peeling bark, you can remove this if you are tidy minded and do not like the shaggy effect, but on no account should the under layers be peeled off, as removal of these will leave a dark brown scar for many years. Selected named clones with white bark include the following; they will make trees 10m (33ft) tall, then slowly reaching perhaps 15m (50ft): 'Jermyns'* has creamy-white bark on the trunk and main branches, giving way to orange-brown on the smaller branches. Apart from excellent autumn colour, the male catkins in spring are longer than any other birch and give quite a display; 'Silver Shadow'* also has dazzling white stems and long, attractive catkins but with larger, drooping leaves; and 'Doorenbos'* which is a Dutch selection with a striking white bark which peels to reveal creamy new bark beneath.

Coloured-bark Birches
B. albo-sinensis (Chinese red-bark birch) has one of the best non-white barks. The best form is the Werrington clone, raised from seeds collected by Wilson in western China in 1910. This develops an orange, peeling, papery bark which has been

likened to burnished copper and will reach large tree size. Almost as good is the variety *septentrionalis**, which is more readily available and makes a narrower-crowned tree. Here the bark is dark pink or dark red with a white waxy bloom; peeling in large sheets to reveal chalky white beneath.

*B. nigra** (River birch) has shaggy, pinkish white bark with rhombic leaves which are medium green above, and paler with white soft hairs beneath. Older trees develop dark, almost black bark.

B. alleghaniensis (Yellow birch), also called *B. lutea*, has bark which is a dull bronzy colour and peels in small flakes. The best characteristic of this species is the really bright gold of the autumn colour, unsurpassed by any other birch. The twigs have a strong scent of oil of wintergreen, although this is only evident when the bark is scraped. Yellow birch makes a tree 10–15m (33–50ft) tall and has neat green foliage.

CEANOTHUS

Very beautiful, mainly blue-flowered, evergreen and deciduous shrubs or small trees, the species of ceanothus are native to the Pacific coast area of west and north America, where they contribute substantiallly to the 'chaperral' or dense brushwood vegetation found slightly inland from the sea. They are often known as Californian lilacs.

The ceanothus provide us with perhaps the most spectacular blue-flowered spring and summer-flowering shrubs we can grow. They succeed on all fertile, well-drained soils, and are particularly suitable for sunny walls, or free standing in sheltered walled or fenced gardens if associated with other dense evergreen shrubs. They are excellent seaside shrubs; some are of low mound-like habit and suitable for bankings and low walls.

Regrettably none can be said to be absolutely and reliably hardy in colder

Ceanothus *'Puget Blue'** (C. impressus *'Puget Blue'). Proven among the hardiest of ceanothus, this is perhaps the most satisfactory variety now available for depth of colour, the freedom of its spring display and for its compact growth whether wall-trained or free-standing (see page 158).*

INSTANT REFERENCE

- Shrubs or small trees
- Evergreen and deciduous
- Upright or mound-forming
- Mainly blue, tiny star-shaped flowers in spring and autumn
- Fertile, well-drained soil
- Fairly hardy in warmer areas, but like protection in colder climates and may suffer dieback in severe winters
- Good seaside plants

areas; even in favoured districts, penetrating arctic winds in winter can seriously damage them, causing massive dieback of twigs and branches, notably of the evergreen species. However, where roots have not been severely frozen, well-established specimens will usually regrow satisfactorily in the spring, particularly if new shoots are helped with foliar feeding. The small-leaved species and cultivars seem to be somewhat hardier than those with larger leaves. However, the genus should not be looked upon as long-lived in cooler climates, and as replacements flower when young and are fast growing, the death of an older, mature plant, although disappointing, is not an irreparable loss.

Practical Matters

PLANTING

This is best carried out in spring when danger of severe frost is over, early autumn being rather a second-best time, although it is usually successful for warm, sheltered wall sites in all but the coldest areas; free-standing specimens planted in autumn will require winter protection in all but the warmest climates or favoured coastal districts in cooler ones.

PRUNING

The deciduous hybrids, such as 'Gloire de Versailles', and one or two of the late-summer or autumn-flowering evergreen hybrids ('Autumnal Blue' and 'Burkwoodii'), which flower on growth made that season, are normally pruned back in spring as new growth commences. Evergreen species and cultivars are pruned during summer, when the flowers have faded. Those trained on walls should be pruned annually: cut back laterals to within two or three buds of the previous year's growth if a compact, mat-like wall coverage is desired.

MAKING A CHOICE

Low Growers

Mound-forming or groundcovering ceanothus are suitable for courtyard, patio and foreground planting, and some are adaptable for furnishing bankings and festooning low walls and balustrades and for covering inspection covers. All are evergreen.

Ceanothus 'Blue Mound' lives up to its name, producing bright blue flowers in late spring and early summer. It is a small-leaved variety, possibly a variety of *C. prostratus*, a reasonably hardy creeping species with holly-like leaves from the Cascade and Siskiyou mountains where it is known as Squaw Carpet; although both of these seem moderately hardy, *C. thyrsiflorus repens**, with pale blue flowers in early summer, is undoubtedly hardier and remarkably vigorous. It will furnish steep banks and is ideal for low walls.

Taller Growers

These are for training on warm, sunny walls or free standing in sheltered gardens. All are evergreen unless otherwise noted.

C. arboreus 'Trewithen Blue'* has a tree-like habit and large, broadly oval leaves 5–10cm (2–4in) long. This fine form of the species carries large panicles of deep blue flowers up to 13cm (5in) long in mid- to late spring, and is suitable for tall walls.

The group of French-raised hybrids known as *C. delilianus* are deciduous and mostly hardy, and suitable as free-standing shrubs in sheltered gardens in all but the coldest areas, where they should be grown against walls of low to medium height. They are best hard pruned each spring, as they flower in summer and autumn on the current season's growth. Large panicles of flower show considerable variation of colour - among the most successful and popular are 'Gloire de Versailles'*, powder blue in large panicles; 'Henri Desfosse'*, violet blue; 'Perle Rose', carmine pink; and 'Topaz'*, indigo blue.

C. 'Puget Blue'* is renowned for the brilliance of its deep-blue floral displays in spring, and distinct in its small oval leaves with impressed veins. When grown as a wall shrub it will respond well to pruning following flowering to maintain a dense, close wall covering. *C. papillosus*, and its variety *roweanus*, is a beautiful and interesting species from the Santa Cruz mountains where it shows a variation in height between 1.5 and about 5m (5–16ft) and is notable for its sticky leaves with glandular teeth and wart-like excrescences. The lower, more spreading *roweanus* has narrower leaves and deep blue flowers in late spring. This species is the parent of one of the hardiest and most spectacular of garden hybrids, the British-raised 'Delight'*, which produces long racemes of rich blue flowers in spring. Derived from the hybrid x *lobbianus*, 'Southmead', a smaller cultivar of rather dense habit, is reasonably hardy and produces bright, rich blue flowers in late spring and early summer. Of similar origin and flowering time is the popular hybrid x *veitchianus*, with clusters of deep blue flowers up to 5cm (2in) in length; both will reach 3m (10ft) on a wall. *C. sorediatus*, known in California as 'Jim Brush', is notable for flowering in both spring and autumn; consequently, this species is most probably involved in the breeding of several popular and useful hybrids which produce their deep blue flowers in summer and autumn, particularly 'Autumnal Blue'* (the hardier), and 'Burkwoodii'*, with flowers in late summer and autumn.

C. thyrsiflorus has the distinction of being the hardiest evergreen species and can be successfully grown against a warm wall in colder areas. Free standing, it will grow rapidly up to 3m (10ft) or more; pale blue flowers are produced freely in the summer on maturing specimens, but not always on young plants. The slightly tender cultivar 'Cascade'* is thought to be a form of this species and makes a tall shrub with arching branches, very spectacular when in flower in the spring.

CLEMATIS

INSTANT REFERENCE

• Mostly climbers, some herbaceous plants
• Evergreen and deciduous
• Flowers at all times of year (according to type) in shades of white, pink, red, purple and blue, some yellow; occasionally scented
• Good garden soil; roots in shade, flowers and foliage in sun
• Mostly hardy
• Excellent for clothing walls and pergolas, and for climbing through shrubs and trees

Clematis is a very popular group of plants, but despite this, few gardeners realise just how many are available. Botanically, there are over 200 species, in addition to the many garden hybrids. Clematis can be chosen to be in flower in any month of the year, whilst a few are attractive in fruit. They range from herbaceous plants to rampant climbers, with evergreen species as well as deciduous ones.

The most common clematis in gardens are either the large-flowered hybrids, such as *C.* 'Jackmanii Superba' and *C.* 'Nelly Moser', or the spring-flowering *C. montana*. These are, rightly, highly valued for the striking displays they provide, but to limit the clematis you grow to this small band is to deny yourself some of the choicest of plants.

Firstly, though, consider the special merits and requirements of these plants. Most clematis are climbers and are very useful for covering walls, scrambling over trellis or through shrubs and small trees. They can also be very effective in formal areas and borders grown on a pyramid of three stout stakes 2–3m (6–9ft) tall, placed a metre apart at the base and tied together near the top. Clematis can also be used to give an extra season of display to a flowering tree, such as when scrambling through a magnolia,

to brighten up a dull feature or add an extra element to heathers and dwarf conifers.

Clematis like to have their flowers and foliage in the sun and roots in cool and shady locations. They will thrive best where these conditions are met; the general recommendation is to have the roots growing beneath a large stone or paving slab, which will keep the soil beneath cool and moist.

Many clematis will, however, grow and flower well in semi-shade and some, such as *C.* 'Nelly Moser', are better for it, as the flowers become bleached and pale in full sunlight. Some grow well in deep shade, but few flower well in these conditions.

In gardens, clematis are mainly grown for the beauty of their flowers, but in a number of species – such as *C. vitalba* (Old man's beard) – this aspect is augmented or even surpassed by the fruits. These are in clusters and have long silky tails; when massed, they give an effective silvery display in autumn and winter.

Another very useful characteristic is that clematis are highly resistant to honey fungus, thus making them suitable plants to grow where this is a problem. For instance, they can be used to cover a fence which has replaced a privet hedge destroyed by honey fungus, or to cover and beautify an old stump.

Practical Matters
PESTS AND DISEASES
Some clematis, mainly the large-flowered hybrids, are susceptible to a wilt fungus, clematis wilt (*Ascochyta spp.*). This invades damaged shoots near ground level, but rarely kills the whole plant if it is well established. Deep planting several centimetres below the normal planting level helps to protect the young plant, as does correct pruning in the early years. Affected plants stand some chance of recovery

Clematis *'Nelly Moser'** remains one of the most popular of large-flowered hybrids – she appreciates some shade and will perform in late spring and often again in autumn.

if the lower part of the stems and the root area are drenched with 'Benlate' (benomyl) at monthly intervals.

PRUNING

Clematis differ widely in the pruning needed for best effect. More than nearly all other common plants, they respond well to correct pruning, yet with inappropriate pruning many become just a mass of foliage. In the garden, they can be classified into three cultural groups:

• Group 1 includes all the early-flowering species such as *C. montana* or *C. armandii*. These produce their flowers from buds laid down during the previous summer's growth. They cannot, therefore, be pruned over winter – at least, not if you want any flowers! With this group, it is actually not necessary to prune to promote flowers; any pruning should be restricted to controlling rampant growth and encouraging the plants to retain young shoots near the base of the plant, rather than have just a twiggy mass of branches at the top. Pruning should take place immediately after flowering to give the subsequent shoots the longest possible growing season.

• Group 2 includes many of the garden hybrids such as 'Barbara Jackman' or 'Nelly Moser'. They produce their main flush of flowers from short shoots growing on the previous season's long growth. As far as possible, these growths should be spaced out and trained during the previous summer. However, pruning of established plants in this group should be carried out in late winter or very early spring. Remove all dead or weak growths and shorten strong growths by up to 30cm (1ft) to just above a strong pair of leaf axil buds. Many of the plants in this category will also produce a flush of flowers at the ends of the current season's shoots, giving two seasons of display.

• Group 3 includes all the herbaceous species and several woody ones, and these produce their flowers entirely at the end of the current season's shoots.

Examples are 'Jackmanii Superba' and *C. tibetana* subsp. *vernayi**. These plants are usually pruned in late winter to early spring, cutting them back to within 30cm (1ft) of the ground. The herbaceous plants will die back naturally in the autumn and can be cut down then. Treated thus, they respond by producing vigorous new shoots and plentiful flowers from midsummer onwards. The woody ones do not, however, *have* to be cut back and with plants growing through trees this is impractical; if left unpruned they will flower earlier in the season, although not so richly.

Further and more detailed siting and pruning recommendations can be found in specialist works on the genus (see Further Reading).

MAKING A CHOICE

Herbaceous and Sub-shrubby Species
These are the Cinderella species of clematis. Perhaps not as showy as some of the others, they can be very useful in the herbaceous and shrubaceous border or to cover the bare lower portion of a wall or trellis beneath taller-growing clematis. Generally, these plants do not cling to or entwine with other plants or supports.

C. heracleifolia (3) is the most common herbaceous clematis and will grow to 75cm–1.5m (2½–5ft). It has large, bold, trifoliate leaves and produces clusters of small, scented, hyacinth-like flowers from midsummer to early autumn from the ends of the shoots and the axils of the upper leaves. In early winter the dead foliage is strongly scented. The clone 'Wyevale'* is the best form, with mid-blue flowers.

C. x eriostemon 'Hendersonii' (3) has deep bluish-purple bell-shaped flowers 5–6cm (2–2½in) across which are carried singly but in great number from midsummer to early autumn. It makes annual growths to 2–2.5m (6–8ft), dying back to ground level in winter.

C. x durandii * (3) also reaches 2–2.5m (6–8ft). The flowers are 7.5–10cm (3–4in) across and dark

violet-blue with contrasting creamy yellow stamens, and are carried from early summer to early autumn.

C. x jouiniana 'Praecox' * (3) is a vigorous hybrid between old man's beard (*C. vitalba*) and *C. heracleifolia*. The flowers are pale lavender and carried from midsummer through to early autumn in large panicles 30–60cm (1–2ft) long. The stems are woody and persistent but do not twine. It will grow up to 2–3m (6–10ft) and is useful for covering mounds, old stumps and the like – a vigorous wide-spreading plant.

Winter-flowering Species
C. cirrhosa (1) is the only winter-flowering species in general cultivation. It needs the shelter of a warm, sunny or sheltered wall in most areas. The flowers are carried from midwinter through to early spring and are 3.5–5cm (1½–2in) in diameter. They are nodding and creamy-yellow with red-purple spotting within. The foliage is evergreen, turning bronzy over winter. *C.* 'Freckles'* has heavily spotted flowers streaked with red, whilst var. *balearica* has the extra feature of deeply cut, fern-like leaves.

Spring-flowering Species
C. montana (1) is the most common of the spring-flowering clematis. The flowers are 5–6cm (2–2½in) across and are borne singly from the axils of the cluster of leaves formed at the base of the new shoots in late spring and early summer, but in such profusion as to hide the foliage. *C. montana* is a very vigorous climber, capable of reaching 10m (30ft) into trees, over shrubs and buildings and along telephone wires and similar items! It also has the ability to flower well in shade as well as in full sun. The plant in the Himalayas has white flowers and usually grows over shrubs, where it looks attractive in late spring. Usually this and similar species in Group 1 form a tangled mass of twigs, leaves and flowers. Alternatively, if they are cut back immediately after flowering, the long arching shoots can be allowed to drape over shrubs without smothering

Clematis rehderiana* is a vigorous autumn-flowering species. Its blooms, with a cowslip-like fragrance, are followed by attractive seed heads suitable for trees and pergolas (see page 162).

them and give an attractive display in spring. 'Alexander' is a form whose creamy-white flowers (purer white in shade) are sweetly scented. 'Elizabeth'* has larger than usual pale pink flowers with an essence-of-vanilla scent. 'Pink Perfection' is rather close to 'Elizabeth', but the flowers are a deeper pink and more fragrant. 'Grandiflora'* is a selection which has larger white flowers, 6–7.5cm (2½–3in) across and is very effective on a shady aspect. 'Picton's Variety' is a selected form with deep rosy-red flowers with up to six sepals. *C. m.* var. *rubens* is a Chinese variant of the species. It differs in the reddish-purple young shoots and petioles and the purplish foliage, and has flowers which are rose-red, 6cm (2½in) across. It is an excellent plant, hence

its universality. 'Tetrarose'* has purplish-pink, scented, fleshy flowers up to 7.5cm (3in) across.

C. chrysocoma (1) is similar to *C. montana* and although a little less vigorous, climbs to 6m (20ft). The soft pink or white flowers are carried in great abundance in late spring and early summer, with a spasmodic crop later in the year.

C. alpina (1) makes a low-growing climber, rarely attaining more than 2–3m (6–10ft), and is an admirable species for a low fence or the lower part of a wall. It is best in a semi-shaded position. The flowers, carried in mid- to late spring, are open, nodding bells 2.5–3.5cm (1–1½in) long with usually pale to deep blue or lilac-blue sepals (clematis flowers do not have petals, but the attractive

coloured parts being sepals). This and *C. macropetala* (see below) are unusual in having a cluster of petal-like stamens (called staminoides) inside the ring of sepals and these are white, contrasting well with the blue sepals. Each leaf has three sets of three leaflets. 'Frances Rivis'* is a particularly good form, with deep blue and rather larger flowers. 'Helsingborg'* is a blue-flowered selection. 'Ruby' has reddish-purple flowers and a white centre and 'White Moth' is a white-flowered selection.

C. macropetala (1) makes a climber to 3–4m (10–13ft) tall with prettily divided leaves. The flowers are composed of four petals and numerous staminoides which grade into the white stamens. 'Maidwell Hall' is a form with pure blue flowers. In

'Markham's Pink'* they are rosy-mauve, flushed with purple at the base of the sepals.

C. armandii (1) is a vigorous ever-green species capable of reaching 6–9m (20–30ft) in mild areas, though needing the protection of a wall or similar shelter in colder districts. The leaves are deep, glossy green, in threes and 7.5–15cm (3–6in) long. The 5–6cm (2–2½in) diameter flowers are pro-duced in mid- to late spring in dense clusters. In 'Apple Blossom' they are white, softly flushed with pink, and the new foliage is bronze coloured. 'Snowdrift' has pure white flowers.

Summer-flowering Species
C. campaniflora (3) is a vigorous climber to 6m (20ft). It has small, bowl-shaped flowers only 2–3cm (¾–1in) across but carried in large numbers. They are white with a blue tint, and carried from midsummer into early autumn.

C. florida (3) is mainly represented in gardens by the clone 'Sieboldii', which has white flowers with purple staminoides, similar to a passion flower. They are 8cm (3in) across and are borne in summer; the plant makes a climber up to 2.5m (8ft). It should be given a warm sheltered position. 'Alba Plena' has greenish-white flowers which are fully double and carried over an extended period.

C. viticella (3) is a semi-woody climber to 4m (13ft) but often dying down in winter. The flowers are around 3.5cm (1½in) in diameter, car-ried from midsummer to early autumn and with four to six spoon-shaped petals. It can be used in both full sunlight and shade. In addition to the following cultivars, several of the large-flowered forms (see below) belong to or are derived from this species. 'Alba Luxurians'* has long-lasting white flowers white with a mauve tint. In 'Little Nell' they are very profuse and pale rose with a white margin. 'Madame Julia Correvon'* has large flowers to 7.5cm (3in) and deep wine-red in colour. 'Minuet'* differs in its upright, creamy-white flowers which have a

broad band of purple on each sepal. 'Purpurea Plena Elegans'* has large flowers with many sepals which are lilac-purple in colour. In 'Royal Velours'* the flowers are a deep vel-vety purple.

Autumn-flowering Species
C. flammula (3) is a rampant climber attaining 4–5m (13–16ft). It has the most strongly scented flowers of any clematis and these are pure white, occurring in large clusters from late summer into mid-autumn.

C. rehderiana* (3) has fragrant flowers, smelling of cowslips. They are pale primrose in colour and carried in large, erect clusters of nodding bells, 1.5–2cm (½–¾in) long. It has bright green pinnate leaves and can grow to 8m (26ft) up a tree if not cut back.

C. tangutica (3) has large lemon-yellow lantern-like flowers. These are carried over a long season, from mid-summer to mid-autumn. The sepals are thick and fleshy. It will grow and flower in full sun, and equally well in shady sites.

C. tibetana subsp. vernayi* (3) is commonly called C. orientalis but is not this species. It is known as the 'orange-peel' clematis because of the very thick and fleshy sepals. The flowers are open bells, from 2–3.5cm (¾–1½in) across and carried in late summer and early autumn. The leaves are bluish-green and deeply pinnate to bipinnate.

C. 'Bill MacKenzie'* is a hybrid of C. tangutica, probably with C. tibetana subsp. vernayi, which has bright yellow flowers that open wide to dis-play the purple filaments. Avoid seed-raised plants of this hybrid – they are likely to be inferior to the true form, which should always be vegetatively propagated.

Fruit Effect
Many clematis are very attractive in fruit, when the fine hairs on the per-sistent styles give a silky effect to the seedheads. C. alpina is the first reli-able species in fruit, lasting from early summer into the autumn before the seeds are shed. C. tangutica retains

them longer over winter and, with C. tibetana subsp. vernayi will be in both fruit and flower in the autumn. C. vitalba (Old man's beard) gives a very effective display in hedgerows and can be used to hide unwanted eyesores. It is too vigorous for most gardens.

Large-flowered Hybrids
These hybrids have been selected for the size of the flowers, usually 10–15cm (4–6in) in diameter. They lose some of the charm of the species but can be used to give a bold display of colour, several having two seasons of flower. The foliage is generally uninteresting. Most will make plants 3–4m (10–13ft) tall. Here is a selection of some of the best varieties available.

'Barbara Dibley' (2) has flowers of a petunia red; it flowers in late spring/early summer, and again in early autumn. It is not suitable for shady locations.

'Barbara Jackman' (2) has flowers of deep violet with a petunia or magenta strip running along the sepals. The flowers are 15cm (6in) across and carried in late spring and early summer. Do not use it in sunny situations.

'Beauty of Worcester' (2) has lavender or blue-violet flowers with creamy white stamens carried from late spring to late summer.

'Bee's Jubilee'* (2) has blush-pink flowers with a paler central strip to the overlapping sepals, flowering in late spring/early summer and again in late summer. It is not for a sunny spot.

'Blue Gem' (2) has sky-blue flowers from early summer through to mid-autumn.

'Carnaby' (2) is a compact and free-flowering cultivar which does well in shade. It has deep raspberry-pink flowers.

'Comtesse de Bouchaud'* (3) is a free-flowering plant with soft rose-pink flowers in mid- to late summer.

'Dr. Ruppel'* (2) has flowers which have deep pink sepals with a carmine bar and yellow stamens and are car-ried from early to late summer.

'Elsa Späth'* (2) has red stamens contrasting with the large lavender-blue flowers, which are borne in late spring/early summer and again in early autumn.

'Ernest Markham'* (3) flowers from early summer to early autumn, carrying glowing petunia-red rounded sepals with a velvety sheen. It is not suited to shady aspects.

'Hagley Hybrid' (3) has shell pink or rosy-mauve flowers with chocolate-coloured stamens. They are produced from early summer to early autumn. It does not appreciate full exposure to the sun.

'Henryi'* (2) has large creamy-white flowers carried in late spring/early summer and again in late summer/early autumn.

'H. F. Young'* (2) is a compact plant with wedgwood-blue flowers in late spring/early summer and again in late summer.

'Huldine' (3) has pearly white flowers 5–10cm (2–4in) across from midsummer to early autumn.

'Jackmanii Alba' (3) is similar, but the flowers are white with veins of blue. The early flowers are double, while those produced later in the season are single.

'Jackmanii Superba' (3) is a larger-flowered form of the well-known original *jackmanii (anuginosa x viticella)* hybrid. The flowers are dark purple, carried in profusion in mid- to late summer. It is suitable for conditions from full sunlight to full shade.'Lady Betty Balfour' (3) has purple flowers with yellow anthers and is late flowering, from the end summer into autumn. It does not suit a shady position and is best in full sun.

'Lasurstern' (2) has deep lavender-blue flowers with white stamens. It flowers in late spring/early summer and again in late summer/early autumn. It should not be put in full sunlight and is suitable for full or semi-shaded sites.

'Marie Boisselot'* (2) is perhaps the best white-flowered cultivar, with large white flowers with conspicuous yellow stamens. It flowers from early summer until mid-autumn and has better foliage than most cultivars.

'Mrs Chomondeley'* (2) is a vig-

Always producing a spectacular display from mid-summer to early autumn, Clematis *'Perle d'Azur'* is excellent growing in a small tree or large shrub.*

orous plant which freely produces masses of light blue flowers from late spring to early autumn. It is appropriate for semi-shade and full shade conditions.

'Mrs N. Thompson' (2) has pretty flowers with violet sepals with a scarlet bar and red stamens. It flowers in late spring/early summer and again in late summer, but should not be exposed to full sun.

'Nelly Moser'* (2) is a very popular cultivar but it should not be planted in full sun as the flowers are quickly bleached to an off-white. In the shade they are mauve-pink with a carmine bar, and it will tolerate full shade. Flowers are borne in late spring/early summer and late summer/ early autumn.

'Niobe'*(2) is often considered the best large-flowered red clematis. It is free flowering from late spring to early autumn in most situations.

'Perle d'Azur'* (3) has light blue or azure-coloured flowers which are

somewhat bell-shaped. They are carried from midsummer to early autumn.

'The President'* (2) has rich purple flowers which are silvery on the outside and produced from late spring to early autumn. It is a reliable cultivar and suitable for positions in full sunlight, as the flowers scarcely fade.

'Ville de Lyon' (3) should be placed to avoid both shade and strong sunlight. The sepals are bright carmine-red with a deeper margin, and it flowers from the middle to the end of summer.

'Vyvyan Pennell'* (2) has double flowers in late spring and early summer, but carries a flush of single flowers on the new growths in late summer. The sepals are lavender-coloured, suffused with purple and carmine in the centre. It should not be planted in shade.

'Wada's Primrose' (2) has pale creamy-yellow flowers which are best displayed in shade.

CONIFERS

INSTANT REFERENCE

- Dwarf to large trees
- Mostly evergreen, a few deciduous
- Wide range of foliage colours and textures, plus some with decorative cones
- Types available to suit most soils
- Mostly hardy
- Good hedging and screening plants; dwarf types suitable for the rock or heather garden

It is a measure of their adaptability and beauty that more tree-growing conifers are planted in gardens than all other trees put together. Admittedly, many are used for hedging or for shelter, but a substantial number are planted as specimen trees.

However, conifers are not just tall-growing species. A number are naturally low growing in character, and in cultivation all the conifer genera have produced a wide assortment of dwarf cultivars. As a group, they provide a large reservoir of attractive plants with many possible uses in the garden and those profiled here represent just a part of this resource.

Most conifers are evergreen, remaining fully clothed with foliage throughout the year, although there are a number of deciduous types. They are hardy plants and thrive on a very wide range of soils. Coupled with an ability to withstand clipping, this makes them very suitable for hedges and screens which are needed for twelve months of the year. Although the pines (Pinus) are not appropriate for hedges, their toughness and dense foliage make them excellent plants for shelterbelts and screens. The foliage which forms the screen can also provide an excellent backdrop for planting, as well as visual separation between two areas.

As specimen trees, conifers add height and scale to the garden, a wide variety of different foliage colours and textures, and also features such as attractive barks, fruits and flowers.

They provide homes for a wide range of wild animals, from insects which feed on them to safe nesting sites and roosting havens for birds.

Dwarf conifers offer the same attractive features as the larger-growing sorts but in miniature scale, making them appropriate for small gardens and as small features in a larger whole. They include many 'character' plants, which give charm and maturity to a restricted layout, as well as some outstanding groundcover plants.

Conifers will grow on a wide range of soils: some are appropriate for very wet soils, and some are suitable for very dry or sandy soils, especially the pines. Many will also grow well on soils derived from chalk or limestone, including the cypresses (Chamaecyparis and Cupressus), junipers (Juniperus) and Thuja, although some members of the pine family are not long lived in these conditions.

The foliage on pines is carried in bundles, called fascicles. These are short lateral shoots and contain two, three or five leaves or needles, from 5–40cm (2–16in) in length. In the cypresses and junipers, the leaves are small and either minute and scale-like, or short awl-shaped needles, less than 1cm (1/2in) long. In between these, most conifers have linear needle-like leaves from 1–4cm (1/2–11/2in) in length.

MAKING A CHOICE

Hedges

Leyland cypress (x Cupressocyparis leylandii) is the ubiquitous hedging conifer of today. It cannot be denied that this tree has many attributes which make it a candidate for any hedge – it grows on almost all soils, is quick to establish and tolerates clipping. However, in most situations its defects so vastly outweigh its attributes – it grows so fast for so long that it will outgrow any screening requirement and become an eyesore or nuisance; it is dull and formless, is unsuited to shade and requires considerable clipping – that there are better choices available.

The first thing to consider is what is wanted from the hedge or screen. This may well lead to the conclusion that a conifer is not the correct choice; perhaps an evergreen cotoneaster, such as C. lacteus, or close-clipped box (Buxus sempervirens), would be more suited to the scale of the situation.

The next consideration is the 'format' of the hedge. A formal, close-clipped hedge may be the best option in some situations, though an informal planting may actually look better whilst achieving the desired result. The best genera for formal clipped hedges are yew (Taxus), Western red cedar (Thuja) and False cypress (Chamaecyparis), although on acid soil only Western hemlock (Tsuga heterophylla*) can make a most delightful hedge.

Yew (Taxus baccata*) used to be the traditional hedging conifer, with good reason. It withstands clipping and can be used to form hedges from 1m (3ft) to 10m (33ft); it is extremely long lived, and of moderate growth rate; it tolerates shade denser than almost any other tree (although it must not be clipped too strongly in dense shade); it grows on all but waterlogged soils, and has the great advantage over all other candidate conifers in that it will make new growth if cut back into bare wood. Almost all other conifers, especially the cypresses, will simply die if there is no live foliage on the shoot below the point of cutting.

Why, then, aren't we surrounded by yew hedges? Impatience! It does not grow as fast as Leyland and Lawson cypresses, and a 2m (6ft) high hedge will take a couple of years longer to establish – that it will take far less effort in maintenance thereafter is frequently forgotten in the haste to obliterate the neighbours from the view. If a quick screen is needed, the best solution is to plant the hedge close to the boundary (50cm/20in) and erect a temporary screen, such as chainlink fencing, 2–3m (6–10ft) back from the boundary. Quick-growing plants such as clematis or evergreen Japanese honeysuckle (*Lonicera japonica* and cvs) can be grown on this whilst the yew becomes established. Placing the temporary screen on the boundary is not as good as it will cause the hedge to grow more slowly, although if the hedge is established within the garden it will allow for maintenance from both sides. Yew is poisonous to horses and cattle and should not be used where the foliage will stray over the boundary.

T. baccata 'Fastigiata'* (Irish yew), is an upright-growing form and will need less trimming in semi-formal hedges. 'Fastigiata Aureomarginata'* is a form with the leaves margined yellow, but should not be mixed with the dark green of 'Fastigiata'.

T. x *media* 'Hicksii'* makes an upright, broadly conical bush. It is a hybrid between common yew and the Japanese yew (*T. cuspidata*) and was developed in the USA as being more winter hardy than yew. It is a female plant and produces attractive red fruits. The red, fleshy portion of the fruit is sweet and edible, at least in small quantities. All the remaining parts of all yew trees are poisonous if eaten, especially the seed within the red fruit.

Chamaecyparis lawsoniana (Lawson cypress) can make good hedges and will tolerate clipping. It is not as fast growing as Leyland cypress but is better for light to medium shade, and has the added attraction of male catkins in spring. These are maroon or brick red and can make a delightful display. Several of the cultivars selected for their narrow crowns can be used to make hedges which need less trimming, such as 'Green Hedger'* which has rich green foliage and was selected for just this purpose; 'Fletcheri'* whose soft leaves are a grey-green, bronzed in winter; and 'Allumigold', with erect sprays of soft grey foliage edged golden yellow. Be very wary of mixing two or more selected cultivars in one hedge or screen: in theory, having alternate plants or groups with different foliage colours or textures may sound attractive, but the end result usually looks contrived and is rarely effective in the garden – the plants grow at differing rates and the colours do not naturally match in such formal situations.

Thuja plicata (Western red cedar) is also excellent for hedges. The foliage is somewhat more open but is carried in depth, thus giving as dense an effect. This has the advantage, moreover, that should the hedge become overgrown or need reducing in width, there is live foliage within the hedge to which it can be reduced. The best feature of Western red cedar is the fruity pineapple fragrance of the foliage, especially strong when cut or crushed, and which (almost) makes trimming the hedge a delight.

Several junipers will tolerate clipping, but do not grow sufficiently fast or large to make them really suitable as hedging. However, if you are planning an informal hedge to mark a boundary or define a space but not totally separate two areas, then several of the slower growing or dwarf cultivars of both *Juniperus* and *Pinus* could be used, such as *J.* 'Pfitzeriana'* or *P. nigra* 'Hornibrookiana', as well as similar dwarf forms of *Chamaecyparis*.

Screening, Shelter and Backcloth
Trees used for these purposes will be allowed or needed to grow taller than a hedge. They will serve to cut out wind or sun (thus providing shelter), neighbours and other eyesores (screening), or light (as a backcloth). Obviously, the one planting can easily achieve all three functions if correctly placed and planned.

Aspects of shelter and the need for it were dealt with earlier (see pp25–26). As with hedges, when contemplating screening consider what exactly you wish to block out: if it is only your neighbour's ground-floor windows, the height required is much less than for a three-storey block of flats. There is little sense in planting trees which will reliably grow 20m (66ft) tall in 20 years (eg, Leyland cypress) when you only need a screen 5m (16ft) tall, unless you have a masochistic desire to trim hedges.

If the belt is going to have a role as backcloth, to help display other plants whose foliage or flowers tend to get lost when seen against a bright sky (such as precocious flowering magnolia), the choice of foliage colour can be very important. Conifers offer a range of leaf colour unrivalled by other plants, especially in the blues and golds. These colours, however, do not make the best backcloths, being too strong in themselves for most plants, although a golden conifer such as *Chamaecyparis lawsoniana* 'Lane'* or *Thuja plicata* 'Aurea'* or 'Zebrina' is the appropriate backdrop for purple foliage such as that of *Betula pendula* 'Purpurea' or *Cercis canadensis* 'Forest Pansy'*.

Ch. lawsoniana makes a very useful tree for these functions. The natural foliage colour is grey-green, which is both restful to the eye and excellent as a backcloth. It grows somewhat denser than is desirable for optimum reduction of wind speed, but is not so dense as to cause extra turbulence. It has a reasonable growth rate, averaging 30–50cm (12–20in) per annum over 20–30 years, and is easily moved and often available at sizes up to 2m (6¹/₂ft).

Selected clones can be used for screens. Those with blue foliage include 'Van Pelt'* and 'Pembury Blue'*, which is the best blue foliage form. 'Fletcheri'* is a smaller-growing plant with grey-green soft foliage. Plants with distinctive green foliage are 'Witzeliana', with a narrow habit and long erect sprays of bright green foliage; 'Green Hedger'* with ascending bright green foliage; and 'Pottenii'*. The latter may look interesting for a period, with its very dense growth of sea-green leaves in feathery sprays, but the veneer of foliage is shallow and if branches are dislodged as the tree grows older (which is inevitable, especially in a shelter planting), the dead brown foliage beneath can look unpleasant. It is, therefore, sensible to look upon it as a tree for 15–20 years and to replace it when it starts to decline in beauty. Forms with golden foliage include 'Lane'*, 'Stewartii', 'Stardust'* and

Ginkgo biloba *(Maidenhair tree) here seen as a fine middle-aged specimen at Sherborne Castle, Dorset (see page 169).*

'Winston Churchill'. All of these selected forms do, however, look excessively formal when used *en masse*. Seed-raised plants do not make such uniform features and this is usually an advantage, creating not just a screen but also a feature which changes with time and the seasons.

Ch. nootkatensis (Nootka cypress) can be used, but the pronounced conical habit may be too strong for most situations.

Juniperus (Junipers) include a number of small trees which can be used for low screens etc, where a top height of no more than 4–6m (13–20ft) in 10–15 years is required. They are perhaps too small and slow-growing for boundary screens, but are suitable for internal divisions in the garden. Several forms of *J. chinensis* are suitable for this purpose, such as 'Obelisk'*, with its tight, erect habit, and 'Pyramidalis'*, slow growing with a rather dense, conical habit composed of awl-like juvenile foliage. *J. scopulorum* has various forms with silvery or greyish-blue foliage on upright, small trees to 6–8m (20–26ft), such as 'Springbank', 'Moonglow' and 'Blue Heaven'*.

Pinus (Pines) are excellent for shelter, as the foliage approaches the ideal of 50 per cent porosity. They also give good screening as, although the crowns are open, the foliage is carried in depth. They tend to develop broader crowns than the cypresses, but as young trees they are similarly narrow. They are also less amenable to clipping to control their spread.

P. contorta subsp. *latifolia** (Lodgepole pine) makes an attractive tree, with bright green leaves and massed yellow male cones in early summer. It is very tolerant of waterlogged soils and exposed windy situations and is an obvious choice for shelter planting in such locations, but is not tolerant of chalky or alkaline soils.

*P. nigra** (Austrian pine) has dense, dark green leaves in pairs and makes a good shelter or screening tree. The old foliage will appear dark in spring when deciduous trees are bursting into leaf but looks much lighter-coloured in late winter; the pine makes its new foliage in early summer at a time when the deciduous trees have settled down into their less flamboyant summer foliage. The closely related *P. leucodermis**(Bosnian pine) is similar but smaller and has more attractive cones. These are bright cobalt blue during their second summer (pine cones take two seasons to grow), whilst the shoots have a white bark (hence leuco-white, dermis-skin). Both of these pines are suitable for chalk and limestone soils.

*P. pinaster** (Maritime pine) has a rather open crown but is good for planting on sandy soils, and has grey-green or glossy deep-green leaves and large bright brown cones which are prominently displayed on the tree.

*P. sylvestris** (Scots pine) has blue-green leaves and two-tone bark, which in the upper bole flakes in small, papery orange scales. It makes a good screen when young, becoming a majestic tree with a rounded crown.

*P. radiata** (Monterey pine) is very good for shelter, especially in windswept coastal areas, though it is not reliably hardy in cold districts. It is one of the fastest growing of all trees, soon averaging 1m (3ft) per annum. The leaves are grassy green, but in the distance appear almost black. The large cones remain unopened on the tree for twenty or more years, in nature only opening after a forest fire to release the seeds. It is not for alkaline soils.

P. wallichiana *(Blue pine) makes an excellent screening tree but is not suited to exposed positions. The long, soft leaves are bluish and hang in bundles of five. It will grow on limestone and chalk soils.

Thuja plicata (Western red cedar) is excellent for screening, shelter and backcloth purposes, especially 'Fastigiata'*, with its naturally slender crown. It can, therefore, be used to make a screen 1–2m (3–6ft) wide without any trimming, although some may be needed after trees have attained 10–15m (33–50ft) as it will by then have become wider at the base.

'Aurea'* is a form with rich, old-gold-coloured foliage, whilst in 'Irish Gold'* and 'Zebrina' the foliage is banded with yellow or creamy-yellow respectively.

Tsuga heterophylla (Western hemlock) will make an attractive backcloth and screening plant but does not take exposure. The leaves are mid-green above and silvery beneath and dense, whilst the branches are pendulous at the tips. It is not suitable for alkaline soils where *T. canadensis* (Eastern hemlock) is more tolerant.

Specimen Trees

The role of a specimen tree is to provide a focal point, such as at the end of a vista, to complement a lawn area, or in the front garden to 'mark' the property in the street.

Chamaecyparis lawsoniana provides a wide range of specimen trees, and most of the taller-growing named forms are good for this purpose. Narrow, columnar-growing forms include 'Allumigold', with blue-grey foliage edged golden yellow, and 'Kilmacurragh'*, with dark green foliage. These plants are appropriate where a pillar or 'exclamation mark' is required, or to create a focal point in a small area. Broader-growing forms include 'Pembury Blue'*, one of the best of all blue-foliaged trees, and the golden-foliaged trees mentioned under screening. 'Wissellii'* has blue-grey or dark blue-green foliage held in tight three-dimensional sprays, which are carried on spaced branches and give a curiously effective tree. It is particularly striking in mid-spring, when the massed pink male cones are displayed against the leaves.

Ch. obtusa 'Crippsii'* is the best gold-foliaged conifer; it slowly makes a broadly conical tree to 10–15m (33–50ft) at a medium growth rate per year of 20–30cm (8–12in) and has dense sprays of bright gold foliage.

Ch. nootkatensis (Nootka cypress), with its remarkably regular conical crown, makes a good formal specimen tree. Where informality is required, this species offers the cultivar 'Pendula'* (Afghan hound tree), with

an attractive, gaunt, open crown, the spreading branches arching up at the tips and curtained with hanging flat sprays. 'Lutea' ('Aurea') has yellow young foliage becoming yellow-green.

Juniperus drupacea (Syrian juniper) makes a distinctive columnar tree with large, crowded, awl-shaped leaves which have silver, waxy bands of stomata.

J. recurva var. *coxii* (Drooping juniper) makes a small conical tree with spreading branches, gracefully pendulous at the tips, and bright sage-green leaves. The foliage is dry in texture and rustles in the wind.

J. scopulorum (Rocky Mountain juniper) includes a number of good small trees with blue or silvery-blue foliage, such as 'Springbank' and 'Moonglow', with conical habits. It also includes the very narrow-crowned and appropriately named 'Skyrocket', although this is sometimes listed as a form of *J. virginiana*. This makes a narrow, upright plant which is approximately ten times as tall as it is wide. The foliage is blue-grey and it will grow to 8m (26ft) in 20 years. It can be very effective for creating an avenue in a small space, such as to join two parts of a garden, or to give continuity along a border, but trimming of the sides is necessary to prevent specimens becoming ragged.

The Pines usually carry their foliage in bundles of two, three or five leaves. As this affects their appearance and approximately equates to their affinities to each other, it is simpler to look at a range of the commercially available pines under these headings.

FIVE-NEEDLED AND SOFT PINES

P. aristata (Bristlecone pine) belongs to a group called 'foxtail pines' which are unusual in that the needles are kept for many years, usually 15–20 and occasionally longer, against two to three (less often up to five) in other species. This results in the crown being dense like a fox's brush, due to the typically spaced pine branches being clothed with foliage along their length instead of only at the tips. It also has the attraction that it makes a small tree, only growing 8–10m (26–33ft) tall, and thus suitable for front gardens and other small spaces. The leaves are bluish-green and in the second and succeeding years are covered with white flecks of resin.

P. armandii (Armand's pine) makes a medium-sized tree with drooping bluish needles and large cones which are green whilst developing in the summer of the second year before ripening brown. *P. wallichiana* (Blue pine) is similar but with narrower cones. These makes excellent specimen trees with their relatively long, soft foliage of a neat bluish-green colour and crowns which are rather open.

*P. cembra** (Arolla pine) has a dense and narrowly columnar crown with leaves dark, shiny green on the outer face and bluish white on the inner surfaces. It makes a small, slow-growing tree on a wide range of soils and situations. It has rusty-red, hairy shoots.

*P. parviflora** (Japanese white pine) is a small tree with bluish foliage set on tiered branches, particularly in 'Tempelhof'. It is an interesting plant, appropriate for sites where only a small tree or large shrub is needed.

P. bungeana (Lace-bark pine) is remarkable for its bark. This is grey-green and smooth but flakes in small round scales to reveal creamy-white or yellow which gradually darkens to green, olive-brown, red or purple. It is a soft pine but has the needles in threes and makes a small, rather slow-growing tree. The seeds are edible.

THREE-NEEDLED PINES

*P. coulteri** (Big-cone pine) has stout, greyish-blue needles which are held pointing stiffly forwards all around the shoot, and are up to 30cm (12in) long. The cones are bright brown with prominent hooked spines and are enormous, weighing up to 2kg (4.4lb). *P. jeffreyi** (Jeffrey pine) is similar but with smaller cones, more bloomed shoots and a denser crown. *P. ponderosa** (Western yellow pine) has greyer-green and shorter leaves of only 10–25cm (4–10in) and mature bark which has deep fissures between

broad, flat, flaking plates which are yellow-brown, red-brown or pinky-grey. The cones can be an attractive purplish colour during the summer. These three species will make vigorous, bold, large trees and thrive on a wide range of sites, including heavy clay soils.

*P. radiata** (Monterey pine) is discussed above as a screening plant, but also makes a good and quick specimen tree for acid lowland and coastal sites.

*P. patula** is an incredibly beautiful Mexican pine but is not absolutely hardy and needs a sheltered and sunny spot in all but the most favoured areas. The bark is reddish to yellow-brown and scaly. The leaves are slender and droop down; they are light or yellow-green in colour and 15–30cm (6–12in) long. In the right place it is outstanding, but is not suitable on chalky or alkaline soils.

TWO-NEEDLED PINES

*P. sylvestris**(Scots pine) when old has a rounded, billowing crown but in young trees it is narrowly conical. 'Aurea'* is a delectable form in which the foliage is more or less the normal blue-green during the summer months; come the winter, however, it turns a bright gold, remaining so from then until mid-spring. 'Edwin Hillier' ('Argentea') has bluer needles but makes a rather squat, small tree. 'Fastigiata' forms an 'exclamation mark' to 8m (26ft) tall with erect branches and can be used to accentuate a vista or mark a small space.

P. densiflora (Japanese red pine) is similar to Scots pine in the reddish and flaky bark of the upper bole, but has bright green and forward-pointing leaves. In the selection 'Oculis-draconis'* each needle has two yellow bands, appearing like a dragon's eyes. This effect is strongest after good summers. It makes a small tree.

*P. leucodermis** (Bosnian pine) has white shoots, ash-coloured bark and rigid, dark green needles. The cones are outstanding during the summer of their second season, when they are a bright cobalt-blue.

P. montezumae (Montezuma pine) is another most attractive and imposing species from Mexico, but is only reliably hardy in mild areas. It has stout shoots which carry the long, pendulous needles in bundles of five, but it is not a soft pine (see above). A number of related species are cultivated under this name, some of them being hardier than others.

OTHER SPECIMEN CONIFERS

Abies concolor 'Candicans' is a form of Colorado white fir which has vivid grey leaves, silvery white when young. It forms a medium to large tree and is suitable for a wide range of sites, including fairly hot, dry ones once established.

*A. nordmanniana** (Caucasian fir) has dense foliage of a mid- to dark green above with two silvery bands beneath. It forms a large columnar tree with tiered branches which are down-swept at the tips. It tolerates a wide range of conditions and is perhaps the best silver fir for general planting. The cones are erect candles, yellow-green when young but ripening to brown; however, these are only borne on the upper whorls of foliage.

A. pinsapo (Spanish fir) has radially arranged leaves which stand out rigidly from the shoots. These are bluish green in colour, especially in the cultivar 'Glauca'*. It forms a large tree and will tolerate all sites except for waterlogged ones, but is especially suitable for chalk soils.

*A. procera** (Noble fir) has a very tiered crown, producing an open tree when young. The foliage is pressed tightly down on the shoots but spreads at the sides and is blue-green. The cones are carried when the tree is fairly young, often by the time it is 5m (16ft) tall (which is unusual in such a large growing tree, capable of 20m (66ft) or more), and are enormous, barrel-shaped in outline and up to 25cm (10in) long. The bark is silvery grey. It is at its best in moist situations on acid soils and is not long-lived on dry sites. It does not tolerate chalk soils.

*Cedrus atlantica** (Atlas cedar) is frequently offered in the variety *glauca**, which has foliage of a beautiful silvery blue throughout the year except when very young, when it is almost silver. It forms a large and long-lived tree, growing to 15–25m (50–80ft) or so. The male catkins open in late summer and are erect, yellow-brown and create their own display. The bark is silvery grey. It is a tree which matures, becoming steadily more attractive as it reaches 25 years plus, being rather a spiky stick for the first five years. Atlas cedar is excellent on all soils, especially chalk or limestone. 'Aurea' is a form with golden yellow foliage and can be effective in the right setting but must not be crowded. Also requiring correct siting is 'Glauca Pendula', a weeping form which needs training so that the branches hang down to best effect, or it will form a mound of little beauty.

*C. deodara** (Deodar cedar) has tiered and spaced branches which are pendulous at the tips. The foliage is the longest of any cedar, grey-green to green in colour. It is an early achiever, needing a cool, moist, setting for long-term beauty. However, as a young tree – for 25 years or so – it is excellent and a much better choice than the other cedars over this timespan.

*C. libani** (Cedar of Lebanon) has spiky growths when young and is a tree for large parkland settings, needing space and a couple of generations to develop. It is a tree to plant for the great-grandchildren to enjoy, as we can now appreciate those planted in the eighteenth century.

*Ginkgo biloba** is not actually a conifer, being the last survivor of its own family. It is deciduous, although this feature is also shown by several conifers, especially the exquisite golden larch listed below. The leaves are bi-lobed and fan-like, oily green during the summer but assuming clear golden yellow in autumn. As a young tree it has a narrow, columnar, conic crown, broadening out erratically in its second century. It is long lived, the 1753 original introduction to England still thriving at Kew.

Larix (Larches) are another genus of deciduous conifers, harbingers of

Three conifers still developing are already prominent in this view of the golden garden at Crathes Castle near Aberdeen. On the left Taxus baccata *'Fastigiata Aureomarginata'**, the Golden Irish yew; in the centre* Chamaecyparis nootkatensis *'Lutea' with yellow young foliage – a form of the Nootka cypress (see page 167) – and behind the seat are the jutting branches of* Juniperus x media *'Pfitzerana Aurea'**, a golden yellow form of Pfitzer juniper (see page 171).*

spring with their fresh green new foliage. They also have excellent autumn colour. The twigs of *L. kaempferi** are reddish purple, whilst those of *L. decidua** are yellow, providing a haze of colour over the winter season.

*Metasequoia glyptostroboides** (Dawn redwood) has lush green foliage set in feathery sprays. It is another deciduous conifer, producing good autumn colour. It quickly forms a tree 10m (30ft) or so tall on almost any soil, but needs a damp one for optimum further growth. It is capable of growing in standing water, although not as vigorously as in well-

drained, moist sites.

*Picea breweriana** (Brewer's weeping spruce) has a columnar crown with more or less horizontal main branches. On these the branchlets hang vertically, in curtains of foliage. Old trees can be particularly effective, when the pendulous shoots are up to a metre or so long.

P. likiangensis has a more normal spruce habit and is chiefly grown for its brilliant red-purple cones set off against the short, bluish foliage. It tolerates a very wide range of soils, but is perhaps at its best on dry acid sands, as these induce more prolific and earlier flowering.

P. omorika* (Serbian spruce) is a tree which develops a very narrow, tall crown; it is not so much that the branches are shorter than in other spruces, but that they hang down at an angle to the erect trunk. The foliage is dark green above and silvery beneath. It will grow on all soils, from dry chalk to wet, acidic sites.

P. orientalis* (Oriental spruce) is similar in habit to the ubiquitous Norway spruce but infinitely superior. The leaves are very short, in the range 0.6–1cm (¼–½in) and furnish the branches densely. The best characteristic, however, are the brick-red male cones in spring, and the purple-red female cones.

P. smithiana* (West Himalayan spruce) needs a moist site for best growth and may be slow to get going. However, as a mature tree the branches are horizontal and spaced, with pendulous branchlets filling the intervening space.

Pseudolarix amabilis* (Golden larch) makes a medium, spreading tree, much wider than most other conifers except cedars. The foliage turns a lovely gold in autumn. It will grow on a wide range of sites, but is rather slow to get established and is not for the impatient. However, it is worth the wait. The cones are similar in outline to larch cones but break up to release the seeds, as in firs and cedars.

Taxodium distichum* (Swamp cypress), despite its name, is not as well adapted to growing in standing water as the Dawn redwood (*Metasequoia*), naturally occurring in land which is only flooded for part of the year. The best position is within 0.5m (1½ft) of a stream or pond, when it will produce its curious aerial roots 'knees' (pneumatophores). These are specially adapted roots which rise up to 60cm (2ft) above soil level and function to allow the exchange of gases – venting carbon dioxide, taking in oxygen – so that the roots can respire in their otherwise inhospitable habitat. However, they are only produced on trees within a few feet of water. The tree is capable of growing on ordinary soils, even dry ones – it is just specially adapted to tolerating waterlogged ones. It is another deciduous conifer, with the foliage turning brick red in late autumn. The new foliage is also late, often not opening fully until early summer.

Sciadopitys verticillata* (Umbrella pine) makes a conical small to medium tree of slow but steady growth. The foliage is in whorls at the shoot tips, appearing like the spokes of an umbrella, hence the common name. The leaves are curious, long and leathery in texture and believed to be two needles fused together. It tolerates a wide range of conditions, including very moist sites.

Sequoia sempervirens* (Coastal redwood) includes the tallest living tree: at 112m (364ft) it is as tall as the dome of St Paul's Cathedral. It is very fast growing but will only maintain this growth in sheltered, moist locations. With exposure it only makes a medium tree – just quickly. The bark is thick and soft, probing niches in which tree creepers can retreat during cold weather. It is one of the few conifers which will coppice. 'Adpressa' is a somewhat slower-growing form in which the needles are thicker and darker green, except the on young shoots, which are creamy-white at the tips.

Sequoiadendron giganteum* (Sierra redwood or Wellingtonia), whilst not as tall as its coastal cousin, includes the largest living trees, and some examples in the Sierra Nevada of eastern California are truly vast. It too has thick, soft bark, although not as soft as in Coastal redwood, which is utilised by birds who hollow out roosting sites. The foliage is awl-shaped, green or slightly bluish-green and carried on down-swept branches in a dense, conical or columnar crown. It is better adapted to exposure and colder sites than Coastal redwood. 'Pendulum' is a remarkable form. It makes a leader of sorts, on which all the branches and branchlets are pendulous, forming hanging curtains. However, the leading shoot is rather like a rumba-dance and most erratic in its sense of direction, creating a wonderful, weird-looking tree.

Dwarf conifers

Dwarf conifers include both naturally small-growing plants and genetic oddities which for some reason, perhaps due to an excess of growth-restricting hormone, do not attain full stature. There is a full range of dwarf conifers available, from plants growing 5cm (2in) in 10 years to those making 10–15cm (4–6in) of growth annually. The most dwarf are not garden plants but need to be grown in the favourable conditions of an alpine house, and are not reviewed here. At the larger end of the spectrum, dwarf conifers give way to slow-growing conifers; there is no absolute difference between the two, and many of the slow-growing varieties are very attractive for a number of years if used as dwarf types.

Dwarf conifers can be valuable in several ways in the garden. Perhaps the current favourite application is as ground-cover, and there are several dwarf conifers capable of attractively suppressing weeds over a square metre or more of ground. They can be very useful for disguising unsightly objects such as manhole covers (see p.108–9); this is because (like ground-cover roses) they root at a single point and grow outwards, whereas most low groundcover plants root as they grow over the surface and are therefore not able effectively to cover such barren objects. As with all groundcovers, the site does need to be free of perennial weeds before the conifers are planted.

Another use is to provide an element of scale in an otherwise formless feature, such as a heather garden. Here the conifer can be used to punctuate the heathers, whilst not growing so fast as to dwarf them. Dwarf conifers can also be used effectively on a rockery, as dwarf trees or in prostrate forms to clamber over rocks. The larger forms can make isolated specimens in a lawn, as plant islands in a sea of grass; obviously for this to be effective the plants need to be isolated, and only in the very largest lawns is there room for more than one.

Finally, they can make interesting collections in their own right as, apart from size, dwarf conifers provide the full range of textures, habits and colours of their larger progenitors, permitting a host of different features to be fitted into a limited space.

Abies koreana is a slow-growing rather than a dwarf tree. It has short leaves which are vividly silver beneath and carries its erect cones when only a metre or so tall. These open purple and spend the summer violet, before ripening to brown in later autumn and breaking apart to release the seeds. A dwarfer selection is 'Silverlocke'* in which the leaves are twisted up to display the silvery white undersides.

A. nordmanniana 'Golden Spreader'* is a slow-growing form of Caucasian fir in which the foliage is bright, light gold or yellow.

Chamaecyparis lawsoniana has given rise to over 200 different cultivars, but only a few of these are good dwarf forms. 'Minima Aurea'* makes an ovoid plant without a stem but with erect sprays of golden-yellow foliage. 'Minima Glauca'* has glaucous or sea-green foliage and forms a rounded bush. Both will very slowly make a plant up to 1m (3ft) high. 'Gimbornii'* is globose or oval with a conical apex. The new foliage has a purplish tinge for the first year, thereafter becoming glaucous blue-green. 'Pygmaea Argentea'* makes a globose bun. The shoots are creamy-white at the tips. It is best in light shade, as full sun will scorch the foliage. 'Lutea Nana'* is a slow-growing, narrowly conical dwarf which has dense, golden-yellow fern-like foliage.

Ch. obtusa has spawned a number of dwarf forms: 'Aurora' makes a compact small shrub with its yellow-green foliage held in shell-like sprays. 'Nana Aurea'* is slow growing, eventually capable of 2m (6ft), and has golden-yellow foliage. 'Nana Gracilis'* forms a dense, conical plant with a rugged shape and glossy foliage.

Ch. pisifera includes several slow-growing cultivars. 'Boulevard'* is a summer-bedding conifer. It has steel-blue foliage which is soft to the touch

and at its best looks very attractive. It will grow to make a small tree but, unless the site is moist throughout the year, after three or four years it deteriorates in condition as the inner foliage hangs dead and brown within the plant, and it is then better replaced. 'Gold Spangle' is a narrow upright shrub with thread- or whiplike golden-yellow foliage. 'Golden Mop'* has similar bright yellow foliage but makes a mound-shaped plant. 'Sungold' also has threadlike foliage but forms a larger bush. It tolerates full sunlight.

Juniperus chinensis has given a number of low- to medium-growing dwarf forms which are often listed under the name *J. x media*. Of these, 'Blaauw'* has short ascending, spreading branches with feathery sprays of bluish-green foliage and will grow to 1m (3ft) or so tall. 'Carberry Gold' slowly makes a prostrate shrub with creamy-yellow foliage. 'Pfitzeriana Aurea'* has golden-yellow new foliage and makes a spreading, flat-topped bush. 'Pfitzeriana Compacta'* is similar in habit but has more prickly juvenile foliage of a grey-blue green, whilst in 'Gold Coast' the foliage remains golden yellow throughout the year. 'Mint Julep'* has bright green foliage and a more vase-shaped habit. In 'Plumosa Aurea'*, the foliage is bronze-gold during the winter, whilst 'Sulphur Spray'* has the foliage pale sulphur-yellow in the spring but brighter yellow during the summer months. All of these forms of juniper are excellent as groundcovers, particularly for banks and the like, where a fairly vigorous plant is required if maintenance is to be reduced.

J. communis (Common juniper) is a variable shrub or occasionally a small tree. 'Compressa'* makes a dwarf 'exclamation mark', growing at the rate of 2–3cm (3/4–1¼in) per annum to a maximum of 80cm (32in). 'Hibernica'* is big brother, with a similar exclamation-mark habit, but making 3–5m (10–16ft) at annual rates of up to 20cm (8in). 'Sentinel' is a dense form with a very narrow habit and purplish shoots. These three

selections have bluish-grey leaves with silvery bands on the inside. Similar clones, but with bright yellow or golden foliage, are 'Gold Cone', with a more conical habit, and 'Golden Rod', which forms a slender column of bright young foliage, turning to green in winter. 'Depressa Aurea' is a spreading form in which the new growths are yellow, becoming bronze as they mature. 'Hornibrookii'* is a ground-hugging form which slowly builds up a series of layers of foliage. 'Repanda'* is similar but more vigorous, making mounds of spreading foliage to 30cm (1ft) thick. 'Green Carpet' is a selection of similar habit but with bright green foliage. These last four selections are good ground-cover plants.

J. conferta is a prickly, prostrate species with glossy green leaves and 'Blue Pacific' a form with blue-green foliage.

J. horizontalis is possibly the best groundcover conifer. It spreads over the soil surface and completely covers it, precluding weed growth. All the named forms are good plants. Foliage colour ranges from 'Blue Chip', with bright blue foliage throughout the year, to 'Hughes', in which it is grey-green (and the habit of the shoots somewhat ascending), and to 'Wiltonii'* – whose leaves retain their bluish-grey colour over winter.

J. procumbens makes a spreading plant 2m (6ft) across and up to 75cm (2½ft) high. 'Nana'* is a smaller, mat-forming clone.

J. sabina 'Tam No Blight' ('New Blue') is a disease-resistant selection of the old clone 'Tamariscifolia'. It is a spreading, 'table-forming' bush which builds up a series of tiers of bright green or bluish-green foliage. It makes a good, tall groundcover plant.

J. squamata 'Blue Carpet'* and 'Blue Star'* are two selections of 'Meyeri' which have steely-blue foliage. 'Blue Carpet' is vigorous and prostrate, growing no more than 30cm (1ft) high, whilst 'Blue Star' makes a dwarf, rounded bush.

Microbiota decussata * is a vigorous, spreading relative of junipers.

It forms a dense cover as a series of overlapping layers of foliage sprays, which are slightly yellow-green, turning bronze during the winter.

Picea abies 'Nidiformis'* is a slow-growing selection of Norway spruce which makes a flat-topped bush with spreading layers of horizontal branches. The centre tends to be lower, thus becoming 'nest' like. It is a suitable candidate for an isolated slow-growing plant in a sea of grass.

P. glauca var. *albertiana* 'Conica'* makes a neat, dense cone of mid-green foliage. It is slow-growing but steady - after forty or so years it may attain 6m (20ft). Like other spruces, it is susceptible to aphid attack and may need spraying to keep it in good condition.

P. mariana 'Nana'* is a small, bun-shaped conifer with bluish-green foliage, appropriate for the rock garden.

Pinus koraiensis 'Compacta Glauca' forms a slow-growing plant with stout branches and blue-green foliage. It is a soft pine, similar to *P. cembra* discussed above, but with longer foliage.

P. leucodermis 'Schmidtii'* has bright green foliage and slowly makes a dense rounded bush.

P. mugo is a dwarf mountain species which can grow to a maximum of 5–8m (16–26ft). Much dwarfer is 'Gnom', a squat selection, gradually becoming a globose bush. 'Mops'* is similar, but quicker to make a rounded shape. 'Ophir' has a dwarf, rounded habit and the foliage turns golden yellow in winter. 'Winter Gold' has similar bright winter foliage but is somewhat taller growing.

P. nigra 'Hornibrookiana' has stout, ascending branches which bear stiff, glossy dark green leaves.

P. parviflora 'Adcock's Dwarf'* is a dense, slow-growing bush with short, grey-green needles.

P. sylvestris 'Beuvronensis'* grows to 1m (3ft) and develops as a low, rounded bush; the annual growth is 5–7cm (2–3in) with bluish-green leaves. 'Gold Coin' is a dwarf selection of the tree form 'Aurea'; it makes a bun-shaped bush for the rockery, with foliage turning pale golden yellow during the winter months. 'Moseri'* is similar but a taller, globose bush or eventually a small tree. With 'Watereri' (whose leaves remain blue-green over winter), it is a possible selection for use as an isolated conifer in an expanse of lawn.

Taxus baccata has given several slow-growing selections, including 'Repens Aurea'*, whose foliage is yellow margined at first, becoming cream margined later, and which makes a low-spreading shrub, and 'Standishii'* which is a dwarf form of the Irish yew ('Fastigiata') with an upright habit and golden-coloured leaves.

Thuja occidentalis has given 'Little Gem', which makes a squat, rounded bush with dense sprays of deep, somewhat yellow-green foliage; 'Rheingold'* with its ovoid or conical habit and rich golden-amber foliage, eventually making a sprawling bush 2–3m (6–10ft) across; 'Sunkist', with golden yellow foliage, which is better in full sun and makes a slow-growing bush; and green foliage forms such as 'Woodwardii'. The foliage in all of these is delightfully fragrant if rubbed or crushed.

T. plicata has given two excellent dense, conical dwarf forms of slow growth rate, and golden foliage with bronze tips in 'Rogersii' and 'Stoneham Gold'*.

T. orientalis (sometimes treated as a separate genus as *Platycladus orientalis*) does not have the fragrant foliage of true thuja species, but is better suited to hot, dry situations. Dwarf forms include 'Aurea Nana'*, which has a dense rounded habit and erect or splayed sprays of light yellow-green foliage, and 'Rosedalis', with an ovoid crown and soft juvenile foliage which changes from canary yellow when new in spring, to sea-green in summer and plum-purple over winter. Taller-growing forms include 'Elegantissima'*, with bright yellow-green sprays which are green during the winter.

CORNUS

INSTANT REFERENCE

• Shrubs and small trees
• Deciduous
• Distinctive white or yellow flowers in winter, spring or early summer, coloured winter-effective stems and variegated foliage, all according to variety
• Any good garden soil (most)
• Hardy
• Coloured-stem varieties make an excellent waterside planting

The Dogwoods, or Cornels, comprise a truly noble genus of plants. In most other genera a horticulturalist selects and propagates the best species and varieties for gardens. In the case of *Cornus*, however, nearly all the species possess some good ornamental qualities in one form or another. The majority are small trees and shrubs of elegant habit. Botanically they have unusual features: the flowers of the showy species have conspicuous bracts, the petals being largely insignificant and they are star-shaped, rather like a clematis in appearance. All the species have leaves arranged opposite each other on their stems, with the exception of *C. alternifolia* and *controversa*.

Practical Matters
SOIL
Most cornus are easy to cultivate and generally grow in any good garden soil. The large-flowered varieties are not, however, successful on poor, shallow, chalk soils. The creeping *C. canadensis* requires an acid sandy peat or leaf mould for success.

Apart from the general elegance of the plants in this genus, there are those which are particularly spectacular in flower, leaf colour, beauty of their stem colour, and in the habit of their horizontal branches. Many possess all of these characteristics.

Cornus 'Norman Hadden'* in flower at Sir Harold Hillier Arboretum in midsummer; inset shows fruits freely produced in late summer and autumn.

MAKING A CHOICE

For flowers

C. *nuttallii* (Pacific dogwood) is a medium-sized tree of generally upright habit, and can reach 15m (50ft). It has large floral bracts, at first cream coloured, becoming white and then occasionally flushed pink; the foliage turns yellow, occasionally red in autumn. It is best planted in a rich soil that does not get too dry.

C. *florida* (Flowering dogwood) and its varieties, as the common name suggests, are grown specifically for their conspicuous flower-like bracts. Unfortunately, they are susceptible to spring frosts and indifferent ripening of the wood in cooler climates. It does, however, thrive when well situated. The variety 'Apple Blossom' is coloured as its name suggests; 'Cherokee Chief'* is a deep rose colour; and 'White Cloud' has brilliant white flowers and bronze foliage. These are the best of the selected varieties.

A mature specimen of C. *kousa* var. *chinensis** in full flower is a sight to be cherished. It is a large and truly ele-gant shrub, sometimes growing to small-tree size. It flowers in great profusion along the gracefully arching horizontal branches in early summer, and remains in flower for several weeks. This is another great asset, as few trees are in flower at this time. The flowers become cream coloured with age and are followed by unusual hanging strawberry-like fruit, with the leaves turning rich bronze and crimson in the autumn.

C. 'Norman Hadden'* is another small hybrid tree, usually multi-stemmed and of spreading, arching habit, producing quantities of creamy-white bracts in early summer. These turn deep pink by midsummer and are followed in early autumn by crops of large, hanging, strawberry-like fruits. A maturing specimen is sensational for much of the summer and autumn. 'Porlock'* is very similar while 'Eddies' White Wonder'* (*florida* x *nuttallii)*, is a superb spring-flowering small tree or large shrub of American origin, and has proved its reliability. Its leaves also colour well in autumn.

C. *mas** (Cornelian cherry) produces yellow flowers which are quite small individually but are produced in quantity on the leafless stems in late winter and early spring. It is, therefore, a most valuable shrub in the garden and develops into a large shrub or small, bushy tree, particularly worth considering to cheer up the wild garden in the depths of winter. The autumn fruits which are occasionally produced are bright cherry-red and edible. Of several cultivars, C. *m.* 'Variegata'* is perhaps the best, the neat, white-margined leaves looking good in combination with the red Cornelian cherry fruits.

Coloured Bark

Cornus alba (Red-barked dogwood) is a well-known, wide-spreading shrub that thrives in wet or dry situations. It is a vigorous plant, quickly forming a thicket of stems, and requires plenty of space to avoid swamping other less vigorous plants. It is, however, ideal for mass planting, and the red stems in winter are particularly effective as a waterside planting. These coloured stems can be encouraged by hard pruning in conjunction with some feeding (farmyard manure is ideal) every other year in early spring. There are a number of cultivars that have been selected specifically for their coloured stems, and some also for their variegated foliage, including:

'Elegantissima'*. This fine, adaptable plant has spectacular, bright silvery variegation and can very effectively be used as a contrast to purple-foliaged plants. It is also ideal for brightening up dark corners. The variegation is white, both marginal and mottled, while the stems are red.

'Kesselringii'. Branches are dark brownish-purple, the unfolding leaves reddish.

'Sibirica'*. The shoots of this variety are a bright crimson colour. It is not a vigorous plant and should therefore be given a damp, well-cultivated soil to maximise its growth.

'Spaethii'*. The foliage of this plant is extremely bright. The leaves are yellow, variegated and considered by some to make this shrub one of the very best yellow-leaved plants. It has the advantage that the leaves are not scorched by bright sunshine nor do they lose the brightness of their colour during the season, as other yellow-foliaged plants tend to.

C. stolonifera 'Flaviramea'* is similar in growth to *C. alba* but perhaps more rampant in wet conditions, which it favours. The young stem colour is greenish-yellow and an excellent contrast to the red-stemmed *C. alba* varieties.

All of these shrubs are effective for their winter stems and should be considered in conjunction with the willow (*Salix*) species and varieties which include those with yellow and orange stems. These and the white-stemmed brambles (*Rubus*) can make a colourful winter-garden display.

Architectural Effect

Finally, there are two rather more distinct species of the *Cornus* family which display a remarkable horizontal branching. These are *C. controversa* and *C. alternifolia*.

C. controversa is a small specimen tree and has slender and regularly forked branches which are clothed during early summer with broad clusters of cream-coloured flowers. In autumn small black fruits are produced, and the foliage colour is often a rich purple-red. Even in winter the branches are a rich red colour. The cultivar 'Variegata'* is a particularly striking plant with irregular silvery variegation that draws even more attention to the horizontal branches. It is slow growing and best positioned as an isolated specimen to display its branching habit effectively and prevent its growing out of shape by competing with adjacent shrubs.

C. alternifolia is a smaller plant of shrub rather than tree size. It displays similar characteristics to *controversa* but is dense in habit. 'Argentea'* makes a spreading, flat-topped shrub 2.5–3m (8–10ft) high, the leaves having a creamy-white margin. This is one of the most striking of variegated shrubs for specimen or focal point.

*C. canadensis*ial* is really a bit of an exception to the genus, being a low-growing, creeping plant only 15cm (6in) high. It dies back to ground level annually. The plant has delightful small, starry white flowers set amid a rosette of pale green leaves. On acid, peaty or leafy soil it will form an attractive carpet of flower succeeded by vivid red fruits. A distinctive plant which makes excellent and unusual ground cover.

Cornus *'Eddie's White Wonder'** (C. Nuttallii x florida). A superb hardy and reliable small tree with autumn leaf colour a bonus to the spring display of blossom.

COTONEASTERS

There must be very few ornamental gardens which do not possess a cotoneaster of some description. They are truly the most indispensable of hardy ornamental shrubs, ranging from prostrate creepers and mound-forming small bushes, to large shrubs, some even growing to small tree proportions. Their two greatest attributes are their ability to grow almost anywhere and in any soil, and the reliability and profusion of berries they produce in autumn. In addition, they all flower equally profusely, even if not spectacularly – being spring-blossoming plants, they have to compete with the cherries and rhododendrons and tend

therefore to be rather overshadowed. They are nevertheless quite pretty in their own right, especially the smaller-growing varieties.

The deciduous species produce excellent autumn colour, along with their berries. Cotoneasters, like other genera containing evergreen and deciduous varieties, include a number of species that are neither truly evergreen nor truly deciduous, and vary with the severity of the winter and the local environment. In a sheltered garden a specimen may be quite evergreen, whilst the same plant in another garden in an exposed position may be leafless.

For the plantsman, the variety of different sizes and habits of the cotoneaster, coupled with the ability

Cotoneaster floccosus* (salicifolia floccosus). A graceful evergreen attaining up to 3m (10ft). Perhaps the best taller cotoneaster, elegant and attractive all year, particularly notable in autumn when in berry (see page 176).

INSTANT REFERENCE

- Prostrate to large shrubs
- Evergreen or deciduous
- Small but profuse spring flowers (favourites with bees), good autumn berries and leaf colour
- Any soil
- Hardy
- Varieties to suit almost any space or purpose

to grow in most situations, gives him the opportunity to plant this genus in almost any part of the garden. There is a cotoneaster to suit almost any space, large or small – the garden designer's true friend. If you want to cover a manhole, clothe a steep bank or screen an unsightly object, cotoneaster can do the job, and evergreen species and cultivars continue to do so all year.

MAKING A CHOICE

Large Shrubs for Screening

The larger cotoneasters tend to be those which are variable in their evergreen hardiness. Possibly the finest of these is 'Cornubia'*, which will grow over 6m (20ft) high and, given the space, equally wide. By pruning to one or more stems it can be cultivated into a most attractive small tree. It is one of the semi-evergreen species and produces huge, pendulous crops of large brilliant red fruits which weigh down the branches in autumn. Closely related to this cotoneaster are four similarly tall plants: 'Rothschildianus'*; which has the distinction of being creamy-yellow fruited and is a wide-spreading shrub when young; 'Exburiensis', similar to 'Rothschildianus', but with apricot-yellow fruits, becoming pink tinged in winter; x Watereri 'John Waterer'*, with red fruits and a wide-spreading habit; and 'Pink Champagne', an equally large, vigorous plant, with more slender, arching branches, narrow leaves and smaller fruits, at first yellow, then becoming pink tinged.

Medium to Small Shrubs

Cotoneaster sternianus* (franchetii sternianus) is an extremely hardy, medium-sized plant, rapidly reaching a height of 1.8m (6ft) or more with a graceful habit. The leaves are sage green above and silvery-white beneath, the berries a bright orange red. This plant is evergreen or very nearly so.

C. lacteus* is a fine evergreen shrub which grows to 3m (10ft). The young shoots are pleasantly covered with a dense white down. The flowers are more attractive than many cotoneasters and are a milky-white in colour.

C. serotinus* is another impressive cotoneaster, with the advantage of being late in flower and very late fruiting. The orange-red berries will persist throughout winter and on into spring.

C. bullatus* is one of the best deciduous large cotoneasters, growing to 3m (10ft) with handsome, conspicuously corrugated leaves. It has no great floral beauty but provides rich autumn leaf colour and has clusters of large red fruit early in the season.

The popular C. 'Hybridus Pendulus' is a cultural form which can be used most effectively as a lawn specimen or focal point. Here the cotoneaster, which would normally be prostrate groundcover is usually grafted on to a stem to make a small, weeping tree. It is certainly a striking evergreen, with its glossy leaves and pendulous branches clothed with brilliant red berries in autumn and winter.

For flower and fruit, C. conspicuus 'Highlight' is a spectacular shrub of medium size. The plant is spreading and mound-forming, gradually reaching its ultimate height of 2m (6ft). It produces a mass of flower, followed by large orange-red fruits. The berries are not attractive to birds and will usually persist throughout the winter.

Cotoneasters generally cannot be considered the most beautiful in their shape and habit alone; they may have other attributes, but grace and elegance is not really one of them. There is, however, one variety that is distinctly more elegant than the others, C. floccosus* (salicifolius var. floccosus). Often considered an aristocrat among the cotoneasters, this species is fully evergreen, with narrow, shiny dark green leaves, white woolly beneath, which are held on slender, drooping, fan-like stems. The bright red berries are smaller than most, but possibly more attractive.

C. splendens* (s. 'Sabrina')(distichus tongolensis) is slightly unusual, having grey-green, rounded leaves. It grows to 2m (6ft) with arching shoots, and freely produces large orange-red fruit. Handsome and very garden worthy.

Groundcover

There are a variety of ground-smothering cotoneasters, the most well-known of which is the deciduous C. horizontalis* with its herringbone-pattern branches. The autumn colour is undoubtedly very fine, but the variety 'Variegatus'*, with its leaves edged with white, is one of the most charming variegated shrubs. In autumn the cream-variegated leaves become suffused with red.

For the clothing of dry banks, even chalky ones, there is no better than C. integrifolius* (microphyllus). A dwarf, glossy-leaved evergreen, it is extremely hardy and tolerant of the most adverse conditions. It rarely grows more than 75cm (2½ft) high and forms a dense, low thicket. The fruits are scarlet-red. C. cochleatus* (microphyllus cochleatus), now considered a distinct species, although slow growing is more prostrate, and the berries have particularly good colour. Reliably evergreen.

Of the many other groundcovering cotoneasters, C. 'Coral Beauty' and 'Gnom' are good prostrate, branching varieties.

C. dammeri* is one of the better-known evergreen groundcovering cotoneasters; it is prostrate in growth and has sealing-wax-red fruit. One of the disadvantages of this plant as a weed suppressor is its low growth, as weeds very easily push through the thin foliage layer. The variety 'Skogholm', which grows to 45cm (18in), is rather better in this respect. It is particularly vigorous and wide-spreading. These are all useful plants and may be grown in the open or as groundcover beneath other shrubs.

DAPHNE

INSTANT REFERENCE

• Dwarf to small shrubs
• Mostly evergreen
• Beautifully scented flowers, midwinter to early summer
• Any well-drained soil
• Not all are hardy
• Choice dwarf kinds are excellent for raised beds, rock gardens or the alpine house

This is a fascinating and delightful genus of mainly dwarf and predominantly evergreen shrubs found in mountainous areas of Europe and Asia. Daphnes are notable for the great diversity and beauty of their shape and form and, above all, for their deliciously scented flowers, produced from mid-winter to early summer.

Plantsmen, connoisseurs and particularly Alpine enthusiasts, prize daphnes very highly, growing the rarer dwarf or miniature kinds in pots and pans to a very high standard of perfection. Indeed, the rarer species of the genus have acquired the revered status of pampered primadonnas – perhaps due to the scarcity of propagation material and the subsequent high price asked by nurserymen. In nature daphnes are often found on the fringe of woods, or on the shaded side of a rock or boulder, and such a situation in the garden is likely to suit them better than an isolated, sunbaked site. If these conditions can be found, the sceptical grower may be pleasantly surprised by the successful growth and comparative longevity of his daphnes. When handling daphnes, care should be taken to avoid contact with the sap as it can be an irritant. All parts of daphnes are toxic if ingested.

Practical Matters
SOIL
Many daphnes are perverse and unpredictable in their performance and have a reputation for sudden inexplicable demise, or at least for being

Daphne bholua 'Jacqueline Postill'* is perhaps the most exciting and rewarding daphne introduction of recent years from Hillier propagator, Alan Postill. A vigorous upright evergreen to 2–3m (6 1/2–10ft), it has scented winter flowers in quantity. Select a sheltered sunny spot (see page 178).

short lived in cultivation. In spite of this, most of the hardy species can be grown in open positions in the garden in any well-drained soil, whether acid or alkaline. Good drainage is very important, but equally there should be adequate water-retaining matter in the soil – peat, leaf mould, bark, etc – to ensure that the plant does not dry out at the roots. Placing stones over the root area if open to sunshine is a further method of ensuring a cool, moist root-run.

DISEASES
Daphnes do have their problems and can suffer decline and dieback of whole or part of the shrub, often resulting in a fairly rapid death. A number of causes can be responsible, with the presence of virus disease heading the list. This may be spread by aphids or eelworm and will cause weakness and poor growth, with noticeable distortion, mottling, spotting or streaking of the leaves. It is best to destroy the affected plant and

remove the soil from the area it has occupied. The use of poorly grown, often pot-bound and sometimes incompatible species of seedling daphne as rootstocks for grafted specimens of the more desirable species and cultivars is another source of deterioration and demise.

MAKING A CHOICE
Raised Beds, Rock Garden or Alpine House
There are a few choice daphnes which, by reason of considerable rarity, slowness of growth and resulting comparative high cost (or a combination of all three) seem to be grown largely by the connoisseur or

alpine garden specialist. Most of these are not just botanical oddities but are very desirable, often spectacular, flowering plants. Until supplies become more readily available, perhaps with the increase of micropropagation facilities, fortunate would-be growers would be best advised to cosset them for safety's sake in a raised bed or well-protected scree or rock garden reserved for such aristocratic alpines. Several adapt well to pan culture; such gems include *Daphne arbuscula** from the Carpathian mountains, which forms a dense, narrow-leaved evergreen hummock up to about 20cm (8in) high. It is closely related to *D. petraea* and is reported to be easier to cultivate. The fragrant, usually deep pink but variably coloured flowers, are produced in dense terminal clusters and can be effective for up to six weeks in the spring. While it is much in demand for the alpine show bench as a pan plant, *D. arbuscula* is quite hardy and will make a fine, small specimen shrublet for a well-chosen rock garden site.

Essentially a collector's plant for alpine house culture, the slightly tender *D. jasminea* from Greece has incredibly brittle branches and is very subject to accidental damage. It is a variable species growing in nature as a gnarled crevice plant on limestone rock. The neat blue-green leaves are evergreen and a good foil for the beautiful and very fragrant flowers, which are purple-pink with white centres.

A relatively recent but exciting and hardy introduction from Northern Japan, *D. jezoensis*, seems to have a future outside for the specialist's rock garden. A small shrublet slowly reaching about 30cm (1ft), it produces fresh green leaves during autumn; then remarkably frost-resistant deep yellow flowers, sometimes lemon-scented, follow during the winter. The leaves fall in late spring. *D. jezoensis* appears to be happy on well-drained acid or slightly alkaline, leafy soil which does not dry out, or equally as a pan plant for the alpine house.

Finally, in this group we must not forget to include *D. petraea*, extolled by Farrer and other distinguished alpine authors for its spectacular disply of deep pink flowers painting the crevices of limestone cliffs of Northern Italy. Given sunshine and moisture at the root at all times, with impeccably good drainage, successful cultivation is not too difficult outside in a raised bed or tufa boulder, as well as in an alpine house pan, and is certainly a challenge worth rising to. *D. petraea* and its larger-flowered form 'Grandiflora' rarely exceed 15cm (6in) in cultivation, forming a dense evergreen shrublet covered for a long period between late spring and midsummer with exquisite waxy, fragrant, rose-pink blooms.

The Open Garden
Here is a selection from those daphnes which are usually available and are more easily grown and established in the open garden. Again, well-drained conditions and moisture at the roots at all times is the best recipe for success with these beautiful shrubs.

Among several newcomers to cultivation we have the very desirable winter-flowering *D. bholua* from the eastern Himalayas, making an upright shrub of 2–3m (6–10ft) or more. In Nepal its pulverised bark is used for paper and rope making. The two hardy cultivars now in commmerce are the deciduous 'Gurkha'* (H3), with purple-rose fragrant and frost-resistant flowers, and the evergreen 'Jacqueline Postill'* (H3), with a more compact habit and fragrant reddish-mauve flowers, which are white within and are produced from early winter to early spring.

D. blagayana*, with deliciously fragrant creamy-white blooms, is an evergreen of rather low and trailing habit found widely in light woodland over limestone throughout south-east Europe. It is recommended by Farrer, among others, that its stems are layered by placing stones or boulders on them.

D. cneorum*, the garland flower, has justly earned its reputation for reliability amongst daphnes, and is one of the most spectacular in flower as well as one of the easiest to grow in sun or semi-shade on rock garden, raised bed or at the front of a well-drained border, where it will quickly form a prostrate, evergreen mat densely covered in spring with rose-pink fragrant flowers. 'Eximia'*, selected by A. T. Johnson, is considered the finest form with its larger, deep rose-pink flowers, crimson in bud; 'Variegata', with golden margins to the leaves, is remarkably vigorous, if shyer in flower. The species, crossed with *D. caucasica*, has produced the popular and reliable semi-evergreen garden hybrid x *burkwoodii**; its cultivar 'Albert Burkwood' ('Somerset' is very similar) has fragrant pale-pink flowers in late spring or early summer which look good against the fresh green foliage on bushes up to 1m (3ft) high and as much across. *D. x. b.* 'Carol Mackie' is a vigorous variegated form, with leaves neatly margined yellow and later creamy-white.

The evergreen *D. collina** from the hills near Naples in Italy is also reliable. It forms a dome-shaped bush about 60cm (2ft) tall with very fragrant purple-rose flowers in spring. *D. c.* var. *neapolitana* (correctly x *napolitana**) is considered to be most probably a hybrid of *collina* with *cneorum*, and in effect is an equally worthy narrow-leaved *collina*, with scented rose-pink flowers opening from mid-spring to early summer.

There are two well-known and frequently planted species producing very welcome scented flowers in winter and early spring. The first is *D. mezereum** (Mesereon), a beautiful and much-loved deciduous species from woods in northern Europe and a rare British native. It will reach about 1m (3ft), the purple-red scented blooms covering bare branches in late winter and early spring, followed by attractive red fruits in summer. There are several variants, most notably 'Alba' ('Bowles White') of more upright, taller habit and with white flowers and amber fruits. Alas, *D. mezereum* is very prone to virus; foliar feeding in early summer may help lightly affected plants.

The other winter-flowering species is the evergreen and slightly tender *D. odora*, which is ideal as a patio plant near the house, where the heady scent of its purplish pink and white flowers can be enjoyed early in the year. Even when out of flower this is a handsome, mounded shrub with large lanceolate leaves up to 7.5cm (3in) long. It adapts well as a conservatory plant in cold districts; the variegated form 'Aureomarginata' has a reputation for greater hardiness.

D. retusa* and the closely related species *tangutica** are both hardy and from China, and are excellent small evergreen shrubs for patio or rock garden planting. *D. retusa* has a dense, compact habit to 60cm (2ft) and rose-purple flowers, scented like lilac, in late spring or early summer, followed by red fruits, while *tangutica* is taller and more open in habit, with larger leaves and white, purple-tinted flowers in early spring followed by larger red fruits. An exciting new hybrid of *retusa* with x *burkwoodii* raised in western Canada is now becoming available. *D. x mantensiana* 'Manten' makes a dwarf, compact evergreen shrub, combining the best of its two distinguished parents. The rose-purple, scented flowers persist well into the summer. This is an excellent new daphne for patio or court-yard planting.

Finally, there are two excellent new Hillier introductions, *D. longilobata* 'Peter Moore', a near-hardy semi-evergreen shrub reaching 1.5–2.5m (5–8ft) and effectively extending the range of variegated daphnes. It has narrow grey-green leaves, conspicuously margined creamy-white and white flowers in summer, followed by red fruits. This daphne shows promise as a container or conservatory shrub. 'Valerie Hillier', (*D. cneorum* x *longilobata*) raised in 1984 by Hillier propagator Alan Postill forms a dwarf spreading evergreen shrub with narrow glossy green leaves and terminal clusters of fragrant flowers opening pale pink from purple pink buds and produced continuously from late spring until autumn.

HARDY FERNS

Much loved by the Victorians for decoration of both garden and conservatory, ferns went out of fashion during the middle of this century, and indeed for some years after World War II it was difficult to obtain plants of any but the commonest species. Happily today we have a resurgence of appreciation of these delightful shade-loving plants, and many of the most desirable species and forms are again being propagated.

Hardy ferns are good perennials and are not difficult to please in the garden, thriving in most fertile, well-drained soils, particularly where there is a high humus content. Cool, moist, shady conditions are ideal, but several, such as *Blechnum* and *Asplenium*, will tolerate quite dry, shady conditions and are found naturally inhabiting cracks and crevices of shady walls and mossy roofs.

For the beauty they can inject into an otherwise dark, perhaps featureless area of the garden, ferns have much to commend them. The unfurling leaves of several species appear in the spring like exquisite felt-covered shepherd's crooks, or croziers, and there is great diversity and delicacy of shape in their leaves, some having fronds of the finest filigree. Throughout summer and well into autumn they make a perfect foil for trees, shrubs and other plants, with which they may be safely associated. A clump of *Polystichum* (Shield fern) or *Athyrium* (Lady fern) will often look 'just right' at the foot of a shady wall or by a stone seat. Some hardy ferns, such as *Phyllitis* (Hart's tongue fern) and *Polypodium* (Common polypody) are near-evergreen in sheltered areas and several species will turn bronze, gold or russet in the autumn, others like *Blechnum* (Hard fern) and *Osmunda* (Royal fern) producing unusual erect, spore-bearing fronds.

MAKING A CHOICE
Cool Glades
Ferns can be used as groundcover, as specimens by tree boles, or to blend

---

INSTANT REFERENCE

- Herbaceous perennials, some evergreen
- Beautiful fronds in a variety of shapes and sizes
- Fertile, well-drained soil in cool, moist, shady conditions
- Hardy
- Excellent for adding interest to dark, featureless garden areas

---

with shade-tolerant shrubs and associate with other groundcovers like ivies and pachysandra, and herbaceous plants such as hosta, brunnera, bergenia, dicentra, epimedium, pulmonaria and hardy geranium, among many others. Most will blend well with early-flowering bulbs, such as aconite, snowdrop and crocus.

Adiantum pedatum* is the hardiest of the maidenhair ferns, producing its typical dainty leaflets beautifully poised on 25–50cm (10–20in) slender, wiry black stems. It needs a sheltered, wind-free, shaded spot and will make an imposing clump when happily sited. Several very desirable dwarf, compact geographic forms of this North American and Asiatic species are now becoming available.

Athyrium filix-femina* (Lady fern) is a delightful and elegant woodland species; the light green, much-divided fronds show great variation and rise from shallow, creeping stems to a height of about 30cm (1ft). For those who enjoy the unusual, the Japanese painted fern, *A. goeringianum* 'Pictum'* (H3) (*A. niponicum* 'Pictum') is unique and a delight – pale grey-green, broadly triangular fronds contrast superbly with dark red stems and leaf stalks, and there is a subtle suffusion of this reddish hue into the bases of the leaflets. A compact grower for a sheltered position, spreading slowly to form a clump ultimately up to 50–60cm (1½–2ft) high.

Of the Buckler ferns (*Dryopteris*), *D. dilatata* (Broad Buckler) reaches 60cm (2½–3ft) and forms mounds of broad, delicately divided fronds, seen well on a shady hedge bank, while

The Ostrich plume fern, Matteucia struthiopteris* *in spring at Longstock Water Garden, Hampshire.*

*D. filix-mas** (Male fern) makes bold clumps of sturdy fronds like giant shuttlecocks, and grows well in most conditions in sun or shade – a useful filler in difficult corners.

One of the most handsome of the European ferns, is *Matteuccia struthiopteris** (Ostrich-feather fern) which requires a sheltered, moist, but well-drained site to display its magnificent, fresh green shuttlecocks that can reach 90cm (3ft) high. It rambles gently by spreading underground rhizomes and looks good among taller shrubs, such as hydrangea or deciduous azalea.

Less demanding, and easily cultivated in semi-shaded woodland, are the evergreen shield ferns, particularly *Polystichium aculeatum** (Hard shield fern), with its dark green leathery fronds to 50–60cm (2–2½ft). *P. setiferum** (Soft shield fern) has soft lacy fronds of more arching habit and a similar height. New unfurling fronds, their leaf stalks densely covered with pale brown scales, emerge delightfully in spring from a mound of old russet-brown leaves; a number of uncommon forms and cultivars are available, particularly 'Plumoso-divisilobum' with very finely divided, feather-like fronds.

Waterside

Above all others, *Osmunda regalis** (Royal fern), a truly regal species, is worthy of a permanent position at the water's edge. Here it will slowly form mounds of brown osmunda fibre (once keenly sought by orchid growers) from which emerge each spring strong, white, silky unfurling fronds, which open to display blunt-ended leaflets and usually attain a height of 1.2–2m (4–6ft). Narrow brown spore-carrying leaflets appear at the apex of most fronds. This is one of the most stately of all ferns, the leaves turning warm golden-brown in the autumn.

*Matteuccia struthiopteris** (Ostrich-plume fern) will also perform well in a shady waterside position, as long as it is sheltered and free draining, while *Onoclea sensibilis** (Sensitive fern), an American species, will colonise rapidly by underground stolons and is happier in boggy, acid conditions. The fresh green fronds reach 30–60cm (1–2ft) with broad, coarsely scalloped or lobed leaflets, and there are forms with both red and green stems.

Shady Paved Areas, Walls, Mossy Stumps and Tree Branches

The hardy evergreen *Asplenium trichomanes* (Maidenhair spleenwort) is a pleasing and familiar inhabitant of cracks and mortar crevices in shady walls; indeed, it seems to enjoy well-drained limy conditions, its delightful rosettes crowding together, usually 7.5–10cm (3–4in) high. The sterile evergreen fronds with thread-like black stalks and small green lobes are reminiscent of the Maidenhair fern. It is often found in association with *Cetarach officinarum* (Rusty-back fern) which has larger, 10–15cm (4–6in) long leaves with conspicuous brown scales covering the undersides. *Phyllitis scolopendrium** (*Scolopendrium vulgare*) (Hart's tongue fern) can often be found in similar situations, though it will grow much more luxuriantly up to 50cm (1½ft) in moist positions almost anywhere in sun or shade. The leathery, tongue-like fronds are undivided, pale green in colour and up to 45cm (1½ft) long – a distinct and conspicuous, if common, plant making a pleasing contrast with other ferns in the garden.

Distinct again is *Blechnum spicant** (Hard fern), a native of acid soil and frequently seen slowly colonising shady, dry banks. The sterile evergreen fronds are divided to the mid-rib and form rosettes from which emerge bright, fertile fronds with narrower leaflets – very attractive and useful in the garden in dry shade. *B. penna-marina* from southern-hemisphere temperate regions and Antarctica, is not fully hardy but is a delightful small and neat little plant for a sheltered, shady banking or mossy wall top. The young fronds are attractively copper-tinted and grow 7.5–10cm (3–4in) high, while *B. spicant* will reach 25–30cm (10–12in). Both require acid soil.

Finally, for a variety of similar situations, including mossy tree boughs, hedge bankings and wall tops, the evergreen *Polypodium vulgare* (Common polypody) is very adaptable. A ubiquitous fern with creeping roots, it is found on mossy banks in chalk, limestone or gravelly areas. The lance-shaped fronds growing to 15–30cm (6–12in) high are deeply cut, with widely spaced comb-like teeth.

HARDY ORNAMENTAL GRASSES AND BAMBOOS

INSTANT REFERENCE

• BAMBOOS: Excellent architectural plants and for screening

• GRASSES: Useful groundcover and elegant leaves to contrast with other plants

• Low, groundcovering grasses to towering bamboos
• Grasses mostly herbaceous, bamboos mostly evergreen
• Beautiful leaves in a variety of colours and sizes
• Any fertile, well-drained soil
• Hardy

There are a number of highly ornamental hardy grasses and bamboos for gardens, ranging from excellent groundcovering grasses a few inches high to bamboos towering to 4.5–5.5m (15–18ft) or more. Together they offer architectural grace and elegance, often combined with artistically satisfying and unusual floral effects – though perhaps without the flamboyance of other garden plants grown more particularly for their flowers. The foliage of many species of both grass and bamboo can be attractively variegated, while the flower plumes or spikelets of *Cortaderia* (Pampas grass), *Miscanthus* and *Stipa*, among others, provide welcome material for floral arranging and winter decoration. A number of dwarf grasses make excellent groundcover in both sun and shade, associating with and complementing such elegant shrubs as hydrangea, Japanese maple, azalea and rhododendron.

While most perennial grass species are herbaceous, growth being renewed annually from below ground, bamboos are strictly evergreen and perennial woody grasses. The taller species such as *Arundinaria simonii*

Chusquea couleou* – *an unusual solid-stemmed bamboo from South America here seen growing well at RHS Garden, Wisley, Surrey (see page 184).*

makes good screens in sheltered areas, while dwarf sorts provide excellent evergreen and often variegated groundcover, particularly near the waterside in sun or semi-shade. While many are clump forming, several species of both bamboos and ornamental grasses, once established, can be both vigorous and invasive, and need careful siting or they will engulf valued weaker plants. Such ornamental grasses as *Phalaris arundinacea* 'Picta'* (Gardeners' garters) or the dwarf bamboo *Arundinaria auricoma (viridistriata)* should not be planted in conventional herbaceous borders for this reason. Such beautiful but vigorous species are best given a vacant corner or isolated area, perhaps surrounded by mown grass, where their brightly variegated foliage can be highlighted and form a striking focal point of beauty and interest.

Practical Matters
SOIL AND PLANTING
Both bamboos and ornamental grasses grow well in any well-drained, fertile soil, though more rampantly in moist conditions. However, permanently wet land or an exposed situation should be avoided for bamboos. Most are now provided container grown by nurserymen for planting at all seasons; even so, avoid planting bamboos in cold districts from early winter to early spring.

AFTERCARE
The occasional flowering of bamboos is a curious phenomenon not yet fully understood, in that all plants of one particular species tend to flower simultaneously over a wide area, including other parts of the world. Regrettably, this often results in the death of the colony concerned. Some regeneration of growth has been

Hakonechloa macra *'Aureola'* is the aristocrat of dwarf variegated grasses (see below).*

achieved with certain species by cutting all canes down to ground level when flowering spikelets are first noted, followed by copious mulching with well-rotted farmyard manure and the addition of a good slow-release fertiliser. However, such action can be devastating, destroying any screening value the plant or colony may have had and, if left, can result in a forest of unsightly dead canes. In these circumstances, it is perhaps better to plant bamboos in small groups or as isolated specimens, rather than to use one species as an important evergreen screen. Fortunately, groundcovering species seem less affected and less inclined to flower, while a group of single specimens of several choicer species can make an impressive planting and if they flower, will not all flower at once!

MAKING A CHOICE
Small Gardens
Ornamental grasses and bamboos can be used with trees, shrubs, ferns and herbaceous plants in sun or semi-shade. With this in mind, there are two or three first-class, low growing perennial grasses and one sedge which should be included here. All have brightly variegated or golden leaves. *Hakonechloa macra* 'Aureola'* is perhaps the most striking of hardy, low-growing, variegated grasses. It comes from Japan and has arching, narrow leaves, conspicuously striped golden yellow and tinted with bronze. It has a neat tufted habit, slowly spreading and reaching a height of 30cm (1ft).

Milium effusum 'Aureum' (Bowles' golden grass) is a delightful bright golden-leaved form of the wood millet, growing to 45–60cm (1¹/₂–2ft). All parts of this elegant little plant are golden, and it naturalises readily – not invasively – breeding true from seed.

The dwarf variegated sedge *Carex hachijoensis (morrowii)* 'Evergold'*, although slightly less hardy, has the

advantage of being evergreen. Small mounds of stiff, narrow leaves are creamy-yellow variegated, and reach 30cm (1ft).

These beauties look well in association with Japanese maples (*Acer palmatum* and *p.* 'Dissectum' cvs), mahonias, *Danae racemosa*, and viburnums. Plant them in groups of three or more grasses between the shrubs. Shade-tolerant herbaceous plants will live-in well with both shrub and grass, including particularly *Ajuga reptans* 'Burgundy Glow', *Lysimachia nummularia* 'Aurea', *Gentiana asclepiadea*, bergenia, epimedium, hosta and helleborus, and ferns.

Specimen Plants
Planted singly, or in groups of three or more of a kind, a number of grasses and bamboos can be very effective as focal or accent points in the garden. The familiar and stately tuffet-forming *Cortaderia selloana* (*argentea*) (Pampas grass) makes a superb lawn specimen; sited well spaced from a dark background such as yew or cypress or

other evergreen hedge, its tall, silvery-grey plumes reach 1.8–2.5m (6–8ft) and are magnificent from late summer well into the autumn; healthy, mature plants can produce fifty or more plumes at once. Where space is limited the smaller, more compact 'Pumila'* will do useful duty. There is also an interesting new cultivar from New Zealand, 'Gold Band'*, with narrow, golden-variegated leaves and plumes to 1.5m (5ft). The taller-growing 'Sunningdale Silver'* has looser, more feathery plumes of great beauty. When tidying these plants in late autumn it is worth remembering to wear gloves, as the long, arching, evergreen leaves have razor-sharp edges.

In favoured sheltered areas, particularly by waterside, *Arundo donax* 'Macrophylla' (Provence reed) makes an imposing specimen 2.5–3.5m (8–12ft) tall. Broad, arching blue-grey leaves are born on equally glaucous stout stems, and there is a superb white-variegated and rather more tender form 'Variegata', 3m (10ft). In cold districts this makes an exciting and different conservatory plant. In similar vein, there is the elegant, if somewhat invasive, *Miscanthus*. Taller growing *M. floridulus (sacchariflorus)**, with grey-green sugar-cane-like growth, will reach 1.8–2.5m (6–8ft) and make a good summer windbreak. The slender *M. sinensis* 'Gracillimus' is perhaps the doyenne of the genus, with narrow, greyish arching leaves with white central veins growing 1.5–2m (5–6ft) tall, while 'Zebrinus' is slightly taller and distinct in its cross-wise zebra stripes of golden yellow.

Among the many hardy bamboos, a few are particularly suitable as evergreen specimens for moist, well-drained focal points in sun or shade, often combining beauty and elegance in a most subtle and satisfying manner. Bamboos will also adapt admirably to container and tub culture, making impressive and evergreen patio or terrace specimens. For either purpose *Thamnocalamus spathaceus* (*Arundinaria murieliae*) is considered to be one of the most beau-

The dwarfer more compact pampas grass Cortedera selloana *'Pumila'* makes an excellent focal point in the small garden.*

tiful species in cultivation; indeed it was thought worthy to be named after the daughter of the great plant-hunter Ernest Wilson, who introduced it from China. Its graceful, arching stems can reach 2.5–3.5m (8–12ft), but less if restricted in large tub or container. *A. Humilis* 'Gauntletti', a clump-forming hybrid bamboo, has large, handsome leaves and young canes which are bright green, becoming purple-tinted with age, and grow to 1.5–2m (5–6ft). The generally taller-growing *Phyllostachys* differ from *Arundinaria* in their less invasive habit and zig-zag stems. *P. aurea** forms clumps up to 3.5m (12ft) high of canes which mature to a distinct creamy-yellow and are used for walking sticks and fishing rods. *P. nigra** (Chinese black bamboo) produces quantities of graceful, arching, leafy stems up to 4m (13ft) high, at first green and then changing to yellow splashed with purple, mottled brown or black in warm, sunny sites.

A rare and distinct species often difficult to obtain, the Chilean *Chusquea culeou** is unique among hardy bamboos in its solid stems (they do not flag if cut for floral arranging), and unusual bottle-brush-like, leafy branchlets which are produced throughout the length of the tall, olive-green stems. This is a beautiful and desirable bamboo, particularly for those who collect the rare and uncommon.

Finally, another unique and contrasting bamboo for an especially prominent position in the garden can be found in *Indocalamus (Sasa) tessellatus* (*Arundinaria ragamowskii*), whose shining green leaves up to 60cm (2ft) long are the largest of all hardy bamboos, and are borne impressively on arching canes, not usually above 2m (6ft) long. It is comforting to learn that this elegant species has not been known to flower in cultivation.

Paved Areas and Patios

There are several tufted or clump-forming grasses which make exciting specimens, effective in both foliage and flower, when grown in small pockets in well-drained, sunny areas which are paved or gravelled. *Helictotrichon sempervirens** (*Avena candida*) has semi-evergreen, blue-grey mounds of arching leaves from which erupt silvery, oak-like inflorescences to a height of about 60cm (2ft). Much smaller, perhaps 15–20cm (6–8in) high, and a popular paving or edging plant, *Festuca glauca* (Blue fescue grass) forms delicate tufts of inrolled leaves. Spring division every other year and regular trimming ensures a good performance.

Molinia caerulea 'Variegata'* is another most desirable tufted small grass for a prominent position in paving; its creamy-white marginal variegation is effective throughout the growing season, and in late summer and autumn purple-brown flower spikes are produced to contrast subtly with the foliage.

Stipa calamagrostis, 60cm (2–2½ft) can be relied on for a long season of display, the arching green foliage and graceful, glistening silvery plumes opening in midsummer and deepening in colour as they fade in the autumn. *S. gigantea**, the largest of the genus, needs space to set it off and is too big for the small patio, but is very worthy of a prominent position elsewhere in the garden. A sunny, and above all well-drained focal point is essential for this splendid grass. Semi-evergreen, tough pointed leaves form a basal mound from which arise 2m (6ft) stems of glistening golden spikelets. Divide clumps every other year in spring.

Groundcover

These grasses and bamboos are for banks, pond or stream side and under trees with light canopies. There are several notable plants which are both good to look at and efficient and functional as labour-saving groundcover, albeit somewhat invasive. However, if correctly sited they are usually controllable, particularly if isolated in mown grass or confined to banks or areas where they cannot swamp weaker or immature plants or shrubs.

Among the grasses are two strikingly variegated plants: *Glyceria maxima* 'Variegata' (*aquatica* 'Variegata'), best grown as a waterside plant, where it will reach about 45–60cm (1½–2ft). Its strap-like leaves are conspicuously variegated with green, yellow and creamy-white, and are tinted pink in both spring and autumn; *Phalaris arundinacea* 'Picta'* (Gardener's garters) is tolerant of a wide range of soil conditions, growing strongly to about 1m (3ft) whether dry or moist. The bold, upright growth is brightly striped with white and can be most effective if well isolated and seen against a dark background.

Dwarf groundcovering bamboos, once established, are equally invasive, but have the advantage of evergreen foliage, sometimes variegated and effective all year. Several species are now used increasingly as groundcover in town centres and other public places. As with taller varieties, these bamboos make excellent tub or container plants for paved areas.

Arundinaria pumila, with purplish, slender canes, *A. pygmaea* and *Sasa ramosa* (*Arundinaria vagans*) all form green carpets about 45–60cm (1½–2ft) high. Variegated dwarf and groundcovering bamboos are a little taller. *A. viridistriata* (*auricoma*) is clump-forming and less invasive, usually maturing to 1–1.5m (3–5ft). It has predominantly golden-yellow, green-striped leaves, while *A. fortunei variegata* also has a tufted habit, attaining about 1m (3ft) with narrow, comparatively long leaves striped creamy-white and is excellent for containers. One other lower-growing bamboo, *Sasa veitchii* (up to 1.5m or 5ft), creates an unusual effect of variegation by the natural withering of the margins of its large leaves. This produces the effect of parchment-white variegation, and an isolated colony near a waterside can be most effective at all seasons, and particularly during autumn and winter.

Finally, *Shibataea kumasasa* 45–60cm (1½–2ft), a rarely seen low-growing Japanese bamboo, is very worthy of a mention in that it is neat, compact and not invasive, and is one of the most distinct of hardy bamboos, with robust zigzag stems and comparatively wide leaves in relation to their length.

HYDRANGEA

'How do I make my hydrangea as blue as Mrs Jones' plant?' This is the usual starting point when gardeners consider hydrangeas, but is only really appropriate to a very limited view of this valuable group of plants. Some of the Hortensia hydrangeas, when grown on acid soils, can look startling with vivid blue flowers, but these are only a small part of the varied shrubs and climbers offered by this genus.

Although some hydrangeas offer features such as attractive barks, bold foliage and interesting fruit heads for use in flower arranging, the main element for the garden is their flowers. These are borne in large clusters and, in the species, are of two types.

Around the outside of the head are the ray florets. These are individually conspicuous but are sterile, with only three to five large sepals; their role is to attract insects to the flowers, or gardeners to the plant. Some forms, especially the common 'Hortensia' hydrangeas, have flowers which com-

---

INSTANT REFERENCE

• Mostly shrubs, occasionally small trees, some climbers
• Deciduous
• Pink, white or blue flowers, often dependent on soil pH, summer to early autumn
• Any soil, must not dry out in summer
• Hardy
• Good in the shrubaceous border and woodland plantings

---

prise ray florets only. However, in the wild species and in the 'Lacecap' hydrangeas, the centre of the flower head consists of masses of fertile florets. Although individually rather insignificant, when massed they are attractive, creating a haze of their principal colour, which may be white, blue or pink. At their best the Hortensias can look very attractive but may be said to lack the grace of the

wild flower forms. The ray florets do not fall when they have finished but persist to enhance the beauty of the fruiting heads.

In some species the pigment which colours the sterile flowers contains aluminium ions. The availability to the plant of aluminium depends to a very large extent upon the pH of the soil (see Chapter 3); in acid soils aluminium is readily absorbed by the plant, and this gives the well-known bright blue colours. As the pH increases, aluminium becomes less available and the colour changes through purple to pink on alkaline soils. Plants which are naturally pink-flowered on neutral or alkaline soils will become purplish or bluish on acidic soils. Proprietary compounds are available to make aluminium ions available to the plant and these can be very effective where the soil is neutral, but are less effective where the soil is veering towards the alkaline. Generally, either clear blues or clear pinks are attractive, and the colours to avoid are the muddy purples. If your

Hydrangea 'Preziosa'* is a very rewarding cultivar, performing well in sun or semi-shade (see page 187).

Hydrangea serrata 'Blue Bird'* is a splendid dwarf lacecap which lives up to its name on acid soils.

efforts to make hydrangeas blue fail, try going the other way and having clearer pink flowers by applying lime (though check that no other plants in the area will suffer).

Hydrangeas are mainly shrubs, but include a number of climbing species. Several make trees in the wild and there is no reason why they should not be grown as small trees in gardens. This will require an element of training by the removal of unwanted basal shoots but *H. aspera, heteromalla* and *paniculata* can all make unusual small flowering trees.

These climbing species are useful for clothing the walls of houses or clinging to the trunks of trees. They have the considerable advantage of developing aerial roots, which serve to attach the plant to the wall or trunk without the need for extensive artificial supports, although a little early guidance is useful. The shrubby species make good plants in the shrubaceous border, particularly in shaded sites, and as shrubs in woodland gardens.

Practical Matters

Soil

Hydrangeas will grow on all soils, including chalk and limey ones. Most like a good quantity of moisture in the soil and should not be planted where it will dry out during the summer. On chalk and other soils which may dry out, organic matter should be worked into the soil and topped with a mulch to retain moisture. Also, avoid using the plants where they will be exposed to the full effects of the sun.

Pruning

Most hydrangeas require very little pruning. The flowers are produced from buds laid down in the previous summer and severe pruning will result in no flowers the following summer. However, weaker and older stems should be thinned out. The exception to this is *H. paniculata*.

MAKING A CHOICE

Small Shrubs

H. macrophylla makes a small shrub 1–2m (3–6ft) tall. It is excellent for

coastal situations, but needs some shelter in inland gardens if the flower buds are not to be killed over winter. The species has given a multiplicity of different cultivars, which are divided into two groups. The Hortensia cultivars, or Mop-head hydrangeas, have flowers composed exclusively or mainly of sterile ray florets. The flowerheads are generally large and rounded. The second group is known as the Lacecap hydrangeas and these have normal flattened flowerheads, but perhaps with more sterile florets than occurs in the wild species. With these forms, the beauty is partly from the sterile florets and partly from the haze of massed but minute fertile florets. The flowers normally open in midsummer and last into late summer and early autumn.

Mop-head Hydrangeas

'Altona'* naturally has rose-coloured flowers but these can be induced to turn blue. They are carried on strong stems and are long lasting, becoming green and in autumn turning red. It is hardier than most and less likely to be damaged by winter weather. It grows to around 1m (3ft).

'Ami Pasquier'* has deep red or crimson flowers and is low growing, to 60 cm (2ft) or so.

'Ayesha'* will reach 1m (3ft) and has glossy green leaves. The flowers are produced in concave heads and are thick-petalled, slightly fragrant and a greyish lilac-pink in colour. A distinct and unusual hydrangea.

'Générale Vicomtesse de Vibraye'* has good pink or blue flowers, although the stems are rather weak. Along with 'Altona', it is one of the hardiest.

'King George' has rose-pink flowers in large florets and with serrated sepals.

'Marechal Foch' has flowers from rosy-pink through purple to deep blue and is an early and free-flowering form growing up to 1.5m (5ft).

'Madame Emile Mouillère'* is usually considered the best white mophead hydrangea, with large serrated sepals with pink or blue eyes.

LACECAP HYDRANGEAS

'Blue Wave'* has blue fertile flowers and ray florets which may be pink or blue according to the soil pH; at their best they are gentian blue. It will make 2m (6ft) tall and is best in light shade.

'Geoffrey Chadbund'* is an excellent recent introduction, a lacecap with large heads of brick-red flowers on neutral or alkaline soils.

'Lanarth White'* and 'White Wave'* have the ray florets pure white, although the fertile florets may be either blue or pink. Both are free flowering in open, sunny positions and will grow 1–2m (3–6ft) tall.

'Mariesii' has almost invariably pink or mauve-pink ray florets, but instead of being restricted to the periphery of the flowerhead, some are scattered amongst the fertile flowers.

'Tricolor'* has leaves which are variegated green, grey and pale yellow, and pale pink to white flowers.

H. serrata makes a low shrub usually less than 1.5m (5ft) tall. It is related to macrophylla and flowers at the same time, but is generally hardier. 'Bluebird'* has domed flowerheads composed of blue fertile flowers and large red-purple to sea-blue ray florets. It is drought tolerant and rather early flowering. 'Grayswood'* is a selection with blue fertile florets, and in which the ray florets begin white and age through pink and, if grown in sunlight, to bright red. 'Rosalba'* is similar, except the ray florets become blotched with pure crimson and the foliage is dull yellow-green. 'Preziosa'* has flowerheads composed entirely of ray florets, although in smaller heads than in the Hortensia group. The flowers are rose-pink and very long lasting, eventually turning reddish-purple and remaining attractive in autumn. The coarsely toothed leaves are tinged purple when young and the shoots are purplish red. It is an excellent form, flowering very freely either in full sun or light shade.

The above four cultivars, excluding 'Bluebird', do not develop blue ray florets on acidic soils or in response to the application of aluminium compounds.

H. arborescens can make a shrub to 3m (10ft), although it is usually much smaller. It is hardy and mainly represented by 'Annabelle'* with very large hemispherical heads of white flowers, nearly all of which are sterile, and are produced from midsummer into early autumn.

H. quercifolia* has remarkable leaves which are likened to those of the red oak, with five to seven scalloped lobes. The leaves turn crimson, orange or purple in the autumn. This shrub to 2m (6ft) needs a moist soil and a sheltered but not shaded position. The flowers are in erect panicles 10–25cm (4–10in) long and are white. 'Snowflake' is a form with double white flowers.

H. involucrata makes a small shrub to 50cm (1½ft) tall, although taller in mild areas. It is not reliably hardy, but carries blue or rosy-lilac fertile florets surrounded by white or bluish-white ray florets from late summer into mid-autumn. 'Hortensis'* is a selection in which the more numerous ray florets are double and buff-pink in colour, although nearly white in shade. It needs a sheltered position.

Large Shrubs and Trees

These hydrangeas make large shrubs, naturally more than 3m (10ft) tall, or small trees up to 6–10m (20–33ft) tall.

H. aspera has its flowers in large corymbs up to 25cm (10in) across. The fertile florets are blue or purple and the ray florets white, pink or purple. The colour is unaffected by the soil pH, although some forms have much better flowers than others. The leaves are variable but often large, to 25cm (10in), and the stems have a buff-coloured, peeling bark. It flowers in mid- to late summer, creating a bold display. H. aspera grows better on chalk than most other species and appears to need a rather dry soil for best development. The new growths can be susceptible to damage by spring frost. 'Macrophylla'* is a cultivar selected for its exceptionally large leaves and flowerheads; 'Villosa'* is an excellent narrow-leafed form with large lilac-blue flowerheads.

H. aspera subsp. sargentiana* is a magnificent species which has stout, bristly shoots and large corymbs of flowers in mid-to late summer. The ray florets are up to 3cm (1in) across and pinkish white. The fertile flowers are deep rosy-lilac. It needs a moist, rich soil and a position which will give it plenty of sunlight but protection from the full force of the midday sun.

H. heteromalla makes a large shrub or small tree with large corymbs of white, flattened lacecap flowers. The ray florets can be up to 5cm (2in) across. The large flowerheads are borne in early to midsummer; these are pure white at first, fading to light pink. The bark is chestnut-brown and peels. H. heteromalla is a very tough plant, tolerating drought, full sun and exposure. 'Bretschneideri'* and 'Snowcap' are exceptional forms of this species.

H. paniculata is unusual in that it can be pruned in the spring and still give a good floral display, behaving more like Buddleia davidii than other hydrangeas. It can be grown either as a low shrub, a larger bush on a stem or leg, or trained to make a tree. It does not need severe pruning to flower copiously, but pruning can be used to concentrate the growth into a small number of flowers, thus creating larger flowerheads. The wild species has mainly fertile flowers but the normal forms in cultivation mainly have ray florets. The flowers are white, fading to pink, and are carried in conical panicles which can be 50cm (1½ft) tall by 30cm (18in) wide. 'Praecox'* is the first to flower, starting in midsummer. Many of the florets are fertile. 'Grandiflora'* develops the largest flowers and comes into bloom around the end of summer. The flowers die off brown but are still attractive. 'Unique'* is similar but with larger flowerheads; 'Everest' has the flowers first white, then tinged pink. 'Tardiva' is late-flowering in early to mid-autumn. A range of clones can thus be used to give a succession of large white flowers, either in the garden or for indoor decoration.

Climbers

*H. petiolaris** is the commonest climbing hydrangea and is very hardy. It will grow high up a wall or into the crown of a tree and, along with the other climbing hydrangea species, is self-clinging. It can also be very effective if used to grow over a mound. The stems have a peeling bark. The flowers are carried in early summer from short shoots which grow horizontally out from the wall or bank and are white. Young plants may take a couple of seasons before they start to climb vigorously, and a further two or three before flowering well.

H. serratifolia is an uncommon evergreen species with dark green, leathery leaves. In late summer it bears creamy-white flowers composed of small fertile flowers and very few, if any, ray florets. It is hardy on a sheltered wall.

Decumaria is an uncommon genus of self-clinging climbers closely related to *Hydrangea* but lacking ray florets. *D. barbara* is deciduous or semi-evergreen and makes a climber to 9m (30ft). The white flowers are produced in clusters 5–7cm (2–3in) across in early to midsummer. It needs the protection of a wall except in mild areas.

D. sinensis is an evergreen species climbing to 5m (16ft). It has fragrant, yellowish-white flowers in terminal panicles in late spring.

Schizophragma is allied to *Hydrangea*, but differs in the sterile florets being composed of a single sepal or bract, not three to five. The two species climb by aerial roots. They flower best in full sunlight but need a moist, rich, loamy soil. *S. hydrangeoides* makes a deciduous climber capable of attaining 10m (33ft) or more. The flowers are yellowish-white, sweetly scented and in corymbs 20–25cm (8–10in) across; they are carried in midsummer. 'Roseum' has the sterile bracts tinged with rose. *S. integrifolium** is also deciduous and differs in the larger flowerheads, to 30cm (1ft), and the larger sterile bracts, which are up to 9cm long by 5cm wide (3.5in x 2in).

ILEX (HOLLY)

This large genus of trees and shrubs contains a majority of evergreen species which are the most well known in our gardens. Most are hardy, and some may grow up to 21m (70ft) high. One of the greatest attributes is their ability to grow in sun or shade: *Ilex aquifolium** is common as an understorey plant in many beech and oak woods.

The majority of the garden varieties originate from either *Ilex aquifolium* or the hybrid holly, *Ilex x altaclerensis* (Highclere holly). This holly originated from a cross between the common holly and the rather tender Azorean holly (*Ilex perado*) and the resulting *Ilex x altaclerensis* has the advantage of being more vigorous in growth, with rather larger, handsome leaves which tend to have fewer spines. With their greater vigour, most forms of the Highclere holly make excellent medium to tall evergreen screening plants and will tolerate considerable shade. Both the common and Highclere holly varieties make excellent hardy evergreen hedges and are most useful for providing shelter in gardens, being dense-growing even down to ground level, particularly the *aquifolium* varieties.

For preference, hollies like a moist, loamy soil. Male and female flowers, which are relatively insignificant, are usually borne on separate plants, and it is therefore important to ensure that both male (M) and female (F) plants are present in order for the impressive berries to be produced.

MAKING A CHOICE
Good Stem Colour
Within the *I. x altaclerensis* group, due mainly to their extra vigour, there are a number of varieties whose stems are an interesting purplish colour. 'Hodginsii'* (M) has purplish young shoots and is more pyramidal in shape than most varieties; it is very hardy and has dark green, rounded or oval leaves. In older specimens the leaves may have few or no spines. 'Purple Shaft' (F), has been selected purely for

INSTANT REFERENCE

- Shrubs and trees
- Mostly evergreen
- Decorative spiny leaves, many varieties variegated; impressive berries
- Moist, loamy soil
- Hardy
- Excellent hedging or specimen plants

its strong, dark purple young shoots, 'Camelliifolia'* (F) for its purplish shoots and dark, shining green leaves, reddish-purple when young. *Ilex aquifolium* also has varieties with purplish stems, but they are considered as a feature in conjunction with their variegated foliage.

Variegated Foliage
Possibly one of the most satisfactory variegated hollies is *Ilex aquifolium* 'Handsworth New Silver'* (F); the leaf colour is especially good being very dark green with a clear margin of white. This white variegation is most attractive with the purple stems. It is a female plant and therefore has the added berrying effect in winter. 'Madame Briot'* (F) is another fine variety with purple young stems, and the leaves of this variety are strongly armed with thorns, and green with a margin of gold and central mottling of gold and light green. 'Ferox Argentea'* (M) (Silver hedgehog holly) is rather distinct from the other varieties. It has prickles extending to cover the surface of the leaves, and the silver-white leaf margins contrast beautifully with its deep purple twigs. It is a bright and neat variegated holly. The young shoots of 'Silver Queen'* (M) are purplish-black, the foliage dark green, faintly marbled grey, with a clear white marginal variegation, most effective when in active growth; additionally, the young leaves are shrimp pink.

Among variegated cultivars of the Highclere holly the following are particularly noteworthy: *I. x altaclerensis* 'Belgica Aurea'* (F) is a near spineless, upright grower formerly known as

Ilex aquifolium 'Madame Briot'* is one of the best of the widely available variegated
female hollies.

'Silver Sentinel'. The leaves are mottled with grey and margined with creamy-white. 'Golden King'* (F) is perhaps the most popular and widely planted variegated broad-leafed holly. The near spineless leaves are gold-margined. 'Lawsoniana'* (F) has its bright golden variegation as a central splash to each leaf. A beautiful plant.

Habit Forms

In terms of overall shape there are a number of more upright-growing varieties such as I. aquifolium 'Green Pillar'*(F) with its dark green, shiny leaves, and I. x altaclerensis 'Camelliifolia'* (F), 'Purple Shaft' and 'Belgica Aurea'* (F). Ilex aquifolium 'Pyramidalis'* (F) is conical as a young plant, broadening with maturity. There is an equally worthy yellow-fringed form 'Pyramidalis Fructu Luteo'* (F). Both are excellent for free fruiting and bright green leaves.

There are two weeping holly varieties which, although of some interest, can hardly be described as the most elegant of weeping trees, as they tend to form a dense mound of foliage. However, they can be trained on a single stem into a more attractive small tree. These are Ilex aquifolium 'Pendula'(F) with dark green, spring leaves and 'Argentea Marginata Pendula' (F) (Perry's silver weeping holly), making a compact mushroom of silver-margined leaves. Both are free-fruiting.

Coloured Berries

The hollies are of course famous for their red berries. Most female cultivars, green and variegated, when planted near a known male form will produce berries – some more freely than others. However, perhaps the most prolific fruiter is I. aquifolium 'J.C. Van Tol'* (F) ('Polycarpa'). Said to be hermaphrodite or self-pollinating, it reliably produces quantities of glistening scarlet fruits seen well against its dark green, glossy leaves. It makes an excellent hedge.

There are several noteworthy yellow-fruited hollies in addition to I. a. 'Pyramidalis Fructu Luteo'* mentioned above. I. a. 'Bacciflava' (F) makes a handsome large shrub when laden with heavy crops of small yellow berries, while I. a. 'Amber' (F), a Hillier-selected clone, produces very distinct bronze-yellow berries.

Dwarf Hollies

There are silver and gold variegated varieties and small or dwarf species which are useful for the rock garden, scree or formal garden.

Ilex crenata is ideal as a dwarf clipped hedge. This species has tiny leaves very unlike the typical holly and small, shiny black fruit. Its variety 'Convexa'* (F) is even smaller and particularly suitable for a dwarf hedge, the leaves more convex and a glossy mid-green; it fruits reliably. 'Golden Gem'* (F) is a more useful, yellow-leaved, dwarf evergreen shrub for the rock garden. Ilex cornuta rarely attains 2.5m (8ft) high and has leaves of an peculiar rectangular form, mainly five spined; the variety 'Burfordii' is very free fruiting with shiny green leathery leaves. Ilex pernyi is slow growing and usually only seen as a dwarf pyramidal specimen, but, given ideal conditions it may reach small tree size. It has unusual, triangular spined leaves.

Acer palmatum *'Dissectum Atropurpureum' in a woodland garden setting amid azaleas and rhododendrons (see page 193).*

JAPANESE MAPLES

There are perhaps no other small trees or shrubs which, together with variation of shape and colour of foliage, are capable of adding such elegance and distinction to a garden.

As well as great beauty of grace and form, in the manner so typical of and appreciated by the Japanese, the many cultivars of *Acer palmatum* display much subtle diversity of leaf shape, from finely cut filigree to deeply lobed, large palmate leaves. In colour there is even more variation,

---

INSTANT REFERENCE

- Shrubs or small trees
- Deciduous
- Wide range of foliage colours and shapes
- Most fertile soils
- Container-grown specimens need protection below -10°C (14F)
- Excellent for autumn colour

---

with fresh young spring growths appearing in many shades of green, pink and even crimson; one can enjoy summer leaves of bright yellow or cool green, while other forms maintain crimson, red or purple foliage throughout the growing season. All tend to change as autumn comes, greens changing to gold or fiery orange and scarlet, while reds and purples will brighten to subtle tones of crimson and pink. There are an increasing number of variegated varieties now becoming available, finely cut leaves often combining fascinating blends of cream, pink, grey and green with patches of red. These change again as the season advances to autumn.

Although not confined to acid soils, Japanese maples blend superbly with rhododendrons, azaleas, camellias, heathers and their allies, enjoying the shelter and partial shade in which these shrubs thrive; equally, they will grow on ideal rhododendron land – light sandy loam with plenty of organic matter present to improve water-holding capacity. On well-cultivated alkaline soils, where plenty of humus is also present, they make good companions for hydrangeas, particularly species like *aspera*, *villosa*, *paniculata* and *arborescens* and their varieties, with viburnums, euonymous, mahonias and many other shrubs which thrive in light shade. On any fertile soil, shade-tolerant herbaceous groundcovers can be a perfect complement to Japanese maples, and in particular hostas, smilacina, bergenias, hardy geraniums, hellebores, pulmonarias and tiarella, and of course ferns and many of the dwarfer ornamental grasses. More than 250 cultivars of *Acer palmatum* are now thought to be in cultivation. In recent years a considerable number of new cultivars have arrived from Japan and are being tried and tested in nurseries and arboreta. Some of those which have proved most successful and rewarding are now becoming commercially available, and we are struggling to remember a new batch of Japanese names!

Practical Matters

SITING

Like most aristocrats, Japanese maples are a little 'choosy' and careful siting is essential to obtain the best results. Allow adequate room for their ultimate growth, both in height and spread; they enjoy the association of groundcovering plants and shrubs which help to maintain a cool root-run and can usually be resited as the maple grows. Light, dappled tree shade is ideal, and freedom from cold draughts and wind is essential. If a Japanese maple is unhappy in the site you have chosen, it will often show resentment by curling its leaves at the margins, and there may be evidence of dieback of branchlets. If there is reasonable cover of taller trees, frost in the spring may not be a problem, but if your garden is low lying, say in a river valley, a site should be chosen which does not catch early sun following frost.

SOIL PREPARATION

Your carefully chosen site should be equally well prepared, removing roots of nearby trees which may be encountered, and incorporating a slow-release-type fertiliser, perhaps blood, fish and bone, or one of the rose fertilisers, together with plenty of well-made compost, pulverised bark or leaf mould, into an area well cultivated, at least 1m (3ft) wide and 30–50cm (1–1½ft) deep.

PLANTING

Japanese maple cultivars require great skill and specially sheltered circumstances to raise them to the standard required for sale, and to stand the best possible chance of establishment in your garden. Thus they are inevitably more expensive than many other commonly grown shrubs, and you should therefore take extra care when planting. When young Japanese maples in pots or containers are planted out into the open ground in the early spring, particularly if they have overwintered under glass, polythene or wooden slat-houses, they will benefit from the shelter afforded by small branches of evergreens, such as cypress or laurel, cut from a hedge and stuck in closely around the young plant to protect tender unfurling leaves from wind, sun or frost.

AFTERCARE

In subsequent years, if correctly sited the developing shrub should become acclimatised and its leaves will unfurl as weather conditions allow. A 'wigwam' or tripod of bamboo canes is also an excellent addition to safeguard the young plant from any damage.

Finally, a mulch of coarse peat, bark or leaves, applied to moist soil will further aid establishment by maintaining a cool root-run. However, attention to watering will be vital in all times of drought, and in the spring for two or three years following planting.

GROWING IN CONTAINERS

If your soil is really hopeless – solid chalk or undrainable pasty clay, or there is no suitable border position in your garden – do not despair: Japanese maples make excellent tub or container plants, particularly for a sheltered patio in light shade. The majority of the dwarf forms of *Acer palmatum* 'Dissectum' are excellent when grown in this manner or as bonsai specimens. Soil-based compost with a generous amount of extra peat or leaf mould and perlite is an ideal compost. Sharp drainage is necessary, but the medium should also have good water-retaining qualities, and a container should certainly be shaded from hot sunshine. In winter, while Japanese maples will stand quite low temperatures in the open ground, remember to guard against soil freezing of container specimens – roots will be damaged or killed if frozen below minus 10°C (14°F). When such severe weather is due, move your container specimens into the protection of a cool greenhouse or garage or, if this is not possible, wrap the container in some insulating material such as polystyrene, held in place with hessian or burlap.

PESTS AND DISEASES

Japanese maples are not usually subject to serious insect attack. Aphids may affect succulent young growth in the spring, causing distortion of shoots and leaves, and when they infest foliage in summer they will produce quantities of honey-dew, resulting in unsightly stickiness upon leaves and shoots and the growth of sooty mould. A regular spraying with an aphiscide such as permethrin should give adequate control.

Mercifully, Japanese maples are not widely troubled with diseases; however, the dreaded verticillium wilt is one of the causes of dieback of twigs and branches. This disease is not yet fully understood and no cure is known. It is often confused with a natural winter dieback of unripened shoots or twigs. Verticillium causes brown streaking under the bark of shoots and twigs or branches of affected shrubs. Rapid collapse and death of the tree or shrub may occur. The tree or shrub should be removed and burnt and its site sterilised and not replanted. It is very important to sterilise pruning tools as well, as the disease can be spread by the use of contaminated tools on healthy plants.

Leaf scorching, shrivelling and twig dieback may result from a number of causes usually not associated with disease. As mentioned earlier, correct siting is of the greatest importance to avoid damage of this nature, resulting from exposure to wind, hot sunshine, salt-laden gales or spring frosts. Equally, short periods of drought can be enough to cause severe burning and even defoliation, particularly with container-grown shrubs, which can be sensitive to irregular watering; efforts should be made to keep them consistently moist. Leaf burn can also be caused by the excessive use of nitrogenous fertilisers, which produce soft, sappy growth, very vulnerable to damage. Also, foliage which is wetted, even accidentally, during periods of hot sunshine can be quite severely damaged and the shrub's appearance spoilt for that season. Fortunately, provided remedial action is taken, no permanent damage is done to established maples, though very young plants may receive a severe check, if not fatal damage.

MAKING A CHOICE
Acer palmatum Forms
YELLOW AND GREEN LEAVES
The *Acer palmatum* cultivars are often divided into a number of groups according to the dominant characteristics of the foliage. The 'Dissectum' group typically exhibits delicate, finely-cut leaves; indeed with its elegant filigree foliage 'Dissectum' itself has well earned the name of 'Lace-leaf maple'. This is one of the indispensables; while the shape and colour of individual leaves may show some variation, the typical plant of commerce forms a mound of cascading branches up to 1.5–2m (5–6ft) high, rarely more,

the shrub maturing broader than it is tall. Finely cut leaves usually open a delightful pale green, progressing to darker shades as the season advances and changing spectacularly to orange and scarlet before falling.

'Osakazuki'* (Heptalobum group) is perhaps the most popular cultivar – not without good reason has it been offered by nurserymen since the middle of the last century. An excellent and vigorous variety, enjoying more sunshine than most other cultivars, ultimately it will make a small round-headed tree of 6m (20ft) or more. The large, seven-lobed, rich green summer leaves are of lasting texture and turn the most brilliant and intense scarlet and crimson in autumn. A carefully sited tree will perform spectacularly and reliably each year.

'Lineariloba'* forms a small tree of upright, slightly arching habit, ultimately perhaps 4m (13ft) or more; this seems to be just the right habit of growth to set off the bright green leaves with long, narrow, strap-like lobes which give this cultivar a distinct elegance and charm.

Quite unique among Japanese maples is 'Ribesifolium' ('Shishigashira'), a small tree of unusual architectural form, slowly reaching 2–3m (6–10ft). Its habit is upright, slightly spreading, but compact; the deep green, seven-lobed leaves are curled and crimpled, each lobe elongated to a point. Autumn colour is usually a rich gold, some leaves suffused with crimson. Long cultivated, it makes an excellent specimen for the larger rock garden and adapts well to bonsai and container growing.

'Seiryu'* is a delightful newcomer, in effect an upright growing form of 'Dissectum'. Quite quickly attaining perhaps 4m (13ft) or more in ultimate height, 'Seiryu' makes a pleasing contrast to the more common mound-forming cultivars of 'Dissectum'. Its spectacular autumn tints can vary from deep yellow to scarlet and crimson.

'Senkaki'* ('Sango-kaku') (Coral-bark maple) has long been popular,

especially for its delightful coral-red stems which are such a striking winter feature. It is very handsome too in its summer cloak of bright green leaves with five to seven lobes, which turn in the autumn to a pleasing blend of golden yellow with subtle overtones of apricot and orange. A vigorous, upright grower, spreading at this summit with age, it will, if well sited, often attain 6m or 7m (about 20ft) and has considerable potential as a focal point for garden or landscape.

MOTTLED OR VARIEGATED LEAVES
Of elegant upright habit and dense twiggy growth, 'Butterfly'* is proving to be one of the most worthwhile of the variegated cultivars now becoming available. It is not slow in growth, and makes a large shrub or small tree up to 3–4m (10–13ft). The pale or bluish-green summer foliage has five to seven irregularly shaped lobes and is generously variegated with creamy-white. In spring the newly unfurled leaves are marked with pink, and in autumn they assume vivid shades of crimson or magenta. Altogether, this is a charming and dainty addition to a collection.

'Corallinum' is no newcomer, but has always been scarce, slow and difficult to propagate; nonetheless, it is an absolute gem among Japanese maples. It makes a small, compact, slow-growing shrub, very suitable for foreground focal points in semi-shade. In spring and early summer the mainly five-lobed leaves and young stems are unique in their remarkable coloration, which has been described as shrimp pink; this changes to a mottled or variegated green during the summer and often assumes crimson or scarlet tones in the autumn – in all, a magnificent small maple.

'Shishio Improved' is an elegant maple often described as a more vigorous form of 'Corallinum', but the leaf colour is more crimson than pink. It is an ideal maple for a sheltered patio, ultimately reaching 2–3m (6–10ft) when unrestricted at the root. It will also adapt well to container growing or bonsai culture.

Acer palmatum 'Bloodgood'*, a splendid recent introduction from USA. The bright red-winged seeds are an added attraction, contrasting well with the deep purple leaves. Pictured here at the Savill Garden, Windsor.

RED, PURPLE OR BRONZE LEAVES

There are now several additions to the excellent range of red/purple maples which contrast so well with the green forms. However, there will always be a place for the long-established stalwarts, such as 'Atropurpureum'; although often showing variation in shape, size and colour of leaf when raised from seed, it remains a magnificent and reliable purple-leaved, round-headed landscape tree up to 10m (30ft). The autumn leaves are usually plain red to crimson. Dwarfer, mound-forming 'Dissectum Atropurpureum' is equally worthy with bronze-purple leaves through the season.

Of the many newer selected cultivars within this colour range, those which follow are particularly good.

'Beni-maiko'. This is a fascinating dwarf, bushy maple, ideal for a shady patio or for container growing. The spring and early summer foliage is a startling scarlet-red, turning reddish-green as the season advances. An added interest is the small irregular leaves with strangely curving lobes.

'Bloodgood'*. A magnificent selection from 'Atropurpureum', now very popular, both in the USA and in Europe. Its large, typically palmate leaves, up to 12cm (4¹/₂in) wide, maintain a rich, deep, almost black-red hue well into late summer, paling to crimson before falling. The bright scarlet winged seeds make a striking contrast with the darker foliage.

It forms a vigorous tree with a broad crown and eventually reaches 5–6m (15–20ft) high.

'Burgundy Lace'*. A magnificent recent introduction, this is ultimately a small tree of spreading habit. The rich wine-red leaves are deeply cut into narrow, sharp-toothed lobes.

'Crimson Queen'* ('Dissectum' group). The persistence throughout the growing season of a good, deep ox-blood-red leaf colour is the special quality of this fine cultivar of American origin. This is a vigorous plant with large, finely-divided, notched leaves, the lobes up to 9cm (3½in) long. A change to scarlet heralds the arrival of autumn. 'Crimson Queen' may ultimately attain up to 3m (10ft) and forms a large mound of cascading branches.

'Inaba-shidare'* ('Dissectum' group). Although known in Japan for more than a hundred years, this is a newcomer to western gardens. Again, its deep purple-red leaf colour is well maintained throughout summer, turning to crimson before falling. The seven-lobed well-divided leaves are exceptionally large, up to 15cm (6in) long and wide, and the tree has more substance than most of the group. It forms an erect, strong-growing tree with some cascading branches.

'Red Pygmy'*. Another recent introduction of merit, which was selected in Holland and seems to be a miniature edition of 'Linearilobum Atropurpureum'. Slow-growing and bushy, the red-purple leaves keep their colour well and are frequently divided to the base into long, slender lobes.

'Trompenburg'. A review of the best Japanese maples commercially available today would not be complete without reference to this superb cultivar from the Trompenburg Arboretum, near Rotterdam. The leaves, with seven to nine lobes, are distinct in their unusual and attractive lobe formation. The deep purple-red leaf colour is well maintained to the end of summer, before turning bronze and then finally crimson before leaf fall. In all, this tree presents a unique and very pleasing aspect. With its vig-orous upright, somewhat arching habit and an estimated ultimate height of 4–5m (13–16ft), 'Trompen-burg' will make a magnificent specimen for garden or landscape.

Acer japonicum Forms
The following two forms of *Acer japonicum*, plus the similar *A. shirasawanum*, are widely available and remain among the most reliable and rewarding of Japanese maples.

'Aconitifolium'* ('Filicifolium') makes a strongly-branched, round-headed small tree up to 5m (15ft). Its dark green, deeply-lobed leaves are of good substance and are shaped like those of the herbaceous genus *Aconitum* (Monkshood) – hence its cultivar name. Confusingly, its synonym 'Filicifolium' refers to the fern-like appearance of its leaves and appears to provide its official common name of 'Fern-leaved maple'. Regardless of this confusion, its autumn colour is spectacular and persists longer than average, combining scarlet or crimson with touches of purple.

With 'Vitifolium'* we have yet a further botanical reference, in the large, broad, vine-like mid-green leaves of this cultivar. Forming a strongly branched tree ultimately up to 7m (22ft) or more in height, mature specimens are one of the autumn glories, when the colour of the falling leaves usually combines gold with scarlet, orange and crimson. This is perhaps the most robust and worthy of Japanese maples for general landscape planting.

A. shirasawanum 'Aureum'*, known (wrongly) as *A. japonicum* 'Aureum', although slow in growth, ultimately forms a large, dense, compact bush up to 5m (15ft) high and as much across. It is very rewarding and well earns its common name of 'Golden full-moon maple', displaying unfailingly, from early spring until autumn, its soft, pale golden-yellow leaves, 6–8cm (2–3in) wide with sharply pointed lobes. In some areas the tips of the leaves are splashed with scarlet in the autumn.

LIGUSTRUM (PRIVET)

INSTANT REFERENCE

- Shrubs and trees
- Evergreen
- White, sometimes fragrant, flowers in summer; variety of foliage colours
- Any garden soil, very easy to grow
- Excellent hedging plant

This genus has been sadly neglected by gardeners and the horticultural trade. Surprisingly, there are some extremely interesting plants related to the well-known hedging privet (Oval-leaved privet) *Ligustrum ovalifolium*. This plant itself, if allowed to develop unclipped into a large shrub will produce a mass of flowers in midsummer in panicles 5–10cm (2–4in) long. The hedging privet is not in fact the common privet (*Ligustrum vulgare*), which is not so gardenworthy and is less evergreen than *Ligustrum ovalifolium*, a plant that originated from Japan.

Although privet might be rather dull as a hedge, it is undoubtedly a very amenable plant. It is after all one of the fastest evergreen hedges (it may lose its leaves in winter in cold, exposed areas), it tolerates all soils, including chalk, and will grow in dry or wet shade. If nothing else will grow, try privet – it will inevitably succeed. It is a pity in some respects that it has gone out of fashion and been replaced by the ever-increasing lines of Leyland cypress, a plant that is very much more difficult to clip and would far rather be a forest tree.

The golden privet, *Ligustrum ovalifolium* 'Aureum'*, is a reliably bright, quick-growing hedge, and it too is able to grow in the most hostile environments. It is slightly more graceful in habit than the green type, the evergreen leaves being completely gold or yellow-margined. Free-standing bushes can be effective in foliage throughout the year, and particularly

A form of golden privet, Ligustrum ovalifolium *'Aureum'*; in autumn blue-black berries are seen well against the variegated foliage.*

in autumn when carrying crops of blue-black berries, seen well against the golden leaves.

It should be noted that all parts, and especially berries/seed of all privets are poisonous if ingested.

MAKING A CHOICE

Trees or Large Shrubs

Given reasonably sheltered positions, the privet family can offer some particularly handsome small trees. *Ligustrum lucidum** may grow to a height of 12m (40ft) or more, with a rounded crown and an attractive fluted trunk. For a non-coniferous plant this is certainly a very good-sized evergreen tree. Only in severe winters may it lose its leaves, but in general it can be regarded as fully evergreen. It has large, lustrous, long, pointed leaves and handsome panicles of white flowers in late summer and early autumn, up to 15–20cm (6–8in) in length. There are three desirable varieties of *L. lucidum*: 'Excelsum Superbum'*, an excellent quick-growing, variegated form, the leaves

margined and mottled deep yellow and creamy white; 'Tricolor', with narrow leaves with an irregular border of white, tinged pink when young; and 'Latifolium', with large camellia-like leaves.

Medium to Large Shrubs

The slightly smaller-growing *L. sinense* will also grow to small tree proportions as a rounded tree to 10m (33ft) high. It is not, however, completely evergreen except in mild winters. For flower display it ranks as one of the best, having long, dense sprays of white flowers in midsummer. The dark purple fruits are equally produced *en masse* and will remain on the branches into midwinter. The variety 'Pendulum' is smaller and has attractive hanging branches.

One of the best privets for foliage and flower is *L. japonicum*, Japanese privet. This plant is ideal for screening or hedging, reaching 2–3m (6–10ft). It has camellia-like leaves of a shining olive green, 10cm (4in) long. It too carries quantities of white flowers in

bloom from midsummer to early autumn. 'Rotundifolium' is more compact and rigid in growth, with round, leathery, dark glossy green leaves. 'Macrophyllum' has larger, broad, glossy black-green leaves and is more vigorous.

L. quihoui* is perhaps the most elegant privet in bloom and is very much overlooked; the flowers are produced in late summer and early autumn at a time when most trees and shrubs are well over. The flower panicles may be up to 50cm (20in) long and are pleasantly fragrant – unlike most privet flowers, which are rather unpleasant in odour. A warm, sheltered position for this plant is preferred to ensure that there is sufficient warmth at this late time of year to open the flowers. In similar vein and equally overlooked is *L. chenaultii*, a semi-evergreen large shrub or small tree with striking long, lance-shaped leaves and lilac-like flower panicles in late summer. A beautiful and uncommon species worthy of wider planting.

MAGNOLIA

INSTANT REFERENCE

• Shrubs to large trees
• Mostly deciduous, some evergreen
• Beautiful, sometimes scented, flowers in white, pink or purple from very early spring to autumn
• Most soils
• Hardy, but early flowers can be damaged by frost
• Magnificent specimen shrubs or trees

Magnolias are planted for the beauty of their flowers and rarely for any other reason. Yet the fruits of some can be attractive, many make bold, leafy shrubs or trees, and several have flowers which are deliciously fragrant. The flowers are composed of two or more rings of sepals and petals, but as it is impossible to determine which is which, they are collectively called tepals! These are thick and fleshy, and easily bruised or damaged by frost. Inside the tepals is a mass of stamens and the carpels which enlarge into the fruit; both stamens and fruits can add to the display. Undoubtedly magnolias add an air of distinction to our gardens.

Magnolia x *soulangeana* is the hybrid much overused in horticulture. This plant can, of course, look excellent and there are many different cultivars of it, ranging from those with large, globular pure white flowers, such as 'Lennei Alba'*, to Rustica Rubra, which has cup-shaped, rose-red blooms. However, *M.* x *soulangeana* is only one hybrid of several which have much to offer.

Magnolias range in size from shrubs growing a metre or so tall (*M. stellata*) to trees growing to 15–20m (50–60ft) and needing up to 25 years before they flower. Flowering ranges from plants which bloom precociously early before the leaves emerge, through to those plants which bear their last flowers late into the autumn.

Most are deciduous, but several of the best are evergreen.

Practical Matters
SITING
The flowering season and the plant's habit greatly affect its use and positioning in the garden. Early flowerers are susceptible to damage by spring frost and therefore need protecting from this as far as is practical: most frost damage occurs to plants exposed to the early morning sun. Side and overhead shelter can be used to reduce the impact of sun and wind, and also to slow down the rate at which the air cools overnight. However, if you garden in a frost pocket, it is probably better to forget about the early-flowering sorts, except perhaps *M. cylindrica* and *M. salicifolia*, or accept that you will only get an adequate display every fourth or fifth season. In addition, some varieties may come into leaf too early, so the floral display is offset by the new foliage; this is especially so with some forms of *M.* x *soulangeana* and *M.* x *veitchii*, where a cooler aspect which will delay leaf emergence may improve the display.

The flowers of *M. wilsonii* and its allies are carried in late spring or early summer and hang down. To be seen effectively, these need to be viewed from below, either by planting at the top of a bank or allowing them to grow over a path – they make much less of a display if sited in the distance in a shrub bed. Other early-summer-flowering plants, such as *M. officinalis*, tend to hide the fragrant flowers amidst their large, bold foliage; these are better sited where the flowers can either be sniffed or be seen from above.

The evergreen species can be damaged by severe winters and are often planted against a wall for protection.

SOIL
Magnolias will thrive on nearly all soils. A few do not like shallow, chalky soils and they do not particularly like light sandy soils, but most will grow on these, albeit more slowly. They are excellent for heavy soils and prefer an adequate amount of moisture with satisfactory drainage.

PLANTING
Magnolias will not tolerate soil disturbance and will suffer if the roots are disturbed by digging or deep hoeing. The roots are thick and fleshy, and if damaged are inclined to rot. For this reason, they can be difficult to move and establish. They should be planted out when the roots are capable of making new growth, preferably in early autumn or late spring so that any damage is repaired by the plant's own defence mechanism. Generally, container-grown plants are best, as these permit the new bush to be planted out without losing roots and with the minimum of disturbance.

MAKING A CHOICE
Early-flowering Types
SHRUBS AND SMALL TREES
These are the most common magnolias in gardens and give very effective floral displays in mid- to late spring.

M. x *soulangeana* (Saucer magnolia) is the ubiquitous one, although not suited to shallow soils over chalk. The form offered as plain *M.* x *soulangeana*, particularly by the cheaper outlets, often has large, tulip-shaped white flowers which are stained with a slightly muddy rose-purple. It forms a large spreading bush, ultimately making a small tree. In some seasons the flowers are not fully precocious and the new foliage detracts from the display. The foliage is reasonable, but the plants do tend to look dull through the summer months. Growing summer-flowering climbers, such as *Clematis tibetana* subsp. *vernayi* or *C. viticella* cultivars, to scramble through the maturing magnolia, will add interest and summer colour, and as these can be cut back to near ground level in late winter they will not interfere with the magnolia's display.

A better result will be obtained by using one of the named cultivars or species described below. 'Alba Superba' is a form with very fragrant white flowers composed of nine tepals

Magnolia 'Heaven Scent'* (x veitchii x liliflora 'Nigra'). One of the most rewarding of the newer Gresham hybrids has fragrant blooms produced in spring. It makes a small- to medium-sized tree, flowering when young.

which makes a dense, erect bush. 'Brozzonii'* is another white-flowered form whose petals are flushed purple at the base. The flowers, however, are very large, to 25cm (10in) across, and they open later than in most forms. 'Lennei'* is probably the best form of this hybrid. It carries large, richly-coloured flowers in late spring, often with a small flush of flowers in the autumn. These are a beautiful rose-purple on the outside and white within. The tepals are obovate and 10cm (4in) long and broad, whilst the leaves are up to 20 x 12cm (8 x 5in). 'Lennei Alba'* is a form with ivory-white, goblet-shaped flowers. 'Picture' has large, reddish-purple flowers which are white within and fade to rosy-pink on the outside. It forms a vigorous, erect shrub or small tree with rounded leaves, and flowers from

a very early age. 'Rustica Rubra'* has faintly scented, cup-shaped flowers which are rosy-red and up to 15cm (6in) across. 'San Jose' carries large, deep pink blooms which are creamy white on the inside of the tepals.

M. liliiflora (*M. quinquepeta*) is one of the parents of *M.* x *soulangeana* and is mainly represented by the clone 'Nigra'*. This has flowers which are very dark purple on the outside and paler or white within and near the tips outside, with the individual tepals 10–12cm (4–5in) long. They are carried in late spring and early summer, often with a late flush in the autumn. The flowers are quite striking in shape and colour, but some of the effect is lost as the leaves are partly, or with later blooms fully, formed when they are displayed. It makes a moderately compact bush.

M. denudata* (Yulan) (*M. heptapeta*) is the other parent of *M.* x *soulangeana*. It has pure white, cup-shaped flowers which are slightly fragrant. They are carried from early to late spring, depending upon the vagaries of the season but, if tempted into bloom too early, are often damaged by frosts. *M. denudata* makes a low, wide-spreading tree, majestic when fully covered in flower.

M. stellata* (Star magnolia) makes a dwarf bush from 1–5m (3–16ft) tall. It is closely allied to *M. kobus* and is sometimes treated as a variety of it. The flowers have from 12 to 18 strap-like tepals which are spreading when the flowers open, then reflexed, giving the star outline. They are easily bruised or damaged by frost, but as they open in succession in early to mid-spring, they give an effective dis-

Magnolia grandiflora *is the classic evergreen wall shrub. Cultivars which produce flowers within a few years of planting include 'Exmouth'* and the very hardy 'Samuel Sommer' (see page 200).*

play for some weeks. 'Water Lily'* has longer and narrower tepals and makes a taller shrub than the normally offered form of *M. stellata*, reaching 3–4m (10–13ft) tall.

Hybrids between *M. kobus* and *M. stellata* have been named *M. x loebneri*. They are more suited to chalky soils than the *M. x soulangeana* selections and make excellent and very floriferous small trees or large shrubs worthy of space in any size of garden. 'Leonard Messel'* has flowers with strap-like tepals which are lilac pink and deeper in bud. 'Merrill'* carries masses of fragrant, pure white flowers.

M. cylindrica* is a delightful small tree or large shrub which deserves much wider planting. It flowers when less than 1m (3ft) tall and carries many white, erect cylindrical flowers in mid-spring, followed by cylindrical fruits. The flowers are tolerant of

some frost and the twigs when crushed smell of aniseed.

M. salicifolia* (Willow-leaf magnolia) makes an upright, small tree which bears pure white flowers in mid-spring on the bare branches. The flowers are more tolerant of frost than others, and the twigs and leaves smell strongly of lemon-scented verbena when bruised. *M. salicifolia* is not very tolerant of chalky soils.

M. 'Kewensis' is a hybrid between *M. salicifolia* and *M. kobus*. It makes a narrow, upright small tree loaded in mid-spring with masses of 6cm (2in) very fragrant white flowers. It is suitable for chalky sites. 'Wada's Memory'* is another form of this cross and is equally delectable.

A large number of hybrids of mixed parentage have been raised from crossing between the above species or with other ones. They make

excellent small trees or large shrubs. They include: 'Betty'* with flowers 20cm (8in) across which are purplish-red on the outside and white within, and which makes a medium shrub; 'Elizabeth' in which the flowers are pale primrose yellow and fragrant, and which forms a small tree; 'Galaxy' which makes a medium-sized tree in time and has white flowers which are strongly streaked with carmine-pink on the outside; 'Heaven Scent'*, forming a medium tree and bearing large, goblet-like white flowers streaked with purple; 'Iolanthe'*, with large cup-shaped flowers of a deep rose-pink on the outer surface and creamy white within, and forming a small tree but flowering as a young plant; 'Jane'*, with her compact, upright habit, forming a medium shrub and carrying fragrant, cup-shaped flowers of red-purple exterior and white interior; 'Peppermint Stick'*, making a medium, upright tree bearing narrow, goblet-shaped flowers which are white, flushed purple at the base; 'Sayanora'*, with large, globular white flowers on a plant which will make a small tree; and 'Susan'*, with fragrant, erect red-purple flowers on a large shrub.

Large trees
The plants described here all make excellent large trees, majestic in late winter and early spring when carrying their flowers. They need woodland conditions and are, unfortunately, too large for most small gardens. The flowers are hardy in bud, but once they have started to open they are susceptible to damage by spring frost, and even in favourable climates, good effective flowering is by no means an annual event.

M. campbellii (Campbell magnolia) makes a vigorous tree to 20m (66ft) with flowers 20–30cm (8–12in) across. Depending upon season, these are carried from late winter into mid- or even late spring. The bark is smooth and grey, finely roughened like an elephant's hide. The leaves are shiny, greyish-green above, and emerge with a reddish-purple tinge. In their native range in the eastern Himalayas the trees have almost exclusively white flowers, but the pink-flowered plant is much more common in cultivation. Seedlings take around 25 years to flower, although grafted plants will flower in less than half this period. *M. campbellii* does not like chalky or limy soils.

'Darjeeling' is a late-flowering selection from Sikkim with dark rose-coloured flowers. 'Ethel Hillier' is a vigorous form, with very large white flowers which have a pinkish tinge at the base of the tepals. The subspecies *mollicomata* differs in producing flowers on trees only 10 or so years old from seed, and in having flowers which are pink to rose-purple, although never with the purity of the best pinks of the type. 'Lanarth' is an outstanding form which has very large, water-lily-like flowers that are cyclamen-purple or deep lilac-purple, and large, rounded leaves. In cold districts it needs shelter on the wall of a house or in woodland.

The typical form (*campbellii*) and subsp. *mollicomata* have been crossed to raise a number of good and very vigorous hardy forms which flower at an early age, including 'Charles Raffill'*, with deep rose flowers which open rose-purple on the outside, paler margins and pinkish-purple within, and 'Kew's Surprise', which has large rich pink flowers.

M. dawsoniana makes a shrubby tree, with large, leathery leaves, and bears attractive pale rose flowers. It grows well on limestone, but may be slow to flower.

M. sargentiana grows into a tall tree, magnificent in mid- to late spring when loaded with large purplish-pink flowers 20cm (8in) across. Even more impressive is its variety *robusta*, which makes a shrubby tree. This has clearer pink flowers and narrower leaves, and has been described as the best of the large tree magnolias.

M. sprengeri var. *diva*, particularly in the selection 'Eric Savill', has spectacular rosy-pink or deep pink flowers. It is worth growing in any woodland garden and flowers in mid-spring,

later than most forms of *M. campbellii*.

M. x *veitchii* is a hybrid between *M. campbellii* and *M. denudata*, and the best form is 'Peter Veitch'. This makes a strong-growing tree with blush-pink flowers on the branches in mid-spring. In most seasons it is glorious, although occasionally the new foliage may emerge with the flowers and detract from their display.

Magnolia wilsonii and allies
This small group of species contains probably the most exquisite of all magnolias. The flowers are carried with the mature new foliage in late spring or early summer, or intermittently until late summer, and therefore are not likely to be damaged by spring frost. They are creamy white and cup-shaped, with a prominent boss of rich red, crimson or purple stamens. Unlike all other species, they are held hanging down (except in *M. sieboldii*, where they face outwards), not carried above the branches. They thus need to be seen from below to be enjoyed fully, preferably at close quarters so that the delightful fragrance can be appreciated. The young flowers are peardrop shaped, reminiscent of a spinning top or the weight on a plumb line. The fruits ripen in early autumn and are pink or pinkish green. The carpels soon open to reveal the pairs of scarlet-coated seeds which are displayed hanging from silken threads.

*M. wilsonii** is the first to flower in late spring and early summer, bearing flowers 7–10cm (3–4in) across. It makes a large shrub or small tree (3–8m/10–26ft) with erect and then arching branches. It will thrive on chalky and other soils.

*M. sinensis** flowers in early summer, producing 10–12cm (4–5in) diameter blooms with a scent of lemons. It has a spreading habit, more so than *M. wilsonii*, and tolerates chalk soils.

*M. sieboldii** is unique in the flowers being held facing outwards; they therefore look you in the face – better marks for presentation, but without the peardrop poise of the other species. They are not produced

in a short flush, but intermittently from late spring to late summer. *M. sieboldii* makes a spreading shrub, ultimately a small tree to 6m (20ft).

Large-leaved and Summer-flowering Types
The following species produce their flowers at the ends of leafy branches during the summer. In some they are rather lost amongst the foliage when seen from below, but this hardly matters, as the foliage itself is large and bold, creating an impact in its own right. Several also have attractive fruits.

*M. hypoleuca** has large leaves up to 45cm (18in) long and half as wide. The flowers are produced in early summer, yellowish-white with maroon stamens, strongly (and nicely) scented of certain proprietary antiseptic creams, and 15–20cm (6–8in) across. The fruits are thick cylinders or egg-shaped, up to 20cm (8in) long by 5cm (2in) wide and brilliant red.

M. macrophylla (Big-leaf magnolia) has the largest leaves of all. They are usually 37–62cm (15–25in) long by 18–30cm (7–12in) wide, but can be up to 90cm (3ft) long. They are oblong ovoid, broadly heart-shaped at the base, bright green above and silvery with soft down beneath. The flowers are not exactly small, being 20–25cm (8–10in) long and up to 35cm (14in), in diameter, fragrant and carried in early summer. This magnolia makes a magnificent foliage tree, but should be planted in a sheltered position as the leaves are fragile and can be torn to shreds by strong winds, and the new growths can be damaged by frosts.

M. acuminata (Cucumber tree) makes a vigorous, conic tree capable of attaining 15–20m (50–70ft). The leaves are elliptic, to 23cm (9in) long and yellowish-green. The flowers are carried in early summer and are dull greenish-yellow and metallic blue – curious, rather than flamboyant. They are followed by the immature fruits which are like small, shocking-red cucumbers and show up well against the foliage. The tree also develops an interesting grey or brown bark which fissures into short, flaking ridges. Var. *subcordata* (*M. cordata*), is smaller-growing with smaller leaves, has flowers which are a soft canary yellow and is a much better garden form. Occasionally it carries an autumn flush.

M. delavayi has one of the largest leaves of any hardy evergreen tree. They are sea-green or bluish-green and may be 35cm (14in) long. The highly fragrant flowers last for only a single day, but an effective display is created as they are carried in succession from midsummer into early autumn and may be 20cm (8in) across. It makes a large shrub or small tree. Unfortunately, it is not reliably hardy, and outside mild areas, it needs the shelter of a wall. Even in favoured districts it is periodically cut back by hard winters, but usually regrows. It is not fussy about soils and will thrive on chalky or limy ones.

*M. grandiflora** (Bull-bay or Evergreen magnolia) is usually grown as a wall shrub, but in warmer climates is sufficiently hardy to grow as a free-standing tree, provided it is placed in a sheltered spot. The enormous flowers are up to 25cm (10in) across and have a spicy fragrance. They terminate the shoots and are produced in a succession from midsummer until stopped by frosts in mid- to late autumn. The leaves are glossy, yellowish-green and evergreen; they are clothed with rusty hairs on the lower surface. *M. grandiflora* will grow on all soils, including chalky ones. 'Exmouth'* is an erect-growing selection with narrow leaves which flowers when young. 'Little Gem' makes only a large shrub of 3m (10ft) or so with a narrow, upright habit. The leaves and flowers are smaller than in other forms. 'St Mary' is a selection which flowers at an early age. The leaves are wavy edged and richly clothed with rufous, felty hairs beneath. 'Samuel Sommer' also flowers when young and carries blooms which may be 30cm (1ft) across when fully expanded. It is a very hardy form introduced in the early 1950s.

RHODODENDRONS AND AZALEAS

INSTANT REFERENCE

- Dwarf shrubs to large trees
- Evergreen and deciduous
- Beautiful spring/early summer flowers in a wide range of colours, some scented
- Acid soils
- Hardiness varies
- Superb specimens for woodland or light shade
- Excellent foliage

Rhododendron is one of the greatest of all garden genera, covering an immense range of attractive plants. These include all the azaleas – a multiplicity of hybrids and named forms as well as several hundred hardy species. Of the species alone, perhaps 400 are in cultivation, and most are available from a nurseryman somewhere. The plants range in size from carpeting alpines growing less than 30cm (1ft) tall to large forest trees, making 15m (50ft) in cultivation but up to 30m (100ft) in the wild. Despite, or perhaps because of, this amazing array, most gardeners grow the less desirable hardy hybrids, which have floral attraction when in bloom but are rather bleak evergreens thereafter.

Most rhododendrons are selected and planted on the basis of flowering time and flower colour. This is the wrong emphasis as flowers, even in the most abundant species with perfect trusses, are but a transient feature, rarely lasting much more than a fortnight or three weeks, and in the early-flowering plants are susceptible to damage by frost, snow or hail. The best use can be made of rhododendrons by considering the permanent features of foliage, bark and habit first, and the flowers as a secondary bonus.

Rhododendrons can be used in a variety of ways in the garden. The winter-flowering ones should be used to give that hint of spring, but need positioning so that the flowers are protected from the early morning sun. The hardy hybrids will tolerate full sun and can be placed almost anywhere in the garden, forming evergreen flowering shrubs and sprawling trees.

Many of the dwarf lepidote (scaly-leaved) species and hybrids will also take some sun, including full sun if the soil is moist, and these can be very effective on a peat garden or in certain positions in association with heathers or dwarf conifers. The azaleas need either full sun or light shade to give their colourful displays, whilst the evergreen types need some shelter from cold winds and light shade. Most of the species and their hybrids are best where they are protected from the full effects of the sun, at least for three or four hours each day; for these plants, light woodland makes the ideal setting.

It should be noted that all parts of all rhododendrons and azaleas, both species and cultivars, can be toxic if ingested. The nectar found in the blossoms is particularly poisonous.

Practical Matters

Soil

The most important requirement of rhododendrons is that the soil does not contain more than a small quantity of free calcium ions. Rhododendrons need calcium just like other plants, but where calcium is freely available it prevents them absorbing iron and other nutrients and poisons them. So if your soil is rich in calcium, such as those derived from chalk, most limestones and some clays in chalky or limestone areas, you are left with two options: either forget about growing rhododendrons and concentrate on other plants, or move! It is possible to ameliorate the soil so that you can grow the plants for a period or in large tubs or isolated or retained raised beds sealed off from the surrounding soil by the use of perforated polythene, However, the effect is far less satisfactory than that which can be achieved from the same effort put into garden plants appropriate to your soil. Altering the soil to make it more acidic only really becomes realistic when it has a pH close to neutral.

In other respects, rhododendrons are undemanding. They. do not like very dry, heavy clay or waterlogged soils, although *Rh. thomsonii* grows in running water in Bhutan! If your soil is in these categories, it is possible to improve it by adding organic matter and draining away surplus water.

SITING

Rhododendrons do not associate well with plants which dry out the soil, and respond by becoming thin and lacking in vigour. Grass is the worst offender and should be removed from at least the plant's rootspread, but other greedy shrubs or trees such as birches and larch can also be a menace. Many of the early-flowering sorts need protection from spring frosts, as does the new foliage of others, whilst some plants also grow late into the autumn and can be damaged by early autumn frosts. These and others will thrive and flower better when grown under dappled shade, such as that provided by oak trees.

PLANTING

More than most plants, rhododendrons do not like being buried. The depth of planting should be no deeper than the nursery soil level, and the roots should then be covered by a generous mulch of organic matter.

AFTERCARE

Rhododendrons do not demand much cultural attention. The very floriferous ones benefit from the removal of the dead flowers (deadheading), so that the plant does not put energy into making unwanted seeds. All species grow better if they are given an annual mulch, but will survive without it if given adequate water during the summer. Watering in early summer on dry sites is important, but overwatering in late summer and early autumn should be avoided, as this prevents flower set and may make the plant grow into the autumn, with an increased risk of frost damage.

Rhododendron *'Mrs. G.W. Leake' is a typical stalwart hardy hybrid of dense habit, producing a magnificent display each spring (see page 204).*

Overgrown plants can be cut back and most will regrow freely from near the base, although some of the larger-growing ones and those with smooth, flaking bark may not. The plants benefit from a light application of compound fertiliser in the spring but not later in the year than early to mid-summer. The nitrogen element should either be ammonium based or from an organic material, eg hoof and horn.

MAKING A CHOICE

With such a bountiful group of plants it is impossible to give more than a brief outline of some of the range available. The approach used here is to discuss the species and primary hybrids under the headings of foliage, bark and habit, with reference made to the flowers and flowering season, and to treat hardy hybrids, azaleas and evergreen azaleas under their own headings.

Rhododendron Species and their Hybrids

The species have the benefit of generally more robust constitutions than many of the hybrids, while making equally good garden plants.

Foliage

As all the rhododendrons in this group are evergreen, foliage is the most prominent aspect of the plant throughout the year. The foliage, however, covers a range of features, and the most striking foliage is exhibited by several of the large-leaved species.

*Rh. sinogrande** has the largest leaves of all, in young plants in moist western gardens they may be 80cm long, although 25–50cm (10–20in) by 15–30cm (6in–1ft) is more usual. The new growths are silvery and very attractive. It also flowers but only on older plants carrying fleshy creamy white or soft yellow blooms in spring. It makes a small tree or large shrub and needs a sheltered moist position; if you can give it this it is well worth growing.

*Rh. falconeri** (H3–4) has prominently veined leaves to 30 x 15cm (1ft x 6in). Underneath they are covered by a dense coat of hairs which are pale buff coloured in young leaves but darken to reddish-brown by the time they are two years old. The flowers in mid-spring are in large trusses of creamy-white or pale yellow. The bark is red-brown and peeling or flaking, and can be most impressive. *Rh. falconeri* makes a large shrub or small tree and, while a much more vigorous plant with woodland shelter, it can grow and produce good but smaller foliage in less sheltered positions.

Rh. arizelum is similar but with smaller and more strongly coloured leaves and a less attractive bark.

Rh. rex has longer leaves which are smooth above and have brown or chocolate downy covering. These all make large shrubs or small trees and whilst they are much more vigorous plants with woodland shelter, they will grow and produce good but smaller foliage in exposed positions.

*Rh. macabeanum** (H3–4) has leaves to 30cm (1ft), thick, leathery and dark glossy green above with white or greyish-cream felt on the lower side. The new growths are very fine, silvery white contrasting with the erect red bud scales. The flowers are yellow or yellowish-white and are borne in mid-spring. This is one of the hardiest of the large-leafed species and makes a plant that is 3–9m (10–30ft) tall.

*Rh. bureavii** (H4) has leaves which are thickly coated with a bright red wool on the lower surface and dark green above. They are 7–13cm (3–5in) long and the plant makes a shrub 2m (6ft) tall. The flowers are white or rose, but *Rh. bureavii* should be planted purely for its foliage, for which it is especially valued.

Rh. mallotum (H4) has leaves 8–17cm (3–7in) long and half as wide. They are dull dark green and wrinkled above, but covered with a soft brownish-red woolly layer beneath. The flowers are carried in rounded trusses in early to mid-spring and are rosy-scarlet or deep crimson.

Rh. (campanulatum subsp.) *aeruginosum* has new foliage which is a rich verdigris-blue above, maturing to midgreen. The underside is covered with cinnamon-brown felt. It makes a low shrub and the older stems have a peeling bark, brown with a coppery tinge. 'Knap Hill'* (H4) is a selection of *Rh. campanulatum* which has lavender-blue flowers, and leaves which have suede-like coating of rust-coloured hairs. It forms a larger shrub.

Rh. cinnabarinum (H4) has beautiful glaucous-blue new foliage for the summer months. The flowers in midspring to early summer are tubular-campanulate with an interesting waxy texture. The colour ranges from orange and apricot to cinnabar-red and occasionally other colours. *Rh. concatenens* (H3) is a particularly good form with very glaucous foliage. It has been crossed with another form of the species to produce the 'Conroy'* group of cultivars. In these, the flowers are carried in pendant trusses of around six blooms, which are narrow, trumpet-shaped and light orange tinged with pink, and they have inherited the glaucous new foliage.

Rh. argyrophyllum subsp. *nankingense* (H4) has leaves which are silvery beneath and a rich shiny green above and puckered with impressed veins. The best form is the attractive 'Chinese Silver'*, in which the new growths are silver, and the flowers in late spring are a lovely clear pink.

Rh. orbiculare (H4) has rounded, heart-shaped leaves which are rather glaucous, particularly beneath. The bell-shaped pink flowers are carried in early or mid-spring. It slowly forms a medium to large shrub.

*Rh. niveum** (H4) has large leaves which are most striking when they flush – first producing erect candles of silver then, as these open, covering the plant in a mass of silvery-white until the hairs on the upper surface are lost. The flowers are in compact heads of rich purple or smoky blue and are borne in mid- to late spring. 'Clyne Castle' is a selection with larger leaves and flowers of a richer purple.

*Rh. fulvum** (H4) is a true foliage plant; the large leaves are dark green above but richly clothed with a cinnamon-coloured indumentum when they first emerge. This is fleeting on the upper surface but persists on the lower one. The flowers are blush to deep rose and open in early to mid-spring. This is a very choice plant for a sheltered woodland setting.

Rh. roxianum (H4) is a slow-growing shrub, although it can eventually attain 3–4m (10–13ft). Flowers are only borne on old plants and, whilst attractive (creamy-white flushed rose), are not the reason this shrub deserves garden space. The foliage is very narrow, particularly in the 'Oreonastes'* group, and with a rich rust or fawn felted covering of hairs beneath.

Rh. 'Sir Charles Lemon'* (H4) is believed to be a natural hybrid of *Rh. arboreum* with *Rh. campanulatum* raised from seeds collected by Joseph Hooker in the middle of the last century. It will make a small tree with time. The leaves are 10–13cm (4–5 in) long by 4–5cm wide (1½–2in) and medium green above; on the underside the blade is covered by a bright coating of rust-coloured hairs. The flowers are produced in mid-spring and are white with purplish spotting on the upper lobes.

Habit

This section is used to 'correct' the imbalance above towards the taller-growing species. It can be divided into two groups, those ultimately making a metre or two (3–6ft) in height, and dwarf forms which will remain below 1m (3ft) tall.

DWARF FORMS

Rh. 'Bow Bells' (H4) forms a low, spreading plant, richly covered with bright pink flowers in late spring and later with bronze new foliage.

Rh. 'Curlew'* (H4) has a dwarf, suckering habit to 30 cm (1ft) tall and carries large, pale yellow flowers in late spring.

Rh. 'Ptarmigan'* (H4) has masses of white flowers in mid-spring and makes a dwarf, spreading shrub.

Rh. impeditum* (H4) makes a low mound up to 60cm (2ft) high with tiny, dark green leaves. The single or paired flowers are bluish-mauve or violet and open in mid- to late spring.

Rh. polycladum 'Scintillans Group' (H4) has an upright, dwarf habit with small green leaves which are greyish beneath. The flowers are carried in terminal clusters of three to six small, deep violet to purple-blue blooms in mid- to late spring and smother the bush.

Rh. williamsianum* (H4) makes a spreading plant to 1m (3ft) tall and 2–3m (6–10ft) across. The flowers are a good shell-pink in mid-spring; the leaves are heart-shaped and glaucous, to 5cm (2in).

Rh. 'Elizabeth', *Rh.* 'Elisabeth Hobbie*, *Rh.* 'Jenny' and *Rh.* 'Scarlet Wonder'* are four hybrids of *Rh. forrestii*, from which they inherit large, deep crimson or scarlet waxy flowers in mid-spring, but unlike their parent these are freely carried. The leaves are dark green above. In 'Elizabeth' the flowers are carried in clusters of five to six and are up to 7.5cm (3¹/2in) across. In the open this forms a low, spreading mound, but may grow taller in shade. 'Elisabeth Hobbie' has looser clusters of six to ten blooms, whilst 'Scarlet Wonder' is dwarfer and more spreading. 'Jenny' is similar to

'Elizabeth', with a more prostrate habit. (All are H4.)

Rh. yakushimanum (H4) has been described as the most perfect rhododendron. It makes a rounded, domed plant, slowly growing to 1.5–2m (5–6ft). The flowers are apple-blossom pink in bud, opening to pure white. The leaves are dark green above, convex and thickly covered with brown wool beneath. The best form is the clone 'Koichiro Wada'* (named after the Japanese nurseryman who first sent seedlings to the West), which has young, silver-white growths.

Rh. yakushimanum has been used in a number of new crosses, collectively known as 'Yak Hybrids'. One example, 'Titan Beauty'*, has neat foliage and turkey red flowers; others include 'Percy Wiseman'*, pearly-pink and larger growing, and 'Surrey Heath'*, a dwarf with rose-pink flowers. (All are H4.)

Rh. racemosum (H4) straddles these two groupings, as it includes both dwarf and medium shrub forms within the species. Generally only a metre or two tall, it can attain 3m (10ft). In any garden, though, it is worth its space when covered with masses of small pink flowers from most of the buds at the ends of the previous season's shoots. It flowers in early or mid-spring. 'Forrest's Dwarf' is a small-growing selection which is truly scintillating.

SMALL TO MEDIUM FORMS

This group includes many plants suitable for small garden spaces, but which with time may grow to 2m (6ft).

Rh. augustinii has flowers in clusters of three or four, but with several carried both on the terminal bud and from axillary buds, clothing the plant in mid- to late spring. The flowers range from light blue to purple. The best form, 'Electra'* (H4), has vivid violet-blue flowers. It forms a shrub 2–3m (6–10ft) tall, but with time in woodland can be drawn up to form a small tree to 6m (20ft). 'St Tudy'(H4) is a hybrid of *Rh. augustinii* with deeper violet-blue flowers and only forms a shrub 2–2.5m (6–8ft) tall.

Rh. davidsonianum* (H3–4) is similar to the above but has flowers of a soft rose-purple. (H3–4). In *Rh. yunnanense* (H4) the flowers are pink but the plant is equally floriferous.

Rh. lutescens (H3–4) is similar but has massed primrose yellow flowers, with lighter green or yellow-green foliage and the tips of the shoots bronze-red or purplish. It forms a rather sprawling bush, much wider than high. 'Bagshot Sands'* (H4) is a selection with slightly larger flowers.

Rh. 'Fabia'* (H4) makes a dome-shaped, rather sprawling shrub with pointed leaves, but the loose trusses have funnel-shaped flowers which are scarlet, with orange within the tube, and speckled brown.

Fragrance

Rh. decorum (H3–4) has large white or pale rose and fragrant flowers in late spring to midsummer. The leaves are medium green above and glaucous beneath. It slowly makes a large shrub and is more tolerant of lime in the soil than most species.

Rh. fortunei (H4) is similar to *Rh. decorum* but with lilac-pink flowers in late spring. It is more tolerant of hot sites. Its subspecies *discolor** (also known as *Rh. discolor*) (H4) is most valuable for its huge trusses of fragrant, funnel-shaped pink flowers from early to midsummer.

Rh. fortunei has also been crossed with *Rh. griffithianum*, which is a rather tender species, to produce the Loderi group of hybrids. These make magnificent large shrubs or small trees for woodland conditions and are extremely free flowering. The flowers are in trusses of nine to twelve and vary in the different forms from pale pink to white. All the forms of this cross are beautiful when in flower, from mid- to late spring, and have the advantage of the flowers being richly fragrant. Especially good forms include 'King George'* which is soft pink in bud opening to pure white, with a pale green inner basal marking 'Pink Diamond'*, which has pale pink flowers with crimson basal markings and holds its colour well; and 'Venus'*, in which the flowers open deep pink and fade to lighter pink with faint green markings in the throat. All these are Loderi hybrids (H4).

Rh. auriculatum (H4) has richly scented white flowers as late as mid- to late summer. The leaves are 10–32cm (4–13in) long and have ear-like lobes at the base. It needs protecting from strong winds, and makes a large shrub or small tree. A hybrid of this species is *Rh.* 'Polar Bear'* (H4). This has trusses of 8–10cm (3–4in) long, fragrant pure white flowers, in mid- to late summer, which individually may be 11cm (4½in) across at the mouth. It is hardy, but needs siting in open woodland. The leaves are light green and up to 30cm (1ft) long.

Rh. ciliatum* (H3–4) has peeling bark and carries fragrant white to lilac-rose flowers in early to mid-spring. The leaves are bristly around the margins and on the upper surface, and it makes a shrub to 1m (3ft). *Rh. ciliatum* needs careful siting to protect it from spring frosts.

Early-flowering Types
With emphasis on the 'all year round' characteristics, some of the plants, whose value is not that they have the best foliage or flowers but simply that they flower in midwinter, have been missed and are discussed here.

Rh. dauricum flowers during mid- to late winter, when it carries rosy-purple blooms. It needs some protection and makes a deciduous or semi-evergreen bush to 1.8m (6ft). Although compared to many later-flowering species the display is modest, it is very valuable for coming in midwinter and a plant or a small group is worth placing where they can be enjoyed at this season. 'Midwinter'* (H4) is the best form of this species.

Rh. mucronulatum is very similar but has larger leaves and flowers and is deciduous. It may open its blooms from midwinter until early spring, depending upon season, and in a series of flushes. A choice form of this species is the clone 'Winter Brightness'*. (H4)

Rh. 'Praecox'* (H4) has flowers of a good rosy-purple and blooms during late winter or early spring. It makes a compact semi-evergreen bush 1.5m (5ft) tall. The flowers are damaged by frost, so it needs siting away from frost-pockets or the early morning sun.

Rh. moupinense* (H3–4) makes a shrub to 60cm–1.2m (2–4ft) high with a low, rounded habit. The pink or white flowers are large and produced in late winter or early spring, but need protecting from frost. It has attractive flaking stems.

HARDY HYBRIDS
These are a group of very tough old hybrids of mixed parentage which includes the common rhododendron, *Rh. ponticum*, and Rh. *catawbiense*. They will grow in full sun and on rather drier or less acidic soils than the species and their hybrids discussed above. They can be very useful for providing a bright splash of colour, but are rather graceless after flowering is over for the year. All those listed are H4.

'Alice'* forms a large shrub of vigorous, upright habit, producing conical trusses of rose-pink flowers with paler centres in late spring.

'Betty Wormald'* is a fine medium-sized shrub. The rose-pink flowers are crimson in bud and marked with deep crimson in the throat. Late spring.

'Britannia'* has soft pinkish-scarlet flowers in late spring or early summer and pale green leaves larger than average, to 22cm (9in) long. Compact and slow-growing.

'Cynthia'* has deep rose-pink flowers in large trusses in late spring.

'Fastuosum Flore Pleno'* has pale bluish-mauve double flowers with a greenish or golden-brown flare. A vigorous, dome-shaped, large shrub.

'Gomer Waterer'* has fragrant flowers, mauve in bud and opening nearly white with a mauvish-pink margin. A reliable dense, medium-sized hybrid of *Rh. catawbiense*.

'Lady Clementine Mitford'* has peach-pink flowers which fade to blush along the centre and makes a large, dense shrub. It flowers in early summer.

'Mrs. Charles E. Pearson'* is a robust shrub of erect habit. Large, conical trusses of mauve-pink flowers with brown markings are produced in late spring.

'Nobleanum' is an old hybrid of *Rh. arboreum*. It flowers some time from early winter to early spring, depending upon the weather, and can be very attractive if the flowers are not damaged by frost. It is a slow-growing, erect shrub or tree with rose-coloured flowers. 'Venustum'* has a more dome-shaped habit and pink flowers shading to white. These open in late winter. 'Mrs G. W. Leake' makes a large dense shrub with imposing leaves; rose-pink flowers with crimson markings are produced in spring.

'Purple Splendour'* has deep purple flowers with black flare markings. The leaves are blackish green. It makes a vigorous medium-sized plant of dense growth and flowers in late spring or early summer.

'Sappho'* has flowers mauve in bud but opening white, with a heavy purple-and-black flare. The central lobe is often duplicated, giving two flares to guide bees. It is inclined to become leggy with time.

Azaleas
Azaleas were at one time put in a separate genus from *Rhododendron*. In horticulture they divide into two groups, the deciduous azaleas and the evergreen azaleas.

Deciduous azaleas
These add the dimension of autumn colour to their repertoire. Most are complex hybrids and bloom in late spring and into early summer with large, flamboyant and fragrant flowers, and need either light woodland or open situations with some shelter.

Rh. luteum* (H4) makes a shrub 2–3m (6–10ft) tall. The flowers are very fragrant and yellow. A tough plant.

The hybrid selections of this and other species are too numerous to mention more than to give a range for an indication of the colour forms. Particularly noteworthy are those known as Knaphill and Exbury Hybrids: 'Ballerina'*(Kn-Ex), white with orange flash; 'Exquisitum'*, flesh pink with deeper pink on the outside and an orange flare, corolla has a frilly edge; 'Gibraltar'*, flame orange with yellow flare, deeper in bud; 'Homebush'* rose-madder semi-double flowers in rounded trusses; 'Persil'*, white with an orange flare and 'Royal Lodge'*, deep vermilion-red turning to crimson red. Average height about 2m (6ft). (All H4)

The following is a selection of azalea species which deserve wider planting, possessing a great deal of charm. Most flower at different times from the commonly cultivated hybrids.

*Rh. albrechtii** (H4) has an open habit and bears purplish rose flowers with or before the leaves in mid- to late spring. The leaves are usually in clusters of five and turn yellow in autumn.

*Rh. kaempferi** (H4) is a low-growing, deciduous or semi-evergreen species which bears flowers in late spring to early summer that range in colour from pale yellow-brown through to salmon to red and rose scarlet. A select form is 'Mikado' (H4), in which the flowers are apricot-salmon and open late, mid-to late summer.

*Rh. kiusianum** (H4) has a more spreading, dense habit and red to lilac-purple flowers.

*Rh. occidentale** (H4) carries trusses of from six to twelve widely funnel-shaped flowers after the leaves. The flowers are white with a yellow blotch and strongly fragrant, whilst in autumn the leaves colour richly.

*Rh. quinquefolium** (H4) has its leaves in whorls of five, with white flowers in mid-spring. The foliage is a bright pale green with a purple edge in spring, colouring well in autumn. It makes a low shrub.

*Rh. schlippenbachii** (H4) has new leaves which are suffused with purple and makes a rounded shrub 2–4m (6–13ft) tall. The saucer-shaped flowers are white or soft rose-pink and carried in mid- to late spring. It will grow well on drier sites than many other species and does not like strongly acidic soils.

*Rh. viscosum** (H4) is the swamp honeysuckle of the eastern United States. The flowers are viscous and produced in early to late summer. They are strongly fragrant and white or pink. *Rh. viscosum* makes a bush to 2m (6ft) or so and will thrive on wet soils.

Evergreen azaleas
These are hybrids or forms of several mainly Japanese species and make low-spreading evergreen bushes from 60cm–1.5m (2–5ft) tall. They need some shade and shelter from the worst of winter weather. They flower in mid- to late spring and may be trimmed periodically to encourage flowering and prevent them growing too large. The following is a selection of the best readily available cultivars:

'Addy Wery'*, deep vermilion flowers in late spring; 'Betty'*, salmon-pink with a deeper centre; 'Blaauw's Pink'*, salmon-pink with pale shading, flowers early and is a hose-in-hose, ie it has two complete sets of petals one inside the other; 'Hatsugiri'*, free flowering in mid- to late spring with magenta-purple blooms; 'Hino Crimson'*, crimson-scarlet flowers; Hinodegiri'*, bright red flowers contrasting with light glossy green foliage in mid- to late spring; 'Hinomayo'*, masses of phlox-pink flowers, dense habit; 'Kirin'*, silvery-pink flowers but slightly tender and often used as a pot plant; 'Kure-no-yuki'*, very hardy and free-flowering dwarf, compact plant with white hose-in-hose blooms; 'Palestrina'*, erect shrub, covered in late spring with 5cm (2in) white flowers with a faint green ray; 'Rosebud'*, double rose-pink hose-in-hose; late spring; 'Vuyk's Rosyred'*, deep rosy-red flowers around 7cm (3in) in diameter in late spring or early summer, compact spreading habit; 'Vuyk's Scarlet'*, low-growing with carmine-red flowers in late spring. (All are H4)

ROSES

INSTANT REFERENCE

- Shrubs and climbers
- Nearly all deciduous
- Beautiful late spring and summer flowers, many fragrant; some carry decorative autumn hips
- Most fertile garden soils, some will grow in poorer conditions
- Types to suit most situations and uses

As noted in the introduction to this chapter, one recent survey of garden plants found that hybrid tea (large-flowered) and floribunda roses (cluster-flowered) were grown in 96 per cent of all gardens. This, perhaps, suggests there is no need for a profile on roses. However, the genus *Rosa* contains far more than just hybrid teas! This profile will, therefore, concentrate on the species and their hybrids, as well as the modern and old-fashioned shrub roses, only mentioning hybrid tea and floribunda roses where they relate to these. Firstly, though, a brief review of these two groups is appropriate.

The characteristic which makes hybrid tea and floribunda roses so universally acclaimed is that they bear a large number of flowers as a series of flushes throughout the summer months. They are also amenable to growing in a wide range of soils and situations, and will bloom freely despite a degree of benign neglect. Some have the added attraction of being strongly and pleasantly fragrant.

However, it is fair to say that few have any beauty in foliage or fruit, and the pruning regimes needed to give the best flowers result in the rose bed resembling a battlefield for all the interest it contains over winter. Also, many of them are susceptible to diseases such as mildew and blackspot, and insect pests like aphids, requiring constant spraying or the acceptance of a less perfect result – they have been described as a wonderful gift to the manufacturers of garden chemicals.

The cultivars of hybrid tea and floribunda roses are constantly changing as new ones are selected and become the 'in' rose for that year. Of course, a few old favourites such as 'Queen Elizabeth' and 'Peace' remain from year to year, but a profile of hybrid tea and floribunda roses in a book such as this will quickly become dated and irrelevant – it is best to consult the catalogues of rose nurseries for a review of what is currently 'in'.

As already mentioned, the groups of roses which are profiled here are the species and their hybrids, modern shrub roses, and some of the old-fashioned varieties, such as bourbons and hybrid musks. These are all plants which require little pruning, have reasonable to good foliage, and mostly provide more than one season of display. They are all vigorous plants, little affected by diseases such as mildew, and do not need molly-coddling. The fact that they usually only flower once is scarcely to be held against them: after all, what other group of garden plants is required to flower throughout the year?

The roses profiled here range from dwarf shrubs to vigorous climbers. Their roles in gardens vary: they are used as climbing plants (for pergolas, fences and over trees and shrubs), in borders, for hedges, as groundcover (especially for banks) and as specimen plants. Together they provide flowers from late spring through to autumn, attractive foliage for as long (a couple are reliably evergreen), fruits for both summer and autumn effect, and one or two have unusual barks or other features.

Practical Matters
SOIL
As a group, these roses are very tolerant of soil, although not all will grow on all soils. There are, for example, species which are especially suitable for sandy, barren soils, like the *R. pimpinellifolia* and *R. rugosa* forms. Most will grow on clay and chalk soils, although waterlogged soils are best avoided or drained.

PRUNING
These roses vary in their pruning requirements. The species and shrub roses require very little; mostly what is needed is to keep the plants within bounds and perhaps to remove older, less vigorous shoots. Fortunately, the taller-growing climbers get on very well without any attention once they have been induced to grow into the right tree, which is just as well, as they can grow 15m (50ft) up it! Some of the old-fashioned varieties benefit from the removal of older wood and its replacement with young shoots from the base, but only a few will either tolerate or benefit from the heavy pruning given to their vulgar relatives. There are few horticultural sights more pathetic than attractive species roses like *R. moyesii* hard pruned near to ground level in spring, thus ensuring copious foliage but no floral or fruiting beauty.

MAKING A CHOICE
Species, their Forms and Primary Hybrids
EARLY YELLOW-FLOWERED SHRUB ROSES
These make shrubs usually 2–3m (6–10ft) tall. The flowers are single and carried in late spring or early summer. Were they never to flower, they would still be worth growing for their dense, feathery or fern-like foliage in a bright or grey-green.

*R. hugonis** is a neat shrub to 2–3m (6–10ft) which carries abundant soft yellow flowers on the graceful, arching branches. The branches may bear large translucent thorns and the fruits are blackish red.

*R. 'Canary Bird'** (*xanthina* x *hugonis*) makes a marvellous shrub which bears 5cm (2in) canary-yellow flowers. These open over a period of a month or so from late spring, often with a scattered flush later in the summer. The feathery foliage is a fresh green in colour, whilst the shoots are almost without thorns.

R. 'Cantabrigiensis' is a hybrid of *R. hugonis* with *R. sericea*. It has fragrant fern-like leaves with seven to eleven leaflets. Forming a medium-sized shrub with an arching habit and

bristly shoots, it carries masses of soft yellow or cream flowers 5cm (2in) in diameter.

R. sericea and *R. omeiensis* are unique in that the flowers have only four petals, although occasionally flowers with five are found. These two attractive species show considerable variation throughout their range in the Himalayas and China, but always have interesting fern-like foliage with nine to thirteen leaflets. The flowers are pure white or pale yellow and can make an interesting if rather short-lived display in late spring. They are followed by the shiny bright red or orange heps which colour in midsummer.

R. sericea 'Pteracantha' (*omeiensis Pteracantha*) is the most common form in cultivation. It is outstanding for the large, flattened thorns or spines which give it its name (literally, 'wingthorn'). These may be 5cm (2in) long on the most vigorous shoots, although shorter on weaker twigs. They are bright red, crimson or purple, depending upon whether seen in transmitted or reflected light. They can be particularly effective when the shrub is located where it can be viewed with the sun behind it. The thorns turn grey-brown in the second year, so for best thorn effect, the older shoots should be removed in early summer; however, the flowers are only carried on last year's shoots and most freely on the side branches which grew last year from the strongest shoots; for optimum flower and fruit, therefore, the strong shoots should be kept for three seasons.

LARGE-FRUITED ROSES
R. moyesii is the most common species of this group in gardens and very attractive both in early summer when carrying the 5cm (2in) single pink or blood-red flowers and in the autumn when laden with the flagon-shaped heps, which are 4–5cm (1½–2in) long and covered with glandular bristles. The leaves are pale or glaucous green with seven to thirteen leaflets. *R. moyesii* makes a desirable shrub capable of growing 3–4m

Rosa pimpinellifolia, *the Scotch or Burnet rose, growing in the limestone pavement of one of its natural haunts, The Burren, Western Ireland.*

(10–13ft) tall and as broad. 'Geranium'* is a selection for the geranium-red flowers and also with large, smooth fruits. It makes a more compact plant with lighter green foliage. 'Arthur Hillier' is a hybrid of *R. moyesii* with a vigorous, semi-erect habit on which are displayed the large rose-crimson flowers, followed by the large, bright red flask-shaped fruits.

SANDY SOILS AND GROUNDCOVER
Many species are especially useful for dry, sandy soils. They will also make effective groundcover, smothering weeds through their dense, shrubby growth.

R. pimpinellifolia (Scotch or Burnet rose) is a small suckering shrub which occurs naturally on sand dunes near the sea, limestone heaths and other dry sites. It grows to a maximum of 1m (3ft) tall and produces single white or pale pink flowers in late spring which are followed by small, dark, brown or blackish heps. 'Double White'* is a selection which describes itself, although it will also grow to 2m (6ft). 'Glory of Edzell' is a low shrub with masses of pink flowers

with yellow centres. 'William III' has a dense, bushy, suckering habit. The leaves are grey-green and provide a foil for the semi-double flowers. In colour these are magenta-crimson, changing to rich plum purple, but paler on the reverse. 'Grandiflora' (var. *altaica*) is a beautiful and very hardy form introduced from Siberia early last century. It reaches about 2m (6ft) and has large, creamy-white single flowers. This geographical form is notable as the parent of several reliable hardy hybrid modern shrub roses, particularly 'Frühlingsgold'* and 'Frühlingsmorgen'.

R. nitida is a small, suckering shrub which has rose-red flowers and shining green leaves that turn purplish red in autumn. *R. virginiana** is similar but has bright pink flowers from early to late summer and small, rounded pink heps. *R. foliolosa* has fragrant and larger flowers, 5–6cm (2–2¹/₂in) across, produced from early summer onwards.

R. rugosa is noted for its glossy rich green leaves, strongly prickly stems and large white or pink flowers with thin, papery petals. The fruits are

large and rich red or maroon; the flesh is tasty and rich in vitamin C. The flowers are carried from early summer onwards and the fruits colour from midsummer till late autumn, when the foliage turns yellow. It flowers on the current season's growths, so can be cut back hard, unlike almost all other species roses. It will grow 3m (10ft) tall if left untrimmed, but only 2m (6ft) if cut back to ground level in late winter. It is the hedging rose *par excellence*. 'Alba'* is the white-flowered form and comes true from seed. 'Rubra'* is a good crimson-flowered selection. Three forms or hybrids of *R. rugosa* are: 'Blanc Double de Coubert'*, which has semi-double white flowers which in bud are tinted blush; 'Fru Dagmar Hastrup'*, which has flowers vividly pink in bud, opening to pale rose-pink and revealing creamy coloured stamens, and has a dense, compact habit, making a smaller shrub, to 1.2m (4ft); and 'Roseraie de l'Haÿ'*, a very vigorous form which carries double crimson-purple flowers with cream-coloured stamens and 10–12cm (4–5in) across.

OTHER SHRUB ROSES

These are attractive shrubs, mainly flowering in midsummer, and several have fragrant foliage.

R. x *alba* is the white rose of York, and therefore of historical interest. It makes a shrub 2–2.5m (6–8ft) tall and has semi-double white flowers followed by oblong-shaped red heps. Among several hybrids or cultivars are 'Maxima'* and 'Semiplena'*.

R. *chinensis* is also of historical interest, as the China or 'monthly' roses were used to give recurrent flowering to the modern rose cultivars. 'Mutabilis'* (H3–4) '(*odorata* 'Mutabilis') has strongly purplish new foliage and makes a small to medium, slender shrub. The blooms are orange in bud, opening to buff shaded with carmine, before maturing through rose to crimson; they are also strongly tea-scented. 'Old Blush' has pink flowers produced in monthly flushes through the summer which are scented of tea.

R. *damascena* 'Versicolor' is a semi-double form in which the flowers are loosely double and strongly fragrant. They are white but irregularly blotched with flakes of rose or pink, and thus this is also known as the 'York and Lancaster rose'. It is a very old cultivar, being recorded in cultivation prior to 1629. R. *damascena* is cultivated for the perfume 'attar of roses', which mainly comes from the dried petals of the cultivar 'Trigentipetala'.

R. *eleganteria** (R. *rubiginosa*) has pale pink flowers but is grown for the sweet fragrance of the foliage. This is a feature particularly when the air or leaves are damp. It can be hard pruned as a hedge, providing a barrier of aromatic leaves.

R. *gallica* makes a suckering shrub to 1m (3ft) tall. The flowers are rosy-pink or crimson and are aromatic, smelling of balsam. R. *g.* var *officinalis** is the 'Apothecary's Rose', with semi-double rose-crimson flowers. A sport from this, 'Versicolor'* (also known as 'Rosa Mundi') has semi-double flowers which are either white blotched with rose or rose blotched

Rosa gallica *var.* officinalis* – *the long-cultivated apothecary's rose – makes excellent balsam-scented flowering groundcover (see below).*

with white. Both were cultivated in the sixteenth century or earlier.

R. *glauca** (R. *rubrifolia*) has foliage which is glaucous with a coppery or purplish hue. It is very effective as a foliage plant amongst other shrubs, although the small flowers are also attractive and clear pink.

TREE-GROWING ROSES

The logical name for these would be climbers, but this would be confusing as it is used for taller-growing large-flowered derivatives of hybrid teas, and floribunda roses, whereas the plants discussed here are much healthier and more vigorous. They are capable of growing high into trees or over shrubs, less promising if kept restrained on a pergola or fence.

R. *filipes* makes a most majestic climber, particularly in the form 'Kiftsgate'*, which is capable of reaching 15m (50ft). This species and its forms have the flowers carried on short lateral shoots in large clusters of 50–100 or more flowers. They are pinkish in bud, opening white, 4cm (1½in) in diameter and very fragrant. It creates a very strong impression in midsummer, and again in autumn

when the masses of small heps ripen through orange to crimson scarlet. Young plants are slow to get going unless sited in full sun, preferably some distance away from the bole of the tree through which they are to climb.

R. *mulliganii** (usually distributed as R. *longicuspis*) makes a strong climber, growing 8m (26ft) or more into trees. It has very fragrant flowers in midsummer. These are 5cm (2in) across with pure white petals and a yolk-coloured boss of stamens. They are carried in clusters of eight to fifteen flowers. The leaves are glossy bright green, darkening with age but remaining shiny and are usually evergreen in all but the coldest areas. The plant will quickly grow up through an old apple tree or over similar support and is more shade tolerant than R. *filipes*. It can be used very effectively to make an evergreen screen by growing it through deciduous trees and has the advantage over conifers in this situation in the fragrant massed flowers in summer and orange-coloured fruits which remain on the tree over winter.

R. *banksiae* makes a strong-growing climber in warm and sunny places. In cooler climates it needs the shelter of a sunny wall to flourish. The flowers are carried in large clusters on the almost thornless stems, whilst the leaves persist green well into winter. The hardiest form is the clone 'Lutea'* (H3) which has double yellow and slightly fragrant flowers. 'Lutescens' has single yellow and more strongly scented flowers. In 'Alba Plena' the flowers are white, in dense rosette-like clusters. Each flower is up to 3cm (1¹/4in) in diameter and carried in late spring to early summer. *R.b.* var. *normalis* is the wild form and has very fragrant, single creamy-white flowers.

R. 'Mermaid'* (H3–4) is the result of crossing a hybrid tea rose and *R. bracteata*. It needs a sheltered position such as a sunny wall. The 10cm (4in) single yellow flowers are carried in succession from midsummer until the autumn and are set off by the glossy foliage.

R. 'Wedding Day' is a strong-growing climbing cultivar capable of making 10m (33ft). It has rich, lustrous green leaves and large clusters of very fragrant flowers in midsummer. These are yolk-coloured in bud, opening to creamy white.

GROUNDCOVER AND LANDSCAPE ROSES
These roses have low, spreading habits and can be used as groundcover. They are especially useful for covering banks, where their long trailing stems can cover large areas, particularly if planted at the top. Initially the ground needs to be weed-free, but once established they will control weeds effectively. Several other roses can be used for ground-cover, such as the suckering species discussed above. Many of the roses discussed here can be trained up pergolas or into trees and several were originally developed as rambler roses.

R. *wichuraiana* makes a prostrate, spreading shrub. The unbranched shoots snake across the ground, growing 2–4m (6–13ft) in a season. They branch in the second year and it is at this time that they start to smother weeds. The leaves are evergreen in mild districts. Flowers are

Rosa mulliganii* (longicuspis) *festooning an old thorn tree. This species is usually evergreen and is spectacular in flower at midsummer (see page 206).*

carried on the lateral shoots from midsummer into early autumn, and are pure white and 5cm (2in) across.

R. 'Max Graf' is a hybrid of *R. wichuraiana* with *R. rugosa* and, like its parents, will control weeds once established. It makes a mound of spreading, prickly stems growing to 1m (3ft) high. It has large clusters of small and fragrant pink flowers in midsummer. There is also a red-flowered form, 'Red Max Graf', while 'White Max Graf' is a white flowered form with large single flowers. These

can be trained as groundcover or up a tree, if desired.

The excellent vigorous, mound-forming 'Rosy Cushion'* provides a recurrent display of single pink flowers with ivory centres. In 'Swany' the blooms are double white and the prostrate growth of medium vigour. 'The Fairy'* is a tough, reliable variety with soft pink double flowers continuously produced on graceful, spreading branches. These last two are neater in habit and ideal for patio planting.

Rosa *'Graham Thomas'* English shrub.*

Modern Shrub Roses

These are colourful large shrubs. They can look good in borders but do suffer from the problems of all prickly plants in such situations, such as access for maintenance. They are a healthy bunch requiring little formative pruning. Shrub roses make very good informal hedges but are at their best when used, along with many species roses, as specimen shrubs in grass areas or at focal points in the garden.

R. 'Cerise Bouquet'* has brilliant cerise-crimson double flowers set against a backcloth of dull green leaves. It will make a large, spreading bush, 4m (13ft) high and wider.

R. 'Frühlingsgold'* is a tough, reliable, early-flowering shrub with pale yellow, large single flowers on arching branches, growing to 2–2.5m (6–8ft). 'R. Frühlingsmorgen' is free-flowering, with very beautiful, large single rose-pink flowers with yellow centres and purple stamens. It grows to 2m (6ft).

R. 'Golden Wings'* makes an upright bush to 2m (6ft) which has recurrent crops of 10cm (4in) clear yellow and strongly fragrant blooms.

R. 'Graham Thomas'*, one of the best of the new English shrub roses and well worthy of the distinguished name it bears. Strong growing to 1.2m (4ft) the blooms are tea-scented and combine the traditional beauty of the old-fashioned rose with the longer flowering season and healthiness of the moderns.

R. 'Jacquelin du Pré' has semi-double, musk-scented white flowers with a central boss of golden stamens, produced in summer and autumn.

R. 'Nevada'* makes a very attractive mound of light green foliage, growing 2–2.5m (6–8ft) high and across. The flowers are semi-double, 7–10cm (3–4in) across, creamy-white and carried in profusion along the branches in late spring to early summer, with a smattering of blooms throughout the rest of the summer. 'Marguerite Hilling'* is a sport of 'Nevada' with deep, flesh-pink single and more fully recurrent flowers.

R. 'Yesterday'* has very fragrant flowers throughout the summer. They are lilac-pink with golden stamens and semi-double.

Bourbon Roses

The Bourbon roses are a group developed in the nineteenth century. They make strong-growing shrubs with smooth, pointed foliage and globular blooms. Several are recurrent flowerers, producing a succession of blooms. The old, weak shoots should be culled in late winter.

R. 'Boule de Neige' has leathery leaves and pink flowerbuds that open to give pure white double flowers which are very fragrant and recurrent. It needs a good soil.

R. 'Gypsy Boy'* ('Zigeunerknabe') has a robust, arching habit, making a handsome bush with its dark, crimson-purple flowers which are rather flat with reflexed petals.

R. 'Madame Isaac Pereire'* makes a large, free-growing bush. The flowers are rose-carmine and richly scented. They are fully double and large.

R. 'Souvenir de la Malmaison' has flowers which are a soft creamy- or blush-pink and carried in two flushes in midsummer and autumn. It is at its best in a hot summer. It has produced a climbing sport reaching 3m (10ft).

R. 'Zephirine Drouhin'* has thornless stems and coppery new foliage. The flowers are cerise-pink, fragrant and semi-double, and carried continuously from midsummer on into autumn. It can be trained as a shrub, but is naturally a climber to 3m (10ft).

Rosa *'Constance Spry'*.

Old-fashioned Roses

These were the 'in' roses of yesteryear and have a certain charm of their own. They flower in early and midsummer, when they are deliciously scented.

R. 'Cardinal de Richelieu'* has deep crimson flowers, fading to maroon purple, which are velvety in texture.

R. 'Comte de Chambord'* has flat, fragrant clear pink flowers with a hint of lilac, carried throughout the summer and autumn and set on a backdrop of light green foliage.

R. 'Constance Spry'* remains one of the most popular of all modern shrub roses. Its midsummer flowers are myrrh-scented, and it may be grown as a lax free-standing bush to 2m (6ft) or adapts well to wall-training as seen here at Mottisfont Abbey, Hampshire.

R. 'Fantin-Latour'* has double flowers which are pale pink. It makes a vigorous, branching bush to 2m (6ft).

R. 'Königin von Dänemark'* has dark blue-green leaves which serve as a foil for the carmine flowers, whose petals are edged pink.

R. 'Madame Hardy'* has blooms which open creamy white, soon becoming pure white.

R. 'Maiden's Blush' has sweetly scented, blush-pink flowers in dense clusters. The foliage is grey-green.

R. 'Rose de Meaux' has clear pink, double pompon flowers. It is a small, erect shrub to 1.2m (4ft) and has small leaves.

R. 'Shailer's White Moss'* has full flowers which are white tinged pink and with mossy sepals. The flowers are freely carried.

R. 'William Lobb'* has flowers which are crimson, passing to a slate blue, and carried in clusters. It is strong growing to 2m (6ft) and appropriate for the back of a border.

Hybrid Musk Roses

These make shrubs 1–2m (3–6ft) tall and have fragrant flowers carried in clusters from early summer into late autumn. Those formed in autumn on the strong growths of the current season contain many more flowers than the early clusters.

R. 'Ballerina'* freely produces large clusters of many small apple-blossom-pink flowers with a white eye, making a fragrant, choice bush.

R. 'Buff Beauty'* has apricot-yellow flowers scented of tea. The new foliage is coppery. It can be trained to climb into trees or over hedges and fences.

R. 'Cornelia'* has a strong scent and lustrous dark green leaves. The flowers are coppery-pink with a hint of apricot.

R. 'Felicia'* makes a well-rounded bush and is excellent for a hedge. The flowers are salmon or apricot pink, fading to silver pink.

R. 'Penelope'* makes a sturdy bush or hedge with broad, glossy dark green leaves. The flowers are salmon-orange in bud, opening to creamy pink.

SALIX (WILLOW)

INSTANT REFERENCE

• Small alpines to large trees
• Deciduous
• Range of shapes, forms and colours of foliage, twigs and branches, with catkins in spring
• Hardy
• Any fertile soil, and particularly damp situations
• Good seaside plants

The willows form a numerous, diverse and fascinating genus of more than 300 species, ranging from small, creeping alpines to large, stately trees. Surprisingly, they are strangely under-used in our gardens, with the exception perhaps of the large hybrid 'Weeping willow' (*Salix* x *sepulcralis* 'Chrysocoma'), which is perhaps not only the most planted but often the only willow known to some gardeners. It may well be that the characteristically weeping habit of this tree, large and dominating as it is, has tended to overshadow the other species, which show great diversity of shape, form, size and colour of foliage, twigs and branches, as well as of spring catkins. Regrettably, *Salix* x *sepulcralis* 'Chrysocoma' ultimately forms a large tree, growing (if not pruned and restricted, thereby ruining its natural shape and beauty) to over 18m (60ft) – not a tree for the small garden, but one for parks, landscape and riverside planting in particular.

Most willows flourish in any fertile garden soil and particularly in damp situations, though many adapt to dry soil conditions if not heavily chalky. Others are useful in difficult situations where the soil is sandy or poor, such as coastal areas, where they make good soil stabilisers, especially such species as *Salix alba*, *S. purpurea* and *S. viminalis*.

A wide variety of shape and size is offered by the willow genus, from the tall, billowing, upright 'White willow'

Salix alba *'Britzensis'* *'Chermesina' – scarlet willow – one of the glories of the winter garden (see page 213).*

(*Salix alba*) through to bush species like the 'Hoary willow' (*Salix elaeagnos*) and on to the creeping stems of the semi-prostrate *Salix repens argentea*, with attractive grey leaves, so useful in pondside situations in moist, sand soils.

One feature of most of the more commonly planted species is the rapidity of their growth following establishment. A number of the shrubby willows are particularly useful in attaining rapid and attractive growth ideal for quick summer screening at low level. Notable species include *Salix caprea*, *S. cinerea*, *S. daphnoides* and *S. viminalis*, all of which are ideal for this purpose. They can be very usefully employed as

short-term planting when mixed with other trees and shrubs that are due to last for many years but are slower to establish – for example, oaks, pines and beech.

Practical Matters
PESTS AND DISEASES
While some dwarf and small shrubby species are likely to have their foliage shrivelled in midsummer in hot, dry gardens, this can usually be overcome by avoiding dry locations if irrigation is not possible. The tree-like and large shrub species are particularly susceptible to willow anthracnose and other scab diseases, the large Weeping willow *S.* x *sepulcralis* 'Chrysocoma' being the most susceptible. These dis-

eases are most serious in a very wet spring and cause severe damage to leaf and branchlets. Small trees or specimens may be sprayed with a copper-based fungicide such as Bordeaux mixture as soon as leaves unfurl, and monthly thereafter until leaf fall. Regretfully, there is little one can do in terms of spraying a large tree but await its subsequent natural recovery.

MAKING A CHOICE
Small Gardens
As stressed above, many gardens are too small for the large-growing hybrid Chinese weeping willow (*Salix x sepulcralis* 'Chrysocoma'*). Fortunately there are now several weeping willows readily available commercially and more appropriate to the small garden. Although ultimately a medium-size tree up to 12–14m (40–45ft), *S. babylonica* 'Pendula' (*S. matsudana* 'Pendula') is both graceful and gardenworthy, and furthermore shows resistance to the familiar willow disease which so disfigures the leaves and twigs of 'Chrysocoma'. *Salix purpurea* 'Pendula'*, a weeping form of the 'Purple osier', has long purplish shoots on which are carried glossy green leaves that are vividly blue/white beneath; it grows in a weeping mound to 5m (16ft) in height and as much in spread if unrestricted. Finally in this section we must mention the smallest of weeping willows, *S. caprea* 'Kilmarnock'*, attaining only 3m (10ft) and most suitable for a patio or small paved area or to complement a small garden pool. It has a dense head of stiffly pendulous branches, and is most attractive in early spring with its bright yellow male catkins.

Coloured Stems
Although none of the willows are evergreen, they do provide us with the most beautiful coloured branches during the winter – red, yellow, orange, purple and some with a white bloom like whitewashed brambles.

S. acutifolia 'Blue Streak'* is a graceful shrub, often a small tree, with polished black-purple stems covered with vivid blue-white bloom.

S. alba 'Britzensis'* ('Chermesina') (Scarlet willow) has brilliant orange-scarlet branches, while *S. alba* var. *vitellina** (Golden willow) has brilliant egg-yolk yellow shoots.

S. x rubens 'Basfordiana'* forms a medium to large tree with conspicuous orange-red twigs in winter.

S. daphnoides (Violet willow) has its purple-violet shoots overlaid with white bloom.

S. purpurea (Purple osier) has long, arching purple tinted shoots. It has a dwarf, compact, slender-branched cultivar 'Nana Gracilis' very suitable for the pondside.

To encourage the production of young, vigorous shoots that display the most vivid colour, hard pruning with some compensatory feeding is necessary at least in alternate years in early spring. Alternatively, *S. alba* 'Chermesina' or var. *vitellina* can be allowed to develop as larger specimens and are most charming when seen at a distance catching the winter sunlight.

All the above willows can be most effectively planted in arrangements with other coloured-stem trees and shrubs such as the white-stemmed birches and polished-bark cherry species (*Prunus serrula* and *maackii*), as well as the coloured dogwoods (*Cornus alba* cultivars) and the white-stemmed brambles (*Rubus cockburnianus* and *thibetanus*). With these and other evergreen and variegated shrub planting such as *Elaeagnus pungens* 'Maculata' and *Ilex x altaclerensis* variegated cultivars, it is possible to make a truly effective winter garden.

Catkins
Although willows are not the most ornamental of plants in flower, many do have fine catkins, generally appearing in late winter or early spring before or with the young leaves. Male and female catkins are usually produced on different trees, with the male generally the more ornamental. *Salix caprea* (Goat willow) illustrates the difference, the male plant producing large yellow catkins known as

'palm', the female silver catkins known as 'Pussy willow'. Even more ornamental are the male catkins of *Salix daphnoides* 'Aglaia'*. Of the various small, shrubby willows displaying good catkins, few can equal *Salix lanata** (Woolly willow), whose yellow-grey catkins look particularly well with the emerging silvery foliage. In similar vein is *S. helvetica** from the European Alps, which has its leaves grey-green above and white beneath. *Salix hastata* 'Wehrahnii'* is of similar habit although slightly taller, displaying its silvery-grey catkins on brown-purple upright stems. Very different is *Salix gracilistyla*, a vigorous medium-sized shrub which has silky grey catkins with red anthers preceding the grey, downy young leaves, while its cultivar 'Melanostachys'* is remarkable and unusual; its catkins, which appear before the leaves, are very dark with blackish scales and brick-red anthers opening to shed yellow pollen.

Diversity of Habit
The leaves of these willows are white/grey or bold and corrugated, and the stems contorted or polished.

Among the most striking foliage trees must be *Salix alba* (White willow). Fortunately, there is a less vigorous form now available, *S. alba* var. *serica* *, which attains 10–15m (30–50ft). The leaves have an intense silver-white hue throughout the growing season, a great advantage over many other silver foliage trees such as the whitebeam, which tends to become greener as the leaves age. In similar vein, equally attractive, ultimately smaller and with even narrower silky-silver leaves is the West North American *Salix exigua* (Coyote willow). This striking newcomer is worthy of wider planting.

The shrubby *Salix elaeagnos** (Hoary willow) has leaves that are particularly narrow, like elongated rosemary leaves – it was indeed formerly known as *S. rosmarinifolia*. This plant is extremely effective in waterside planting schemes, as it exhibits a dense, shrubby habit, growing rapidly but not becoming over-large.

The leaves of *S. babylonica* 'Tortuosa'* (*S. matsudana* 'Tortuosa') (Contorted or Dragon's-claw willow) are likewise narrow in shape but distinctly crisped and curled, and pale yellow-green in colour, particularly in the spring. The twisted, contorted branches and twigs give this plant a unique appearance, and its rather upright growth makes it a useful contrasting shape when planted with horizontally branched subjects such as *Viburnum plicatum* 'Mariesii'. Although making a tree 15–20m (50–66ft) tall, it can be hard pruned or coppiced in a similar manner to those species grown for winter stem colour. There is also an interesting hybrid willow *S.* x *sepulcralis* 'Erythroflexuosa' which provides a like effect of twisted stems and contorted leaves, and in addition a pendulous habit with small ultimate growth. The vigorous, pendulous shoots are orange-yellow.

S. pentandra (Bay willow) has quite bold foliage, shining dark glossy green on the upper surface. It is a large shrub or small tree worthy of wider planting; its leaves are aromatic when crushed and are used in Norway as a substitute for bay.

Very handsome and different are the glossy deep green leaves of *S. fargesii**, up to 18cm (7in) long and wrinkled, with veins that are deeply impressed on the upper surface. In addition, this species has reddish-brown shoots that are stout and polished in their second year. Furthermore, the winter buds are red, large and conspicuous and it has a wide, spreading habit ultimately to 3m (10ft) high. *S. magnifica** has the largest and boldest leaves of all, up to 10–20cm (4–8in) long and very reminiscent of magnolia foliage. This species makes a large shrub, 3–5m (10–16ft) tall, and has purplish young twigs. The foliage is glaucous beneath.

*Salix lanata** (Woolly willow), as its common name implies, has downy, silver-grey rounded leaves – a slow-growing but very attractive species, usually up to about 1m (3ft) in height.

SORBUS (ROWANS AND WHITEBEAMS)

INSTANT REFERENCE

- Mostly small to medium trees
- Deciduous
- Flowers, usually white, in late spring/early summer; brilliant autumn leaves and berries in a range of colours
- Most soils
- Hardy
- Many are excellent all-round trees for small gardens

Sorbus is a very large genus, renowned for the rowans and whitebeams which make neat and colourful small to medium trees. Although primarily a genus of trees, the genus includes some shrubs, which can be used to associate with heathers or to add variety to a group of dwarf conifers.

The species can conveniently be divided into the rowans (or Mountain ashes) and the whitebeams, although there are a few species intermediate between these groups. The rowans have feathery leaves with many leaflets, which in most develop brilliant autumn colours, and white, red or amber coloured berries. They thrive on acidic and neutral sites, and will grow on chalk or limestone soils but are less reliable here. They prefer a rich, moisture-retentive soil but tolerate poor sands and the like. The whitebeams have simple leaves; in most, the underside of the leaf blade is covered by a cobweb of fine hairs which give the leaf a silver colour. In autumn, they often assume russet colours. The fruits are usually red, or greenish orange. Whitebeams are particularly useful for growing well on alkaline soils, such as over chalk, although they also thrive on acidic sands and neutral soils. They are more drought tolerant than the rowans. In both groups, the flowers are in large clusters, usually in late spring or early summer, and in the occasional species they are pink, not white. As members of the apple family they can be affected by the disease fireblight, which may kill or disfigure them. Otherwise, they are largely disease free.

Sorbus should be planted either in full sun or partial shade, such as afforded by light woodland. They will not tolerate deep shade. The taller sorts are useful as small trees to give an element of scale in the garden setting, they also make possible sites for climbing plants such as roses. They are always changing with the seasons, from the new foliage to the flowers in early summer, the mature foliage, the fruits and the autumn leaf colour, giving way finally to the winter silhouette. The rowans with white or amber berries are often left untouched by the birds until well into the winter, although they and all the other species have berries which are valuable for the food they provide for birds. The shrubby species can be used in borders, but are better placed within a sylvan setting.

Sorbus are easy to establish and most are available at sizes up to heavy-standard trees 5m (16ft) tall. They are therefore a good choice for the impatient, or where an immediate tree is needed.

MAKING A CHOICE
Rowans
Red and vermilion fruits
S. aucuparia (Rowan) scarcely needs an introduction. It is a tough, small to medium tree capable of growing in cold and exposed districts, yet attractive for its white flowers in late spring, bright red berries which begin to ripen around midsummer, and a reasonable display of autumn colour. Unfortunately, the birds often seem to discover the berries within a couple of weeks and in some years none last into early autumn. 'Fructu Luteo'* ('Xanthocarpa') has yellow fruits and these last much longer than the red berries, ensuring a more reliable fruit display. 'Asplenifolia' has fern-like and deeply cut leaves and makes a good

garden tree. 'Beissneri' has similar leaves but with red stalks and turning a good yellow in autumn. The main feature is the coppery-brown bark, which appears redder when wetted by rain. It is an interesting form, although the crown is rather open and too narrowly upright. 'Edulis' has larger berries which can be used to make jams and jellies. 'Cardinal Royal' is an upright form which carries massed large clusters of bright red fruits. 'Sheerwater Seedling'* has large clusters of orange-red berries and is a tree of vigorous, upright habit.

S. *commixta* makes a narrow-crowned tree which assumes brilliant autumn colour, ranging from deep purple through to scarlet. The berries are bright red or vermilion. 'Embley'* is an excellent selection of this species and has steeply ascending branches forming a narrow, upright crown. The autumn leaf colour is scarlet, then deep red.

S. 'Eastern Promise' makes a small tree of upright habit. The berries are rose-pink and produced in large bunches. The leaves turn through purple to flame as they assume their autumnal tints.

S. x *kewensis** is renowned for its large clusters of orange-red fruits. It is perhaps the best fruiting rowan, and ideal as a food source for wild birds. It forms a small, spreading tree.

S. *sargentiana** develops a rounded crown with rigid branches and large, red, rounded buds which are sticky like those of horse chestnut. The leaves are large with large leaflets; they are rich green until turning brilliant red in autumn. The small scarlet berries are in enormous rounded clusters.

S. *scalaris** is an exquisite species. The new foliage is attractively coloured as it opens. The leaves are frond-like with many glossy, medium-sized leaflets closely set like the rungs of a ladder. These act as a foil for the white or creamy flowers and the bright red berries, which are in clusters of up to 200. Finally, the leaves turn orange-yellow and scarlet in

Sorbus cashmiriana* *underplanted with hostas – the white fruits persist until late winter.*

autumn. It grows into a small tree with a spreading and arching habit.

S. 'Winter Cheer' has flat bunches of berries; as they ripen, they colour from chrome-yellow to orange-red. It forms a small to medium open tree.

S. *domestica* (Service tree) differs from the above rowans in having large edible fruits coloured green with a red flush, either pear-shaped (var. *pyrifera*) or apple-shaped (var. *pomifera*). The bark is scaly and it makes a medium to large tree and has been long in cultivation.

White, pink or amber fruits
S. *cashmiriana** makes a large shrub or a small tree to 6m (20ft) with a spreading habit. The flowers are pale pink, unusual in cultivated rowans but apparently frequent amongst the many shrubby species awaiting intro-

duction from the western Himalayas and China. The fruits are glistening white and 1.5cm (^{1}/2in) in diameter. They persist long into the winter, hanging like marbles from the branches, which are bent down under their weight.

S. *hupehensis** is an upright-growing small tree with ascending branches and sea-green kite-shaped leaves. The small berries, usually white or pink tinted, ripen in mid-autumn and usually remain on the trees well into the New Year. In var. *obtusa**, the berries are small and pink; in the form known as S. *oligodonta* they are glistening white and set on red stalks, which together give a pinkish hue, as if the plant is in flower. The leaves also remain green until well into the autumn, often only colouring fully in late autumn.

Sorbus aucuparia 'Sunshine' has dense clusters of golden fruits – a seedling from 'Joseph Rock' raised by Hilliers.

S. 'Joseph Rock'* has a compact, upright habit and berries which are creamy-white, maturing to amber. They look very effective against the fiery autumn colours of red, orange, copper and purple, but last for several weeks after the leaves have fallen. Seedlings or hybrids of 'Joseph Rock' making erect-crowned small trees include 'Ethel's Gold' and 'Sunshine', both with golden-coloured fruits.

S. 'Leonard Messel' is a hybrid of *S. harroviana*, which has large, glistening pink berries. These are carried in massed bevies set on the stout shoots. The upright branches create a dense, ovoid crown. The leaves are large, with nine to eleven large, oblong leaflets, up to 11cm (4½in).

S. *vilmorinii** makes a spreading, low tree, rarely taller than 6m (20ft). The leaves are fern-like, composed of 19 to 29 leaflets, and turn deep red in late autumn. The large 1cm (½in) juicy berries ripen deep maroon and gradually fade to almost white. It needs a moisture-retentive site to flourish

S . 'White Wax' makes a small tree with a conical head of branches. The fruits are pure white, large (up to 1cm/½in) and carried in drooping clusters. The foliage is fern-like with up to 23 feathery leaflets.

Shrubs
S. *reducta** is a suckering shrub to 1m (3ft). It grows well on a moist site sheltered from the midday sun. The leaves have nine to fifteen leaflets and turn bronze and purple in autumn. The flowers are carried in lax clusters in late spring and are followed by globose pink berries in early autumn. It associates well with heathers and dwarf conifers.

Whitebeams

S. *aria* (Whitebeam) is characteristic of chalk and limestone downs, but is also found on sandy areas. The new foliage is vividly silvery due to the covering of hairs on both the upper and lower leaf surfaces, especially in 'Lutescens'*, and although the upper surface soon becomes glabrous, the hairs on the lower surface remain. It forms a dense-crowned, upright tree with large clusters of creamy-white flowers in late spring, bright red fruits in early to mid-autumn and russet autumn colour. 'Chrysophylla' has yellow foliage throughout the season, most strongly so in spring and turning butter-yellow in autumn. It is an excellent form, deserving wider planting.

S. *thibetica* is usually offered as the clone 'John Mitchell'* (formerly called 'Mitchellii'). This has very large leaves which are broad elliptic or nearly rounded, to 12 x 10cm (5 x 4in). They are dark, sub-shiny above and vividly silvered beneath. The autumn colour is the usual mixture of russets from this group of species, but the leaves of this plant are slow to decompose; if left beneath the tree they can be very attractive in the late winter sun, when half will show the russet upper surface and the remainder the still silver lower face. The fruits are brown and 2cm (¾in) across. In time it makes a medium to tall tree, growing to 15–20m (50–70ft).

S. *wardii* has been confused with S. *thibetica*. It makes a narrow, upright-growing tree with berries which ripen yellow or orange. The new leaves are silvery, becoming nearly glabrous and shiny medium green. They are strongly ribbed and 10cm (4in) or so in length. It is excellent where a narrow tree is needed, such as to punctuate a view within the garden, or to provide height without too much breadth.

S. *intermedia* (Swedish whitebeam) is a very tough tree, tolerating coastal conditions, barren sites and atmospheric pollution. The leaves are strongly lobed and grey-green. It is attractive in flower and when laden with bright red fruits, but as a garden tree is surpassed by other species. More suited to a garden is the 'Brouwers'* selection, with ascending branches forming a narrow crown.

S. *alnifolia* makes a small to medium tree with an upright habit and smooth, beech-like bark. The foliage is dense and turns apricot-pink or orange-scarlet in autumn. The pure white flowers are followed by bright red or deep-pink fruits.

S. *folgneri* forms a most attractive small and rather narrow-crowned tree. The tapering leaves are medium green above and very silvery beneath. They are carried on slender shoots and the slightest breeze will display the undersides. In autumn they turn golden-pink. The branches are slightly pendulous at the tips and the new shoots are covered with silvery-white hairs at first. The berries are usually red, but golden yellow in 'Lemon Drop'.

S. *torminalis* (Wild service tree) is a medium-sized tree with dark-brown bark which fissures into scaly plates. The leaves are shiny dark green and distinctly lobed, resembling a maple leaf. They turn crimson or yellow in autumn. The brownish fruits can be eaten after they have been bletted, ie exposed to frost, which starts to decay them, but are rather too small. It will grow in most soils, except poor acidic ones, but is best on heavy loams or clays.

VIBURNUMS

INSTANT REFERENCE

• Small to large shrubs
• Evergreen and deciduous
• Pink or white flowers, some heavily scented, at most times of year depending on variety
• Any soil, very easy to grow
• Hardy
• Good hedging plants

This is a large genus of shrubby plants both evergreen and deciduous, ranging from small to large size and offering a quite remarkable variety of decorative features to enhance our gardens. The flowers – broadly akin to those of hydrangeas – are produced in various shades of pink and white, and many are heavily scented. Other viburnums produce fine crops of berries and autumn colour, particularly deciduous varieties, while others exhibit variation in their foliage between spring and autumn. Perhaps their greatest asset, however, is their tolerance of most growing conditions. They are very easy to grow and only unhappy in dry situations and on the poorest of soils. Indeed, many grow very well on chalk soils, particularly those akin to the 'Wayfaring tree', *Viburnum lantana*, which grows naturally and commonly on chalk downs.

With a few exceptions, all are quite hardy, which for a genus containing so many evergreens is another great advantage to the plantsman. Even the severest of winters, which can brown leaves, rarely causes irreparable damage. Certain species are especially useful in their ability to tolerate shady conditions; the deciduous 'Guelder rose', *Viburnum opulus*, and its varieties, is happy here, as well as in moist conditions.

MAKING A CHOICE

Of the evergreens, *Viburnum davidii** is a low, spreading shrub with large, dark green, leathery and conspicuously veined oval leaves, which makes excellent groundcover in shade or may be grown as an imposing dome-shaped specimen.

The larger *Viburnum tinus* (Laurustinus), is also very tolerant of shady places and will make a good hedge. Its cultivars 'Eve Price'* and 'Gwenllian'* are very handsome in winter and early spring when in flower. Another notable and very hardy evergreen deserving wider planting and recognition is *V.* 'Pragense'*, which forms a medium to large shrub with glossy and corrugated shining dark green leaves, white felted beneath, and creamy-white flowers in late spring.

Shape and Form

Here the viburnums offer a fine range of mainly rounded shrubs such as the medium-sized evergreen *V. cinnamomifolium** (H3), with dark green glossy leaves similar to those of *davidii*, and the Hillier hybrid x *globosum* 'Jermyns Globe', with foliage

similar to that of the *V. tinus*. A number with upright habits, such as *V.* x *bodnantense* and its cultivars 'Dawn'* and 'Charles Lamont'*, exhibit attractive upright stems with exfoliating winter bark, as well as their scented winter flower. Again, great diversity is shown by *Viburnum plicatum* (Japanese snowball) and its cultivars, giving us possibly the most effective horizontally-branched shrub in *V. p.* 'Mariesii'*. This is a selected form with large lacecap flowers which, when fully developed, give the effect of a snow-laden bush; it will grow to 3m (10ft) high and as much across if unrestricted. It is ideal as a lawn specimen, contributing not only shape and form, but very significant floral display and autumn foliage colour.

Although quite different, *V. rhytidophyllum* must be mentioned within this section, for many consider it to be among the most magnificent of large

Two distinct forms of Viburnum *growing together.* Viburnum plicatum *'Mariesii'* on the left, with its typical horizontal branching habit.*

evergreen foliage shrubs, with its elliptical and attractively corrugated leaves reminiscent of large-leaved rhododendrons. It is also excellent on chalk soils and for screening.

Flowers and Fragrance
It is perhaps the beautiful flowers of viburnums that have made the genus so popular in gardens; most of them have white or pale pink flowers, many pink in bud opening to white, while the fragrant pink flowers of *V. carlesii* 'Aurora'* are noticeably red in bud and very sweetly scented. The well-known and formerly much-planted *V. farreri** (*fragrans*) popular for its late-autumn pink flowers continuing into winter, seems now to be largely superseded by its hybrid x *bodnantense* (see above), which produces larger flowers through autumn and winter.

Another popular and well-known variety for its sheer volume of flowers is *V. opulus* 'Roseum'* ('Sterile') (Snowball tree), which produces large, creamy-white rounded heads and is most spectacular in early summer.

Some of the viburnums have flowers that at first glance resemble those of the lacecap hydrangea; this is an unusual feature, where the showy sterile male flowers advertise the blooms to pollinating insects that visit the fertile female flowers in the centre of the inflorescence. Of these, *Viburnum plicatum* and its cultivars are particularly notable: *V. p.* 'Pink Beauty'* has its flowers subtly tinted pink, while 'Lanarth'* is a selection equally spectacular but less horizontally branched than 'Mariesi'.

Mention should be made also of *Viburnum sargentii* 'Onondaga'*, a small to medium size, very distinct shrub, with its large maple-like leaves tinted a delightful red as they open in spring, later to complement the white outer lacecap florets and inner pink-budded flowers. Its garden merits continue in autumn with colouring leaves and wine-red berries – but choose a site sheltered from early frosts to avoid leaf damage.

Finally, among the deciduous viburnums in this section comes *Viburnum* x *juddii**, with reliable sweetly-scented, pink-tinted white flowers in mid- to late spring and freedom from the aphid attacks so often experienced with some forms of the *V. carlesii*. However, *V. c.* 'Aurora'* (see above) is less troubled in this respect.

Of the evergreens notable for both floral display and fragrant flower, *V. x burkwoodii* is both reliable and spectacular, with its fine display of pink-budded white flowers produced between early and late spring. It quickly develops into a very useful medium-size shrub, and the following selected cultivars are particularly notable: 'Anne Russell'*, with fragrant, earlier flowers, and 'Park Farm Hybrid'*, with its strong-growing, spreading habit and slightly later fragrant flowers.

Berries and Autumn Colour
This diverse genus also provides some of the most spectacular leaf colour and berry display available from hardy shrubs. Regrettably, however, many of the most showy berrying plants exhibit the phenomenon of self-incompatibility, making it necessary to plant a number of specimens to achieve cross pollination. *Viburnum davidii*, referred to above for its low-growing habit and dark glossy evergreen leaves, is one such plant – female specimens contributing unusually bright turquoise-blue, egg-shaped berries, effective during the winter months. Another magnificent large shrub requiring grouped planting to achieve a good display of berries is *V. setigerum*. With pollination, its branches in autumn can be heavy with orange-yellow fruits which finally turn brilliant red. Furthermore, this Chinese species gives a bonus in the interesting colour change of its foliage through the growing season from red young leaves through various shades of green to autumn colour in brilliant orange.

However, there is one group of viburnums that will never let you down – *Viburnum opulus* (Guelder Rose) and its cultivars, which are self-fertile and will produce quantities of fruit. Awarded cultivars are available, particularly 'Xanthocarpum'*, which has berries of clear golden yellow, almost translucent when ripe, and 'Notcutt's Variety'*, with larger flowers and fruits and good autumn colour as well.

Viburnum carlesii 'Aurora'*, a strong-growing healthy selection, its flowers are deliciously fragrant.

FURTHER READING

BEALES, PETER
Roses (HarperCollins, 1992)

BEAN, W.J.
Trees and Shrubs Hardy in the British Isles
(vols 1–4) (J.Murray, 1970/80)
(Supplement 1988)

BIRD, RICHARD and KELLY, JOHN
The Complete Book of Alpine Gardening
(Ward Lock, 1992)

BRICKELL, C.D. and MATHEW, B.
Daphne – The Genus in the Wild and in Cultivation
(Alpine Garden Society, 1976)

BRIDGEMAN, P.
Tree Surgery – A Complete Guide
(David & Charles, 1976)

BROOKES, JOHN
The Small Garden
(Marshall Cavendish Ltd, 1984)
The Country Garden
(Dorling Kindersley, 1987)
John Brookes' Garden Design Book
(Dorling Kindersley, 1991)

BROWN, GEORGE E.
The Pruning of Trees, Shrubs & Conifers
(Faber & Faber, 1972)

BUCZACKI, S. & HARRIS, K.
Collins Shorter Guide to the Pests, Diseases & Disorders of Garden Plants
(Collins, Edinburgh, 1983)

CHATTO, BETH
The Damp Garden
(Dent, 1982)
The Dry Garden
(Dent, 1978)

COOMBES, ALLEN J.
Trees. An Eyewitness Handbook
(Dorling Kindersley, 1992)
Collingridge Dictionary of Plant Names
(Newnes Books, 1985)

COX, PETER A.
The Smaller Rhododendrons
(Batsford, 1985)
The Larger Rhododendron Species
(revised edition) (Batsford, 1990)

COX, PETER and KENNETH
Cox's Guide to Choosing Rhododendrons
(Batsford, 1990)

ELLIOTT, JACK
Alpines in the Open Garden
(Christopher Helm, London, 1991
Timber Press, Oregon, USA)

EVISON, RAYMOND J.
Making the Most of Clematis
(Burnell/Floraprint, revised edition 1991)

GARDINER, JIM
Magnolias – their Care and Cultivation
(Cassell, 1989)

HAWORTH-BOOTH, M.
The Hydrangeas (revised edition)
(Constable, 1986)

HILLIER BOOKS
The Hillier Colour Dictionary of Trees & Shrubs
(David & Charles, 1993)
The Hillier Manual of Trees & Shrubs, Sixth Edition
(David & Charles, 1991)

HUXLEY, ANTHONY (Chief Ed.) and GRIFFITHS, MARK (Ed.)
The New RHS Dictionary of Gardening
(Four vols)
(Macmillan Press/RHS, 1992)

INGWERSEN, W.
Manual of Alpines
(W. Ingwersen & Dunns Print Ltd, 1978)

NEWSHOLME, CHRISTOPHER
Willows: The Genus Salix
(Batsford, 1992)

PEARSON, ROBERT (ed)
The Wisley Book of Gardening
(Collingridge, 1981)

PERRY, FRANCES
Water Gardening (Country Life Ltd, 1947)

RUSHFORTH, KEITH
Conifers (Christopher Helm, 1987)
The Hillier Book of Tree Planting & Management
(David & Charles, 1987)

RUSSELL, STANLEY
Stapeley Book of Water Gardens
(David & Charles, 1985)

STRONG, ROY
Creating Small Gardens
(Conran Octopus Ltd, 1986)

THOMAS, GRAHAM S.
The Art of Planting (Dent, 1984)
Perennial Garden Plants for the Modern Florilegium (revised edition)
(Dent, 1986)
Plants for Ground Cover
(revised edition) (Dent, 1986)
Climbing Roses Old & New
(revised edition) (Dent, 1983)
The Old Shrub Roses (Dent, 1979)
Shrub Roses of Today (Dent, 1962)

VERTREES, J.D.
Japanese Maples (revised edition)
(Timber Press, Cambridge, UK and Oregon, USA, 1987)

. . . .

The following publications may also be of use:

Award of Garden Merit Plants
Royal Horticultural Society
(RHS, 1994)

British Agrochemical Association Leaflet
Garden Chemicals – a guide to their safe and effective use

Forestry Commission Leaflets
External Signs of Decay in Trees
Young, C.W.T.
Forest Fencing
Pepper, H.W. and Tee, L.A.
Chemical Repellents Pepper, H.W.

Forestry Commission Arboricultural Research Notes
Tree Shelters Evans, J. and Shanks, C.W.
Tree Shelters – A Guide to their use, and information on suppliers
Shanks, C.W.
Tree Staking Patch, D.

The Plant Finder
Philip, Chris and Lord, Tony
Revised annually
(Royal Horticultural Society)

Wisley Handbooks (Cassells/RHS, 1986)
Whole series, especially
Pruning Ornamental Shrubs,
by J Clayton (revised J. Main) (1980)
Reclaiming the Neglected Garden
by Dennis Woodland (1991)
Shrubs for Small Gardens (1986)
Dwarf and Slow-Growing Conifers
by John Bond (2nd edition, 1993)
Trees for Small Gardens
by Keith Rushforth (1987)

SUPPLIERS AND USEFUL ADDRESSES

SUPPLIERS

Garden labels (plastic and metal)

ANDREW CRACE DESIGNS
Bourne Lane
Much Haddam
Herts SG10 6ER
(0279) 842685

MacPENNY NURSERIES
Bransgore
Christchurch
Dorset
Tel: (0425) 672348

KEITH AND HEATHER RUSHFORTH
32 Park Lane
Fareham
Hants PO16 7JX
Tel: (0329) 284738

Trellis:

TRELLISWORKS LTD
Westmead
Clay Lane
Fishbourne
Chichester
Sussex PO19 3JG
Tel: (0263) 778566

MACHIN DESIGNS LTD
Ransome's Dock
London SW11 4NP
Tel: (081) 223 4383

and in the USA at:

652 Glenbrook Road
Stanford, CT 06906

Pergolas, arches, gazebos, floral screens, fruit cages, etc

AGRI FRAMES LTD
Charlwoods Road
East Grinstead
West Sussex RH19 2HG
Tel: (0342) 328644

ADDRESSES

ALPINE GARDEN SOCIETY
Secretary: Michael Upward
AGS Centre
Avon Bank
Pershore
Worcs WR10 3JP
Tel: (0386) 55479

ARBORICULTURAL ADVISORY
INFORMATION OFFICE
Forestry Commission
Forest Research Station
Alice Holt Lodge
Farnham
Surrey GU10 4LH
Tel: (0420) 22255

ARBORICULTURAL ASSOCIATION
Ampfield House
Ampfield
Romsey
Hants SO51 9PA
Tel: (0794) 368717

HARDY PLANT SOCIETY
Little Orchard
Great Comberton
Pershore
Worcs WR10 3DP
Tel: (0386) 710317

INSTITUTE OF CHARTERED FORESTERS
7a St Colne Street
Edinburgh EH3 6AA
Tel: (031) 225 2705

INSTITUTE OF HORTICULTURE
c/o Royal Horticultural Society
80 Vincent Square
London SW1P 2PE
Tel: (071) 976 5951

NATIONAL COUNCIL FOR
THE CONSERVATION OF PLANTS
AND GARDENS (NCCPG)
The Pines
RHS Garden
Wisley
Woking
Surrey GU23 6QB
Tel: (0483) 211465

ROYAL HORTICULTURAL SOCIETY
(RHS)
80 Vincent Square
London SW1P 2PE
Tel: (071) 834 4333

ROYAL NATIONAL ROSE SOCIETY
Chiswell Green
St Albans
Herts AL2 3NR
Tel: (0727) 50461

SOCIETY OF GARDEN DESIGNERS
6 Borough Road
Kingston-upon-Thames
Surrey KT2 6BD
Tel: (081) 974 9483

GENERAL INDEX

Numbers in **bold** type indicate illustrations.

Acid-loving (calcifuge) plants 102–4
Alpine gardens 14–15
Alpine houses 14
    for daphne 177–8
Alpines 140
Amcide (*Ammonium sulphamate*)
    85
Anemone *see* Anemone
Animal damage, avoiding 90, **90**
    stockproofing 45–7
    tree guards 79–80
Aphids 29
Arrowhead (*Sagittaria*) 143
Arum lily (*Zantedeschia aethiopica*)
    143
Award of Garden Merit (AGM) 152
Azalea *see* Azalea

Badger gates **90**
Bamboos 142, 181–4, **181**
Banks 110
    planting scheme **110–11**
Barrenwort (*Epimedium*) 117–18
Beds
    herbaceous 13
    island 109, 112, **115**
Beech (*Fagus sylvatica*) 96, 134
Bellflower (*Campanula*) 117, 127,
    140
Berberis *see* Berberis
Biological control 29
Birch (*Betula*) 141, 154–7, **155**
Bishop's hat (*Epimedium*) 117–18
Black-eyed Susan (*Rudbeckia*)
    121–2, 128
Bladder senna (*Colutea arborescens*)
    130
Bleeding heart (*Dicentra*) 117, 127,
    146
Borders
    herbaceous 13
    shrub 9–10
    shrubaceous 112–15
Boundaries
    screening 65, **65**, 106, **107**
    stockproofing 45–7
Box (*Buxus*) 96, 109, 110, 133
Bricks, use in design 43–4
Brooklime (*Veronica beccabunga*)
    143
Broom, Moroccan (*Cytisus
    battandieri*) **123**, 124, 137
Bulbs 131
Bulrush (*Scirpus tabernaemontani*)
    143
Burning bush (*Dictamnus albus*)
    127
Bur-reed (*Sparganium ramosum*)
    143
Buying plants 73

Calcium 22, 200
Californian lilac (*Ceanothus*) 110,
    130, 140, 157–8, **157**
    for patios 124
    for walls and frames 136, 137
Camellia *see* Camellia
Cape marigold (*Osteospermum*) 128,
    131
Cascades 52–3
Catmint (*Nepeta*) 121, 127, 131
Cedar (*Cedrus*) 130, 168–9
Clay soils 21, 22, 24
Clematis *see* Clematis

Climate 26, 105
Climbers 123–4, 136–8
Clout (*Alloxydim sodium*) 85
Colour, in design 58
Compost heaps 100–1
Composts 23–4
Coneflower (*Rudbeckia*) 121–2, 128
Conifers 164–72
    for dry situations 130
    for island beds 109
    for rock gardens 139–40
    planting 74–5
Conservatories 12–13
Conserving plants 151
Cornelian cherry (*Cornus mas*) 173
Cotoneaster *see* Cotoneaster
Cotton lavender (*Santolina*) 122, 128
Couch grass (*Agropyron repens*) 85
Courtyards 58
    design plans **38**, **58–9**
    plants for 123–9
Cranesbill (*Geranium*) **98**, 118, 127,
    140, **146**
Croquet lawns 11
Cultivation 23
Cut-and-fill technique **52**

Dalapon 85
Daphne *see* Daphne
Dawn redwood (*Metasequoia
    glyptostroboides*) 142, 169
Day lily (*Hemerocallis*) 118, 143
Deadnettle (*Lamium*) 58, 120, 127
Deer *see* Animal damage
Delphinium *see* Delphinium
Density of planting 58–60
Design plans
    courtyards **38**, **58–9**
    front gardens **40–1**
    inherited gardens **62–3**
    new gardens **34**
    small gardens **33**, **70**, **71**
    terraces **33**
    walled gardens **57**
Dichlobenil 85
Diquat 85
Diseases 89–90
Dogwood (*Cornus*) 58, 95, 129,
    172–4, **173**, **174**
Drainage 23, **23**, 104
Dry situations 130–2
    dry shade 133
Dutchman's breeches (*Dicentra*)
    117, 127, **146**

Earthworms 21
Evergreen screens, 107, **107**

Failing plants 66
False bulrush (*Typha*) 143
Feeding 87–8
    nutrients needed 22
    see also Fertilisers
Fences 45–7, **47**
    plants for 136–7
Ferns 179–80, **180**
    for patios 129
Fertilisers
    artificial 24, 88
    manures 88
Field maple (*Acer campestre*) 133
Fir (*Abies*) 168, 171
Firethorn (*Pyracantha*) 106, 110,
    124, 134, 137

Flowering rush (*Butomus
    umbellatus*) 142
Flower parts **28**
Foam flower (*Tiarella cordifolia*) 122
Focal point planting **102**,
    planting schemes **144–50**
Formality of treatment 35–8
Fountains 52–3
Front gardens 40
    design plan **40–1**
Fruit growing 10, 70
Fuchsia *see* Fuchsia
Fungi 29

Garden centres 73
Garden furniture 50
Gentian (*Gentiana*) 103, 118, 140
Glyphosate (Tumbleweed,
    Roundup) 72, 85
Golden larch (*Pseudolarix amabilis*)
    170
Golden rod (*Solidago*) 66
Grasses 181–4, **182**, **183**
    for dry situations 131
    for patios 129
Gravel 49, **50**
    as a mulch **27**, 86–7
Great spearwort (*Ranunculus
    lingua*) 143
Greenhouses 14
    lean-to 12–13
Groundcover 58, 100
    cotoneaster for 176
    for dry situations 131, 132
    grasses and bamboos for 184
    maintaining 100
Ground elder (*Aegopodium
    podagraria*) 81
Grouping plants 144

Hardy perennials 112, 116–22
Hawthorn (*Crataegus monogyna*)
    134
Hedges 10–11, 133–5
    berberis 154
    conifers 164–5
    for screening 65, 106–7
    maintaining 97
Height, in design 58
Hellebore (*Helleborus*) 118, 127
Hemlock (*Tsuga*) 140, 167
Herbaceous beds 13
Herbaceous borders 13
    maintaining 97–8
Herbaceous perennials
    for dry shade 132
    waterside 143
Herbicides 84–5
Herbs 10
Holly (*Ilex*) 96, 106, 107, 134, 188–9,
    189
Honeysuckle (*Lonicera*) 65, 109
    for hedging 134
    for patios 124
    for walls and frames 137, 138
Hornbeam (*Carpinus betulus*) 96,
    133
Hydrangea *see* Hydrangea

Inherited gardens 15, **15**, 62
    design plan **62–3**
Insecticides 29
Inspection covers, screening 68,
    108–9, **109**

Iris *see* Iris
Iron 22
Irrigation systems 16
Island beds
    for screening 109
    planting scheme **115**
Ivy (*Hedera*) 65, 109, 110
    for dry shade 132
    for patios 124, 125
    for walls 137, 138

Japanese maple (*Acer palmatum*)
    73, 110, 124, 190–4, **190**, **193**
Juniper (*Juniperus*) 66, **109**, 110,
    130, 139, 166, 167, **169**, 171

Kingcup (*Caltha palustris*) 142

Labels 79, **79**
Lady's mantle (*Alchemilla mollis*)
    116, 127
Lamb's ears (*Stachys olympica*) 122,
    128, 131
Larch (*Larix*) 169
Large gardens 67
Lavender (*Lavandula*) **120**, 134, 140
Lawn mowers 80–1
Lawns 9
    croquet 11
    herbicides 85
    maintaining 98–9
    mowing 67, **66–7**, 98–9
    seeding and turfing 53–4
Lawson cypress (*Chamaecyparis
    lawsoniana*) **38**, 139
    dwarf forms 171
    for hedging 133, 165
    for screening 106, 166
Leyland cypress (× *Cupressocyparis
    leylandii*) 107, 134, 164
Lighting 16, 53
Lily of the Nile (*Agapanthus*) 116,
    127, 131
Lime-hating plants *see* Acid-loving
    plants
Loosestrife (*Lysimachia*) 51, 120–1,
    143
Lungwort (*Pulmonaria*) 121, 128

Machinery 80–1
Magnesium 22
Magnolia *see* Magnolia
Mahonia *see* Mahonia
Maidenhair tree (*Ginkgo biloba*)
    130, **166**, 169
Manures, 23–4, 88
Marjoram (*Origanum vulgare*) 128
Marsh marigold (*Caltha palustris*)
    142
Masterwort (*Astrantia major*) 117,
    117
Meadow lawns 99
Michaelmas daisy (*Aster*) 116–7,
    116
Minerals 22
Mock orange (*Philadelphus*) 125
Monkshood (*Aconitum*) 116, **116**
Moroccan broom (*Cytisus
    battandieri*) **123**, 124, 137
Mulching 24, **24**, 77, 86–7, **86**
    gravel **27**
Mullein (*Verbascum*) 128

Neglected gardens 64

New gardens design plan **34**
New Zealand burr (*Acaena*) 127
New Zealand flax (*Phormium*) 125, 131
Nutrients 22

Oak (*Quercus*) 130, 134, 141
Orchards 13
Organic matter 21, 23–4

Paddling pools 12
Paeony (*Paeonia*) 121
Paraquat 85
Patios 8–9, **71**
plants for 123–9
Paving 8–9, 48–9, 66
Pergolas 138
Periwinkle (*Vinca*) 51, 110, 122, 132
Pests and diseases 89–90
insect pests 29
of birch 155–6
of clematis 159–60
of daphne 177
of Japanese maple 192
of willow 213
slugs and snails 119
pH levels 22, 24, 102–4
and hydrangea colour 22, 185
and nutrient uptake 87
Phlox *see Phlox*
Phosphorus 22
Photosynthesis 27
Pickerel weed (*Pontederia cordata*) 143
Pine (*Pinus*) 109, 110, 130, 140, 168, 172
for screening 107, 134, 166–7
Pink (*Dianthus*) 127, 140
Plans, drawing 39–42, **39**
see also Design plans; Planting schemes
three-dimensional 32, **32**
Plantain lily (*Hosta*) **73**, 118–19, 127, 143
Plant biology 26–9
Planting 74–7
preparation 72–3
Planting schemes **54–5**
banks **110–11**
focal point planting **144–50**
inspection covers **109**
raised beds **103**
shrubaceous borders and beds **113**, **114–15**
suburban back garden **60–1**
Play areas 11
Polythene sheeting 80, 87
Pools 12, **12**, **51**

constructing 50–2
maintaining 100–1
paddling 12
swimming 16
Potassium 22
Privet (*Ligustrum*) 96, 134, 195, **195**
Pruning 76, 92–6, **94**, **96**
birch 155
ceanothus 158
clematis 160
hydrangea 186
rose 206
Pumps 51, 52–3
Purple loosestrife (*Lythrum*) 121, 143

Rabbits *see* Animal damage
Raised beds
for calcifuge plants 103
for daphne 177–8
planting scheme **103**
Red hot poker (*Kniphofia*) 119–20, **119**
Redwood (*Sequoia*) 170
Reed-mace (*Typha*) 143
Retaining walls 47
Rhododendron *see Rhododendron*
Rock gardens 13, 139–40
construction 49
daphne in 177–8
Rock rose (*Cistus*) 110, **123**, 124, 130, 137
Rootout (*Ammonium sulphamate*) 85
Rose (*Rosa*) 206–12, **7**, **126**, **135**, **207**, **208**, **209**, **210**, **211**
climbing 123, 136, 137, 138
for banks 110
for hedging 134
for patios 126
planting 74–5
weeping standard 129
Rosemary (*Rosmarinus officinalis*) 110, 126, 134–5
Rough grass 72–3
Rowan (*Sorbus aucuparia*) 129, 214–16, **215**, **216**

Sage (*Salvia officinalis*) 122, 128
Sand pits 11–12
Sandy soils 21, 22
Scabious (*Scabiosa*) 128
Scale, in design 31–2
Scree gardens 14–16, **14**
Screening 10–11, 65, **65**, 106–8, **107**
berberis 152
conifers 165–7
Sculpture 49–50

Sheeting 80, 87
Shelter 11, 25, **25**, **26**
conifers for 165–7
Shrubaceous planting 98–100
borders and island beds 112
hardy perennials for 116–22
planting schemes **113**, **114–15**
Shrub borders 9–10
Shrubs
for banks 110
for dry situations 130–1, 132
for island bed screens 109
for patios 124–6, 129
for rock gardens 140
planting 74–5
pruning 92–6
retaining worthy 64, **64**
waterside 142
Sloping gardens 68–9, **68**
measuring levels 19
Small gardens 69–70
design plans **33**, **70**, **71**
Soil 20–4
fertility 87–8
Soil mounding **53**, 54
Soil organisms 21
Solomon's seal (*Polygonatum*) 121
Speedwell (*Veronica*) 128
Spruce (*Picea*) 110, 140, 169–70, 172
Spurge (*Euphorbia*) 58, 118, 127, 131, 132, **148**
Star of the veldt (*Osteospermum*) 128, 131
Steep gardens *see* Sloping gardens
Steps, construction 47–8, **48**
St John's Wort (*Hypericum*) 110, 125, 131, 138
Stone, use in design 44–5
Storing plants 75
Suburban back gardens 60
planting scheme **60–1**
Suckers 94
Sulphur 22
Summer houses 14
Sun rose (*Helianthemum*) 118, 140
Surveying
gardens 18–19, **30**
surroundings 17, **17**
Swamp cypress (*Taxodium distichum*) 20, 142, 170
Swimming pools 16
Sycamore (*Acer pseudoplatanus*), drop-crotching 92

Tennis courts 16
Terraces
design plan **33**

plants for 123–9
Terracing **52**, **68**
Three-dimensional plans 32, **32**
Thyme (*Thymus*) 128
Tools 80
Torch lily (*Kniphofia*) 119–20, **119**
Tree mallow (*Lavatera*) 127
Trees
for dry situations 130, 132
for patios 129
planting 74–5
protecting 77–80
size 104–5
staking and tying 74, **74–5**, 77–8, **77**, 90–1
surgery 91–2, **91**, **92**, 93, **93**
waterside 141–2
Trellis 47
Triangulation 18, **18**
Turf 72–3

Vegetables 10
in small gardens 70
Viburnum *see Viburnum*
Vine weevil 29

Walled gardens 57
design plan **57**
Walls 42–5
plants for 136–8
Wall shrubs, 124, 136–8
Wand flower (*Dierama*) 127
Water buttercup (*Ranunculus aquatilis*) 141
Water gardens *see* Pools
Watering 77, 89
Water lily (*Nymphaea*) 141
Water mint (*Mentha aquatica*) 143
Water plantain (*Alisma plantago-aquatica*) 142
Water soldier (*Stratiotes aloides*) 141
Weedout (*Alloxydim sodium*) 85
Weeds
biology 27
control 27–8, 66, 80, 82–5
Wellingtonia (*Sequoiadendron giganteum*) 170
Western red cedar (*Thuja plicata*) 96, 107, 135, 140, 165, 167, 172
Whitebeam (*Sorbus aria*) 93, 216
Willow (*Salix*) **13**, 95, 129, 141, 142, 212–14, **212**
Wood, use in design 45–7

Yew (*Taxus baccata*) 96, 97, 109, 110, 135, 164–5, **169**, 172
Yucca *see Yucca*

INDEX OF PLANTS

Abelia 124, 137
Abeliophyllum distichum 124
Abies 168, 171
Abutilon v. 'Veronica Tennant' 136
Acacia 136
Acaena 127, 131, 140
Acanthus 127, 131
Acer 102, 129
   campestre 133
   japonicum 194
   palmatum **73**, 110, 124, 190–4
     'Bloodgood' **193**
     'Dissectum Atropurpureum' **190**
   pseudoplatanus **92**
     'Brilliantissimum' **82**
   shirasawanum 'Aureum' 194
Achillea 116
Aconitum 116
   s. 'Ivorine' **116**
Acorus calamus 142
Actinidia 136, 138
Adiantum pedatum 129, 179
Aegopodium podagraria **81**
Aesculus p. 'Atrosanguinea' 129
Agapanthus 116, 127, 131
Agropyron repens 85
Ajuga 116, 140
Akebia quinata 137
Albizia j. 'Rosea' 129
Alchemilla mollis 116, 127
Alisma plantago-aquatica 142
Allium 131
Alnus 141
Amelanchier 'Ballerina' 141
Andromeda p. 'Macrophylla' 142
Anemone × hybrida 116, 127
   'Queen Charlotte' **112**
Anthemis cupaniana **13**
Anthyllis hermanniae 140
Arabis f.-c. 'Variegata' 140
Aralia elata 129
Arbutus 129, 130
Aristolochia macrophylla 138
Armeria m. 'Vindictive' 140
Artemisia
   a. 'Lambrook Silver' 127, 131
   canescens 116, 131
   'Powis Castle' 110, 130
Arundinaria 142, 181, 183–4
Arundo donax 'Macrophylla' 183
Asplenium trichomanes 180
Aster 116–17
   n.-a. 'Alma Potschke' **116**
Astilbe 117, 143
Astrantia major 117
   'Sunningdale Variegated' **117**
Athyrium filix-femina 129, 179
Atriplex halinus 130
Aubretia 140
Aucuba japonica 106, 109, 132
Azalea 126, 204–5
Azara microphylla 137

Ballota pseudodictamnus 131
Berberidopsis corallina 137
Berberis 133, 152–4
   × *stenophylla* 95, 152
   thunbergii 133, 140, **152**
     'Red Chief' 133, **153**
Bergenia 117
Betula 141, 154–7
   nigra **155**
Blechnum spicant 129, 180
Brunnera macrophylla 117
Buddleia 130, 136

alternifolia 95, 130
   davidii 94, 130
   globosa 95
Butomus umbellatus 142
Buxus
   microphylla 109
   sempervirens 96, 110, 133

Callistemon 137
Callitriche verna 141
Calluna 102, 103
   vulgaris 88
Caltha palustris 142
Camellia 124, 137
   × *w.* 'Donation' **124**
Campanula 117, 127, 140
Campsis × t. 'Madame Galen' 136
Caragana a. 'Lorbergii' 129, 130
Carex h. 'Evergold' 127, 182
Carpenteria californica 130
Carpinus betulus 96, 133
Caryopteris × c. 'Heavenly Blue' 130
Cassinia 130
Ceanothus 110, 130, 137, 157–8
   a. 'Trewithen Blue' 124, 158
   'Blue Mound' 124, 140, 158
   'Puget Blue' 136, **157**, 158
Cedrus 130, 168–9
Celastrus orbiculatus 138
Cerastium tomentosum 110
Ceratophyllum demersum 141
Ceratostigma willmottianum 130
Cercis 130
Cetarach officinarum 180
Chaenomeles 137, 138
Chamaecyparis 167, 171
   lawsoniana 133, 139, 165–6, 167, 171
     'Green Hedger' 106
     'Kilmacurragh' **38**
   nootkatensis 166, 167
     'Lutea' **169**
Choisya ternata 110, 124, 130,
   'Sundance' **145**
Chusquea culeou **181**, 184
Cistus 110, 124, 130, 137
   × *purpureus* **123**
Clematis 123–4, 137, 138, 159–63
   × *jackmanii* 94, 136, 162–3
   montana 65, 95, 160–1
   'Nelly Moser' **7**, **159**
   'Perle D'Azure' **163**
   rehderiana 65, **161**, 162
   tangutica 94, 162
   'Ville de Lyon' 161
Clerodendrum t. var. *fargesii* 130
Colutea arborescens 130
Convolvulus cneorum 124, 130
Cornus 172–4
   alba 58, 95, 142, 173–4
     'Eddie's White Wonder' 129, **174**
     'Norman Hadden' 129, **173**
Corokia cotoneaster 137
Coronilla v. ssp. *glauca* **7**, 137
Cortaderia selloana 182–3
   'Pumila' **183**
Cotinus 'Grace' 129, **145**
Cotoneaster 106, **107**, 109, 110, 129, 133–4, 175–6
   dammeri 51, 66
   floccosus **175**
   'Rothschildianus' **95**
Crambe cordifolia 127
Crataegus monogyna 96, 134
Crinodendron hookerianum 137

Crinum × powellii 127
Crocosmia 117, 127
Cryptomeria japonica 107, 130, 139
× *Cupressocyparis leylandii* 107, 134, 164
Cupressus 130
Cytisus **21**, 102, 110, 130, 140
   battandieri **123**, 124, 137

Danaë racemosa 109, 132
Daphne 124, 130, 140, 177–9
   b. 'Jacqueline Postill' **177**
   cneorum **139**, 178
   o. 'Aureomarginata' 138, 179
Delphinium 117
Deutzia × hybrida 'Mont Rose' **64**
Dianthus 127
   deltoides 140
Diascia **20**, 127, 131, 140
Dicentra 117, 127
   f. 'Luxuriant' 117, **146**
Dictamnus albus 127
Dierama pulcherrima 127
Disanthus cercidifolius **94**
Dorycnium hirsutum 130
Drimys winteri 137
Dryas octopetala 140
Dryopteris 179–80

Eccremocarpus scaber 137
Eleagnus × ebbingei 106, 109
Elodea densa 141
Embothrium c. 'Norquinco Form' 129
Epimedium 117–18, 132
Erica 102, 103
Erigeron karvinskianus **131**
Eriobotrya japonica 137
Eryngium 131
Escallonia 134
   'Donard Radiance' 109
   'Iveyi' **136**, 137
Eucalyptus niphophila 129
Euonymus
   alatus 104
   europaeus 104
   fortunei 109, 124,
     'Emerald 'n' Gold' **108**, 138
     'Silver Queen' 124, 138
Euphorbia 118, 127, 131
   amygdaloides var. *robbiae* 58, 118, 132
   polychroma **148**

Fabiana i. 'Violacea' 124
Fagus sylvatica 96, 134
× *Fatshedera lizei* 124
Festuca glauca 129, 131, 184
Filipendula purpurea 143
Forsythia i. 'Spectabilis' **97**
Fothergilla major **149**
Fremontodendron 'California Glory' 137
Fritillaria 131
Fuchsia 124
   'Prosperity' **125**
   'Tom Thumb' 140

Galtonia viridiflora 131
Garrya e. 'James Roof' 137
Gaultheria shallon 110
Genista
   aetnensis 129, 131
   hispatica 110
Gentiana

asclepiadea 118
   septemfida 140
   sinoörnata 103
Geranium 118, 127, 140
   e. 'A.T. Johnson' **98**, 118
   'Wargrave Pink' **146**
   m. 'Ingwersen's Variety' 118, 132
   sanguineum 'Striatum' **140**
Ginkgo biloba 130, **166**, 169
Glyceria m. 'Variegata' 142, 184
Gunnera manicata 143
Gypsophila
   p. 'Rosy Veil' 118
   r. 'Dorothy Teacher' 140

Hakonechloa m. 'Aureola' 129, 182, **182**
Halesia monticola 129
× *Halimiocistus wintonensis* 125
Halimium ocymoides 125, 140
Hebe 109, 110, 125, 137, 138, 140
   × *f.* 'Blue Gem' 134
   salicifolia **106**
Hedera 125
   c. 'Gloire de Marengo' 124
   colchica 137
   'Dentata Variegata' 109, 124, 132
   helix 65, 109, 124, 137, 138
     'Hibernica' 110
Helianthemum 118, 140
Helichrysum 125, 131
   italicum **123**
   subsp. *serotinum* 131
Helictotrichon sempervirens 129, 131, 184
Helleborus 118, 127
Hemerocallis 118, 143
Hibiscus syriacus 131
Hippophaë rhamnoides 142
Hoheria glabrata 129
Hosta 118–19, 127
   crispula 119
   f. 'Aurea Marginata' **73**
Hottonia palustris 141
Houttuynia c. 'Chamaeleon' **142**
Humulus l. 'Aureus' 138
Hydrangea 125, 138, 185–8
   petiolaris 137, 188
   serrata 'Blue Bird' **186**
   s. 'Preziosa' **185**
Hypericum 125
   calycinum 110
   kouytchense 125, 138
   o. 'Grandiflorum' 131

Ilex 188–9
   × *altaclerensis* 106, 134, 188
   aquifolium 96, 134, 188–9
     'Argenteovariegata' 107
     'Madame Briot' **189**
Indigofera heterantha **130**, 131
Indocalamus tesselatus 184
Iris 119
   foetidissima 119, 132
   kaempferi 142–3
   laevigata 143

Jasminum
   nudiflorum 138
   officinale 136
Juniperus 109, 110, 130, 139, 166, 167, 171
   horizontalis 66, **109**, 171
   × *m.* 'Pfitzerana Aurea' **169**
   s. 'Blue Carpet' 66, 110

Kerria j. 'Pleniflora' 137
Kirengeshoma palmata 119, 127
Kniphofia 119–20
  caulescens **119**

Lamiastrum g. 'Variegatum' 132, **132**
Lamium maculatum 58, 120, 127
Larix 169
Lavandula 120
  angustifolia 134, 140
  stoechas 'Papillon' **120**
Lavatera 'Rosea' 127
Ledum 142
Ligustrum 194–5
  ovalifolium 96, 134, 194
    'Aureum' **195**
Lindera 142
Lippia citriodora 137
Liriope muscari 120, 127
Lithospermum d. 'Heavenly Blue' 140
Lonicera 124, 137, 138
  j. 'Halliana' 65,
  nitida 96, 109, 134
Lysichiton americanum 143
Lysimachia 120–1
  nummularia 51, 120
  punctata 120, 143
Lythrum 121
  p. 'Firecandle' 121, 143

Magnolia 129, 196–200
  grandiflora 137, **198**
  'Heaven Scent' **197**
Mahonia 152–4
  a. 'Apollo' 109, 132, **132**, 152
  japonica 58, 64, 109, 153
  × *media* 'Lionel Fortescue' **154**
Malus 129
Matteuccia struthiopteris 180, **180**
Mentha aquatica 143
Metasequoia glyptostroboides 142, 169
Microbiota decussata 109, 171–2
Milium e. 'Aureum' 129, 182
Mimulus aurantiacus 125
Miscanthus 183
Molinia c. 'Variegata' 129, 184
Morus a. 'Pendula' 129
Myrica gale 142
Myrtus 125

Nandina domestica 125, 140
Neillia thibetica 142
Nepeta 131
  × *faassenii* 121, 127
Nerine bowdenii 127–8, 131
Nymphaea 141

Oenothera missouriensis 128
Olearia × *scilloniensis* 131, 134
Onoclea sensibilis 180
Ophiopogon p. 'Nigrescens' 121, 128
Origanum vulgare 128
Osmanthus × *burkwoodii* 106, 109
Osmunda regalis 143, 180
Osteospermum 128, 131
Ozothamnus 125

Pachysandra terminalis 109, 121, 132
Paeonia 121
  suffruticosa 125
Parahebe catarractae 140
Parthenocissus 137
  quinquefolia 65, 137
Passiflora caerulea 136
Peltyphllum peltatum 143
Penstemon 128, 131
  'Hidcote Pink' **128**
Perovskia a. 'Blue Spire' 125, 131
Persicaria 121
  vacciniifolia 121, 140
Phalaris a. 'Picta' 181, 184
Philadelphus 125
  'Sybille' 96
Phlomis 125, 131
  fruticosa 109
Phlox 121, 140
Phormium 125, 131
Photinia × *f.* 'Red Robin' 125
Phuopsis stylosa 58, **59**
Phygelius 125
  × *r.* 'Winchester Fanfare' **125**
Phyllitis scolopendrium 129, 180
Phyllostachys 142, 184
Physocarpus opulifolius 142
Picea 130, 140, 169–70, 172
Pieris 125
Pileostegia viburnoides 137
Pinus 130, 140, 166–7, 167–8, 172
  mugo pumilio 109, 110, 134
  nigra 134, 166–7
  sylvestris 107, 134
  'Fastigiata' 130, 168
Pittosporum 126, 134
  'Garnetti' 130
  tenuifolium 126, 134, 137
  'Tom Thumb' **105**
Polygonatum × *hybridum* 121
Polygonum see Persicaria
Polypodium vulgare 180
Polystichum 129, 180
Pontederia cordata 143
Populus 141
Potamogeton crispus 141
Potentilla 110, 121, 126, 134
  a. 'Beesii' 126, 140
  fruticosa 97
  'Tangerine' **126**
  nepalensis 121, 128
Prunus 129, 134
  laurocerasus 96, 97, 106, 109, 110, 134
  'Zabeliana' 58
  lusitanica 106
  sargentii **95**
  serrula **95**
  tenella 126
Pseudolarix amabilis 170
Ptelea t. 'Aurea' 129
Pulmonaria 121
  saccharata 128
Pulsatilla vulgaris 140
Punica g. 'Nana' 126
Pyracantha 106, 110, 134, 137
  'Soleil d'Or' 110, 124
Pyrus s. 'Pendula' **10**

Quercus 130, 134, 141

Ranunculus
  aquatilis 141
  lingua 143
Raphiolepis × *delacourii* 'Coates' Crimson' 126
Rhamnus a.
  'Argenteovariegata' 107, 126, 130, 137
Rhododendron 103, 126, 140, 200–5
  'Curlew' **76**
  'Mrs G.W. Leak' **201**
  ponticum 104, 134, 204
Ribes s. 'Brocklebankii' 138
Robinia
  hispida 'Macrophylla' 124
  slavinii 'Hillieri' 129, 130
Rodgersia 121, 143
Romneya coulteri 131
Rosa 110, 123, 126–7, 129, 134, 136, 137, 138, 205–11
  banksiae 'Lutea' **7**, 136
  'Constance Spry' **211**
  gallica var. *officinalis* **208**
  'Graham Thomas' **210**
  mulliganii **209**
  'Nozomi' **126**
  'Penelope' **135**
  pimpinellifolia **207**
  rugosa 97, 134
Rosmarinus officinalis 110, 126, 134–5
Rubus cockburnianus 95
  tricolor 110
Rudbeckia 121–2
  fulgida 128
Rumex acetosella 88
Ruscus aculeatus 132
Ruta graveolens 'Jackman's Blue' 122

Sagittaria 143
Salix 129, 141, 142, 212–14
  alba 'Britzensis' 95, **212**
    var. *sericea* **13**
Salvia 122
  officinalis 122, 128
Sambucus racemosa 'Plumosa Aurea' **112**
Santolina 122
  chamaecyparissus 122, 128
Sarcococca
  confusa 109
  hookeriana 126
Sasa 142, 184
Saxifraga 140
Scabiosa 128
Schisandra g. 'Rubriflora' 136
Schizophragma 137
Schizostylis coccinea 128
Sciadopitys verticillata 170
Scirpus tabernaemontani 143
Sedum 122, 131
Senecio
  'Sunshine' 109, 110
  vulgaris 27
Sequoiadendron giganteum 170
Sequoia sempervirens 170

Shibataea kumasasa 184
Skimmia japonica 109, 126, *confusa* 110
Smilacina racemosa 122
Solanum c. 'Glasnevin' 124, 136
Solidago 66
Sophora t. 'Grandiflora' 130, 137
Sorbus 129, 214–16
  aria 93, 216
  aucuparia 'Sunshine' **216**
  cashmiriana **215**
  sargentiana 102–4, 215
Sparganium ramosum 143
Spirea japonica 126, 140
Stachys
  macrantha 'Robusta' 122, **122**
  olympica 122, 131
  'Silver Carpet' 122, 131
Stipa 129, 131, 184
Stratiotes aloides 141

Tamarix 131
Taxodium
  ascendens 'Nutans' 141
  distichum 20, 142, 170
Taxus baccata 96, 97, 109, 110, 130, 135, 164–5, 172
  'Fastigiata Aureomarginata' **169**
Thamnocalamus spathaceus 183
Thuja 172
  plicata 96, 135, 140, 165, 167, 172
  'Fastigiata' 107, 135
Thymus 128, 140
Tiarella cordifolia 122
Trachelospermum
  asiaticum 137, **137**
  jasminoides 136
Tsuga 167, 140
Tulipa 131
Typha 143

Verbascum 128
Veronica 128
  beccabunga 143
  prostrata 140
Viburnum 106, 126, 217–18
  carlesii 'Aurora' **218**
  plicatum 'Mariesii' 58, **217**
  rhytidophyllum 106, 217–18
  tinus 109, 110, 126, 135, 217
Vinca
  major 110, 122, 132
  minor 51, 122, 132
Viola cornuta 140
Vitis
  coignetiae 138
  vinifera 137, 138

Waldsteinia ternata 122, 128
Weigela f. 'Variegata' 96, **146**
Wisteria sinensis 136, 138

Yucca 126, 131

Zantedeschia aethiopica 143
Zauschneria c. 'Dublin' 131
Zenobia pulverulenta 126